Wontner's Guide to Land Registry Practice

Wontner's Guide to

Land Registry Practice

Twenty-second Edition

David W. Rees

B.Sc.Econ., LL.B.

Assistant Land Registrar

SWEET & MAXWELL THOMSON REUTERS

First edition 1928
Twenty-second edition 2009

Published in 2009 by Thomson Reuters (Legal) Limited
(Registered in England & Wales, Company No. 1679046
Registered Office and address for service:
100 Avenue Road, London NW3 3PF) trading as Sweet & Maxwell Limited
For further information on our products and services, visit
www.sweetandmaxwell.co.uk

Typeset by J.P. Price of Chilcompton, Somerset
Printed in Great Britain by
Ashford Colour Press Ltd, Gosport, Hampshire

No natural forests were destroyed to make this product;
only farmed timber was used and replanted.

A C.I.P. catalogue record for this book
is available from the British Library

ISBN 13 978–0–41404–168–4

Editor's Note

Throughout this book (unless otherwise indicated) references to:

"the Act" and to section numbers relate to the Land Registration Act 2002;
"the Adjudicator" means the Adjudicator to HM Land Registry;
"the Adjudicator Rules" means the Adjudicator to Her Majesty's Land Registry (Practice and Procedure) Rules 2003;
"the Fee Order" relate to the Land Registration Fee Order 2009 (a copy of which is set out in Appendix V);
"conveyancer" has the same meaning as in the Rules i.e. a solicitor, a licensed conveyancer within the meaning of s.11(2) of the Administration of Justice Act 1985, a fellow of the Institute of Legal Executives, a barrister, a duly certificated notary public, or a registered European lawyer (as defined);
"developing estate" means a registered title consisting of land being developed for residential and/or commercial purposes and disposed of in individual plots or flats;
"HMRC" means HM Revenue and Customs;
"Land Registry" means Her Majesty's Land Registry;
"NLIS" means the National Land Information Service;
"PPP" means a public–private partnership;
"the proper office" means the office designated under s.100(3) for the receipt of applications or a specified description of application;
"the Referral Rules" means the Land Registration (Referral to the Adjudicator to HM Land Registry) Rules 2003;
"the Rules" and to individual rules relate to the Land Registration Rules 2003;
"Sch.1 form" means a form contained within Sch.1 to the Rules;
"Sch.3 form" means a form contained within Sch.3 to the Rules;
"SDLT" means stamp duty land tax;
"statement of truth" means a statement of truth which complies with the requirements set out in r.215A;
"TLATA" means the Trusts of Land and Appointment of Trustees Act 1996;
"the 1967 Act" means the Leasehold Reform Act 1967;
"the 1971 Act" means the Powers of Attorney Act 1971;
"the 1977 Act" means the Rentcharges Act 1977;

"the 1986 Act" means the Insolvency Act 1986;
"the 1987 Act" means the Landlord and Tenant Act 1987;
"the 1989 Act" means the Law of Property (Miscellaneous Provisions) Act 1989;
"the 1993 Act" means the Leasehold Reform, Housing and Urban Development Act 1993;
"the 1994 Act" means the Law of Property (Miscellaneous Provisions) Act 1994;
"the 1996 Act" means the Family Law Act 1996.

References to an Act or Statutory Instrument are (if applicable) to that Act or Statutory Instrument as amended. The commentary in this book is that of the author and not that of the Land Registry.

All reasonable care was taken in the preparation of this book, but any person relying on any of the statements, express or implied, in this book does so entirely at their own risk and without liability on the part of either the author or the publisher.

The law is stated as at August 31, 2009, although subsequent changes have been taken into account where possible.

Preface

This 22nd edition is the latest in a long line of editions going back to 1928, when *Wontner* was first published as a guide to Land Registry practice following the great property reform legislation of 1925, which included the Land Registration Act 1925.

At that time, registered land was still in the minority and it was the unregistered conveyancing system which dominated. Some 80 years later the situation has been reversed. Registered titles are now in the majority and it is unregistered conveyancing which is encountered increasingly infrequently. It is to the credit of the land registration system set up in 1925 that the basic framework has remained intact throughout that time.

But the system has not stood still and the enormous social and economic changes which have taken place have necessitated regular amendments both to the underlying legislation and to the practice and procedures applicable to land registration. Those amendments culminated, in 2003, with a complete overhaul of the legislation leading to the coming into force of the Land Registration Act 2002 and the Land Registration Rules 2003.

Six years on, that new legislation has now firmly bedded in, with undoubted benefits to the land registration system and to registered conveyancing in general. However, change continues to occur and this inevitably means that there have been further significant developments in Land Registry law and practice since the 21st edition in 2005. These changes are reflected in this new edition and include a general amendment of the Land Registration Rules 2003 following an extensive review in 2008 and the recent introduction of two new "triggers" for compulsory first registration.

The underlying principles of land registration, however, remain the same: to provide a clear, structured and effective system of registration of title to legal estates and of dispositions of registered titles, backed by the state guarantee of title. Those principles continue to underpin the registered land system as it moves forward in the 21st century.

In preparing this 22nd edition, I hope it will prove as useful and informative as its predecessors have done.

David Rees

October 1, 2009

Contents

6 Lost or Destroyed Title Deeds

7 Adverse Possession

8 Covenants, Easements and Profits à Prendre

9 Inspection, Official Copies and Searches

Table of Cases

Table of Statutes

Table of Statutory Instruments

Chapter 1

General Features

Introduction

1–001 Land registration is carried out principally under the authority of the Land Registration Act 2002 ("the Act") and the Land Registration Rules 2003 ("the Rules"). It is administered by Her Majesty's Land Registry ("Land Registry") in accordance with the Act and the Rules and its own practice and procedures.

Land Registry is a government agency whose main purpose is to register title to land in England and Wales and to record dispositions, such as sales and mortgages, with registered land.

Its published mission is to provide "the world's best service for guaranteeing ownership of land and facilitating property transactions" and its vision is "making property transactions easier for all".

The Act and the Rules

1–002 The Act replaced existing legislation (principally the Land Registration Act 1925) with effect from October 13, 2003. Schedule 12 to the Act contains various transitional provisions, including para.1 which confirms the validity of existing entries in the register as at the date the Act came into force.

The Act contains the primary legislation setting out the main framework within which land registration will operate and the Rules contain provisions regulating the practical implementation of land registration within that framework.

What estates and interests can be registered?

1–003 The Act covers registration of title to legal estates which are interests of any of the following kinds (s.2):

(1) an estate in land. "Land" includes buildings and other structures, mines and minerals (whether or not held with the surface) and land covered with water including the sea-bed up to the territorial limits of England and Wales (ss.130 and 132). Manors (being "lordship of the manor" titles) are not included in the definition; these can no longer be registered and s.119 allows manors registered under earlier legislation to be de-registered. In addition s.90 prohibits the registration of public–private partnership leases relating to transport in London;

(2) a rentcharge (see Chapter 15);

(3) a franchise, which is a right granted by the Crown e.g. to hold a market or fair and which may be an "affecting franchise" (i.e. one affecting a defined area of land) or a "relating franchise" (i.e. a franchise which does not affect a defined area of land and is not therefore is not an affecting franchise);

(4) a profit à prendre in gross, which is a right, e.g. of hunting and fishing, the benefit of which is not attached to land (see para.8–023);

(5) any other interest or charge which subsists for the benefit of, or is a charge on, an interest the title to which is registered e.g. a benefitting easement or a charge by way of legal mortgage; and

(6) interests capable of subsisting at law which are created by a disposition of an interest the title to which is registered. These are interests created by registrable dispositions of a registered title e.g. an easement granted over registered land.

Of these, only (1), (2), (3) and (4) may be substantively registered with their own individual title; (5) and (6) may only be registered by way of entry in the register of a registered title.

Classes of title

1–004 Registration may be with one of the following classes of title (ss.9 and 10):

(1) absolute title;

(2) possessory title;

(3) qualified title;

and additionally for leaseholds only,

(4) good leasehold title.

The reasons why the registrar will on first registration approve a particular class of title and the effect of registration with that class are explained in paras 5–012 and 5–017.

It may subsequently be possible to upgrade the class of title, and the circumstances in which this can be done are explained in Chapter 22.

The register of title

Rules 2 and 3 contain provisions as to how the register is to be kept and how individual registers may be amalgamated or divided. The register is now almost entirely kept in electronic form. **1–005**

Individual registers of title must have a distinguishing number, or series of letters and numbers, known as the title number and must consist of:

(1) a property register;

(2) a proprietorship register; and

(3) where necessary, a charges register (r.4(1) and (2)).

An entry in a register may be made by reference to a plan or other document, in which case the registrar must keep the original or a copy of that document (r.4(3)).

Whenever the registrar considers it desirable in relation to an individual register, he may open a new edition showing only the existing entries, rearrange the entries or alter the title number (r.4(4)).

Property register

This contains a description of the registered property by reference to a plan based on the Ordnance Survey map and known as the title plan (except in the case of profits à prendre in gross and certain franchises) and details of other matters e.g. the inclusion or exclusion of mines and minerals; benefiting easements, rights and privileges (r.5). **1–006**

In addition, the property register of a leasehold estate must contain sufficient particulars of the registered lease to enable that lease to be identified and, if the lease contains a provision prohibiting or restricting dispositions, an entry stating that the lease prohibits or restricts dispositions of the estate (r.6). However, where the lease is a "prescribed clauses lease", the registrar does not need to make such an entry if the provision is not specified or referred to in clause LR8 (see para.12–008).

In the case of a registered rentcharge, franchise or a profit à prendre in gross, where practicable the property register must, if the estate was created by an instrument, also contain sufficient particulars of the instrument to enable it to be identified (r.7).

The benefit of restrictive covenants is not entered in the property register, because the register is a register of legal estates and interests and such covenants are by their nature equitable; the benefit therefore subsists "off the register" (see also para.8–003).

Proprietorship register

1–007 This includes, where appropriate, the class of title, the name of the proprietor, the proprietor's address for service, restrictions, bankruptcy entries, details of positive covenants and indemnity covenants and of modification of implied covenants (r.8(1)). Whenever practicable it will also include details of the price paid or value declared and that entry will remain until there is a change of proprietor, or some other change in the register of title which the registrar considers would result in the entry being misleading (r.8(2) and (3)).

Charges register

1–008 This contains, where appropriate, details of leases, charges, and any other adverse interests; any dealings with or affecting the priority of those interests which are capable of being noted; the name and address for service of the proprietor of any registered charge and any restrictions and bankruptcy entries in relation to a registered charge (r.9).

In the case of the property register and the charges register, the registrar may enter in either of them any matter otherwise required to be entered in any other part of the register if he considers it to be more convenient. Thus it is common to find "combined" entries in the property register containing details both of benefitting easements and of the burden of easements excepted and reserved, where these were originally created within one deed.

Indices (section 68 and rules 10 and 11)

1–009 The *index of proprietors' names* shows for each individual register the name of the proprietor of the registered estate and of the proprietor of any registered charge together with the title number. Until every register is kept electronically the index need not contain the name of any corporate or joint proprietor of an estate or of a charge registered as proprietor prior to May 1, 1972. See para.9–003 as to the procedure under which a search of this index can be made.

The *index map* records whether any parcel of land is registered, or in the process of being registered and the title number. A separate verbal *index of relating franchises and manors* is also kept. Further details, including an explanation of how searches of these indices can be made, are contained in paras 3–014 to 3–018.

The day list (r.12)

The day list is a record of the date and time at which every pending application was made and of every application for an official search with priority. For this purpose "pending application" does not include an application under Pt.13 of the Rules (which covers "Information etc." such as applications for official copies), except an application to designate a document an exempt information document under r.136 or an application for a network access agreement under para.1(4) of Sch.5 to the Act. **1–010**

Notice of an application for an official search with priority remains on the day list until the priority period allowed by the search comes to an end (see para.9–022).

If the registrar proposes to alter the register without having received an application he must enter his proposal on the day list and, when so entered, it will have the same effect as if it were an application made at the date and time of its entry.

Delivery and priority of applications

Land Registry's office at Lincoln's Inn Fields, London, is the administrative head office. The day-to-day work of registration is carried out at the other offices listed in Appendix I. Unless lodged electronically, all applications and correspondence should therefore be delivered to the proper office, as designated by an order of the Lord Chancellor as the proper office for the receipt of applications (s.100(3)). **1–011**

A list of administrative areas and the particular Land Registry office which is responsible for each of them is available from the Land Registry website (see para.1–025).

An application is "received" by Land Registry when it is delivered:

(1) to the proper office; or

(2) in accordance with a written arrangement as to delivery made between the registrar and the applicant or their conveyancer; or

(3) electronically, where that is authorised (r.15(3)).

This does not apply to an application under Pt.13 of the Rules ("Information etc."), other than an application that the registrar designate a document an exempt information document under r.136 (see para.9–013).

An application received on a business day is taken as made at the earlier of:

(1) the time of the day that notice of it is entered in the day list; or

(2) midnight marking the end of:

(a) the day it was received if the application was received before 12 noon; or

(b) the next business day after the day it was received if the application was received at or after 12 noon (r.15(1)).

An application received on a day which is not a business day is taken as made at the earlier of:

(i) the time of the day that notice of it is entered in the day list; or

(ii) midnight marking the end of the next business day after the day it was received (r.15(2)).

A "business day" is a day on which Land Registry is open to the public (r.217(1)). Currently Land Registry is normally open to the public daily except for Saturdays, Sundays and bank holidays and any day certified as an "interrupted day" (r.216(1)). The registrar may certify any day as an interrupted day if he is satisfied that on that day there is likely to be either a general delay or failure relating to a communication service, or any other event or circumstance causing a substantial interruption in the normal operation of Land Registry. This could arise, for example, in severe weather conditions.

The registrar may in the future arrange for Land Registry to be open on Saturdays and if he does he must give at least eight weeks' notice of his decision (r.216(2) to (4)).

Entries made in the register on first registration, or on the registration of a disposition required to be completed by registration or entries made in, removed from or altered as a result of any other application have effect from the time the application is made (s.74 and r.20).

Where two or more applications relating to the same registered title are taken as having been made at the same time the order in which they should rank in priority as between each other is determined in accordance with the provisions of r.55.

Chapter 9 discusses the deemed times of delivery of applications for official searches of the register and the priority conferred on applications for registration by official certificates of search.

Forms (rr.206 to 212)

A document affecting a registered title must refer to the title number (r.212(3)). **1–012**

Prescribed forms which cover most types of transaction are set out in Sch.1 to the Rules ("Sch.1 forms"). Forms of execution are contained in Sch.9 to the Rules.

Miscellaneous forms (e.g. Form 1—certificate as to execution of power of attorney) are set out in Sch.3 to the Rules ("Sch.3 forms").

See also para.10–007 for further discussion on forms.

The registrar also publishes Welsh language versions of the Sch.1 and Sch.3 forms and of the Sch.9 forms of execution, and when they are published they are to be regarded as if they were contained in the relevant Schedule to the Rules.

The registrar may permit a person to make an application relying on a document that is not in the relevant Sch.1 or Sch.3 form, if that person cannot obtain and lodge the relevant scheduled form or it is only possible to do so at unreasonable expense, if he is satisfied that neither the rights of any person nor the keeping of the register are likely to be materially prejudiced by allowing the alternative document to be relied upon.

Any application or document in one of the Sch.1 forms must:

(1) be printed on durable A4 size paper;

(2) be reproduced as set out in Sch.1 as to its wording, layout, ruling, font and point size (except for Forms ST1, ST2, ST3 and ST4 where the special forms of execution provided in r.215A(4) and (5) may be used instead);

(3) contain all the information required in an easily legible form; and

(4) if it consists of more than one sheet of paper, or refers to an attached plan or a continuation sheet, be securely fastened together.

An "additional provisions" panel may be used, where provided within a Sch.1 form.

If (other than in Form DL) the necessary information will not fit in the panel provided, the panel must be continued on a continuation sheet in Form CS.

Where a form is produced electronically:

(a) the depth of a panel may be increased or reduced to fit the material to be comprised in it, and a panel may be divided at a page break;

(b) the text outside of the panels, other than—

(i) the name and description of the form at the top of the page, and
(ii) any text after the final panel,

may be omitted;

(c) inapplicable certificates and statements may be omitted;

(d) the plural may be used instead of the singular and the singular instead of the plural;

(e) panels which would contain only the panel number and the panel heading may be omitted, but such omission must not affect the numbering of subsequent panels;

(f) "X" boxes may be omitted where all inapplicable statements and certificates have been omitted;

(g) the subheadings in an additional provisions panel may be added to, amended, repositioned or omitted;

(h) "Seller" may be substituted for "Transferor" and "Buyer" for "Transferee" in a transfer on sale;

(i) the vertical lines which define the left and right boundaries of the panel may be omitted.

If no form is prescribed the document must be in such form as the registrar may direct or allow.

Fees

Fees are currently prescribed by the current Land Registration Fee Order 2009, referred to in this book as "the Fee Order", the text of which is set out in Appendix V. **1–013**

Fees are normally required to be paid on delivery of the application to which they relate by means of a cheque or postal order crossed and made payable to Land Registry (art.13 of the Fee Order).

Where a fee is paid by a cheque which is not honoured, the application may be cancelled (r.16(4)).

Any person or firm, if authorised by Land Registry, may use a credit account for payment of fees on applications and services of such kinds as the registrar may direct (art.14 of the Fee Order). Certain services are only available to credit account holders e.g. the telephone search service.

Applicants who have made prior arrangements may pay fees for substantive applications by direct debit. Information about setting up such an arrangement can be obtained from Accounts Section, Land Registry, Plumer House, Crownhill, Plymouth PL6 5HY or from Land Registry's website (see para.1.025).

When two or more instruments relating to the same land are delivered for registration as part of the same application, a separate fee is payable in respect of each; but when a sale and a sub-sale are effected by one instrument of transfer only one fee, assessed on the price paid by the purchaser or the sub-purchaser, whichever is the greater is payable (art.3(4) of the Fee Order).

There are special provisions for "large-scale" applications involving large numbers of "land units", as defined in the Fee Order.

Rejection and cancellation of applications, and requisitions raised by Land Registry (rules 16 and 17)

If an application appears to the registrar to be substantially defective, he may reject it on delivery or he may cancel it at any time thereafter. **1–014**

If an application is not in order the registrar may raise such requisitions as he considers necessary and specify a period (being not less than 20 business days) within which the applicant must comply with the requisitions. If the applicant fails to do so, the registrar may cancel the application or may extend the period when this appears to him to be reasonable in the circumstances.

If he considers it necessary or desirable, the registrar may refuse to complete or proceed with an application until further documents or evidence are supplied or notice is given.

If it will not be possible to reply to requisitions in the time specified, an extension must be requested. The request should:

(1) state the reason for the delay;

(2) explain what is being done to resolve the problem; and

(3) indicate when it is expected that a full reply to the requisition can be supplied.

If such a request is made and supported by a proper reason an extension may be allowed, but if no request is made the application will be cancelled.

Land Registry's Practice Guides 49 and 50 contain full details of its policy and practice on the rejection of defective applications and on requisitions and cancellation.

Early completion policy

1–015 A policy of "early completion" was introduced by Land Registry as from August 3, 2009 with the purpose of ensuring that individual applications for registration are, where possible, completed rather than being delayed as a result of failure to provide evidence of satisfaction of an existing registered charge.

The policy applies to all situations where an application for a discharge of whole has been made with another application, but evidence of satisfaction of the charge has not been provided. For example, it applies in the common scenario where an application is made in Form AP1 for the registration of a discharge of an existing charge, a transfer and a new charge. Three distinct applications are being made. Without evidence of satisfaction of the existing charge, Land Registry will reject the application for discharge but complete the other applications where possible. The entries relating to the existing charge will be left in the register until evidence of satisfaction is provided.

Previously, Land Registry would deal with the three applications collectively, with the result that there was a risk of all three applications being cancelled if evidence of discharge of the existing charge could not be lodged, with a consequential risk of loss of priority for the interests of the transferee and new chargee.

If there is a restriction registered in favour of the existing chargee which provides that no disposition and/or that no charge of the registered estate shall be registered without the consent of that chargee, Land Registry will requisition for evidence of discharge or evidence that the terms of the restriction have been met. If the requisition is not dealt with Land Registry will, in the case of a restriction against the registration of any disposition, cancel not only the application for discharge but also the application to register the transfer and charge. In the case of a restriction against the registration of a charge only, Land Registry will complete the registration of the transfer, cancelling the other applications and leaving the entries relating to the existing charge in the register.

A "stand alone" application made only for discharge of a registered charge is substantially defective if evidence of satisfaction is not lodged with the application and will therefore be rejected.

Stamp duty land tax ("SDLT") and stamp duty

SDLT is a tax payable on certain land transactions completed on **1–016** or after December 1, 2003. It was introduced by the Finance Act 2003 and replaced stamp duty for most land transactions.

"Land transaction" means the acquisition of a chargeable interest in land located in the United Kingdom. "Chargeable interest" is defined in s.48(1) of the Finance Act 2003 and includes freehold and leasehold estates in land, and rights over another's land. The definition includes both legal and beneficial interests. A wide range of transactions are therefore within the scope of SDLT.

SDLT is payable in respect of transactions rather than deeds; therefore a liability to SDLT can arise even in cases where no deed has been executed e.g. the surrender of a lease by operation of law (see para.12–038).

Most land transactions are "notifiable", which means HM Revenue and Customs ("HMRC") must be informed about the transaction, even in cases where it is of a type which will not attract SDLT. Land Registry cannot register the transaction unless the application is accompanied by evidence that HMRC have been notified, such evidence being either:

(1) a Land Transaction Return certificate (Form SDLT5); or
(2) a printed submission certificate, as generated when a person applies electronically for an SDLT5 certificate.

Where a Land Transaction Return certificate is required (unless it is covered by an outline application—see para.10–030), the application will be rejected if lodged without it, unless at least 20 business days have passed since completion. If the certificate is not by then available, the application can be lodged but it must be accompanied by a clear statement that the Land Transaction Return has been sent to HMRC. The application will not be cancelled provided that Land Registry is asked, in response to requisitions or reminders, to extend the time because HMRC has not provided the certificate. Failure to respond to Land Registry requisitions or enquiries will result in cancellation.

Certain types of land transaction do not require notification to HMRC. A "self certificate" in Form SDLT60 was previously required for these, but this was abolished with effect from March 12, 2008.

Other transactions which are exempt from SDLT or outside the scope of SDLT do not require notification to HMRC. Exempt interests are described in s.48(2) of the Finance Act 2003 and include, for example, a legal or equitable charge, a discharge of a charge or a contract for sale.

Land Registry can register such transactions without SDLT evidence being lodged, but in cases where the position is not clear, a covering letter confirming the position should be lodged with the application.

There are still a few transactions on which stamp duty is payable. These will mainly be based on pre-July 11, 2003 contracts. Where a document is lodged which is endorsed with stamp duty and, if appropriate, with a "produced" stamp, no query will be raised and no covering letter is necessary. A transfer for value (not relating to a share) dated after November 30, 2003 on which stamp duty would still be payable but which is below the stamp duty threshold, should be lodged with a Form L(A)451 and a covering letter of explanation.

Where appropriate, a transfer may contain a certificate under the Stamp Duty (Exempt Instruments) Regulations 1987 and should be lodged with a covering letter explaining why the certificate is appropriate.

Land and charge certificates

1–017 Before October 13, 2003 in nearly all cases a new or updated land certificate or a charge certificate was issued on completion of first registration applications and applications to register dispositions of registered titles. The exception was where certain mortgage lenders had agreed to dispense with the need for a charge certificate when a charge in their favour was registered.

Since October 13, 2003, land and charge certificates have no longer been issued or required. It is now not necessary to lodge an existing land or charge certificate in connection with any application; if lodged it will be destroyed.

Title Information Document

Although it is not required by the Rules, as a matter of practice Land Registry issues a Title Information Document whenever an application is "marked off" (i.e. completed). The document consists of a frontsheet with an official copy of the register attached. It is envisaged that a conveyancer will pass this document on to their client. **1–018**

Retention and return of documents (rules 203 to 205)

Subject to the delivery of any certified copies required, the registrar must comply with any request made by an applicant or their conveyancer within an application, for the return of all or any of the documents accompanying that application. Except on an application for first registration, a person making such a request must deliver with the application certified copies of the documents which are the subject of the request. On an application for first registration, a person making a request for the return of any statutory declaration, statement of truth, subsisting lease, subsisting charge, certificate relating to SDLT or the latest document of title must deliver with the application certified copies of such documents as are the subject of the request, but is not required to deliver copies of any other documents. **1–019**

Otherwise, on completion of any application the registrar may retain all or any of the documents that accompanied the application.

The registrar may destroy any document which he retains if he is satisfied that he has made and retained a sufficient copy of the document or further retention of the document is unnecessary (r.203).

For a period of five years from October 13, 2003, any person who either:

(1) delivered a document to the registrar on which any entry in the register of title is, or was, founded; or

(2) was the current registered proprietor, where the person who delivered the document was at that time the registered proprietor, or applying to become the registered proprietor,

could request the return of that document.

If, at the date of such a request, the document was kept by the registrar he was obliged to return it to the person making the request unless he received more than one request in respect of the same document, when he might either retain the document or, in his discretion, return it to one of the persons making a request.

At the end of the five-year period, if there was no outstanding request in relation to the document, the registrar could destroy any document if he was satisfied that he had retained a copy of the document, or further retention of the document was unnecessary (r.204(2)).

That period has now expired, but where a request is made following the end of that period, the registrar may treat it as a request under r.204(2).

The registrar may release any document retained by him upon such terms, if any, for its return as he considers appropriate (r.205).

Bulk applications

1–020 When it is propose to make a "large scale application", the applicant should first contact the Commercial Arrangements Section at Land Registry's head office on 020 7917 8888 or email at bulk.apps@landregistry.gsi.gov.uk to discuss the matter. A large scale application is one comprising a common deed or deeds affecting registered and/or unregistered land in areas covered by one or more Land Registry office and which either affects more than 200 properties comprising registered titles only or a combination of registered titles and unregistered titles or affects more than 50 unregistered titles.

The Commercial Arrangements Section will provide guidance as to the preparation and lodging of the application and will also arrange for a nominated Land Registry office to deal with the application. It will also, where necessary, prepare a written order under the current Land Registration (Proper Office) Order permitting the application to be lodged at that nominated office.

When it is proposed to make a "small scale application", the applicant should first contact the customer service manager at the Land Registry office that administers the largest number of affected titles, for further guidance. A small scale application is one comprising a common deed or deeds affecting registered and/or unregistered land in areas covered by more than one Land Registry office, and which affects 200 or fewer registered and/or 50 or fewer unregistered properties. This does not include a follow-up application to an existing large scale application, which must be referred to the Commercial Arrangements Section as above.

Scheme titles

Where a local authority or company or similar purchaser acquires a large extent of land in a piecemeal manner over a period of time, a request may be made to Land Registry for each parcel of land to be incorporated into a single registered title, known as a "scheme title", as and when it is acquired. This avoids the purchaser becoming the proprietor of a large number of individual registered titles and subsequently having to request amalgamation of those titles. **1–021**

A scheme title may be appropriate where, for example, a local authority is in the process of acquiring a large number of individual properties by compulsory purchase, as part of a redevelopment scheme.

Land Registry Direct

Land Registry Direct, which is available to Land Registry account holders only, allows on-line access to registers, title plans and the day list, on-line ordering of official copies and searches and the on-line lodging of certain applications where no fee is payable. **1–022**

Further information can be obtained from: Land Registry Direct, Touthill Close, City Road, Peterborough, PE1 1XN. Tel: 0870 0100299. E-mail: admin@landregistrydirect.gov.uk.

Electronic conveyancing

In 1998 a joint report by the Law Commission and Land Registry entitled *Land Registration for the Twenty First Century* (Law Com. No.254) was published, with a view to developing the concept of an electronic conveyancing system. In consequence, the Act contains provisions which authorise the establishment of a Land Registry network to facilitate a system of e-conveyancing (ss.91 to 95 and Sch.5 to the Act). Various consultation exercises on such a system have been carried out by **1–023**

Land Registry in recent years, as a result of which it has been concluded that the system should be introduced in stages over a period of time rather than in one major change.

Following the introduction of the Electronic Notification of Discharge ("END") whereby mortgage lenders can electronically notify Land Registry of the discharge of a charge (although a formal application to cancel the charge from the register is still required), the first new service to come on stream was electronic discharges ("EDs"), which allows mortgage lenders to electronically signal the discharge of a legal charge direct to Land Registry, computer to computer. Following electronic validation checks, the discharge is reflected in the register automatically.

Currently, new electronic lodgement services are being piloted with certain users through Land Registry's electronic conveyancing portal. These include the "E-DS1", which is an alternative method of electronic discharge to be made available to those mortgage lenders who chose not to join the EDs service. It needs no supporting application or paperwork; it is an application in itself and automatically removes the charge from the register. An electronic charge in standard form (an "e-CSF") has also been piloted in 2009, which is the first electronic deed. See Chapter 14 for further discussion on charges. Land Registry is currently developing the concept of an electronic transfer ("e-TR1") which will initially be used in relation to the transfers on sale of the whole of one registered title by private individuals to private individuals.

During 2009, users of Land Registry Direct are being moved across to Land Registry's portal, so that the service can be withdrawn in early 2010.

The Land Registration (Network Access) Rules 2008 and the Network Access Appeal Rules 2008 are now in force. A number of network access agreements have been entered into Land Registry and certain subscribers pursuant to s.92 and Sch.5 to the Act, to enable such subscribers to use e-conveyancing services.

Up to date information is available at: www.landregistry.gov.uk/e-conveyancing.

Information

Inquiries

1–024 Inquiries as to Land Registry practice may be made in writing, by telephone or by personal visit to the Customer Services Centre at a Land Registry office, which in the case of an inquiry relating to a specific title should be at the proper office.

Land Registry website

Up to date information about Land Registry practice and procedure and copies of Sch.1 forms can be obtained from Land Registry's website at www.landregistry.gov.uk. **1–025**

Find A Property

Land Registry's Find A Property online service is aimed at the general public, enabling a search to be made for registers and title plans that can be identified by an address. Copies of registers and title plans found can be downloaded for a fee in accordance with the Fee Order, payable by credit/debit card. An online search of the index map facility is also available. The service replaced the previous Land Register Online service in May 2009 and can be found at Land Registry's website. **1–026**

National Land Information Service ("NLIS")

The NLIS provides conveyancers with online access to a number of data providers, such as government agencies and local authorities. Various searches necessary when purchasing a property can be carried out through NLIS, including local authority, coal mining and Land Registry searches. Further information can be found at the NLIS website at www.nlis.org.uk. **1–027**

Practical points

- Use the correct forms of disposition and application,
- Lodge applications at the proper office,
- Lodge the correct fee(s),
- Lodge the appropriate SDLT evidence where necessary,
- Request the return of an original document (and lodge a certified copy of it with the application) where required,
- Ensure Land Registry requisitions are dealt with or (where appropriate) a request for an extension of time is made,
- Be aware of Land Registry's "early completion" policy and lodge any necessary discharge with an application where possible.

Chapter 2

Legal and Equitable Estates and Interests

Introduction

The most familiar form of land ownership is the freehold estate. However, various other legal and equitable estates and interests may exist in relation to a piece of land. The land registration aspects are an important element of the law and practice relating to these estates and interests. **2–001**

This chapter provides an overview of the distinction between legal and equitable estates and interests and the effect of the land registration system in relation to them. It covers a number of topics which will be discussed further within individual chapters.

Legal estates

There can only be two legal estates in land (s.1(1) of the Law of Property Act 1925): **2–002**

(1) an estate in fee simple absolute in possession (the freehold estate); and

(2) a term of years absolute (the leasehold estate).

These two legal estates may be registered with their own individual title if they fall within the categories prescribed by the Act (see paras 1–003, 5–002 and 5–003).

Legal interests

There are only five types of legal interest in land (s.1(2) of the Law of Property Act 1925): **2–003**

(1) easements, rights or privileges;
(2) rentcharges;
(3) charges by way of legal mortgage;
(4) certain charges not created by an instrument e.g. a statutory charge;
(5) rights of entry e.g. under the terms of a lease or rentcharge.

These interests are only legal interests if they take effect at law. So, for example, an easement granted by deed may take effect at law and be a legal interest, but if granted in writing (but not by deed) it will take effect only in equity and be an equitable interest.

Of these legal interests, only rentcharges, profits in gross and franchises can be registered with their own individual title (see paras 1–003, 5–002 and 5–003).

The remaining interests, being easements, profits appurtenant (i.e. a profit that exists for the benefit of a piece of land) and charges by way of legal mortgage, can be registered by way of entry in an existing registered title (see para.1–003).

Equitable interests

2–004 Any interest in land that does not qualify as a legal estate or interest is an equitable interest (s.1(3) of the Law of Property Act 1925). Equitable interests include for example:

(1) the interest of a beneficiary under a trust;
(2) interests arising under a contract for sale;
(3) interests that do not meet the formal requirements for the creation of a legal interest e.g. an easement not created by deed; and
(4) restrictive covenants.

The benefit of equitable interests cannot be registered. However, the burden of the interest can be protected by the entry of a notice and/or restriction (as appropriate) in the register of an affected registered title (see Chapter 16).

Differences between legal and equitable interests

2–005 Legal estates and interests take effect at law whereas equitable interests take effect only in equity. This has implications as to their enforceability and the need to protect certain interests in order to maintain their priority and enforceability against others.

The basic rule is that most legal estates and interests are enforceable as of right, whereas equitable interests are enforceable only at the discretion of the court. Therefore, a person who has an equitable interest in land may be refused a remedy by the court to enforce that right, if they have themselves behaved improperly; this is because the equitable maxim "He who comes to equity must come with clean hands" applies. This basic principle has been modified significantly by statute, including the Act.

Some interests can potentially be either legal or equitable interests (such as easements), whereas some interests can only be equitable (such as restrictive covenants).

Creation and disposition

Legal estates and interests

Generally, legal estates and interests must be created and disposed of by deed (s.52(1) of the Law of Property Act 1925) but there are exceptions, e.g. certain leases granted for a term of not more than three years, or easements acquired by prescription. **2–006**

The requirements for a valid deed executed on or after July 31, 1990 are set out in s.1 of the Law of Property (Miscellaneous Provisions) Act 1989 (see para.10–008).

In addition, the Act and the Rules impose additional requirements for the form and registration formalities in respect of certain legal estates and interests relating to registered land. Section 27 sets out those dispositions of a registered estate or charge that are required to be completed by registration (see para.10–002), the main types being a transfer, the grant of a legal charge and the grant of a lease of an estate in land for a term of more than seven years from the date of grant. The Rules prescribe the form of disposition that must be used for certain registrable dispositions, as well as the relevant application forms (see para.10–007).

This means that, for example, a transfer of a registered estate must be in the correct form (such as Form TR1) and be registered at Land Registry using application form AP1 in order to take effect at law. In consequence, a purchaser of registered land will only have an equitable interest until the transfer to them is completed by registration.

Equitable interests

Generally, equitable interests need to be created and disposed of in writing (s.53(1) of the Law of Property Act 1925), but there are exceptions e.g. an equitable interest arising under a constructive trust. **2–007**

Protection of legal and equitable estates and interests on first registration

Registration

2–008 Certain legal estates and interests may be the subject of an application for either voluntary or compulsory first registration (see paras 5–002 and 5–003).

Where a disposition of an unregistered estate is subject to compulsory first registration, an application for registration must be made before the end of two months from the date of the disposition (or any extended period ordered by the registrar), otherwise the disposition becomes void with regard to the transfer, grant or creation of a legal estate (see para.5–004). It is therefore essential to comply with any compulsory first registration requirements in order to "protect" the legal estate in question.

Benefit and burden of certain interests on first registration

2–009 On completion of first registration the registered estate will be vested in the proprietor. Also, any beneficial easements and other interests subsisting for the benefit of the registered estate will automatically vest in the first registered proprietor on first registration (ss.11(3) and 12(3)) and thereafter in any new registered proprietor on registration of a subsequent transfer of the estate, even though they may not have been entered in the register (see para.5–017).

On first registration with title absolute the proprietor will hold the property subject to:

(1) those interests that are the subject of an entry in the register;

(2) any overriding interests set out in Sch.1 to the Act (see para.5–018);

(3) interests acquired under the Limitation Act 1980 of which the proprietor has notice (i.e. certain "squatter's rights"); and

(4) (in the case of a leasehold estate) covenants obligations and liabilities incident to the estate (e.g. tenant's covenants in the lease).

In the case of properties registered with a lesser class of title, the proprietor will also hold the property subject to any interests excepted from the effect of registration e.g. an undisclosed restrictive covenant burdening land registered with possessory freehold title, which existed at the time of first registration. A leasehold property registered with good leasehold title means that the landlord's power to grant the lease is not guaranteed e.g. if evidence of the landlord's unregistered title to grant the lease was not lodged on first registration of the lease.

Trustees will hold the property subject to any interests under the trust of which they are aware.

Overriding interests on first registration

Overriding interests are a defined category of unregistered interests set out in Sch.1 to the Act, which will continue to bind the land upon first registration, even though they do not appear on the register and may not be apparent from the title deeds or even be known to the registered proprietor (see para.5–018). **2–010**

Protection of legal and equitable estates and interests—registered estates

Registration of registrable dispositions

Once a property has been registered, most dispositions relating to the registered title must be completed by registration if they are to take effect at law, i.e. they are "registrable dispositions". Section 27 sets out the various types of registrable dispositions (see para.10–002), which include, for example, not only a transfer of the registered title or the grant of a legal charge, but also the grant of an easement. Schedule 2 to the Act sets out the registration requirements necessary to complete registration. **2–011**

Until completed by registration such dispositions only take effect in equity. For example, the grant of an easement, even if made by deed, will take effect only as an equitable easement until completed by registration and (not being legal) will not be an overriding interest under Sch.3 to the Act (see para.10–028). Until it is protected in the register by entry of a notice, it may be liable to be "overridden" on a subsequent disposition for value, such as a transfer on sale and in consequence may cease to bind the registered estate (see para.2–020).

It is therefore essential to comply with any registration requirements in order to "protect" the legal estate or interest created by a registrable disposition.

Protection of third party interests

Even if a legal or equitable interest does not arise from a registrable disposition, it may still need to be protected in the register if it is to bind third parties and preserve its priority. Under the Act, there are now only two ways of protecting third party rights in the register: **2–012**

(1) by notice; and/or
(2) by restriction.

Further details of these methods of protection are as follows.

2–013 **(1) *Notices*** A notice is an entry in the register in respect of the burden of an interest affecting a registered estate or charge. The fact that an interest is the subject of a notice does not necessarily mean that the interest is valid, but it does mean that if it is valid its priority is protected (s.32).

A notice only protects priority; it does not in itself confer priority.

It should be noted that overreaching (see paras 2–021 and 18–001) never affects legal or equitable estates and interests that affect the legal estate, such as leases, charges, options, estate contracts, easements or restrictive covenants, which may be protected by entry of a notice.

Certain interests cannot be protected by entry of a notice. For example, interests under a trust, leases for three years or less from the date of the grant (except where required to be registered) or restrictive covenants between landlord and tenant relating to the demised premises (s.33).

A notice may be entered by the registrar e.g. on first registration which will be a "registrar's notice", or following a specific application to enter a notice. Such an application may be for an "agreed notice" or a "unilateral notice". A registrar's notice takes effect as an agreed notice.

2–014 *Agreed Notice* This can be entered in the register either:

(a) by or with the consent of the registered proprietor (or a person entitled to be registered as proprietor); or
(b) if the applicant can satisfy the registrar as to the validity of their claim.

Some interests can only be protected by an agreed notice; for example, home rights (r.80—see Chapter 17).

2–015 *Unilateral Notice* Unlike an agreed notice, a unilateral notice:

(a) may be entered without the consent of the registered proprietor; and
(b) the applicant does not have to satisfy the registrar as to the validity of their claim.

Notices are discussed further in Chapter 16.

2–016 **(2) *Restrictions*** A restriction makes it apparent from the register that either the powers of the registered proprietor are limited or a prior condition must be met before a disposition can be registered. Restrictions:

(a) do not confer or protect priority, although a restriction may prevent registration of a disposition, which would adversely affect the priority of an interest;

(b) may not be entered for the purpose of protecting the priority of an interest, which is or could be the subject of a notice (ss.42(2) and 46(2)); however, an application for both may be made where appropriate; and

(c) do not prevent overreaching.

Restrictions are discussed further in Chapter 16.

Some interests (such as a charging order against the legal estate) can be protected by entry of an agreed notice or unilateral notice, because they affect the legal estate. Some interests (such as a charging order against a beneficial share of a joint owner) can only be protected by entry of a restriction, because they only affect an equitable interest under a trust of land. Some interests (such as an option to purchase the legal estate), can be protected by entry of both an agreed or unilateral notice (to protect its priority) and a restriction (e.g. to restrict any further dispositions being registered—if the option contains a "lock out" clause).

Some matters cannot be protected in the register, such as those that do not amount to an interest in the land e.g. an unsecured debt or a personal licence.

Section 77 provides that liability in damages may arise if a notice or restriction is applied for unreasonably.

Overriding interests—registered land

As on first registration, there are certain overriding interests, set out in Sch.3 to the Act, that override registered dispositions and will continue to bind the land even though they do not appear in the register and may not be apparent from the pre-registration title deeds or even known to the registered proprietor (see para.10–028). **2–017**

Once a notice of an overriding interest has been entered in the register that interest loses its overriding status and can never regain it (s.29(3)).

Entries made under the Land Registration Act 1925

Protection in the register under the Land Registration Act 1925 was by means of notice, caution against dealings, restriction or inhibition. The Act contains transitional provisions, so that entries made under the Land Registration Act 1925 will continue to have effect with certain modifications (see para.16–002). **2–018**

Priority of legal and equitable interests—registered estates

Rules of priority

2–019 The basic rule is that the priority of an interest affecting a registered estate or registered charge is not affected by a disposition of that estate or charge whether or not the interest or disposition is registered (s.28), i.e. the first in time prevails.

This basic rule is however significantly altered by ss.29 and 30 which create a special rule of priority in respect of registerable dispositions of a registered estate or registered charge made for valuable consideration. The effect of completion by registration of such a registrable disposition is to postpone to the interest under the disposition any interest affecting the estate or charge immediately before the disposition, if the priority of that interest is not protected at the time of registration.

The priority of an interest is "protected" for this purpose if it is:

(1) a registered charge;

(2) an interest protected by a notice in the register (protection by restriction is not sufficient in this context);

(3) an overriding interest under Sch.3 to the Act (see para.10–028);

(4) an interest excepted from the effect of registration e.g. if the title to the estate is qualified or possessory;

(5) (in the case of a leasehold estate) an interest the burden of which is incident to the estate e.g. tenant's covenants in the lease.

Effect of priority

2–020 If an interest requires protection in order to preserve its priority, failure to do so may mean that, on registration of a registrable disposition for value:

(1) The interest may be overridden completely by the disposition and cease to bind the registered title. For example, on registration of a transfer for value to a purchaser, they will take free of an equitable charge entered into by the vendor which was not protected by a notice in the register, although the vendor themselves may remain contractually liable to the chargee.

Or:

(2) The interest may be overridden by the disposition and lose priority to it, although it may otherwise continue to

> bind the registered title. For example, on registration of a registered charge granted for value to a chargee, the registered chargee will take free of an equitable easement granted by the registered proprietor which was not protected by a notice in the register and was not an overriding interest. Although the equitable easement will otherwise continue to bind the land for the time being, the chargee could sell the land free from the equitable easement if they were to exercise their power of sale.

This does not apply where the registrable disposition is not for value (for example, a transfer by way of gift) and an unprotected interest will therefore continue to bind the registered estate even after such a disposition has been registered and will not lose priority to it.

As between competing equitable interests, priority remains based upon the date of creation and ss.29 and 30, LRA 2002 do not apply as between these interests, as they are not registrable dispositions which have been completed by registration. Therefore, as between two competing equitable charges, where one is protected by a notice in the register and the other is not, they may both bind the registered proprietor and as between themselves, the first in time has priority.

Until completed by registration, a registrable charge takes effect in equity only and ranks against other equitable charges (whether or not protected by a notice in the register) according to the date of creation. Once completed by registration, the charge becomes a registered legal charge and s.29 applies, so that it gains priority over any prior equitable charge not protected in the register at the time of its registration.

As mentioned above, entry of a notice only protects rather than confers priority. Therefore, even if an equitable charge has been protected by a notice at the time of registration of a registrable charge, if the equitable charge post-dates the registered charge, it is the registered charge which will have priority—this is because the equitable charge (being second in time) never had priority over the registered charge and entry of the notice did not alter this.

If the priority of an interest is "protected" even though it is not the subject of an entry on the register, completion of a registrable disposition by registration will not mean that the disposition gains priority over that interest. For example, if the prior interest is an overriding interest or an interest excepted from the effect of registration, a purchaser will take subject to that interest on registration of the transfer to them, even though the prior interest does not appear in the register.

Overreaching

2–021 Overreaching occurs where there is a disposition for value of land, which is subject to a trust (see also paras 18–001 and 19–005). It is the mechanism under which the capital money is paid to two trustees or a trust corporation (or a sole personal representative acting as such), which enables a purchaser of a legal estate in the land to take free from certain equitable interests, whether or not they have notice of those interests (ss.2 and 27 of the Law of Property Act 1925). For the purposes of overreaching, a "purchaser" includes a mortgagee.

The effect of overreaching is that the interests of the beneficiaries under the trust are transferred to the proceeds of sale, leaving the purchaser to take the legal estate free of those interests.

Only certain equitable interests can be overreached; others cannot be overreached, nor can legal estates and interests. Those equitable interests that can be overreached are interests that do not relate to the legal estate in the land; for example an equitable charge on a beneficial share in the land or a contract to buy a beneficial share in the land.

Conversely, those interests that are only equitable, but which do relate to the legal estate in the land cannot be overreached; for example, an equitable charge on the legal estate, a restrictive covenant or an equitable easement. However, a purchaser will take free of them if they are not protected by an entry in the register or (in the case of an equitable easement) it was not an overriding interest under the Land Registration Act 1925 as preserved under the transitional provisions in the Act (see para.10–028).

The purpose of overreaching is to ensure that the purchaser takes free of the beneficial interests, but the trustees remain subject to those interests. For example, on the grant of a legal charge for value, the chargee may overreach any prior beneficial interest (such as a charging order on a beneficial share) enabling the chargee to take free of it, but the registered proprietors (as the trustees) will remain subject to that interest.

Devolution on death

Legal estate

2–022 The general rule is that the legal estate passes to the survivor(s) of joint owners, irrespective of whether they held the equitable interest in the property as beneficial joint tenants or tenants in [illegible]. This is because the legal [illegible] [illegible] and therefore [illegible] where they held the [illegible] [illegible]

[illegible]

[illegible]

[illegible]

Chapter 3

Plans, Maps and Boundaries

Title plans

The property register of each individual registered title contains a description of the registered estate which (in the case of a registered estate in land, rentcharge or affecting franchise) refers to a plan based on the Ordnance Survey map which is called the title plan (r.5). Each title plan is filed in Land Registry's computer system under the unique title number for the individual title to which it relates. **3–001**

Prior to the coming into force of the Act, the title plan was known as the "filed plan".

The title plan is prepared from:

(1) the plans and verbal descriptions in the pre-registration title deeds or registrable disposition, as the case may be;

(2) an inspection survey of the land where necessary; and

(3) the result of any further inquiries made by the registrar to establish the identity and extent of the property.

An applicant for first registration must normally provide sufficient information by plan or by verbal description to enable the land to be identified clearly on the Ordnance Survey map (r.24(1)(a)).

If, as is normally the case, the extent of the land to be registered can be identified on the Ordnance Survey map from the information supplied, the title plan will be prepared without a survey. However, where the extent of land to be included in the title cannot clearly be related to the features shown on the Ordnance Survey map an inspection survey will be carried out either by a Land Registry surveyor or by the Ordnance Survey at the request of Land Registry.

As all Land Registry's plans are based on the Ordnance Survey map, they may not be reproduced without a paper map copying licence from the Ordnance Survey. Any person intending to make copies of any of Land Registry's maps or plans should therefore first make the necessary arrangements by applying to: Customer Contact Centre, Ordnance Survey, Romsey Road, Southampton, SO16 4GU.

What does the title plan show?

3–002 A title plan shows:

(1) The title number of the registered estate.

(2) The extent of the registered estate, normally with "general boundaries" (see para.3–003), marked by red lines. Sometimes the verbal description of the estate in the property register will contain information clarifying the extent. For example, if the title relates to a first floor flat there will be a note in the property register to explain this.

(3) Other colours, which are explained in notes on the title plan or in the register, to identify, for example, land affected by easements or restrictive covenants. If land is coloured green it is not included in the title but is surrounded by land which is in the title. If it is edged green it has been removed from the title and is now registered under a new title number which may also be shown in green.

(4) Black lines, which represent boundary features such as walls, hedges, fences or buildings as shown on the Ordnance Survey map upon which the title plan is based.

(5) The scale to which the plan is drawn. Most plans are at the scale of 1/1250 which is used for land in urban areas, and for developing building estates, small houses, single building plots and so on. 1/2500 scale is used for land in predominantly rural areas, such as farms and other medium-sized units that are unlikely to be developed in the near future. 1/10560 or 1/10000 is sometimes used for the registration of mountain, moorland, marshland and similar areas that are unlikely ever to be developed or actively cultivated. Only the 1/2500 scale Ordnance Survey map shows Ordnance Survey parcel numbers and areas. Where a title plan is based on an extract from the

1/2500 scale map on which the numbers and areas are shown, they will not be deleted, except where only part of a parcel is included in the title. It is important to be aware that the numbers and areas shown on one edition of an Ordnance Survey map may differ from those shown on another.

(6) Dimensions, which may where appropriate be shown so as to tie the positions of unfenced boundaries, or to otherwise to clarify extents of land. However, the fact that such measurements are shown does not mean that the position of the boundary has been fixed or determined for land registration purposes (see para.3–004).

Enlargement plans are sometimes provided as part of a title plan, so as to clarify detail beyond the scope of the normal Ordnance Survey scales e.g. to show small juts in boundary walls and different floor levels. Supplementary plans can be annexed to title plans where appropriate, for example to show parts of buildings at different floor levels or to carry complicated reference markings that would cause confusion if shown on the title plan itself.

General boundaries

Every property, whether or not it is registered, has exact legal boundaries i.e. lines separating the property owned by one person from that owned by their neighbour. But deeds rarely identify these legal boundaries precisely, and often the owners themselves do not know exactly where they are. Trying to fix the boundaries precisely at the time of registration would involve a great deal of expense and could cause a dispute that would not otherwise have occurred. For that reason title plans normally show "general boundaries" (s.60(1)). A general boundary does not determine the exact line of the boundary (s.60(2)). **3–003**

This was also the case prior to the coming into force of the Act (r.278 of the Land Registration Rules 1925).

Registration with general boundaries means that, even though the title plan may show the red edging drawn along a particular wall, hedge, fence or other feature on the ground it does not show the exact line of the legal boundary. As a result the title plan does not define whether the boundary:

(1) runs somewhere within the feature on the plan; or

(2) runs along one particular side of the feature; or

(3) runs beyond the near side or the far side of the feature; or

(4) includes all or any part of an adjoining roadway, river or stream, for example.

As title plans are based on the Ordnance Survey map, they are limited by the precision with which such maps are prepared. As with any map, Ordnance Survey maps are subject to some limitations which depend upon the scale of the map and the accuracy of the surveying techniques used. These limitations are likely to result in some variation between what is shown on the map and what exists on the ground and as a result, title plans cannot be used to establish the precise position of features on the ground simply by scaling from the title plan. In some cases the nature of particular features on the ground can add to the uncertainty. For example, a mature hedge can be several metres wide, so that it can be difficult to relate it to the single line which represents it on the map.

General boundaries therefore allow flexibility in the relationship between the legal boundaries and any physical features on the Ordnance Survey map that Land Registry makes reference to when making a reasonable interpretation of the estate comprised within the title deeds.

The nature and effect of registration with general boundaries was considered by the court in *Lee v Barrey* [1957] Ch.251, CA. Two recent cases, *Derbyshire County Council v Fallon* [2007] EWHC 1326 (Ch) and *Strachey v Ramage* [2008] EWCA Civ 384 have further emphasised the importance of this point.

Determined boundaries

3–004 Under the Land Registration Act 1925 application could be made for a title to be registered with "fixed boundaries". The applicant had to bear the cost of this expensive process, and there was no guarantee that it would be possible, as a result of the investigations made, to fix the boundaries. In practice such applications were extremely rare.

Section 60(3) of the Act contains provision for the exact line of a boundary to be "determined" rather than it being a general boundary.

An application by a registered proprietor for the exact line of their boundary or part of their boundary to be determined must be made in Form DB accompanied by:

(1) a plan, or a plan and a verbal description, identifying the exact line of the boundary claimed and showing sufficient

surrounding physical features to allow the general position of the boundary to be drawn on the Ordnance Survey map; and

(2) evidence to establish the exact line of the boundary (r.118).

If the registrar is satisfied that:

(a) the plan, or plan and verbal description, supplied identifies the exact line of the boundary claimed;

(b) the applicant has shown an arguable case that the exact line of the boundary is in the position shown on the plan, or plan and verbal description; and

(c) he can identify all the owners of the land adjoining the boundary to be determined and has an address at which each owner may be given notice (r.119),

he must give the owners of the land adjoining the boundary to be determined (except the applicant) notice of the application, and of the fact that the exact line of the boundary will be determined if an objection is not received within the notice period.

But the registrar need not give notice of the application to an owner of the land adjoining the boundary where the evidence supplied includes either an agreement in writing as to the exact line of the boundary made with that owner or a court order determining the line of the boundary (r.119(2)).

The notice period is 20 business days or such longer period as the registrar may decide before the issue of the notice. If before the notice period has expired a request setting out why an extension should be allowed is received by the registrar, he may extend the notice period. Any such extension will be for such period as the registrar thinks fit which does not have to be the period requested. In deciding whether to extend the notice period the registrar will take account of all relevant matters including, if he thinks it appropriate, the views of the applicant (r.119(3), (4) and (5)).

If a valid objection to the application is received which cannot be disposed of by agreement, the matter must be referred to the Adjudicator (see Chapter 23).

If the application is completed, the registrar must make entries in the register and on the title plans of any titles affected, stating that the exact line of the boundary has been determined under s.60 and giving particulars of that line (r.120).

Where, when registering a transfer or lease of part of a registered title, the registrar has sufficient evidence to determine the exact line of a common boundary between the land transferred or leased and land which at the date of the transfer or lease was owned by the transferor or landlord he may do so (r.122).

A fee in accordance with the Fee Order is payable.

Deed plans

Use to clarify title plan

3–005 In cases of overlapping floors or party walls, for example, where a surveyor or architect has prepared detailed plans on larger scales, Land Registry will consider referring to those plans as an adjunct to the title plan.

Plan containing a statement of disclaimer

3–006 Plans which bear a statement of disclaimer, for example: "Note: This plan is for reference only and although believed to be correct, its accuracy is in no way guaranteed and it is expressly excluded from any contract" or "For identification only" are not acceptable for use in a disposition relating to registered land, such as a transfer or lease.

Reduced copy plans used in original deeds

3–007 Land Registry will reject any application relating to a lease or other disposition of part of a registered estate which contains plans that have been reduced from their original scale but which still bear the original scale endorsement.

Where it is clear that the plan contained in the disposition is a reduced copy of the original, it is only acceptable if:

(1) the original scale has been deleted; or

(2) it has been endorsed with a statement to the effect that it is a reduced copy (or in the case of a copy deed, a reduced copy of the plan to the original deed); or

(3) the actual scale is stated in place of the original scale.

If the scale on a layout plan is drawn by reference to metres or feet, the reduced image of the drawn scale that appears on the reduced copy plan will satisfactorily indicate the scale of the reduced plan; but an endorsement should always appear on the reduced copy plan.

Discrepancy between Ordnance Survey map and transfer or lease plan

3–008 Although registration is normally with general boundaries, Land Registry relates the boundaries as accurately as possible to the physical features, including fences, hedges and walls shown on the Ordnance Survey map. Where a transfer or lease plan shows detail which does not correspond with that actually existing on the ground, Land Registry may require the plan to be altered so that it does so.

If the plan is to be altered, Land Registry will if possible avoid the need to prepare a formal deed of rectification. So, for example, the parties concerned may be asked to remove the defective plan and substitute and sign a new plan, or to sign a new plan containing a statement that it correctly represents their intentions, and to sign an appropriate endorsement (referring to the new plan) on the defective plan.

Limitation of mapped extent of a registered title

Where part of the land in an application for first registration of an estate in land clearly falls outside the occupied extent of the property which is being registered (as shown on the latest Ordnance Survey map) and it appears to be occupied by another person, or where part of the land in the application is already registered under another registered title, Land Registry may prepare the title plan to exclude the land in question and send a letter to the applicant explaining why the extent registered is different from that applied for. It is then open to the applicant to account for the discrepancy e.g. by producing evidence of a licence or tenancy, or, where appropriate, to apply for alteration of the title plan of an existing registered title (see Chapter 24). **3–009**

Ownership of fences and walls: "T" marks

Land Registry will make an entry in the property register in respect of a declaration as to ownership of fences and other boundary features which is either identified on examination of title on first registration or contained within a disposition of a registered estate in land, as the case may be. **3–010**

Where "T" marks are referred to in positive covenants that are set out in the register (because they are intermixed with restrictive covenants—see para.8–005), explanatory notes are added as necessary, but it is usually unnecessary to reproduce the "T" marks on the title plan. "T" marks may appear on the plan to a deed which contains no fencing covenant or other provision which refers to them. If in such a case the applicant for registration specifically asks for the "T" marks to be reproduced on the title plan, Land Registry will usually comply with the request.

It is important to remember that where the register mentions ownership of walls, fences, hedges and other boundary features, these may have changed. For example, new boundary features might have been built and the neighbouring owners at that time might have agreed who was responsible for them. Regardless of any information given on the register it is usually best for a registered proprietor to discuss the matter with their neighbour and agree who owns a fence, hedge or other boundary feature before doing anything to it.

Accretion and diluvion

3–011 The fact that a registered estate in land is shown in the register as having a particular boundary does not affect the operation of accretion and diluvion (s.61(1)). Land abutting water is susceptible to gradual erosion or increase by deposit of silts etc. over a period of time. In these circumstances, the boundary represented in the title plan may not therefore be static as land may be acquired by accretion or lost by diluvion.

Neighbouring owners may enter into an agreement about the operation of accretion or diluvion in relation to a registered estate in land, but this has effect only if registered (s.61(2)). On registration, the registrar must make a note in the property register that the agreement is registered for the purposes of s.61(2) of the Act (r.123(2)).

Boundary disputes

3–012 Except in those rare cases where the boundary has been fixed or determined, Land Registry cannot decide or confirm where the exact legal boundary between two properties lies.

Therefore, if the exact legal line of the boundary has to be otherwise established, this can only be done:

(1) by the adjoining owners reaching an agreement; or

(2) judicially.

If at all possible, an agreement is usually the best way of bringing a dispute about the line of the boundary to an end. If an agreement is reached and there are significant changes that ought to be recorded, it is normally best to set the terms of the agreement down in a formal document and arrange for it to be noted in the registers of any registered titles affected.

However, such an agreement can only *clarify* the position of an existing boundary; it cannot be used to effect a transfer of property and a transfer in the prescribed form would be required in that regard. Also, such an agreement does not "determine" a boundary for land registration purposes and it would remain a general boundary in the register.

Although Land Registry cannot impose a solution it can sometimes help the parties to reach agreement by providing information which it holds and by offering guidance about land registration practice.

Mistake in a title plan

If a registered proprietor considers that there is a mistake in the title plan for their own and/or another registered title, the matter should be raised with Land Registry to enable it to investigate the matter and confirm whether or not there is such a mistake. **3–013**

Where there is a mistake in a title plan of a minor or uncontentious nature, the registrar may alter the title plan to correct it without a formal application being made. In other cases, it may be necessary for a proprietor to make a formal application for alteration in Form AP1. This would be the case where, for example, the matter was likely to be contentious and it is therefore important that the dispute and adjudication procedure is available in order to resolve any dispute (see Chapter 23).

Where the proposed alteration amounts to "rectification" of a registered estate in land and the proprietor is in possession of the land in question, it is not normally possible to remove that land from their title without their consent (paras 3(2) and 6(2) of Sch.4 to the Act—see Chapter 24).

If a registered proprietor is affected by the mistake or would be affected by the action needed to correct it, the registrar will normally serve notice upon them (r.128(2)). If there is a valid objection, the dispute can only be resolved by agreement or by the Adjudicator or by a court (see Chapter 23).

A person who suffers financial loss as a result of a mistake in a title plan may be entitled to be indemnified. If there is a possibility that there is a mistake which may lead to costs being incurred, the registrar's consent to incur costs should be sought before any costs are incurred; normally indemnity for costs cannot be paid unless the registrar consented to those costs being incurred. Alteration. rectification and indemnity are discussed further in Chapter 24.

Index of registrations

The index (section 68 and rule 10)

3–014 The registrar is obliged to keep an index, which is comprised of two parts.

An *index map* is kept by the registrar from which it can be ascertained, in relation to a parcel of land, whether there is:

(1) a pending application for first registration or for a caution against first registration (other than in respect of a relating franchise);

(2) a registered estate in land or a registered rentcharge, profit à prendre in gross or affecting franchise; or

(3) a caution against first registration (other than in respect of a relating franchise),

and, if there is such a registered estate or caution, the title number.

A separate *index of verbal descriptions* of:

(a) pending applications for first registration or for a caution against first registration in respect of a relating franchise;

(b) registered relating franchises;

(c) registered manors;

(d) cautions against first registration in respect of a relating franchise,

arranged by administrative area and identifying their title numbers is also kept.

Searches of the index (rules 145 and 146)

3–015 Both parts of the index are open to inspection and any person may apply for an official search of the index. A search is made either:

(1) by delivering a Form SIM (for a search of the index map) or Form SIF (for a search of the index of relating franchises and manors) to the proper office;

(2) by telephone or fax if a credit account holder; or

(3) by direct access to the register if a credit account holder and Land Registry Direct subscriber;

(4) through the NLIS.

Description of the property to be searched

An application for a search of the index map must clearly describe the land to which it relates. The description should include the postal number or description, the road name, the locality, the town, the local authority serving the property, the post code and/or Ordnance Survey map reference (if known) and any known title number. **3–016**

If the search is in respect of a particular flat in a block of flats, this should be made clear in the description.

If the registrar so requires, the applicant must provide a copy of an extract from the Ordnance Survey map on the largest published scale showing the land to which the application relates (r.145(3)).

An application for a search of the index of relating franchises and manors must specify whether the search is in respect of manors or relating franchises, and specify the relevant counties and/or unitary authorities.

If a search of a large area is required applicants should contact the proper office in advance so that special arrangements may be made to eliminate unnecessary work.

Search fees

Fees are payable in accordance with the Fee Order. There is now a fee payable for all searches, including those which do not reveal a title number. A credit account can be used for payment of fees on such searches. If it transpires additional fees are required e.g. because of the number of registered titles revealed, the applicant will be notified of this and given the opportunity to withdraw their application without fee if they wish or it will be returned in any event if the additional fees are not lodged. **3–017**

Certificate of result of search (rules 145(4) and 146(3) and Part 1 and Part 2 of Schedule 6 to the Rules)

The result of an official search of the index map will be in paper form and include the following information: **3–018**

(1) the date and time of the official search certificate;

(2) a description of the land searched;

(3) the reference (if any) of the applicant or the person to whom the search is being sent;

(4) whether there is:

(a) a pending application for first registration (other than for a relating franchise);

(b) a pending application for a caution against first registration (other than in respect of a relating franchise);
(c) a registered estate in land;
(d) a registered rentcharge;
(e) a registered profit à prendre in gross;
(f) a registered affecting franchise; or
(g) a caution against first registration (other than in respect of a relating franchise),

and, if there is such a registered estate or caution, the title number.

Where, on a search of a routine nature, the result of the search reveals that either the whole of the land searched is registered under two to five different title numbers or part of the land searched is unregistered and the remainder is registered under one to five different registered titles, Land Registry may issue a plan illustrating the registered properties as shown on the index map.

These plans are illustrative and do not define the extent of the land in a title. If more specific information is required about a title then the applicant must inspect and/or obtain official copies of the register and title plan (see Chapter 9).

There is currently no fee payable for the provision of such a plan. Such plans are not provided when the search relates to a large area or an area of complex registrations.

The result of an official search of the index of relating franchises and manors will contain the information set out in Pt.2 of Sch.6 to the Rules.

Party Wall etc. Act 1996 and party wall agreements

3–019 The purpose of the Party Wall etc. Act 1996 is to regulate the manner in which works to party walls and other works adjacent to boundaries are carried out. In general, the Party Wall etc. Act 1996 does not affect ownership of land and hence no notice or other entry may be made in the register in respect of any of the following arising under that Act:

(1) a party structure notice;

(2) a party wall award;

(3) a notice under s.1(2) of the Act in respect of a proposed new wall.

However s.14 of the Party Wall etc. Act 1996 provides that the expenses of building a party wall or party fence wall or carrying out works under the Act may be apportioned between the building owner and the adjoining owner (as defined in that Act). Until the adjoining owner has paid the appropriate share of the expenses to the building owner, the part of the party wall on the adjoining owner's land vests in the building owner.

If the adjoining owner's estate is registered, the building owner can apply to protect their ownership rights by the entry of a notice in the register (see paras 16–005 and 16–008). The notice should be confined to the land affected and the position of the wall must be described sufficiently to enable a verbal description or a reference on the title plan to be given in the entry for so much of the wall as falls within the adjoining owner's title against which the notice will be entered.

A party wall agreement may be made under the provisions of the Party Wall etc. Act 1996 or under general law; its effect for land registration purposes will depend upon its provisions.

A party wall agreement may providing that ownership of a wall or fence is split longitudinally between two neighbouring registered titles represents a "provision as to boundary structures" and an application may be made in Form AP1 for the register to be altered to include an entry in respect of the agreement.

A party wall agreement may also contain the mutual grant of easements and the appropriate application should be made in respect of them (see Chapter 8). If granted over a registered estate, these may constitute a registrable disposition required to be completed by registration (s.27—see para.10–002).

In addition to or instead of easements, a party wall agreement may also contain restrictive covenants affecting all or part of the wall or fence. Where necessary, application may be made for entry of a notice in the register in respect of them (see paras 16–005 and 16–008).

common. This is because the legal estate can only be held as joint tenants and therefore passes automatically to the survivor(s) even where they held the equitable interest as beneficial tenants in common (see para.19–001).

On the death of a sole owner or the survivor of joint owners, the legal estate passes to their personal representative(s) (see para.19–003).

Equitable interest

The equitable or beneficial interest will pass by survivorship (in the case of beneficial joint tenants) or by will or intestacy (in the case of beneficial tenants in common) (see para.19–001). The registrar is not normally concerned with the equitable interest except in relation to the entry or cancellation of a restriction in Form A (see paras 5–007 and 11–013). **2–023**

Practical points

- Consider the nature of an estate or interest and how it may need to be protected,
- Consider the priority of competing interests where necessary,
- Ensure that overreaching is effected where required,
- Ensure a document is in the form of a deed where necessary, to ensure an estate or interest can take effect at law,
- Be aware of the nature and effect of a notice in the register and the distinction between an agreed notice and a unilateral notice,
- Be aware of the nature and effect of a restriction in the register.

Practical points

- Bear in mind the nature and effect of registration with general boundaries when considering a title plan;
- Ensure a satisfactory plan is used in a transfer, lease or other disposition;
- Remember to carry out a search of the index map where necessary e.g. prior to a purchase of an unregistered estate;
- Take the appropriate action in respect of any party wall agreement.

Chapter 4

Cautions Against First Registration

Nature and effect

A caution against first registration entitles the cautioner to be given notice of an application for first registration of a legal estate to which the caution relates and gives the cautioner the right to object to that application (s.16(1)). **4–001**

The notice period is 15 business days, which may be extended to a period of up to 30 business days if the cautioner applies for an extension and the registrar, after consulting the applicant for cancellation if he thinks it appropriate, agrees to allow it. The extension allowed does not have to be the extension applied for; it can be for any period the registrar thinks fit up to a total period of 30 business days (r.53).

If a valid objection to the application is received which cannot be disposed of by agreement, the matter must be referred to the Adjudicator (see Chapter 23).

A caution against first registration neither guarantees the validity of the interest to which it relates nor confers priority on that interest (s.16(3)). Also, it does not replace the normal requirement to protect an interest by registration as a Land Charge, where necessary.

Who can apply?

A caution against first registration may, subject to the important exception mentioned below, be registered by a person who claims to be the owner of or entitled to an interest affecting a qualifying estate. A "qualifying estate" for this purpose is a legal **4–002** estate relating to the land to which the caution relates and which is an interest of one of the following kinds:

(1) an estate in land;

(2) a rentcharge;

(3) a franchise; or

(4) a profit à prendre in gross.

A broad range of interests affecting such an estate may entitle a person to apply for registration of a caution against first registration; for example, where a person claims the benefit of an easement over an unregistered estate in land.

However, as one of the aims of the Act is to encourage registration of title, the owner of an unregistered freehold estate in land or of an unregistered leasehold estate in land held under a lease of which more than seven years are unexpired is not allowed to protect their interest by the registration of a caution against first registration (s.15(3)). The appropriate way to protect such an estate is to register it.

For a transitional period of two years such an owner was allowed to register a caution against first registration, but any such caution ceased to have any effect after October 12, 2005 (para.14 of Sch.12 to the Act).

Existing cautions against first registration registered before the Act came into force (even if registered to protect a claim to an unregistered freehold estate in land or to an unregistered leasehold estate in land held under a lease of which more than seven years are unexpired) continue to have effect from October 13, 2003, but they are now subject to the same provisions for alteration, withdrawal and cancellation set out below as cautions registered on or after that date (paras 1 and 16 of Sch.12 to the Act).

Method of application

4–003 Application for a caution against first registration must be made in Form CT1 accompanied by a plan or other sufficient description to enable the land to which it relates to be identified on the Ordnance Survey map (r.42).

The application must be supported by a statement of truth made by (or on behalf of) the applicant or by their conveyancer, setting out details of the interest claimed. The form of statement of truth is incorporated within Form CT1. Documents proving the interest should not be lodged with the application nor should they be attached to the statement of truth.

The application may be accompanied by a consent by another person to the registration of the caution, which must be in writing (r.47). Such a consent is relevant if a subsequent application to cancel the caution is lodged (see para.4–008).

A fee in accordance with the Fee Order is payable. But under s.117(2) no fee is payable where the application is to protect an interest which will cease to be an overriding interest on October 12, 2013 (see paras 5–018 and 10–028).

The cautions register

A separate register of cautions against first registration is kept **4–004** by the registrar (s.19) with an individual register for each caution (r.40). It is kept almost entirely in electronic form.

Each individual caution register has its own caution title number and is in two parts:

(1) The *caution property register,* containing a description of the legal estate to which it relates and of the interest claimed. The description will refer to a caution plan based on the Ordnance Survey map, where the caution relates to an estate in land, a rentcharge or an affecting franchise.

(2) The *cautioner's register,* containing:

  (a) the name of the cautioner;
  (b) an address for service (see r.198); and
  (c) (where appropriate) details of any person consenting to the lodging of the caution.

Inspection and copies

The cautions register is open to inspection and official copies **4–005** can be obtained (see Chapter 9).

Alteration of the cautions register

The court may make an order for alteration of the cautions **4–006** register to:

(1) correct a mistake; or

(2) bring the register up to date (s.20).

The registrar also has power to alter the cautions register for the same purposes (s.21).

If the court makes an order for alteration, the registrar must give effect to it when it is served on him (s.20(2)).

If, in any proceedings the court decides, or if on application the registrar is satisfied, that the cautioner does not own the relevant interest, or only owns part, or that such interest either wholly or in part did not exist or has come to an end, the court must make an order for alteration of or, as the case may be, the registrar must on application alter, the cautions register (rr.48 and 49). However, the registrar is not obliged to alter the cautions register under s.21 so as to substitute another person as cautioner unless the whole of the relevant interest is vested in that person by operation of law.

An application to the registrar to alter the cautions register must be made in Form AP1 and must include written details of the alteration required and of the grounds on which it is made, and any supporting document. Before the registrar makes the alteration he must, unless he is satisfied that it is unnecessary, serve notice on the cautioner (r.50).

A person who claims that the whole of the relevant interest described in an individual caution register is vested in them by operation of law as successor to the cautioner may apply for the register to be altered to substitute them as cautioner (r.51(1)). If the registrar does not serve notice, because he is satisfied that it is unnecessary, or if he does serve notice and the cautioner does not object within the time specified in the notice, the registrar must give effect to such an application (r.51(2)).

A successor to the cautioner in other cases may apply for alteration under s.21(1) and r.50 so as to substitute them as cautioner, unless the vesting is the result of a "trigger" inducing compulsory first registration (see para.5–003). Satisfactory evidence of vesting e.g. an assignment, must accompany the application.

If a valid objection to the application is received which cannot be disposed of by agreement, the matter must be referred to the Adjudicator (see Chapter 23).

Where an alteration is made by the registrar, he has a discretion to make a payment in respects of costs reasonably incurred in connection with the alteration (s.21(3)).

A fee in accordance with the Fee Order is payable.

Withdrawal

An application to withdraw a caution against first registration must be made in Form WCT signed by the cautioner or their conveyancer. If the application affects only part of the land to which the caution relates, it must contain sufficient details, by plan or otherwise, to identify that part clearly on the Ordnance Survey map (r.43). **4–007**

Only the cautioner may apply to withdraw the caution. If the cautioner has died, their personal representative must first apply to be shown as cautioner in place of the deceased cautioner (r.51).

No fee is currently payable.

Cancellation

The owner of the legal estate to which a caution against first registration relates, or the owner of a legal estate derived out of that estate, may apply for cancellation of the caution (s.18(1) and r.45). In addition, where the land to which the caution relates is demesne land, Her Majesty or the owner of a legal estate affecting the demesne land may apply (r.45(b)). **4–008**

But where the caution was lodged with the applicant's consent, or with the consent of a person from whom they derive title, the applicant must prove either that the relevant interest has come to an end, or that the consent was induced by fraud, misrepresentation, mistake or undue influence or given under duress (s.18(2) and r.46).

The application must be made in Form CCT and, if the application affects only part of the land to which the caution relates, it must include sufficient details, by plan or otherwise, to identify that part clearly on the Ordnance Survey map (r.44(1) and (2)). It must be accompanied (other than where the applicant is Her Majesty) by evidence to satisfy the registrar that the applicant is entitled to apply (r.44(3)).

The registrar must give the cautioner notice of an application for cancellation (s.18(3)). If the cautioner does not object to the application before the end of the notice period, the registrar must cancel the caution (s.18(4)). The notice period is 15 business days, which may be extended to a period of up to 30 business days if the beneficiary applies for an extension and the registrar, after consulting the applicant for cancellation if he thinks it appropriate, agrees to allow it. The extension allowed does not have to be the extension applied for; it can be for any period the registrar thinks fit up to a total period of 30 business days (r.53).

If a valid objection to cancellation is received which cannot be disposed of by agreement, the matter must be referred to the Adjudicator (see Chapter 23).

No fee is currently payable.

Practical points

- Remember that a caution against first registration cannot now be registered by certain owners of unregistered land,
- Bear in mind that registration of a caution against first registration does not guarantee the validity of an interest or confer priority upon it,
- Registration of the interest as a Land Charge should still be effected, where necessary,
- Use the correct application form when applying to cancel or withdraw a caution against first registration.

Chapter 5

First Registration

Introduction

The Act provides for both voluntary and compulsory first registration of title to an unregistered legal estate of a kind specified in s.2 (see para.1–003). Title to an estate in land may be capable of either voluntary or compulsory first registration as discussed below. Title to a rentcharge, a franchise or a profit à prendre in gross may be capable of voluntary first registration, but is not currently subject to compulsory first registration. **5–001**

Voluntary first registration

An application may be made voluntarily at any time for the registration of the title to an unregistered legal estate which is an interest of any of the following kinds: **5–002**

(1) an estate in land;

(2) a rentcharge;

(3) a franchise (see para.1–003); or

(4) a profit à prendre in gross (see paras 1–003 and 8–023),

if it is vested in the applicant or they are entitled to require it to be vested in them (but not where they have merely contracted to buy under a contract) (s.3(1), (2) and (6)).

The two estates in land which are capable of registration are a fee simple absolute in possession (freehold) and a term of years absolute (leasehold).

No application can be made to register a leasehold estate vested in the applicant as a mortgagee where there is a subsisting right of redemption (s.3(5)).

An application to register a lease may only be made if it was granted for a term of which more than seven years are unexpired, unless the right to possession under the lease is discontinuous e.g. a "timeshare" lease, in which case an application can be made whatever the length of the term (s.3(3) and (4)).

If a person holds both:

(a) a lease in possession; and

(b) a lease of the same land to take effect in possession on, or within a month of, the end of the lease in possession,

in the same capacity, the leases are treated as creating one continuous term for this purpose (s.3(7)).

Under s.118 the Lord Chancellor may by order, after appropriate consultation, reduce the length of a leasehold term which may be the subject of an application for registration, but it is not currently proposed that he should do so.

Section 79 contains provisions whereby Her Majesty may grant a freehold estate out of demesne land to Herself and may register the title to that estate, thereby overcoming the problem that demesne land would not itself be capable of registration.

Compulsory first registration

Duty to apply

5–003 There is a duty to apply for compulsory first registration (s.4) on the occurrence of a specified event or "trigger" in relation to a qualifying estate. For this purpose a "qualifying estate" is an unregistered legal estate which is either a freehold estate in land or a leasehold estate in land for a term which, at the time of the event, has more than seven years to run (s.4(2)). "Land" for this purpose does not include mines and minerals held apart from the surface (s.4(9)).

The events triggering compulsory first registration specified in s.4 are as follows.

(1) The **transfer** (whether by conveyance, assignment, transfer or otherwise) of a **freehold estate in land**:

   (a) for valuable or other consideration (including a negative value); or
   (b) by way of gift (including for the purposes of constituting a trust under which the settlor does not retain the whole of the beneficial interest, or uniting the bare legal title and the beneficial interest in

property held under a trust under which the settlor did not, on constitution, retain the whole beneficial interest); or

(c) in pursuance of an order of any court; or

(d) by means of an assent (including a vesting assent under the Settled Land Act 1925);

(e) giving effect to a partition of land subject to a trust of land;

(f) by a deed that appoints (or by virtue of s.83 of the Charities Act 1993 has effect as if it appointed) a new trustee;

(g) by a vesting order under s.44 of the Trustee Act 1925 that is consequential on the appointment of a new trustee;

(h) in circumstances where s.171A of the Housing Act 1985 applies (disposal by landlord that leads to a person no longer being a secure tenant).

(2) The **transfer** (whether by conveyance, assignment, transfer or otherwise) of an **existing leasehold estate in land** with more than seven years to run at the time of the transfer:

(a) for valuable or other consideration (including a negative value); or

(b) by way of gift (including for the purposes referred to in (1)(b) above); or

(c) in pursuance of an order of any court; or

(d) by means of an assent (including a vesting assent under the Settled Land Act 1925);

(e) giving effect to a partition of land subject to a trust of land;

(f) by a deed that appoints a new trustee (in the circumstances referred to in (1)(f) above);

(g) by a vesting order under s.44 of the Trustee Act 1925 that is consequential on the appointment of a new trustee.

In addition, registration is also compulsory on a transfer in circumstances where s.171A of the Housing Act 1985 applies (disposal by landlord that leads to a person no longer being a secure tenant), regardless of the term of the lease being transferred.

(3) The **grant** of a **new leasehold estate in land** out of a qualifying estate for a term of years absolute which is:

(a) for a term of more than seven years from the date of the grant, and which is:

(b) for valuable or other consideration (including a negative value); or
(c) by way of gift (including for the purposes referred to in (1)(b) above); or
(d) in pursuance of an order of any court.

In addition, registration is also compulsory on the grant out of any unregistered legal estate in land of any new lease (regardless of the length of the term):

(i) in pursuance of Part 5 of the Housing Act 1985 (the right to buy); or
(ii) in circumstances where s.171A of the Housing Act 1985 applies (disposal by landlord that leads to a person no longer being a secure tenant).

(4) The **creation** of a **first legal mortgage** protected by deposit of documents of a qualifying estate (in which event the mortgagee is entitled to apply for registration in the name of the mortgagor whether or not the mortgagor consents (s.6(6) and r.21).

The registrable estate which is subject to compulsory first registration will be either the qualifying estate itself (in the case of a transfer or creation of a mortgage) or the estate created by the event giving rise to compulsory first registration (in the case of the grant of a lease).

Section 80 provides for compulsory first registration of grants out of demesne land.

The duty to apply for compulsory first registration does not arise on:

(a) a transfer by operation of law to which (1) above would otherwise apply, e.g. the vesting of unregistered land in a new trustee under s.40 of the Trustee Act 1925 (s.4(3)); or
(b) the assignment of a mortgage term (s.4(4)(a)); or
(c) the assignment or surrender of a lease to the owner of the immediate reversion where the term is to merge in that reversion (s.4(4)(b)); or
(d) the grant of an estate to a person as mortgagee (s.4(5)).

Some leasehold estates not specified in s.4 can nevertheless be the subject of a voluntary application for first registration, as can an unregistered legal estate which consists of mines and minerals held apart from the surface or which is a rentcharge, profit à prendre in gross or a franchise (see para.5–002).

Time limit for compulsory application

The estate owner or their successor in title must apply for first registration within two months of the date on which occurs the event giving rise to the duty to apply (s.6). If this is not done, the transfer, lease or mortgage will become void as to the transfer, grant or creation of a legal estate (s.7(1)). **5–004**

In that event it will take effect in equity only, so that in the case of:

(1) a transfer, the title to the legal estate reverts to the transferor who holds it on bare trust for the transferee;

(2) the grant or creation of a lease or mortgage, the grant or creation takes effect as a contract for valuable consideration to grant the lease or create the mortgage;

(3) the appointment of a new trustee, the legal estate reverts to the person in whom it was vested immediately before the appointment.

Where necessary, a request (supported by a written explanation) may be made for an order of the registrar extending the time period for registration. If satisfied there is a good reason for the request, an extension will normally be granted and the application when lodged within that extended period will be treated as if s.7(1) had not applied. No fee is currently payable for such an order.

Procedure before completion of a transaction which will result in a duty to apply

There is no special procedure to be adopted before completion of a conveyance or other transaction which will "trigger" compulsory first registration. The transaction proceeds in the way unregistered interests are normally dealt with and it is only upon completion that the additional task of applying for first registration of title needs to be carried out. **5–005**

The document effecting the transaction may either be in a "unregistered" format, e.g. a traditional form of conveyance, or alternatively a form contained in Sch.1 of the Rules such as a transfer in Form TR1, may be used where appropriate. In the case of a lease, this does not have to be in the form of a "prescribed clauses lease" (see para.12–004) although this format can be used if desired.

In the case of an estate in land, the usual local and Land Charges searches will be necessary. A Land Charges search should be carried out against the names of the relevant estate owners, for the relevant period and in respect of the relevant counties; any entries revealed should be accounted for, otherwise the registrar may make a protective entry in the register. In addition, an application should always be made for an official search of the index map, as explained in para.3–015, to discover whether any estates in the land are already registered or the subject of a caution against first registration or the subject of a pending application for first registration of for registration of a caution against first registration.

Bearing in mind that the estate will be the subject of an application for registration for the first time, care should be taken to check that the extent of the land to be registered is accurately defined by reference to boundary walls or fences or other physical features on the ground; and that the transfer, lease or mortgage accurately identifies the land to be registered in relation to the Ordnance Survey map (r.24). It is inadvisable to describe the land by reference to a plan to an earlier document of title unless the plan is known to correspond with the current physical boundaries.

The land should be inspected both to ascertain the boundaries and to discover, so far as this can be done by inspection, any unregistered interests to which it is subject (see para.5–018).

Particular care is required in the case of certain types of property—for example, where a garden is separated from the house to which it belongs by a passage or road, or where rooms or parts of rooms extend into an adjoining property or over a passageway, or where the boundaries are not fully defined by features on the ground. A purchaser or their conveyancer should always ensure that such cases are identified by checking the layout of the property, and the facts should be brought to the attention of Land Registry, preferably by means of a plan, when lodging the application for first registration.

If, while a person is subject to a duty to make an application for compulsory first registration of an unregistered estate, there is a dealing with that estate, that dealing is treated as if it had taken place after the date of first registration. The registration of any such dealing delivered for registration with the application for first registration has effect from the time of the making of that application (r.38).

The application for first registration

5–006 An application for first registration must be made in Form FR1 (r.23) lodged with the appropriate fee in accordance with the Fee Order and accompanied by (r.24):

(1) Sufficient details, by plan or otherwise so that the land can be identified clearly on the Ordnance Survey map.

The land to be identified on an application to register a rentcharge, franchise or profit à prendre in gross is the land affected by that estate or to which it relates.

(2) In the case of a leasehold estate, the lease, if in the possession or control of the applicant, and a certified copy.

(3) All deeds and documents relating to the title that are in the possession or control of the applicant. If the title deeds have been lost or destroyed, see Chapter 6. Deeds and documents which are in the custody of a mortgagee under a mortgage or in respect of which the applicant has only a right to production are not regarded as being under the applicant's control, but the applicant should lodge a sufficient marked abstract or certified copy. The registrar has the power to order the production of documents (s.75) but in practice it is rarely necessary for this power to be exercised.

(4) A list in duplicate in Form DL of all the documents delivered.

Where appropriate the following should also be lodged:

(5) Form DI (see para.5–008).

(6) The appropriate SDLT evidence (see para.1–016).

(7) Any mortgage or charge by the applicant.

(8) Certified copies of any statutory declaration or statement of truth, subsisting lease, subsisting charge, certificate relating to SDLT, or the latest document of title which the applicant has requested be returned to him under r.203(2). The latest document of title is the document by which the applicant or, if vesting was by operation of law, the applicant's predecessor acquired the estate which is being registered (r.203(8)). The registrar is not obliged to return all or any of the documents lodged with the application unless the applicant requests him to do so (r.203(1)). But if the applicant makes such a request on first registration he is not required to lodge certified copies of any documents other than those specified in this paragraph (r.203(4)).

See also para.12–011 as to leases of unregistered land.

Completing Form FR1

When completing Form FR1 the following points should be borne in mind: **5–007**

Property: If the property to be registered has an address including a postcode, it should always be included.

Extent: The "postal address" option cannot be used when registering a flat or cellar, for example and a reference to a plan will be required (see paras 5–009 and 5–010).

Class of title: The box identifying the class of title which is being applied for should be clearly marked with an "X". The class of title actually granted may be different, depending upon the result of the registrar's examination of the title.

Applications, priority and fees: Details of the applications being made should be listed in priority order. See para.1–013 as to the methods of payment of fees. On first registration of land a fee is payable calculated in accordance with the Fee Order, assessed on the present value of land and buildings whether or not the application is based on a recent purchase.

The applicant: Full details of the applicant, including any relevant additional details in respect of any company or limited liability partnership applicant (such as a registered number), should be provided.

Address for service (r.198): At least one and not more than three addresses for service, to which all notices and other communications to the proprietor will be sent by the registrar, must be provided.

One address for service must be a postal address, whether or not in the United Kingdom. If any additional addresses for service are supplied they must be either a postal address, whether or not in the United Kingdom, a box number at a United Kingdom document exchange or an electronic mail address. *It is very important that addresses for service are accurate and kept up to date.* In the case of an ordinary householder who on completion of the purchase moves to the property being registered, the address to be entered on the register will usually be the full postal address of that property. However, if the property has been purchased for rental purposes, the address of the property is not likely to be suitable as the address for service.

Where the applicant is more than one person—declaration of trust: Where there are joint applicants, a trust of land automatically arises and it should therefore be confirmed whether they are holding on trust for themselves (and if so, whether as beneficial joint tenants or tenants in common) or on some other trust. Although the registrar is not affected by notice of a trust (s.77) and is not generally concerned with the beneficial interests, he does need this information to enable him to decide whether or not a restriction in Form A is required in the register pursuant to his obligation under s.44(1) and r.95(2)(a).

The obligation under s.44(1) is that the registrar must enter a restriction in Form A when registering two or more persons as proprietor of a registered estate in land, unless satisfied that the survivor of them can give a valid receipt for capital money arising on a disposition—this will normally only be the case where the proprietors are holding on trust for themselves as beneficial joint tenants (so that the "rule of survivorship" applies—see paras 18–001 and 19–001) or are the personal representatives of an absolute owner, acting as such (so that a receipt by a sole personal representative will be sufficient).

The purpose of the restriction is to ensure that "overreaching" is effected, where required under ss.2 and 27 of the Law of Property Act 1925, with capital monies being paid to at least two trustees, or a sole personal representative acting as such, or to a trust corporation (see paras 2–021, 18–001 and 19–005). It does not obviate the need for an express declaration of trust to be executed where appropriate, the importance of which was the subject of detailed judicial comment in *Stack v Dowden* [2007] UKHL 17.

In the case of other types of registered estate, r.94(2A) provides that where two or more persons apply to be registered as proprietors of an unregistered estate which is a rentcharge, profit à prendre in gross, franchise or manor, they must also apply for entry of a restriction in Form A if a sole (surviving) proprietor will not be able to give a valid receipt for capital money.

Certificate as to other interests: If there are any rights, interests or claims affecting the estate which are known to the applicant, other than those disclosed in the title deeds or Form DI (see para.5–008), these should be disclosed in the Form FR1. This would include, for example, any rights in the course of being acquired over the estate by adverse possession, or a disputed third party claim relating to the estate.

Examination of title: The registrar has a discretion to have regard to any prior examination of the applicant's title by a conveyancer when carrying out his own examination (r.29). Therefore, if the applicant's title has not been examined in the usual way by a conveyancer, this should be confirmed.

Confirmation of identity: This requirement was introduced by Land Registry as part of its strategy to combat property fraud and should be complied with as appropriate, depending upon whether or not the application is being lodged by a conveyancer.

Signature of form: The Form FR1 should be signed by the applicant or by their conveyancer in the name of the firm.

Form DI—Duty to disclose unregistered interests that override first registration (rule 28)

5–008 On an application for first registration, the applicant is under a duty to provide information about any of the interests that override first registration which:

(1) are within the actual knowledge of the applicant; and

(2) affect the estate to which the application relates (r.28).

This information should be provided in Form DI lodged with the application.

However, there is no requirement to provide information about interests which are apparent from the documents lodged with the application nor is it necessary to disclose:

(a) interests that cannot be protected by entry of a notice (see Chapter 16);

(b) public rights;

(c) leases granted for a term not exceeding seven years from the date of the grant, not being a lease which the tenant is under a duty to register, when at the time of the application the term granted by the lease has one year or less to run; and

(d) local land charges.

Form FR1 requires the applicant or their conveyancer to certify either that Form DI accompanies the application or that no disclosable interests affect (see para.5–007).

Where the applicant provides information about such an interest the registrar may enter a notice in the register in respect of that interest (r.28(4) and once noted it will cease to be an interest that overrides (s.29(3)).

Registration of mines and minerals (rule 25)

5–009 An application for first registration of title to mines and materials apart from the surface must be accompanied by:

(1) a plan of the surface under which they lie;

(2) any other sufficient details by plan or otherwise so that they can be identified clearly; and

(3) full details of rights incidental to their working.

Such an application is never compulsory (s.4(9)), but a voluntary application may be made. The application must also be accompanied by evidence of title to the mines and minerals; a normal 15-year root of title will not usually be sufficient in this regard.

Due to the difficulties in establishing a good title to mines and minerals, the registrar will in many cases only be in a position to grant a qualified class of title (see para.5–012). The qualification will be in the following form:

> "QUALIFICATION: The inclusion of all or any of the mines and minerals and powers of working and getting them in this title does not affect or prejudice the enforcement of any estate right or interest therein existing before [*date of first registration*]."

In the case of an application for first registration of a lease of mines and minerals, where the landlord's title to the mines and minerals cannot be satisfactorily established, a good leasehold class of title will be granted, rather than title absolute.

See also paras 11–012 and 12–012 as to further discussion on mines and minerals in relation to registered land.

Registration of cellars, flats, tunnels, etc. (rule 26)

Unless all of the land above and below the surface (except **5–010** where only mines and minerals are excluded) is included in the application, the applicant must provide a plan of the surface on, under or over which the land to be registered lies, and sufficient information to define the vertical and horizontal extents of the land which is to be registered.

Official examination of title

Before completing an application for first registration, the **5–011** registrar will examine the evidence of title lodged in order to satisfy himself as to the quality of the applicant's unregistered title to the estate. In the context of an unregistered estate, title is essentially based upon the right to possession of the estate or to the receipt of the rents and profits from it; that right is normally established by lodging a full documentary title commencing with a good root of title which is at least 15 years old.

Rule 24 requires all the available deeds and documents to be lodged and, if any title deeds which are essential to proving title are not lodged, the applicant must satisfactorily account for their absence otherwise this could result in a lesser class of title being granted and/or a protective entry being made in the register e.g. if the missing deed contained restrictive covenants (see also Chapter 6).

In examining title the registrar may have regard to any examination by a conveyancer prior to the application and to the nature of the property (r.29).

The registrar may (r.30):

(1) make searches and enquiries and give notices to other persons;

(2) direct that searches and enquiries be made by the applicant; and

(3) advertise the application (although this is very unusual).

Classes of title

5–012 The Act provides for several different classes of title to be granted.

(1) Absolute freehold title may be approved if the registrar is of the opinion that the title is one which a willing buyer could properly be advised to accept by a competent professional adviser (s.9(2)). In deciding whether such a title has been shown the registrar may disregard the fact that the title is open to objection if he is of the opinion that the defect will not cause the holding under the title to be disturbed (s.9(3)).

(2) Absolute leasehold title or good leasehold title may be approved if the registrar is of the opinion that the title is one which a willing buyer could properly be advised to accept by a competent professional adviser (s.10(2)(a) and (3)). In addition, for the grant of absolute leasehold title the registrar must approve the landlord's title to grant the lease (s.10(2)(b)). Again, the registrar may disregard the fact that the title is open to objection if he is of the opinion that the defect will not cause the holding under the title to be disturbed (s.10(4)).

In examining the applicant's title to a lease which is a sub-lease, the registrar must also approve the title to any intermediate leasehold title.

Since June 19, 2006, Land Registry will grant absolute leasehold title on:

(a) Registration of a sub-lease where the consent of the head-landlord is not lodged. However, a protective entry will be made in the property register of the applicant's title stating that:

> "The registrar has not seen any consent to the grant of this sub-lease that the superior lease, out of which it was granted, may have required".

This reflects the fact that, whilst the grant of the sub-lease without consent may not render it invalid and prevent the grant of absolute title, the grant of such a title would not prevent forfeiture of the head lease and determination of the sub-lease.

(b) Registration of a lease where the consent of any mortgagee is not lodged, where this appears to be required. However, a protective entry will be made in the property register of the applicant's title stating that:

> "The title to the lease is, during the subsistence of the charge dated [. . .] in favour of [. . .] affecting the lessor's title (and to the extent permitted by law, any charge replacing or varying this charge or any further charge in respect of all or part of the sum secured by this charge), subject to any rights that may have arisen by reason of the absence of chargee's consent, unless the lease is authorised by section 99 of the Law of Property Act 1925".

The purpose of the entry is to warn of the potential vulnerability of the registered lease and to reduce the possibility of the mortgagee's right to determine the lease being lost as a result of the operation of s.29 (see paras 2–020 and 10–003).

(3) Qualified title may be approved if the registrar is of the opinion that the applicant's title (or in the case of leasehold title, the landlord's title to the reversion) has been established only for a limited period or subject to certain reservations which cannot be disregarded (ss.9(4) and 10(5)). Qualified titles are in practice rarely granted but could arise where, for example, the title depended upon a conveyance in breach of trust; the title would then be qualified so as to preserve any interest of the beneficiaries under the trust which might be lost if absolute title were granted.

(4) Possessory title may be approved if the registrar is of the opinion that:

(a) the applicant is in actual possession of the land or in receipt of the rents and profits of the land (or in the case of a rentcharge, in receipt of the rent (r.196A)), by virtue of the estate which is being registered; and
(b) there is no other class of title with which they may be registered (ss.9(5) and 10(6)).

This might arise where, for example, the applicant's title was based upon lost deeds (see Chapter 6) or adverse possession (see Chapter 7).

The effect of registration with a particular class of title is discussed in para.5–017.

Additional entries

5–013 On first registration, as a result of the registrar's examination of title, additional entries may be made in the register as follows:

(1) An entry as to a beneficial right may be made if:

(a) on examination of the title; or
(b) on receipt of an application providing details of the right and evidence of its existence,

the registrar is satisfied that the right subsists as a legal estate i.e. as an easement or profit à prendre appurtenant and benefits the registered estate (r.33(1)). If he is not so satisfied, he may enter details of the right claimed with such qualification as he considers appropriate (r.33(2)). (See also paras 8–007 to 8–013.)

(2) A notice must be entered by the registrar as to the burden of an interest (such as a restrictive covenant) which appears from his examination of title to affect the registered estate. However, this does not apply to:

(a) an interest that cannot be protected by a notice (see para.16–003);
(b) a public right;
(c) a local land charge;
(d) an interest which appears to the registrar to be of a trivial or obvious character, or the entry of notice in respect of which would be likely to cause confusion or inconvenience (r.35).

(3) An entry as to any agreement that prevents the acquisition of rights of light or air for the benefit of the registered estate may be made (r.36).

(4) A notice of a lease which is the subject of an application for first registration may be made in the register of a registered reversionary title, where such a notice does not already appear in the register (r.37—see para.12–011).

Public authorities: certificates of title

The registrar has made arrangements with a number of local and other public authorities whereby when the authority sells land, it gives the purchaser a certificate as to the title in an agreed form, instead of deducing title in the ordinary way. The certificate is effective at the date of the completion of the sale and it contains a statement of the incumbrances that affect the land on that day. Land Registry accepts this statement, and accordingly, when the purchaser applies for first registration of their title, they need not produce the normal conveyancing evidence of the authority's title. This procedure will be used, for example, on purchases of property under the right to buy scheme. **5–014**

Public sector housing/Right to buy

Under s.154(2) of the Housing Act 1985 a landlord is obliged to give to a tenant who exercises their right to buy under that Act a certificate of title in a form approved by the registrar. Three such forms of certificate of title have been so approved: **5–015**

(1) PSD1 (where the landlord conveys a freehold dwelling house);

(2) PSD2 (where the landlord owns the freehold and grants a lease of a house or grants a shared ownership lease of a house or flat); and

(3) PSD3 (where the landlord does not own the freehold and grants an underlease of a house or flat).

Similarly, Forms PSD13, PSD14 and PSD15 have been approved for use in preserved right to buy cases and Form PSD16 has been approved for use in extended right to buy cases.

Form PSD17 has been approved for use on the conveyance, lease or assignment of housing land or buildings, where the disposal is subject to a preserved right to buy or is a voluntary disposal with the consent of the Secretary of State, or is a disposal by the Housing Action Trust or Development Board for Rural Wales.

These forms of certificate of title are only for use in the specified cases and should not be used in any other circumstances. The certificate must be signed as provided and, in the case of a local authority, by the chief executive officer or by some other officer approved by the registrar.

The certificate of title procedure entirely replaces the need for a normal examination of title. Not only does it obviate the need for production of the title deeds but it also makes it unnecessary for a Land Charges search to be made by the purchaser against the name of the authority.

In reliance upon the certificate, the property will be registered subject to any incumbrances specified in the certificate, any contained in the deed inducing registration, and any created by the applicant. The authority is responsible for the accuracy of the certificate and must refund to Land Registry any indemnity paid because the certificate was incorrect.

A lease granted pursuant to the right to buy must be registered whether or not the lease is granted for a term of more than seven years (s.4(1)(e)).

When applying for first registration following the exercise of the right to buy, an "X" should be placed in the box provided in Panel 14 in Form FR1 to show that title has not been examined and reliance has been placed on the certificate of title lodged with the application.

Where the title to a property acquired in exercise of the right to buy is already registered, the normal provisions as to registration of a disposition of registered land will apply (see Chapters 10 and 11).

The fee payable in accordance with the Fee Order upon any application following a sale at a discount under the right to buy provisions is assessed on the price actually paid and not on the full market value.

Similarly on first registration of a shared ownership lease granted under the Housing Act 1985, a fee will be payable on an amount equal to the sum of the premium actually paid plus the rent reserved at the time of granting the lease.

Housing defects (Part XVI of the Housing Act 1985)

5–016 Paragraph 17 of Sch.20 to the Housing Act 1985 extends the provisions for compulsory registration of title to defective dwellings repurchased under that Act. It is provided that the acquiring authority must supply a certificate of title in a form approved by the registrar. Two such forms have been approved; PSD11 (freehold dwelling) and PSD12 (leasehold dwelling).

Again, the authority is responsible for the accuracy of the certificate and in reliance upon it, the property will be registered subject to any incumbrances specified in the certificate and any subsequently created by the applicant authority.

No application for the first registration of a leasehold interest is necessary where the acquiring authority is the owner of the reversion. If the title to the reversion is registered, an application should be made for cancellation of notice of the lease acquired from the reversionary title (see para.12–031). If the reversion is not registered, the leasehold deeds should merely be placed with the title deeds to the reversion.

If the title to a repurchased dwelling is already registered, application for registration of the disposition should be made in the normal way (see Chapters 10 and 11).

The effect of first registration (sections 11 and 12)

When an application for first registration is completed, the applicant becomes the registered proprietor and the legal estate is vested in them, together with all interests (such as benefitting easements) subsisting for the benefit of the estate whether or not entered in the register. The precise effect of first registration will depend upon the class of title granted. **5–017**

(1) When registration is of a *freehold estate* with *absolute title* it is vested in the proprietor with all interests subsisting for the benefit of the estate, subject only to the following interests affecting the estate at the time of registration:

   (a) interests which are the subject of an entry in the register;
   (b) unregistered interests that override first registration (see para.5–018); and
   (c) interests acquired under the Limitation Act 1980 of which the proprietor has notice.

If the proprietor is not entitled to the estate for their own benefit, or not solely for their own benefit, then, as between themselves and the persons beneficially entitled, the estate is vested in the proprietor subject to such of their interests as the proprietor has notice of (s.11(5)).

(2) When registration is of a *leasehold estate* with *absolute title* it is vested in the proprietor with the same effect as registration under (1) above except that it is subject also to implied and express covenants, obligations and liabilities incident to the estate (such as tenant's covenants in the lease).

(3) Registration with *good leasehold title* has the same effect as registration with absolute leasehold title, except that it does not affect the enforcement of any estate, right or

interest affecting, or in derogation of, the title of the landlord to grant the lease.

(4) Registration with *qualified title* has the same effect as registration with absolute title except that it does not affect the enforcement of any estate, right or interest which appears from the register to be excepted from the effect of registration. Thus the estate will be subject to matters which are the subject of the qualification in the register.

(5) Registration with *possessory title* has the same effect as registration with absolute title, except that it does not affect the enforcement of any estate, right or interest adverse to, or in derogation of, the proprietor's title subsisting at the time of registration or then capable of arising. Thus the estate will be subject to any undisclosed mortgages subsisting at the date of first registration where the unregistered title deeds had been lost or destroyed, for example (see Chapter 6).

Unregistered interests that override first registration (sections 11 and 12 and Schedule 1 to the Act)

5–018 The Act distinguishes between those interests which override first registration (as set out in Sch.1 to the Act) and those that override registered dispositions (as set out in Sch.3 to the Act). Under the Land Registration Act 1925, which did not make that distinction, these were generically referred to as "overriding interests" and are still commonly referred to as such.

On first registration the proprietor is subject to any of the following interests which affect the registered estate even though they are not the subject of a notice in the register:

(1) A leasehold estate in land granted for a term not exceeding seven years from the date of the grant, except for a lease which the tenant is under a duty to register (see para.5–003). This includes any lease which was formerly an overriding interest under s.70(1)(k) of the Land Registration Act 1925 immediately prior to October 13, 2003 (para.12 of Sch.12 to the Act).

(2) An interest belonging to a person in actual occupation, relating to land of which they are in actual occupation, except for an interest under a settlement under the Settled Land Act 1925.

(3) A legal easement or profit à prendre.

(4) A customary right.

(5) A public right.

(6) A local land charge.

(7) An interest in any coal or coal mine, the rights attached to any such interest and the rights of any person under ss.38, 49 or 51 of the Coal Industry Act 1994.

(8) In the case of land to which title was registered before 1898, rights to mines and minerals (and incidental rights) created before 1898.

(9) In the case of land to which title was registered between 1898 and 1925 inclusive, rights to mines and minerals (and incidental rights) created before the date of registration of the title.

(10) A franchise.

(11) A manorial right.

(12) A right to rent which was reserved to the Crown on the granting of any freehold estate (whether or not the right is still vested in the Crown).

(13) A non-statutory right in respect of an embankment or sea or river wall.

(14) A right to payment in lieu of tithe.

(15) (for a period of three years from October 13, 2003) a right acquired under the Limitation Act 1980 before that date (para.7 of Sch.12 to the Act).

(16) A right in respect of the repair of a church chancel.

At the end of a period of 10 years beginning on October 13, 2003, (9) to (14) and (16) above will cease to be interests that override first registration (s.117). It is therefore important that an application to either register a caution against first registration (see Chapter 4) or enter a notice to protect such interests in the registers of all titles affected (see Chapter 16) is made before that 10-year period expires. No fee is payable.

It is important to bear in mind that the proprietor will on first registration be subject to any interests which override even though they are not entered in the register and regardless of whether or not the proprietor knows about them.

The following well-known judicial decisions (made under s.70(1) of the Land Registration Act 1925) illustrate the importance of the overriding interests of persons "in actual occupation". **5–019**

***Williams & Glyns Bank Limited v Boland; Williams & Glyns Bank Limited v Brown* [1980] 2 All E.R. 408, HL.** Two appeals on similar facts. In each case the wife had contributed substantially to the purchase of a house and she and her husband were living in it as their matrimonial home. The husband was the sole registered proprietor. The wife had registered no caution, restriction or notice and the husband without her knowledge charged the land to the bank, which made no inquiry of the wife. The husband defaulted on the mortgage and the bank sought to enforce its security. Held: that the wife was in actual occupation—therefore her equitable interest, as tenant in common, was protected as an overriding interest under s.70(1)(g) of the 1925 Act and prevailed against the bank.

***City of London Building Society v Flegg* [1987] 3 All E.R. 435, HL.** "Bleak House" was purchased in the joint names of Mr and Mrs Flegg. More than half the purchase money was provided by the wife's parents and the balance from a building society mortgage. Unknown to the wife's parents, who were in occupation, the Fleggs first created two further charges and then borrowed sufficient funds from the plaintiffs to pay off the original building society and two further loans. The plaintiffs sought an order for possession against the wife's parents. Held: that the wife's parents' interest, as equitable tenants in common, was not an overriding interest under s.70(1)(g) of the 1925 Act and it was overreached under Part I of the Law of Property Act 1925 because the charge had been executed by two trustees for sale.

It should be noted that, unlike the position under the Land Registration Act 1925, the receipt of rents and profits is not sufficient for the purposes of para.2 of Sch.1 to the Act. Also, that the limitations under para.2 of Sch.3 to the Act relating to the interests of persons in actual occupation (see para.10–028) do not apply to para.2 of Sch.1.

Compulsory purchase and statutory vesting

5–020 A compulsory purchase order my be required to enable the acquisition of a piece of land. The land may be acquired by:

(1) agreement; or
(2) deed poll; or
(3) general vesting declaration.

In the case of unregistered land, where the land is acquired by agreement, an application for compulsory first registration should be made as necessary. Where the land is acquired by deed poll or general vesting declaration, it vests in the acquiring authority by operation of law and so an application for first registration will not be compulsory (s.4(3)), but a voluntary application may be made.

There are a number of statutory provisions under which land may be transferred automatically and vest in a particular person or body by operation of law. In the case of unregistered land, a vesting by operation of law will not "trigger" compulsory first registration (s.4(3)), but a voluntary application may be made.

A transfer of unregistered land pursuant to a court order will be a "trigger" for compulsory first registration and the appropriate application should therefore be made, as necessary.

Practical points

- Be aware of the new "triggers" for first registration,
- Ensure that any compulsory application for first registration is made within two months of the "trigger" event,
- Ensure that any necessary Land Charges search is lodged and any entries accounted for,
- Provide confirmation of the trusts upon which joint proprietors are to hold the registered estate, to avoid unnecessary entry of a restriction in Form A by default and/or unnecessary problems in the future,
- Remember to carry out a search of the index map when entering a purchase or other disposition of an unregistered estate,
- Ensure the correct address(es) for service are provided on first registration and kept up to date subsequently,
- Check for the existence of interests which override and ensure any such interests are disclosed in Form DI where appropriate.

Chapter 6

Lost or Destroyed Title Deeds

Introduction

It sometimes happens that unregistered title deeds are lost or destroyed, for example whilst in the custody of a conveyancer or a bank, or as a result of fire or theft. When this occurs, an application for first registration of the title may nevertheless be made. However, in addition to the normal requirements for such an application (see Chapter 5), it must also be supported by evidence: **6–001**

(1) to satisfy the registrar that the applicant is entitled to apply voluntarily for first registration under s.3(2) (i.e. that the unregistered legal estate sought to be registered is vested in them or they are entitled to require the estate to be vested in them), or that they are required to apply for compulsory first registration under s.6(1) (i.e. on the occurrence of one of the "trigger" events listed in s.4—see para.5–003), and

(2) to account for the absence of documentary evidence of title (r.27(1)).

This evidence will normally consist of, or include, a statutory declaration or statement of truth which may be in Form ST3. Although the use of Form ST3 is not compulsory, it will help to ensure that all the relevant information is provided. Alternatively a certificate by a conveyancer or suitably authorised official of a bank or building society (as the case may be) may be provided, where the deeds were lost or destroyed in their custody; a conveyancer must sign their certificate personally and not in the name of their firm.

The evidence lodged will need to cover:

(a) the circumstances of the loss or destruction;

(b) the reconstruction of the title;

(c) possession of the estate; and

(d) evidence of identity of the applicant in some cases (see para.6–010).

Application

6–002 An application for first registration where the title deeds have been lost or destroyed must be made in Form FR1 accompanied by Form DL, Form DI (if necessary) and a fee in accordance with the Fee Order (see Chapter 5), as well as the additional supporting evidence required by r.27. The estate to be registered will need to be clearly identified, by reference to a plan if necessary (see para.5–006).

The applicant or their conveyancer should also enclose with the application an undertaking to produce the title deeds to Land Registry if they are subsequently discovered. Any favourable or unfavourable evidence of title which comes to light after first registration should be produced to Land Registry, together with Form UT1 if an application to upgrade the title is appropriate (see Chapter 22).

Circumstances of the loss or destruction

6–003 It is not just the fact of loss or destruction of the deeds which is important; equally important are the circumstances of that loss or destruction, including details of who held the deeds at the time and why. This is usually proved by a statutory declaration, statement of truth or suitable certificate by a person or persons with first hand knowledge of the facts. What must be shown is:

(1) where and by whom the deeds were held immediately before their loss or destruction;

(2) why the person in possession had custody of the deeds, e.g. were they held for safekeeping or as security for a loan;

(3) the full circumstances of their loss or destruction;

(4) the efforts made to recover the deeds;

(5) whether or not at the time of the loss or destruction the owner had created any mortgage, charge or lien on the property or deposited the deeds with any person, firm or body as security for money;

(6) whether the applicant is in occupation of the estate or in receipt of the rents and profits from it; and

(7) that the applicant is entitled to apply for first registration as the legal estate is vested in them or they are entitled to require it to be vested in them.

If the deeds were lost or destroyed whilst in the custody of (or being sent in the post from) a conveyancer, building society, bank or other well-known institution, the above information should normally be supplied by a member of that firm or organisation.

Reconstruction of the title

The best available secondary evidence of how title has devolved to the applicant must be produced. The nature and quality of this will vary depending on the circumstances of the particular case. What follows are suggestions that may sometimes be useful. **6–004**

A certified copy or a completed draft of the conveyance or assignment to the applicant (and of any subsisting mortgage) should be lodged if possible, together with completed drafts or examined abstracts of as much of the earlier title as possible. These documents can be exhibited to a statutory declaration or statement of truth or a certificate by the conveyancer who acted when the applicant purchased the property, declaring that the title was investigated in the usual way, indicating from where the copy documents came, and confirming the due execution and stamping of the conveyance or assignment and any mortgage.

If all original deeds and copies or other evidence of them have been lost or destroyed, it is sometimes possible to obtain copies, abstracts or drafts from the conveyancer who acted for the applicant's vendor. A receipted schedule of deeds, if its source and origin are satisfactorily proved, may provide some evidence of custody and title. Copies of "particulars delivered" pursuant to s.28 of the Finance Act 1931 (obtained from the appropriate district valuer), copies of documents relating to capital gains tax or inheritance tax, fire insurance policies, and receipts for rates, other taxes and insurance premiums, may be useful as confirmation of ownership.

If the deeds were held by a mortgagee when they were lost or destroyed, it is useful to have a declaration by the conveyancer who acted for the mortgagee as to investigation of the title prior to the making of the loan. The evidence provided should also either declare that the mortgage is still subsisting, or give an account of its repayment.

If the estate was not in mortgage when the deeds were lost or destroyed, the evidence provided should confirm this and include an explicit statement that at the time of the loss or destruction the owner had not created any mortgage, charge or lien on the estate and had not deposited any of the title deeds with any person, firm or body as security for money.

If the property is leasehold and the lease has been lost or destroyed, a certified copy of the counterpart can usually be obtained; and the landlord may be able to provide information relating to licences to assign and production of documents by lessees for registration. In any event, the landlord will be able to confirm who has paid the rent.

As regards land in an area formerly covered by the Middlesex or one of the Yorkshire Deeds Registries, a statutory declaration, statement of truth or certificate by a conveyancer who has examined memorials of deeds may help to establish a chain of title. The records of the former deeds registries (which have now closed) can be inspected as follows.

County of Middlesex

6–005 The registers of the Middlesex Deeds Registry, being copy memorials 1709 to 1938 with covering indexes, may be inspected at the London Metropolitan Archives, 40 Northampton Road, London EC1R 0HB. (Telephone: 020 7332 3820.)

East Riding of Yorkshire

6–006 The records of the former East Riding Registry of Deeds, including memorials and indexes and covering the period 1708 to 1974, are now in the custody of the East Riding of Yorkshire Archives and Record Service, County Hall, Champney Road, Beverley, East Yorkshire HU17 9BA. (Telephone: 01482 392790.)

North Riding of Yorkshire

6–007 The North Riding Register of Deeds, which contains copies and memorials of deeds made between 1736 and 1970, is now in the custody of the North Yorkshire County Record Office held by the County Archivist, whose address for correspondence is County Hall, Northallerton, North Yorkshire DL7 8AF. (Telephone: 01609 777585.)

West Riding of Yorkshire

The records of the former West Riding Registry of Deeds, including copies and memorials of documents of title for the period 1704 to 1970, are now in the custody of the West Yorkshire Archive Service, Registry of Deeds Building, Newstead Road, Wakefield WF1 2DE. (Telephone: 01924 305980.) **6–008**

N.B. The City of York did not fall within the areas formerly covered by the Yorkshire Deeds Registries.

Land Charges searches against the applicant and all other known estate owners must also be lodged and any entries accounted for. If there is any risk of the non-disclosure of restrictive covenants, the registrar will make an entry in the register to the effect that the registered estate is subject to such restrictive covenants as may have been imposed on it before the date of first registration so far as they still subsist and are capable of being enforced. This protective entry will be extended to include rentcharges in areas where these are common.

Where unverified copies of restrictive covenants are supplied, Land Registry will not be able to rely upon these for the purposes of making an entry in the register unless the risk of the particulars being defective is considered slight; each case will be considered upon its merits, but if the particulars are not considered sufficient, a protective entry will have to be made in the register instead. Where such particulars are lodged with an application lodged by a solicitor then, in agreement with the Law Society, the registrar may where requested enter a notice in the register to refer to the unverified particulars.

An entry will also be made in respect of any easements adversely affecting the title which are revealed in the reconstructed title or disclosed as overriding interests within the application (see para.5–008). In addition, if there is a risk that the estate may be subject to easements which are not apparent from the application, a protective entry will be made.

An entry in respect of the benefit of legal easements will only be made in the register if the applicant has shown satisfactory evidence of title to them (r.33—see para.5–013).

Possession of the estate

The applicant is usually expected to provide satisfactory evidence that since the date of acquisition they have been in actual occupation of the whole of the estate or in receipt of its rents and profits (particulars of which, supported by copies of rent books or receipts, should be given) without any adverse claim. Any other relevant facts should be provided. **6–009**

The registrar may, where appropriate, arrange for an inspection survey in cases where he considers it necessary.

The evidence of possession is important, both to assist in satisfying the registrar that the applicant is entitled to apply for registration and also because a possessory title (which is most commonly granted in these circumstances) can only be granted where the registrar is satisfied that the applicant is in actual possession of the land or in receipt of the rents and profits from it (ss.9(5) and 10(6)).

Evidence of identity

6–010 Where title deeds have been lost or destroyed, Land Registry may require evidence of identity. This helps to both demonstrate the fact that the applicant does hold the legal estate and combat property fraud. Such evidence is not required when the application is lodged by:

(1) a conveyancer who is applying for registration because the title deeds were lost or destroyed whilst in their custody; or

(2) a major mortgage lender, where the deeds were being held as security for the lender's mortgage and were lost whilst in their custody; or

(3) a duly authorised official of a local authority, government department or nationally well known body, where the deeds relating to their land, or land on which they hold a mortgage, were lost whilst in their custody; or

(4) a receiver or liquidator of a company, where evidence of the appointment is supplied with a certified copy of the mortgage or charge, where the applicant is a receiver appointed under such a deed.

Where the applicant is an individual, evidence of identity in Form ID1 must be completed (for each applicant, where there are more than one).

For corporate applicants, or those applicants which are some other kind of institution, evidence of identity of the individual giving instructions on behalf of the corporate body must be provided in Form ID2.

In all cases, Land Registry requires a recent passport-sized photograph of each applicant or individual, which must be affixed to Form ID1 or ID2 where indicated. A conveyancer must personally certify (not in the name of the firm) that the photograph is a true likeness of the applicant or individual.

Class of title

Where the evidence of title is unavailable or incomplete, an applicant may nevertheless be granted a registered title if the registrar is satisfied as to the applicant's title and the circumstances of the loss or destruction. If Land Registry's requirements have been satisfactorily dealt with, a possessory title may be granted. Each application is considered on its merits, but normally absolute or good leasehold title will not be granted where the loss or destruction of the deeds cannot be adequately explained, bearing in mind the potential for a claim for indemnity if an absolute title is granted which subsequently transpires to be a mistake (see Chapter 24). **6–011**

Lost or destroyed land or charge certificates

Since October 13, 2003, no new land or charge certificates have been issued and they no longer have any legal status or effect. It is no longer possible to apply for a replacement certificate where a certificate issued prior to that date has been lost or destroyed. **6–012**

Other situations

In cases where the estate forms part of the "ancient possessions" of the applicant (such as land forming part of the endowment of a long-established charity) and there are no title deeds known to have existed, the above procedures will not be applicable. Instead, a statutory declaration, statement of truth or conveyancer's certificate may be provided in support of an application for first registration, confirming: **6–013**

(1) how the estate came to be vested in the applicant;

(2) that there are no title deeds known to have existed;

(3) that the applicant has throughout been, and remains, in occupation of the estate or in receipt of the rents and profits from it; and

(4) whether there are any incumbrances on the estate.

If satisfied as to the applicant's title, the registrar may be willing to grant a possessory title or possibly an absolute title, although this will depend upon the individual circumstances including the status of the applicant and the nature of the estate and the evidence lodged. Where appropriate, the registrar may make a protective entry in respect of the possibility of the estate being affected by restrictive covenants, subjective easements or rentcharges (see above), unless he considers it unnecessary.

For an application based upon a title acquired by adverse possession, see Chapter 7.

Practical points

- Make sure to cover all the necessary elements in an application based upon lost or destroyed title deeds,
- Bear in mind that a possessory rather than an absolute title may be granted if the application is successful,
- Ensure that any necessary Land Charges search is lodged and any entries accounted for,
- Remember to lodge evidence of identity where required.

Chapter 7

Adverse Possession

Introduction

Adverse possession is the mechanism by which a person "squatting" on land may (in the case of unregistered land) acquire an unregistered legal estate in that land and extinguish that of the documentary title owner or (in the case of registered land) become entitled to be registered as proprietor of the land in place of the existing proprietor. **7–001**

In the leading case of *JA Pye (Oxford) Ltd v Graham* [2002] UKHL30, the House of Lords reviewed the law relating to adverse possession and Lord Hope of Craighead dismissed a popular misconception about what is required for adverse possession:

> "At first sight, it might be thought that the word 'adverse' describes the nature of the possession that the squatter needs to demonstrate. It suggests that an element of aggression, hostility or subterfuge is required. But an examination of the context makes it clear that this is not so. It is used as a convenient label only, in recognition simply of the fact that the possession is adverse to the interests of the paper owner or, in the case of registered land, of the registered proprietor."

There are different principles and procedures applicable to an application for registration based upon adverse possession, depending upon whether the application:

(1) is for first registration; or

(2) relates to registered land and is made under the transitional provisions of para.18 of Sch.12 to the Act; or

(3) relates to registered land and is made under the provisions of Sch.6 to the Act.

The different types of application are discussed separately below. However, the underlying principles of adverse possession will be applicable to each of them. Essentially, an application based upon adverse possession must be supported by evidence to satisfy the registrar that:

(a) the squatter has factual possession of the land;

(b) the squatter has the necessary intention to possess the land;

(c) the squatter's possession is without the owner's consent; and

(d) all of the above have been true of the squatter (and any predecessors through whom they claim) for at least the minimum requisite period.

Factual possession

7–002 The *Pye v Graham* case strongly endorses the decision in *Powell v McFarlane* (1977) 38 P. & C.R. 452 where Slade J. stated:

> "Factual possession signifies an appropriate degree of physical control. It must be a single and [exclusive] possession, though there can be a single possession exercised by or on behalf of several persons jointly. Thus an owner of land and a person intruding on that land without his consent cannot both be in possession of the land at the same time. The question what acts constitute a sufficient degree of exclusive physical control must depend on the circumstances, in particular the nature of the land and the manner in which land of that nature is commonly used or enjoyed . . . Everything must depend on the particular circumstances, but broadly, I think what must be shown as constituting factual possession is that the alleged possessor has been dealing with the land in question as an occupying owner might have been expected to deal with it and that no-one else has done so."

Intention to possess

7–003 A squatter must not only be in possession of the land; they must also have the necessary "intention to possess" the land.

In *Buckinghamshire County Council v Moran* (1988) 86 L.G.R. 472 Hoffman J. stated that what is required is:

> "not an intention to own or even an intention to acquire ownership but an intention to possess".

In *Powell v McFarlane* Slade J. defined the "intention to possess" by stating that it is the:

> "intention, in one's own name and on one's own behalf, to exclude the world at large, including the owner with the paper title if he be not himself the possessor, so far as is reasonably practicable and so far as the processes of the law will allow."

In *Pye v Graham* Lord Hutton in endorsing Slade J.'s judgment, stated:

> "Where the evidence establishes that the person claiming title under the Limitation Act 1980 has occupied the land and made full use of it in the way in which an owner would, I consider that in the normal case he will not have to adduce additional evidence to establish that he had the intention to possess. It is in cases where the acts in relation to the land of a person claiming title by adverse possession are equivocal and are open to more than one interpretation, that those acts will be insufficient to establish the intention to possess."

Possession without the owner's consent

The squatter must not be in possession of the land with the owner's consent. In *Buckinghamshire County Council v Moran* Slade L.J. stated that: **7–004**

> "Possession is never 'adverse' within the meaning of the [Limitation Act] 1980 if it is enjoyed under a lawful title. If, therefore, a person occupies or uses land by licence of the owner with the paper title and his licence has not been duly determined, he cannot be treated as having been in 'adverse possession' as against the owner of the paper title."

Period of adverse possession

The squatter must have fulfilled the above criteria for a period of not less than the requisite period, and the dates of such possession may also be relevant. The requisite period and dates of possession will depend upon the type of application, as discussed below. **7–005**

The House of Lords decision in Pye v Graham was the subject of an application to the European Court of Human Rights (*JA Pye (Oxford) Limited v The United Kingdom* [2009] (app. No. 44302/02)) and ultimately the Grand Chamber of that court found that English law on adverse possession is not contrary to the European Convention on Human Rights. That decision was in relation to the law applicable prior to the coming into force of the Act; a new regime relating specifically to registered land has been introduced by Sch.6 to the Act (see para.7–010).

It should be borne in mind that neither an application to Land Registry for registration based upon adverse possession nor an objection to such an application, even if it is referred to the Adjudicator (see Chapter 23) will prevent any limitation period from continuing to accrue, as proceedings before the registrar or the Adjudicator do not represent an "action" for the purposes of the Limitation Act 1980.

Adverse possession of unregistered land

7–006 If a person has acquired title to unregistered land by adverse possession under the Limitation Act 1980 they may make an application for first registration of that title in Form FR1 (see Chapter 5). The application must be supported by evidence of adverse possession, as discussed above, to satisfy the registrar that the applicant is entitled to apply (r.27(1)).

The evidence will consist of a statutory declaration or statement of truth by the applicant and others (e.g. the applicant's vendor where relevant), setting out the facts relied on to support the claim to title by adverse possession. Any other relevant documentation available, such as old photographs of the land or evidence of the paper title, should also be lodged.

The evidence may consist of, or include, a statement of truth which may be in Form ST1 (relating to adverse possession of land) or ST2 (relating to adverse possession of a rentcharge); use of these forms is not compulsory, but their use will help to ensure that all the relevant information is provided.

The normal limitation period under the Limitation Act 1980 is 12 years (although an extended period may apply in certain cases) and there must have been no acknowledgement of the documentary owner's title during that period. The evidence lodged must therefore cover a continuous period of at least that duration up to the date of the application.

Land Charge searches against the names of the applicant and (if known) the documentary owner and their predecessors should be lodged, along with any other relevant searches, such as a company search or commons registration search where appropriate.

Land Registry will normally inspect the land (where the application relates to an estate in land) and may serve notice of the application upon such adjoining owners and others as it considers appropriate (r.30). If a valid objection is received which cannot be disposed of by agreement, the matter will have to be referred to the Adjudicator (see Chapter 23).

A fee in accordance with the Fee Order is payable. The applicant may be called upon to pay an additional fee to meet the cost of a survey or special enquiries.

Any application based upon adverse possession will be considered upon its individual merits. If the application is successful, the registrar will normally only grant a possessory title because he will not be in a position to be satisfied with certainty that the adverse possession by the applicant has extinguished the documentary owner's title. A protective entry may be entered in the register if the registrar considers there is a risk that the land may be subject to undisclosed restrictive covenants, easements or rentcharges.

Special considerations apply where there are any known existing mortgages on the estate and also where the application relates to leasehold land or where the squatter has encroached from their own leasehold land onto other land.

Adverse possession of registered land: transitional provisions

Previous law

Where title to registered land was acquired by adverse possession, the registered proprietor of the land held the title to that land in trust for the adverse possessor under the provisions of s.75 of the Land Registration Act 1925. **7–007**

Transitional provisions

The Act introduced a new regime for adverse possession of registered land, so that the trust referred to above no longer arises. However, if immediately before October 13, 2003, a registered title to land was held in trust by virtue of s.75 of the Land Registration Act 1925, the adverse possessor is entitled to be registered as proprietor of that land (para.18(1) of Sch.12 to the Act). **7–008**

Such an adverse possessor has a defence to any action for the possession of the land and if a court decides that a person is entitled to such a defence, it must order the registrar to register the adverse possessor as the proprietor of the title to that land (para.18(2) and (3) of Sch.12 to the Act).

For a period of three years from October 13, 2003, where a person was entitled to be registered as proprietor of a registered estate under s.75 of the Land Registration Act 1925, that right will have been an interest which was overriding in respect of registered dispositions, notwithstanding that the adverse possessor was not in actual occupation at the time the disposition was registered (para.11 of Sch.12 to the Act—see para.5–018). That period has now expired but, if such an adverse possessor was in occupation at the relevant time then their interest may have overridden a registered disposition in certain circumstances (see para.10–028).

The application

7–009 An application under the transitional provisions of para.18(1) of Sch.12 to the Act must be made in Form AP1, accompanied by similar supporting evidence to that required on an application for first registration based upon adverse possession (see para.7–006). Similar limitation periods also apply, but the evidence lodged must *also* demonstrate that the minimum limitation period had expired before October 13, 2003 so that a trust under s.75 of the Land Registration Act 1925 had arisen by that date. In addition, the title to the land must have been registered prior to that date, although not necessarily for the entire period of the adverse possession.

A fee in accordance with the Fee Order is payable, which includes the cost of a survey.

Land Registry will normally inspect the land and will serve notice upon the registered proprietor and any registered chargee of the existing registered title. If a valid objection is received which cannot be resolved by agreement, the matter will have to be referred to the Adjudicator (see Chapter 23).

Any application based upon adverse possession under the transitional provisions will be considered on its individual merits. If the application is successful, the applicant will be registered as proprietor of the land in place of the existing proprietor, with the same class of title.

Special considerations apply where there are any existing charges and also where the application relates to leasehold land or where the squatter has encroached from their own leasehold land onto other land.

Where the requisite limitation period had expired prior to October 13, 2003 but the land only became registered on or after that date, application cannot be made under the transitional provisions. Instead, application may be made in Form AP1 (accompanied by supporting evidence as above) for alteration of the register to reflect the fact that the documentary owner's title had already been extinguished at the time of first registration of the estate.

Adverse possession of registered land: Schedule 6 to the Act

The law

7–010 Under the Limitation Act 1980, if a person is in adverse possession of unregistered land, the owner's title will be extinguished after the requisite period of limitation has elapsed.

The periods of limitation under the Limitation Act 1980 do not now apply to registered land (subject to the transitional provisions referred to above), so that time cannot run against a registered proprietor so as to extinguish his registered title or create a trust in favour of the squatter (s.96).

Title to registered land can still be acquired as a result of adverse possession, but only under the provisions of the Act. If a person in adverse possession makes a successful application under Sch.6 to the Act, they will be registered as proprietor in place of the existing registered proprietor.

The underlying principles of adverse possession (see above) therefore remain relevant to such an application.

Who can apply?

A person may apply to be registered as the proprietor of a registered estate in land (in place of the existing registered proprietor) if they have been in adverse possession for the period of 10 years ending on the date of the application (para.1(1) of Sch.6 to the Act). The land need not have been registered for the whole period of the adverse possession. **7–011**

A person may apply even if, within the period of six months ending on the date of the application, they have been evicted by the registered proprietor or a person claiming under that proprietor, and:

(1) on the day before their eviction they were entitled to make such an application for registration; and

(2) the eviction was not pursuant to a judgment for possession (para.1(2) of Sch.6 to the Act).

However, a person cannot apply:

(a) when there are possession proceedings against them or judgment for possession was given against them in the last two years (para.1(3) of Sch.6 to the Act); or

(b) during any period when the registered proprietor (in wartime) is an enemy or a prisoner of war (nor before the end of 12 months after the end of such a period) or, in certain circumstances, they are under a mental disability or suffering from a physical impairment (para.8 of Sch.6 to the Act).

At any time when a property is held in trust and the beneficiaries' interests are not in possession, no-one can be regarded as in adverse possession (para.12 of Sch.6 to the Act).

Successive periods of adverse possession count as one period (see para.11 of Sch.6 to the Act).

In the case of Crown foreshore the requisite period of adverse possession is 60 years, not 10 years.

The application (rule 188)

7–012 Application must be made in Form ADV1, accompanied by a statutory declaration or statement of truth made by the applicant not more than one month before the application and containing the additional details required by r.188(2)(a) (including the facts which would enable the applicant to rely on one or more of the conditions set out in para.5 of Sch.6 to the Act, if required—see para.7–014), together with:

(1) any supporting statutory declaration(s) or statement(s) of truth; and

(2) any additional evidence which the applicant considers necessary to support the claim,

so as to provide evidence of adverse possession for the requisite period and evidence that the applicant is a person entitled to apply.

A statement of truth may be in Form ST1 (relating to adverse possession of land) or ST2 (relating to adverse possession of a rentcharge); use of these forms is not compulsory, but their use will help to ensure that all the relevant information is provided.

A fee in accordance with the Fee Order is payable, which includes the cost of a survey.

Service of notice of the application

7–013 If satisfied with the evidence provided (normally after a site inspection has been carried out) the registrar must serve notice of the application on:

(1) the registered proprietor of the land;

(2) any registered chargee;

(3) (where the estate is leasehold) the registered proprietor of any superior registered estate;

(4) any person who is registered as a person to be notified of such an application (see para.7–016); and

(5) (where the registered proprietor is a dissolved company) the Treasury solicitor (or the solicitor for the affairs of the Duchy of Lancaster or the Duke of Cornwall, where appropriate).

Response to the notice

If none of the recipients of the notice respond to the notice or they all consent, the applicant will be registered as proprietor in place of the existing proprietor free of any existing registered charge. **7–014**

If a recipient of the notice objects (in Form NAP or otherwise in writing) on the basis that the applicant is not in adverse possession or the applicant is not entitled to apply, then the matter will, if not disposed of by agreement, have to be referred to the Adjudicator to HM Land Registry (see Chapter 23).

If a recipient of a notice serves a "counter notice" upon the registrar in Form NAP during the notice period (being 65 business days (r.189)), requiring the application to be dealt with under para.5 of Sch.6 to the Act, the application will be rejected unless the applicant can establish that one of the following three conditions is met:

(1) it would be unconscionable because of an equity by estoppel for the proprietor to seek to dispossess the applicant and the circumstances are such that the applicant ought to be registered. An example might be where the applicant has built on registered land believing it was their land and the registered proprietor has knowingly acquiesced in the mistake; or

(2) the applicant is for some other reason entitled to be registered. An example might be if they had contracted to buy and paid the purchase price but never taken a conveyance or transfer; or

(3) it is a "mistaken boundary" case, for which there are four requirements:

 (a) the land concerned must adjoin land owned by the applicant;
 (b) the exact line of the boundary must not have already been determined (see para.3–004);
 (c) the applicant (or any predecessor in title) must have reasonably believed the land belonged to them for at least 10 years of the period of adverse possession ending on the date of the application; and
 (d) the land must have been registered for more than one year prior to the date of the application.

An example of where this condition might apply is where the boundary fences on a developing estate were erected in the wrong place by the developer contrary to the estate layout plan.

If an applicant intends to rely on one of these conditions, they must set out the relevant facts in their supporting statutory declaration or statement of truth and tick the appropriate box in Form ADV1.

If the recipient of the notice objects on the grounds that the applicant has not established that one of the three conditions has been met, then the matter will, if not disposed of by agreement, have to be referred to the Adjudicator (see Chapter 23).

If the applicant successfully establishes that one of the three conditions has been met, they will be registered in place of the existing proprietor subject to any registered charge. If that charge also affects other land, the applicant may require the charge to be apportioned on the basis of the respective values of the two areas of land charged. Rules 194A–194G contain procedures relating to apportionment. Once the charge has been apportioned the land can be discharged from the charge by payment of the amount apportioned to it and the costs of apportionment (para.10 of Sch.6 to the Act).

Special considerations apply where the application relates to leasehold land or where the squatter has encroached from their own leasehold land onto other land.

Right to make a further application for registration

7–015 Where the original application is rejected because the applicant did not establish that one of the three conditions in para.5 of Sch.6 to the Act was met (see para.7–014), they may make a further application if they are in adverse possession of the land from the date of the original application until the last day of the period of two years beginning with the date of its rejection, provided:

(1) the restrictions in para.8 of Sch.6 to the Act do not apply (see para.7–011);

(2) no possession proceedings are pending against them;

(3) no judgment for possession has been given against them in the last two years; and

(4) they have not been evicted pursuant to a judgment for possession.

The application must be in Form ADV1 accompanied by the documents, evidence and fee as set out at para.7–012 above, except that the additional details to be included in the applicant's statutory declaration or statement of truth (including full details of the previous rejected application) are those required under r.188(3).

Under r.17, 15 business days' notice of the application will be served on:

(a) the registered proprietor of the land;

(b) any registered chargee;

(c) (where the estate is leasehold) the registered proprietor of any superior registered estate;

(d) any person who is registered as a person to be notified of such an application (see para.7–016); and

(e) any other person the registrar considers it appropriate to notify.

If the applicant is successful, they will be registered in place of the existing proprietor, free of any existing registered charge.

Registration as a person entitled to be notified of an application for adverse possession (rule 194)

If a person can satisfy the registrar that they have an interest in a registered estate in land or a registered rentcharge which would be prejudiced by the registration of any other person as proprietor of that estate or rentcharge by adverse possession under Sch.6 to the Act (or under Sch.6 as applied to rentcharges by r.191), they may apply in Form ADV2 to be registered as a person to be notified of such an application (r.194). An example of such a person might be a beneficiary under a trust who is not in possession. **7–016**

The name of such a person who successfully applies will be entered in the proprietorship register as a person entitled to be notified under para.2 of Sch.6 to the Act.

Adverse possession of a rentcharge

Rule 191, made pursuant to the power contained in para.14 of Sch.6 of the Act, applies the provisions of Sch.6 of the Act to rentcharges in the modified form set out in Sch.8 to the Rules. **7–017**

Rule 192 contains provisions which apply where adverse possession is based on non-payment of rent and r.193 sets out provisions which prohibit recovery of rent after adverse possession of a rentcharge.

Under r.224 and para.18(5) of Sch.12 to the Act, if title to a rentcharge was acquired by adverse possession prior to October 13, 2003, and it was held in trust under s.75(1) of the Land Registration Act 1925 immediately before that date, the beneficiary of that trust may apply either to be registered as proprietor of the rentcharge, or for the registration of the rentcharge to be cancelled.

Practical points

- Consider which method of application is appropriate and use the correct application form,
- Ensure the requisite evidence is lodged with the application,
- In an application under Sch.6 to the Act, ensure the applicant's statutory declaration or statement of truth is dated not more than one month before the date of the application and contains the required confirmations and facts.

Chapter 8

Covenants, Easements and Profits à Prendre

Covenants

Burden of restrictive covenants—first registration

When the deeds and documents accompanying an application for first registration show that the estate is subject to restrictive covenants (other than covenants between landlord and tenant affecting the demised premises in the lease (s.33(c)), notice of the covenants will be entered in the register (r.35(1)). The entry in the charges register will refer to the deed containing the covenants and provide details of the covenants (including any covenanting clause) by either setting out the covenants verbatim in the register or by referring to a filed document containing them. **8–001**

Sometimes neither the original deed nor a certified copy nor examined abstract will accompany the application. The action taken by the registrar will then depend on the circumstances:

(1) If an unverified copy or abstract of the covenants accompanies the application and the registrar considers the risk of it being inaccurate to be so small that it can properly be treated as though it were verified e.g. if the evidence consists of an apparently accurate typewritten copy or a photocopy, it will be so treated and an entry made in the register as above.

(2) If an unverified copy or abstract of the covenants accompanies the application but cannot properly be treated as though it were verified and, if a solicitor so requests, an entry will (in accordance with an agreement made between the Law Society and Land Registry) be made in the charges register along the following lines:

> "A [Conveyance] of the land in this title [and other land] dated . . . made between . . . contains restrictive covenants but no verified particulars of them were produced on first registration. The details set out [in the schedule of restrictive covenants hereto] of what purport to be the said covenants were provided by (*solicitor*) acting for a vendor in . . .".

As this entry is qualified, no indemnity (see Chapter 24) will be payable if the details referred to are not complete or correct.

(3) If an unverified copy or abstract of the covenants accompanies the application, but cannot be treated as verified and is not the subject of a request by a solicitor as in (2) above, an entry will be made in the register referring to the deed containing the covenants and stating that it contains restrictive covenants but that:

> ". . . neither the original deed nor a certified copy nor an examined abstract thereof was produced on first registration."

Such an entry will also be made when no particulars, verified or unverified, of the covenants or stipulations accompany the application.

Particulars of the words of covenant should be provided whenever possible, but when only particulars of restrictive stipulations without the words of covenant accompany an application, a modified form of entry indicating that the words of covenant were not available, will be used.

The documents lodged with some types of application for first registration may not contain adequate information as to whether or not restrictive covenants affect the estate. This situation will commonly arise where an application is based upon either:

(1) a title to unregistered land acquired by adverse possession (see Chapter 7);

(2) lost title deeds (see Chapter 6); or

(3) ancient possessions (see Chapter 6).

The registrar, when completing such an application, will normally make a protective entry in the register to the effect that the registered estate is subject to such restrictive covenants as may have been imposed thereon before a specified date (normally the date of the application) so far as they are subsisting and capable of being enforced. However, the entry will not be made if the registrar is satisfied that there are no restrictive covenants which are likely to affect the estate.

For restrictive covenants in leases, see para.12–020.

Burden of restrictive covenants—registered estates

Restrictive covenants (other than those between landlord and tenant affecting the demised premises (s.33(c)) imposed on a registered estate must be protected by entry of a notice in the register of the burdened title (see Chapter 16). The notice may set out the covenants verbatim in the register or refer to a filed document containing them. **8–002**

If a transfer of whole or part, or other registrable disposition of a registered estate under s.27(2) imposes restrictive covenants, a notice of these covenants will be entered automatically in the register of the burdened title upon registration of the transfer or other disposition. However, if the transfer or other disposition imposes restrictive covenants on any other title, the relevant title number(s) must be given in panel 2 of the Form AP1, otherwise the registrar is not obliged to make any entry in that title and a specific application for entry of a notice of the covenants on that title is necessary (rr.72(5) and 72C(3)).

If restrictive covenants are imposed upon a registered estate otherwise than in a transfer or other registrable disposition, e.g. by a deed of covenant, an application must be made for entry of a notice of the instrument imposing them in the register of title to the burdened estate. It is important to identify the burdened estate clearly (by plan if necessary) and also to identify the estate intended to be benefited by the covenants.

For restrictive covenants in leases see para.12–020.

Benefit of restrictive covenants

The Act does not provide for the entry of the benefit of equitable rights in the register. Consequently, no entry can be made in the register of the benefit of restrictive covenants as such a benefit is an equitable not a legal right. Entitlement to the benefit of restrictive covenants must therefore subsist "off the register". **8–003**

Release, waiver or modification of restrictive covenants

An application for entry of a notice in respect of a deed of release or variation should be made in Form AN1 (for an agreed notice—see para.16–005) or Form UN1 (for a unilateral notice—see para.16–008) if made by the person claiming the benefit of the covenants; or in Form AP1 if made by the registered proprietor of the burdened estate. **8–004**

An application for cancellation of an existing notice (other than a unilateral notice—see below) in respect of restrictive covenants based upon a deed of release should be made in Form CN1 (see para.16–006).

In practice it is usually difficult, if not impossible, to prove that a deed purporting to release, waive, discharge or modify restrictive covenants is fully effective, because of the difficulty in identifying the extent of the estate having the benefit of the covenants and ensuring that all parties having an interest in the covenants have joined into the deed. It is thefore Land Registry's practice in most cases (unless the position is beyond doubt) to retain the original notice of the covenants in the register and enter a notice of such a deed in the register stating that it is "expressed" to release or vary the covenants (r.87(4)).

Where it is claimed that restrictive covenants protected in the register by a notice (other than a unilateral notice) are void for non-registration as a Land Charge following first registration, application may be made in Form CN1 to cancel the notice (see para.16–006), accompanied by evidence to satisfy the registrar that the covenants are void (r.87(1)).

If the existing notice in respect of restrictive covenants is a unilateral notice, application may be made in Form UN2 for removal or in Form UN4 for cancellation of the notice (see paras 16–010 and 16–011).

When the Upper Tribunal (Lands Chamber)—formerly the Lands Tribunal—has made an order under s.84 of the Law of Property Act 1925 as to modification or discharge of restrictive covenants, application may be made for this to be reflected in the register. The action taken by the registrar will depend upon the terms of the order.

Personal covenants: indemnity covenants and positive covenants

8–005 Under rr.64 and 65 the registrar may make an appropriate entry in the proprietorship register of any positive covenant given by the registered proprietor or any previous proprietor, or of any indemnity covenant given by the registered proprietor. Such an entry must, where practicable, refer to the deed containing the covenant and must be deleted if it appears to the registrar that it does not bind the current registered proprietor.

Where a deed contains positive covenants which are intermixed with restrictive covenants, these will not normally be edited out and entered separately, but will instead be entered in the register as part of the entry of a notice of the restrictive covenants. If they are not so intermixed they will be the subject of a note in the proprietorship register, referring to a "schedule of personal covenants", where they will be set out verbatim or reference made to a filed deed containing them.

Where a transfer contains indemnity covenants in respect of restrictive or positive covenants referred to in the register, a note will be entered in the proprietorship register stating that the transfer to the proprietor contains a covenant to observe and perform the covenants and of indemnity in respect of them. If the transferee has not covenanted to observe and perform the original covenants the note will merely state that the transfer to the proprietor contains a covenant of indemnity in respect of them.

Implied covenants

In a conveyance, transfer, charge or lease, certain covenants for title by the disponor may be implied into the deed effecting the disposition by virtue of s.1(1) of the Law of Property (Miscellaneous Provisions) Act 1994 ("the 1994 Act"), depending upon whether the disposition (which need not be for valuable consideration) is expressed to be made with "full title guarantee" or "limited title guarantee". **8–006**

A registrable disposition may be expressed to be made either with full title guarantee or with limited title guarantee (r.67(1)). However, "right to buy" leases must be made with full title guarantee, which should not be modified.

Rule 67(2) makes provision for dispositions made before July 1, 1995 or made after that date in pursuance of a contract or option entered into before that date (unless there has been an intervening disposition expressed to have been made with full title guarantee).

Where a disposition of leasehold land limits or extends the covenant implied under s.4 of the 1994 Act a reference to that fact may be made in the register (r.67(6)).

A registrable disposition of leasehold land containing a provision limiting or extending any covenant implied under s.4(1)(b) of the 1994 Act must do so by express reference to that section (r.68). The registrar will make the following entry in the register to reflect this (r.67(6)):

> "The covenant implied under s.4(1)(b) of the Law of Property (Miscellaneous Provisions) Act 1994 in the disposition to the proprietor is modified."

However, no other reference to any covenant implied by virtue of Pt.1 of the 1994 Act can be made in the register (r.67(5)).

Paragraph 20 of Sch.12 to the Act sets out the indemnity covenants which are implied on the transfer of a pre-1996 lease, being an "old tenancy" for the purposes of the Landlord and Tenant (Covenants) Act 1995. Where a transfer of a registered lease which is an old tenancy modifies or negatives any covenants implied by para.20(2) and (3) of Sch.12 to the Act, an entry that the covenants have been so modified or negatived must be made in the register (r.66).

For implied covenants in a transfer of a rentcharge, see para.15–009.

Easements

Easements on first registration

8–007 ***Beneficial easements*** On first registration the registered estate is vested in the registered proprietor together with the benefit of all easements subsisting for the benefit of the registered estate (ss.11(3) and s.12(3)), whether or not the easement is shown in the register. However, the registrar may enter the benefit of a benefitting easement on first registration of an estate if he is satisfied the easement subsists at law for the benefit of the estate (r.33(1)).

The applicant must therefore lodge evidence that the grantor had power to grant the easement, otherwise the registrar may either omit the right or enter a qualification note to an entry in the register (r.33(2)).

If the easement was granted over an unregistered estate that has since been registered, it may be necessary for a notice as to the burden of the easement to be entered in the register of the burdened title at the same time as the benefit is entered in the register of the benefitting title. This will be done by the registrar as part of the first registration, normally after service of notice on the proprietor of the burdened title.

8–008 ***Subjective easements*** The registrar must enter a notice in the register of the burden of all easements, whether legal or equitable, which are apparent from the documents lodged with the application (r.35).

Proving the grantor's power to make the grant

(1) *Burdened estate is registered*

8–009 (a) *Charges* The consent of any chargee of the burdened estate, whose charge has priority over the grant of the easement and who has not joined in the grant, should be lodged. If the chargee has not consented to the grant, the easement is liable to be overridden if the chargee exercises their power of sale. If the consent cannot be lodged, the application may (unless there is a restriction in favour of the chargee—see below) be completed but with a note along the following lines being added to the register entry for the benefitting title:

> "NOTE: The consent of the proprietor of the charge dated . . . in favour of . . . affecting title(s) . . . was not produced on registration and the rights . . . may be overridden in the event of the exercise of the power of sale."

The note can be cancelled without fee if an application is subsequently made in Form AP1 enclosing the consent.

(b) Restrictions Any restriction (including a restriction in favour of a chargee) in the register of the burdened title must be complied with so far as necessary. **8–010**

(c) Cautions against dealings and notices of (intended) deposit If there is a caution against dealings or a notice of (intended) deposit in the register of the burdened title and the consent to the registration of the easement does not accompany the application, the registrar may serve notice upon the cautioner or depositee (see paras 14–026 and 16–016). **8–011**

(2) Burdened estate is unregistered

(a) Evidence of grantor's title Evidence of the grantor's title to the burdened estate, commencing with a good root more than 15 years old at the date of the application, must accompany the application. **8–012**

(b) Charges The consent of any legal mortgagee of the burdened estate to the grant of the easement should be lodged, unless they have joined in the grant. If this consent is not lodged, the application may be completed but with a note being added to the register entry for the benefitting title in the form referred to in para.8–009. **8–013**

Registrable dispositions—transfers and deeds of grant

The express grant or reservation of an easement over a registered estate is a registrable disposition required to be completed by registration (s.27(2)(d), LRA 2002) if it is to take effect at law. This is so even if it is contained in a lease where the lease itself cannot be registered or noted. **8–014**

The registration requirements are set out in para.7 of Sch.2 to the Act. A notice must be entered in the register of the burdened estate and, if the benefitting estate is also registered, the benefit must be entered in the register of that estate. An application to register an easement **must** be made in Form AP1 (r.13) in order to meet the registration requirements.

This is the case even if only the burdened land is registered (r.90). Therefore an application for entry of an agreed or unilateral notice in Form AN1 or Form UN1 will **not** meet the registration requirements. In the case of an agreed notice, the following note will be added to the entry to reflect this:

> "NOTE: The grant or reservation of the rights . . . has not been completed by registration in accordance with section 27 of the Land Registration Act 2002 and so does not operate at law."

In that event, a subsequent application may be made in Form AP1 to complete the easement by registration so that it does take effect at law. Until then, it takes effect in equity only and the benefit cannot be registered in the register of the benefiting title (if registered).

The nature of an application relating to an easement will therefore depend upon whether it is a registrable disposition and whether both the benefiting land and burdened land are registered or only one of them is registered. In each case, the application should include:

(1) the original deed and a certified copy if the return of the original deed is required;

(2) the appropriate SDLT evidence, if applicable (see para.1–016);

(3) any consents or certificates required in respect of mortgages, charges or restrictions relating to the burdened title (see paras 8–009 to 8–013);

(4) a fee in accordance with the Fee Order.

8–015 ***Benefitting and burdened estates registered*** The grant or reservation of the easement will be a registrable disposition. Application must therefore be made in Form AP1 to complete the easement by registration. The title numbers of all the registered titles involved must be specified in panel 2, otherwise the registrar is not obliged to make any entry unless separate application is made (r.72C(3)). The easement will be completed by registration, with entries being made in the registers of both the benefitting title and the burdened title (r.72C(2)).

Where the easement is contained in a transfer of a registered title, only an application to register the transfer is necessary; no separate application in respect of the easements is required. The registrar will make the necessary entries as a matter of course when registering the transfer, provided the relevant title numbers are provided in panel 2 of the Form AP1 or separate application is made (r.72(4) and (5)).

8–016 ***Benefitting estate is unregistered and burdened estate is registered*** The grant or reservation of the easement will be a registrable disposition. Application must therefore be made in Form AP1 to complete the easement by registration. The title numbers of all the registered titles involved must be specified in panel 2, otherwise the registrar is not obliged to make any entry unless separate application is made (r.72C(3)). The easement will be completed by registration, with the entry of a notice of the burden of the easement in the register of the burdened title (r.72C(2)).

Benefitting estate is registered and burdened estate is unregistered The grant or reservation will not be a registrable disposition, so it will be effective at law when made. An application may be made under r.73A(1)(a) for the benefit of the easement to be registered as appurtenant to the registered benefitting estate. The application must be made in Form AP1. **8–017**

Equitable easements

If an easement is granted or reserved in writing other than by deed, or other than for a period equivalent to a fee simple absolute in possession or a term of years absolute, it will be equitable. Also, where the grant or reservation is a registrable disposition but is not completed by registration, it will take effect in equity only. **8–018**

(1) *Benefit of equitable easements* The Act makes provision only for the registration of *legal* interests (s.2) and therefore the registrar will not enter the benefit of an equitable interest in the register of the benefitting estate, either on first registration or subsequently.

(2) *Burden of equitable easements* The burden of an equitable easement will, if it is disclosed within the application, be the subject of a notice in the register on first registration of the burdened estate (r.35). If the burdened estate is already registered, an application may be made in Form AN1 to enter an agreed notice or in Form UN1 to enter a unilateral notice in respect of the burden of the equitable easement (see paras 16–005 and 16–008).

Where an equitable easement is granted in a transfer or other disposition of registered land, the registrar will enter a notice of the burden of the easement in the register of a registered burdened estate, providing the title number is entered in panel 2 of the Form AP1 otherwise a separate application must be made (rr.72(4) and (5) and 72C(2) and (3)).

Easements in leases

See paras 12–013 to 12–019. **8–019**

Easements as overriding interests

See paras 5–018 and 10–028. **8–020**

Extinguishment of easements

When an easement is referred to in the register of title and has been extinguished, an appropriate application may be made for the relevant entry or entries to be removed. Extinguishment may **8–021** arise where, for example, there has been a deed of release, or through unity of ownership of both the benefitting and burdened estates, or through abandonment. The application should be accompanied by evidence to satisfy the registrar that the easement has been extinguished.

Where the benefit of the easement has been registered in a registered benefiting title, the application should be made in Form AP1; otherwise (where only the burden has been noted in the register of a registered burdened title), the application should be in Form CN1 or Form UN2 or Form UN4 as appropriate (see paras 16–006, 16–010 and 16–011).

If a valid objection is received to a notice of the application served by the registrar which cannot be disposed of by agreement, the matter will have to be referred to the Adjudicator (see Chapter 23).

Prescriptive easements

8–022 Prescription is the acquisition of a right through long use or enjoyment ("user") so that the law presumes that the right was lawfully granted. There are three methods of acquiring an easement by prescription:

(1) at common law;

(2) by lost modern grant; and

(3) under the Prescription Act 1832.

Whichever method is relied on, the user must have been exercised:

(a) for at least 20 years;

(b) as of right i.e. without force, without secrecy and without permission;

(c) by or on behalf of a freehold owner against another freehold owner, so that where the burdened land is occupied by a tenant, the user must normally have started before the tenancy began; and

(d) continuously i.e. with no long, unexplained periods of non-user. Where the claim is made under the Prescription Act 1832, a break is not treated as an "interruption" in user for the purposes of that Act until acquiesced in for one year.

In addition, the right claimed must be one that could have been lawfully granted. This point was considered by the House of

Lords in *Bakewell Management Ltd v Brandwood* [2004] UKHL. In consequence, if the right could not have been lawfully granted by deed e.g. a right to pollute a river contrary to a statutory prohibition, then it cannot be acquired by prescription.

Section 193(4) of the Law of Property Act 1925 makes it a criminal offence to drive a vehicle over a common. Section 34 of the Road Traffic Act 1988 makes it a criminal offence to drive a motor vehicle over land that is not a road and that is a restricted byway or over which a public footpath or bridleway runs. However, both offences are only committed if driving over the land is "without lawful authority". Since a right to drive over the land concerned *could* in most cases have been lawfully granted, it can in those cases be acquired by prescription.

Previously, the Vehicular Access Across Common and Other Land (England) Regulations 2002 and the Vehicular Access Across Common and Other Land (Wales) Regulations 2004 (made under s.68 of the Countryside and Rights of Way Act 2000), provided for the creation of a legal easement, giving a right of way for vehicles, in cases where the user would have given rise to a prescriptive easement had it not constituted an offence. Those regulations lapsed when s.51 of the Commons Act 2006 came into force on October 1, 2006.

A prescriptive easement over a registered estate that has arisen by prescription does not have to be completed by registration to take effect at law and it will subsist for the benefit of any registered or unregistered estate to which it is appurtenant, notwithstanding that it is not the subject of an entry in the register. However, its validity will only be guaranteed for registration purposes of it is registered as appurtenant to a registered estate.

An application for registration of the benefit of a prescriptive easement may be made in either:

(1) Form FR1 at the time of an application for first registration of the benefiting estate (r.33); or

(2) Form AP1 at any time subsequently (r.73A).

If the burdened land is registered, the title number must be given in the application form.

Where the application is only to note the burden of an easement, the application should be made in Form AN1 for entry of an agreed notice or Form UN1 for entry of a unilateral notice, as appropriate (see paras 16–005 and 16–008).

The application must be accompanied by satisfactory supporting evidence, normally in the form of a statement of truth or statutory declaration by the applicant and any predecessors in title setting out the relevant details of the user of the easement claimed, for the requisite period of 20 years or more. Form ST4 is a statement of truth designed for such an application; its use is not compulsory, but its use will help ensure that all the relevant information is provided.

If the title to the applicant's estate is unregistered, they should lodge evidence of their title. Similarly, the applicant should lodge evidence of title in respect of the burdened estate if the title to that estate is unregistered.

A fee in accordance with the Fee Order is payable. If an inspection of the land is necessary, an additional fee to cover the cost of this will also be payable.

If the application is completed, the register entries made by the registrar will depend upon:

(a) whether both the benefiting land and burdened land are registered or only one of them is registered; and

(b) where the burdened land is unregistered, whether satisfactory evidence of title to it has been produced.

Where both the benefiting estate and burdened estate are registered, notice of the application will be served upon the registered proprietor and any registered chargee of the burdened title. If no objection is received, the benefit of the easement will be registered as appurtenant to the benefitting title and a notice as to the burden will be entered in the burdened title.

Where the benefitting estate is registered but the burdened estate is unregistered, if the applicant lodges evidence of title to the burdened estate and the address of the freehold owner, notice of the application will be served on the freehold owner and any other person who may have an interest in the burdened estate.

If no objection is received, the benefit of the easement will be registered as appurtenant to the benefitting title.

However, if (as is often the case) the applicant is not able to lodge evidence of title to the burdened estate and the address of the freehold owner, the registrar is likely to make only a note in the register to the effect that the applicant claims the benefit of the easement (r.73A(5)). This entry will be in the following form:

> "[Date] The registered proprietor claims that the land has the benefit of a right [terms of right as claimed by claimant]. The right claimed is not included in this registration. The claim is supported by [dates and details of statement(s) of truth or statutory declaration(s) and who has made them].
> NOTE: Copy/copies filed."

Where the burdened estate is registered but the benefitting estate is unregistered, notice of the application will be served upon the registered proprietor and any registered chargee of the burdened title. If no objection is received, a notice as to the burden will be entered in the burdened title in the appropriate form, depending upon whether the application is for an agreed notice or a unilateral notice.

Where the benefit of a prescriptive easement is entered in the register of a registered benefitting title, the entry will indicate that the right was acquired through long user and will refer to the statement(s) of truth or statutory declaration(s) lodged in support of the application, which will be open to inspection and copying (see Chapter 9).

If a valid objection is received in response to a notice served in respect of an application which cannot be disposed of by agreement, the matter will have to be referred to the Adjudicator (see Chapter 23).

Profits à prendre

A profit à prendre is a right to take something from another **8–023**
person's land e.g. sporting rights or grazing rights.

Before October 13, 2003, the benefit of a profit à prendre appurtenant (i.e. one attached to land) could be registered as appurtenant to a registered estate in land, but the benefit of a profit in gross (i.e. not attached to any land) could not be registered. However, the Act now provides for profits à prendre in gross to be capable of substantive registration in their own right (s.2—see para.1–003).

For the first registration of title to a profit à prendre in gross, see Chapter 5.

Any profit à prendre in gross granted out of a registered estate on or after October 13, 2003 is a registrable disposition which must be completed by registration to operate at law (s.27(2)(d)—see para.10–002). An application should therefore be made in Form AP1, accompanied by the original grant (together with a copy if the applicant wishes the original deed to be returned) and a fee in accordance with the Fee Order.

The proprietor of a registered profit à prendre in gross may transfer or lease it subject to any rule of law, express provision in the grant of the profit, or entry in the register to the contrary (s.23—see para.10–001).

A lease of a registered profit à prendre in gross is a registrable disposition, regardless of the length of the term (s.27(2)(d)—see para.12–007).

A "right of common" is a form of profit à prendre and some rights of common will be profits à prendre in gross. However, not all profits à prendre in gross will be rights of common. This distinction is important, because rights of common over land capable of being registered under the Commons Registration Act 1965 **cannot** be registered under the Act. Nor can the burden of such rights be the subject of a notice in the register of land subject to them (s.33(d)).

The property register of a registered profit à prendre in gross must contain a description of the profit (r.5) and, where practicable, sufficient particulars of any instrument which created it to enable it to be identified (r.7).

A notice of the burden of a profit à prendre is entered in the register of a registered estate affected by it in the same way as notice of the burden of an easement (see above).

As to the overriding status of legal profits à prendre see paras 5–018 and 10–028.

A profit à prendre in gross may, like an easement, be acquired by prescription in certain circumstances (see para.8–022). Any application based upon common law prescription or lost modern grant will be considered upon its merits; the Prescription Act 1832 does not apply to profits à prendre in gross.

A profit à prendre may, like an easement, be extinguished in certain circumstances (see para.8–021). In that event, application may be made for removal of the relevant entry or entries and/or (in the case of a registered estate consisting of a profit à prendre in gross), closure of the registered title. The application must be accompanied by evidence to satisfy the registrar that the profit à prendre has been extinguished. This may occur by virtue of:

(1) statute;

(2) release (express or implied); or

(3) merger by unity of ownership and possession.

If a valid objection is received in response to a notice of the application served by the registrar which cannot be disposed of by agreement, the matter will have to be referred to the Adjudicator (see Chapter 23).

Practical points

- Ensure satisfactory details of restrictive covenants are lodged with an application for first registration, to avoid a protective entry being made,
- Ensure that an application in Form AP1 is made to complete the grant of an easement by registration (where it is a registrable disposition) and that panel 2 of the form refers to all relevant title numbers,
- Ensure that all relevant evidence is lodged with an application relating to a prescriptive easement,
- Check the wording of easement entries carefully, to ascertain whether the benefit of the easement is "guaranteed" for registration purposes and confers all necessary rights,
- Do not confuse adverse easements with benefiting easements where these are intermixed in the property register.

Chapter 9

Inspection, Official Copies and Searches

Introduction

As well as applications for registration, a person may need to make an application to inspect and/or make copies of or obtain official copies of the register, documents referred to in the register and other documents. A person may also need to make an official search of the indexes or the register. The relevant procedures are discussed below. **9–001**

Inspection of the register

Section 66(1) provides that subject to formalities and fee, any person may, inspect and make copies of: **9–002**

(1) the register of any individual registered title (including any title plan);

(2) any document kept by the registrar which is referred to in the register;

(3) any other document kept by the registrar which relates to an application to him; and

(4) the caution register of an individual caution against first registration (including any caution plan).

This general right to inspect and make copies ("the general right under s.66(1)") is now much wider than was the case under the Land Registration Act 1925. This is in line with the Freedom of

Information Act 2000 ("the Freedom of Information Act"). Although that Act only came into force on January 1, 2005 the Act and the Rules were drafted to take account of its provisions. This means that, where the information is available as of right under s.66(1), it cannot be requested under the Freedom of Information Act as it is "reasonably accessible" for the purposes of that Act (see para.9–014).

However, the general right to inspect and make copies is subject to rr.133 and 135 which provide that the following "excepted documents" are excepted from the general right:

(a) exempt information documents;

(b) an edited information document which has been replaced by another edited information document under rr.136(6) or 138(4);

(c) Form EX1A;

(d) Form CIT and any form which has been attached to Form CIT, together with any documents or copy documents prepared by the registrar in connection with the application;

(e) any document relating to an application for a network access agreement under para.1(4) of Sch.5 to the Act;

(f) an "identity document" i.e. any document within s.66(1)(c) provided to, or prepared or obtained by, the registrar as evidence of identity of any person (such as an applicant);

(g) an "investigation of crime document" i.e. any document within s.66(1)(c) (other than an identity document) which relates to the prevention or detection of crime—**unless** it is a document:

   (i) lodged as part of or in support of either an application to the registrar or an objection to an application; or

   (ii) prepared by, or at the request of, the registrar as part of the process of considering an application or objection but which is not prepared principally in connection with the prevention or detection of crime.

In addition, correspondence and documents relating to claims for indemnity under Sch.8 to the Act are also excepted from the general right. Also, the general right to inspect does not extend to the index of proprietors' names (see para.9–003).

However, these exceptions are in turn subject to special provision under r.140, in relation to applications made in Form

CIT in connection with court proceedings, insolvency and tax liability (see para.9–012).

Inspection of the index of proprietors' names

The index of proprietors' names (see para.1–009) is not open to general inspection. However, in addition to the special right to a search made in Form CIT discussed in para.9–012, any person may apply in Form PN1 for a search to be made of the index in respect of either their own name, the name of a corporation aggregate, or the name of some other person in whose property they are able to satisfy the registrar that they are interested generally, e.g. as trustee in bankruptcy or personal representative (r.11(3)). **9–003**

Separate applications should be made in respect of any former or alternative names, and every address which may have been used as an address for service in the register should be stated.

The reply to the application will state whether or not the person named in the search appears in the index and, if they do, the reply will also give the relevant title number(s). The reply does not constitute an official search for the purposes of the Act.

A fee in accordance with the Fee Order is payable.

Personal inspection

Land Registry offices are open to the public between the hours of 8.30am and 6pm Mondays to Fridays, excluding public holidays. During those hours anyone may apply in Form PIC to make a personal inspection of the register and the documents referred to in s.66(1), subject to the exceptions referred to in para.9–002. Fees are payable for inspection, depending upon the subject matter (Part 2(2) of Sch.3 to the Fee Order). If the title number is not known, an additional fee may be payable. It is advisable to make an appointment to inspect, and to confirm the subject matter of what is to be inspected, in advance of a visit to a Land Registry office. **9–004**

Official copies

Rules 134 and 135 provide that a person may apply for: **9–005**

(1) an official copy of an individual register and title plan;

(2) an official copy of an individual caution register and caution plan;

(3) a certificate of inspection of any title plan (see paras 9–010 and 21–010);

(4) any document referred to in the register and kept by the registrar; and

(5) any other document kept by the registrar which relates to an application to him.

Rule 135 provides that the "excepted documents" referred to in r.133 (see para.9–002) are also excepted from the right to obtain official copies.

Application for official copies

9–006 An application should be made in Form OC1 for an official copy of a register, title plan, caution register and caution plan or for a certificate of inspection of the title plan (see para.9–010). An application should be made in Form OC2 for an official copy of a document referred to in the register and kept by the registrar or for any other document kept by the registrar that relate to an application to him.

In Form OC2 it is essential that documents referred to in the register which are required are listed specifically with their nature and dates being given. The title number(s) under which the documents are kept must be given and the number of copies required stated. Generalised requests will not be accepted. Where documents which are not referred to in the register are required, as much detail as possible should be supplied.

The application should be lodged at the proper office. If the title number is not known the words "Please supply the title number" should be written boldly at the head of the Form OC1 (an additional fee may then be payable—see para.9–008). Separate applications in Form OC1 should be made in respect of each individual registered title or individual caution register.

Form EX2 is used for requests for official copies of exempt information documents (see para.9–013).

Delivery of the application

9–007 The application can be delivered by post, in person or by document exchange. Credit account holders can also make application by fax or by telephone. Telephone applications may only be made between 8.30am and 6pm Monday to Friday and 8.30am to 1pm on Saturday, excluding public holidays, to Land Registry's Telephone Services on 0844 892 0307 (for properties in England) or 0844 892 0308 (for properties in Wales).

A telephone application for an official copy of a document can only be made if that document is one which is referred to in the register. Land Registry Direct and NLIS applicants are able to order official copies from their own computer direct to Land Registry's computer and may request the official copies to be in electronic form, where the original is held in electronic form.

Fees for official copies

Fees are payable in accordance with Pt.2 of Sch.3 to the Fee Order. **9–008**

A credit account (see para.1–013) can be used for payment of fees for official copies.

Issue of official copies

Official copies of registers and title plans are always timed and dated to show that they represent a true record at that specific time. Where there are pending substantive applications, the date and time will be backdated to immediately before receipt of the earliest pending application. An official search can also be made, to provide details of the pending application(s) if required. **9–009**

Official copies of documents are not dated because, once registered or otherwise referred to in the register, documents are not normally altered.

Official copies are admissible in evidence to the same extent as the original (s.67(1)). A person who relies on an official copy in which there is a mistake is not liable for loss suffered by another by reason of the mistake (s.67(2)). Accuracy of an official copy is guaranteed and indemnity may be payable as a result of any mistake in an official copy (s.103 and para.1(1)(d) of Sch.8 to the Act).

Certificate of official inspection of the title plan

Instead of an official copy of the title plan a "certificate of official inspection of the title plan" may be obtained (r.134(1)(d)). **9–010**

When a transaction relates to only part of the estate in a large registered title and a certificate in Form CI would give the applicant all the information about the title plan that they need, the use of such a certificate can save the additional expense and delay entailed in obtaining an official copy of the title plan. The main use of certificates in Form CI is in connection with registered developing estates (see Chapter 21), but the procedure may be used in relation to any title plan.

A paper application should be made in Form OC1. A fee in accordance with the Fee Order is payable.

The application is normally made by reference to an estate layout plan approved by Land Registry (see para.21–003) and involves the use of recognised plot numbers. In the case of postal applications only, application may be made by reference to a plan annexed to the application; the plan should be prepared on the same basis as a plan for use with a search of part (see para.9–019). Where an estate plan has been approved, only the plot number need be given. Otherwise, an accurate plan must be lodged in duplicate (at 1/2500 scale or greater) showing, in relation to the detail shown on the title plan, the precise position and extent of the plot of land in question.

The certificate will be in Form CI (r.143) and will state that the land to which it relates is within the title concerned and what, if any, colour or other references shown on the title plan and mentioned in the register entries affect it. The accuracy of the certificate will be guaranteed, but it will not confer on the applicant priority for the registration of any disposition.

Historical information

9–011 The register of title only provides current details of the title at a particular point in time—it does not show how the title has changed historically. Section 69 and r.144 provide a mechanism for a person to obtain such information. This will only apply where the registrar holds previous editions of a registered title, or a registered title which has been closed, in electronic form. He is not under an obligation to keep such records, and register history information *may* be available for dates after May 4, 1993 and title plan information *may* be available for dates after October 13, 2003. Limited information is held about title plans before this date.

Application can be made in Form HC1 for a copy of either :

(1) the last edition of the register or title plan of a specified title that existed on a specified date; or

(2) all editions of the register or title plan of a specified title that existed on a specified date,

where these are kept by the registrar in electronic form. If the application is in order, the registrar will issue the requested copies.

It should be borne in mind that historical copies of a registered title may not provide a complete record of all alterations and dispositions made. For example, a single application containing more than one transaction or a number of applications processed at the same time may result in the register reflecting the final transaction only on that date.

If the required information is not held in electronic form, the registrar may hold paper copies of earlier editions of the register or title plan and may be able to provide copies of these in response to an application under the Freedom of Information Act (see para.9–014). Such an application should provide as much information as possible about the enquiry and the reason why the information is required. This will enable Land Registry to determine if it is able to provide the information required.

Inspection in connection with court proceedings, insolvency and tax liability

Under r.140 certain specified officials responsible for either investigating crime and recovering the proceeds of crime, acting as receiver in special circumstances, administering the affairs of insolvent individuals or corporations, or assessing tax liability may by using Form CIT apply: **9–012**

(1) to inspect, make copies of, or obtain official copies of excepted documents as referred to in rr.133 and 135 (see paras 9–002 and 9–005); and
(2) for a search in the index of proprietors' names in respect of the name of a person specified in the application (see para.9–003).

Schedule 5 to the Rules sets out who can apply and the appropriate certificate which must be given in Form CIT.

Such an application should be made in the relevant Form PIC, OC2 or PN1, with Form CIT attached. Form CIT sets out the nature of the application and the appropriate certificate.

The form can also be attached to Forms PIC, OC1, OC2, HC1, SIM and SIF when used for applying for documents to which the general right under s.66(1) applies, or for historical editions of registered titles, or for official searches of the index map and index of relating franchises and manors (see para.3–015).

Under rr.133 and 135, Form CIT, any form to which it has been attached as indicated above and any document or copy of a document prepared by the registrar in connection with an application in a form to which Form CIT has been attached, are all excepted documents which are excepted from the general right under s.66(1).

Exempt information documents

These documents are one of the categories of "excepted documents" which are excepted from the general right under s.66(1) (see paras 9–002 and 9–005). Under r.136 a person who claims a **9–013** relevant document contains prejudicial information can apply to the registrar to designate it as an "exempt information document".

A "relevant document" is defined in r.136(7) as a document which is referred to in the register of title or which relates to an application to the registrar, where the original or a copy has been kept by the registrar, or which will be so referred to as a result of an accompanying application or which relates to that accompanying application and the original or a copy will be or is for the time being kept by the registrar.

"Prejudicial information" is defined in r.131 as:

(1) information that relates to an individual who is the applicant for designation and if disclosed to other persons (whether to the public generally or specific persons) would, or would be likely to, cause substantial unwarranted damage or substantial unwarranted distress to the applicant or another; or

(2) information that if disclosed to other persons (whether to the public generally or specific persons) would, or would be likely to, prejudice the commercial interests of the applicant for designation.

If designated as an exempt information document, the document is subject to special provisions that except it from the general right under s.66(1) and regulate the circumstances in which the registrar may allow inspection and copying or the provision of official copies of it.

Application for designation should be made in Forms EX1 and EX1A. Form EX1A must state the grounds upon which the applicant claims that the document contains prejudicial information. It should be borne in mind that Form EX1A is excepted from the general right under s.66(1), but Form EX1 is not, nor are any accompanying letters. A fee in accordance with the Fee Order is payable.

The application must be accompanied by a copy of the document with the prejudicial information edited out and the words "excluded information" inserted instead wherever information has been excluded within the document ("the edited information document"). The edited information document must be certified as being a true copy of the relevant document, except that it excludes the prejudicial information and includes the above wording instead.

Provided the application is in order and the registrar is satisfied that the applicant's claim is not groundless, he must designate the relevant document as an exempt information document and may make an appropriate entry in the register of any affected registered title. However, if the registrar considers that designating the document as an exempt information document would prejudice the keeping of the register, he can cancel the application. This would be the case where, for example, the excluded information consisted of the price paid in a transfer or lease or a clause containing an easement or restrictive covenant.

A subsequent application may be made in respect of the same document and may even relate to the same excluded information. This could occur where, for example, the subsequent applicant was concerned that the original applicant might later apply to withdraw the designation (see below). Where a subsequent application is made for exemption in respect of further information in the document, the registrar must prepare another edited information document which excludes the information excluded from the existing edited information document and any further information excluded from the edited information document lodged by the subsequent applicant.

The benefit of the designation of an exempt information document cannot be transferred to another person; for example on a transfer of the registered estate to which it relates.

An application in Form OC2 for an official copy of an exempt information document will provide only a copy of the edited information document. Subject to the effect of the Freedom of Information Act (see para.9–014), a person can only obtain an official copy of the complete document if they apply under r.137 in Form EX2, stating why an official copy of the edited information document is not sufficient for their purposes and (if such be the case) why they consider that the information claimed to be prejudicial information is not such information or, if they accept that all or some of the information is prejudicial information, why they consider that the public interest in providing an official copy of the exempt information document outweighs the public interest in not doing so. Application for an official copy of an exempt information document may also be made under r.140 using Form CIT, in connection with court proceedings, insolvency or tax liability (see para.9–012). A fee in accordance with the Fee Order is payable. Form EX2 is not excepted from the general right under s.66(1).

Where application is made under r.137, the registrar must serve notice on the applicant for the exempt information document designation unless he is satisfied that such notice is unnecessary or impracticable. He may consider any information the recipient provides in response to the notice in reaching his decision.

If the registrar decides that either:

(a) none of the information claimed to be prejudicial information is prejudicial information; or

(b) although the information is prejudicial information in whole or in part, the public interest in providing an official copy of the exempt information document to the applicant outweighs the public interest in not doing so,

he must provide an official copy of the exempt information document to the applicant. In the case of (a), he must also remove the designation and any entry in the register which relates to that designation.

Under r.138, the person who applied for designation of a document as an exempt information document may apply for the designation to be removed. The application should be in Form EX3.

The registrar must remove the designation and any entry in the register which relates to that designation, if he is satisfied that the application is in order. Where a document has been made an exempt document as a result of more than one application by different persons, the registrar must replace the existing edited information document with one that reflects only the current exemptions.

Freedom of Information Act 2000

9–014 The Freedom of Information Act came into force mainly on January 1, 2005 and generally allows inspection of all documents held by Land Registry as a "public authority".

Any person now has the right to ask a public authority for information and, if that authority holds it, to have that information disclosed to them unless there are justifiable reasons why this should not be done. Under the right of access provisions of the Freedom of Information Act:

(1) a request must be in writing (which includes e-mail or fax) and must include a name and address to which a response can be sent;

(2) the request does not have to mention the Freedom of Information Act;

(3) the request can be made to any part of the public authority;

(4) the authority must reply within 20 working days;

(5) the authority has a duty to provide assistance to the applicant; and

(6) the authority may charge a fee for providing the information.

A request to Land Registry for information covered by the Freedom of Information Act may only be refused in the following circumstances:

(a) where Land Registry reasonably requires further information to identify and locate the information requested but the applicant has failed to supply it; or
(b) where the request is "vexatious" or repeated, for example where Land Registry has previously complied with an identical or similar request from the same applicant and a reasonable time has not elapsed between compliance with the previous request and the making of the current request; or
(c) where Land Registry estimates that the cost of complying with the request would exceed the "appropriate limit", currently £600; or
(d) where an exemption applies and applying the "public interest test" (if applicable) leads to the decision that it is not in the public interest to disclose the information (see below).

Exemptions from the obligation to disclose information can be absolute or non-absolute. If an absolute exemption applies, the information requested need not be disclosed and, in many cases, Land Registry is not obliged to comply with the duty to confirm or deny whether it holds the requested information. Absolute exemption applies to requests for information reasonably accessible by other means. This means that the Freedom of Information Act does not apply, for example, to requests for official copies of registers, title plans, and documents relating to applications or to requests for historical copies of registers, as these are available under the general right under s.66(1). Applications in that regard should therefore be made in the appropriate form i.e. Form OC1 or as the case may be (see above).

Information covered by Land Registry's Publication Scheme is also absolutely exempt. The Freedom of Information Act requires Land Registry to adopt and maintain a publication scheme setting out classes of information which it intends to make available to the public as a matter of course, the manner in which the information is to be made available and whether the information will be provided free or for a charge. Land Registry's Publication Scheme is available on its website (see para.1–025). Other examples of information covered by absolute exemption are information supplied by or relating to court records.

In the case of non-absolute exemptions, the Freedom of Information Act requires Land Registry to consider whether or not the exemption applies and, if it does, then to consider the "public interest test" before withholding or disclosing information. Examples of information covered by the non-absolute exemptions are personal information about third parties and information that constitutes a trade secret or the disclosure of which would, or would be likely to, prejudice the commercial interests of any person. Under the public interest test there is likely to be a public interest in disclosing information where it:

(i) facilitates the accountability and transparency in the spending of public money; or

(ii) allows individuals to understand decisions affecting their lives and, in some cases, assists individuals in challenging those decisions; or

(iii) brings to light information affecting public safety.

As indicated in para.9–002, the Act and the Rules were drafted to take account of the provisions of the Freedom of Information Act, so it appears unlikely that inspection of exempt information would be allowed under that Act where it would not be allowed under the Rules. However it remains a possibility, which should be borne in mind when drafting documents relating to registered land.

In relation to a request under the Freedom of Information Act for personal inspection and copying, or for a copy of a document, or for historical information (as opposed to an application under r.11 in Form PIC or under r.135 in Form OC2 or under r.144 in Form HC1), the request should be made in accordance with the requirements set out above, for consideration by Land Registry. There is no requirement to provide reasons for the request, but it may assist in cases where the public interest test needs to be applied.

In relation to a request for an official copy of an exempt information document under the Freedom of Information Act (as opposed to an application under r.137 in Form EX2), the request should be made in accordance with the requirements set out above, for consideration by Land Registry. Again, there is no requirement to provide reasons for the request, but it may assist the registrar in deciding whether the full copy of the document can be provided.

Under the Freedom of Information Act, the registrar may need to determine whether the excluded information is "personal data" for the purposes of the Data Protection Act 1998 (see para.9–015), the disclosure of which would contravene any of the data protection principles in that Act. If it is, the information is exempt from the general right of access under the Freedom of Information Act. If it is not, the registrar has to apply the public interest test in deciding whether a full copy of the document can be provided. The registrar will normally serve notice of the request upon any third party who may be affected by the decision and they will have the opportunity to make representations, which the registrar will take into account in making his decision.

A fee may be payable for a request under the Freedom of Information Act. If the information cannot be provided within 20 working days, Land Registry will inform the applicant in advance and provide an estimated time for dealing with the request. If the registrar decides to refuse a request for information, the applicant will be informed of this and the reasons for the decision.

Data Protection Act 1998

The Data Protection Act 1998 affects Land Registry, but does not apply to the majority of the data that it holds because s.34 of that Act exempts information that is already publicly available; for example under the general right under s.66(1). An application relating to such information should be made in the appropriate form i.e. Form OC1 or as the case may be (see above). **9–015**

If a person as a "data subject" makes a request under the Data Protection Act 1998 for personal data that is not already publicly available, it must be made in writing, accompanied by sufficient details to enable Land Registry to locate the data, evidence of identity, and a fee of (currently) £10.

Under the Data Protection Act 1998, Land Registry must deal with the request within 40 days. The response will provide details of the personal data held about the applicant, the purposes for which it is being used, and those to whom the data may be disclosed. If the data requested contains details about other living persons, Land Registry may need to obtain their consent to divulge the data or it may edit the data to exclude those details. In this case, the 40-day period may be extended.

Official searches of the register

In order to obtain up-to-date information as to all subsisting entries in the register of a title, it is not enough to read what appears in a land or charge certificate, a Title Information **9–016**

Document or an official copy, as this may no longer be current. Entries may have been made in the register since the date (shown on the inside cover of the certificate) on which a land or charge certificate was last officially made to correspond with the register or since the date when the Title Information Document or official copy was issued. For example, the registration of a second charge may not appear in a first charge certificate. Entries relating to cautions against dealings and bankruptcy commonly do not appear in any certificate, because it was not necessary for this to be lodged at Land Registry before such entries could be made. Also, land and charge certificates have not been issued since October 13, 2003 (see para.1–017), so any in existence at that time may be out of date. All these matters, however, could be the subject of entries in the register.

At any time, an up-to-date official copy of the register may be obtained. But however recent the date on which the Title Information Document or official copy was issued, it is never safe to assume that no new entry has been made in the register since that date. It is clearly of great importance to persons dealing with a registered title that they are not bound by adverse entries of which they were unaware; to protect against this the Act provides for a system of official searches of the register, which is operated in accordance with the Rules.

Official searches of the register with priority

Purpose

9–017 The purpose of these searches is to enable a "purchaser", defined in r.131 as "a person who has entered into or who intends to enter into a 'protectable disposition' as disponee", to obtain an official certificate as to the entries in the register of the disponor's title immediately before completion and to ensure that (if they apply to register the disposition within the priority period conferred by the search) they will be unaffected by any entry made between the date of this certificate and the registration of their protectable disposition.

"Protectable disposition" is defined in r.131 as "a registrable disposition (including one by virtue of r.38) of a registered estate or registered charge made for valuable consideration". See para.10–002 for further information about what constitutes a registrable disposition under s.27.

Who may apply?

9–018 Official searches with priority are available only to a "purchaser" as defined by r.131 (see para.9–017). This will include not only a person purchasing a registered estate, but also a person taking a charge over a registered estate or acquiring an easement over it by way of deed of grant for valuable consideration. However, these searches are not available to a mortgagee who intends to protect the mortgage in the register by a notice under s.32, for example, as that will not constitute a registrable disposition. Other persons may, however, apply for an official search without priority by using Form OS3 (see para.9–032).

The application

Application for an official search with priority may be made in paper form ("a paper search"), by fax, by telephone, orally or through Land Registry Direct or the NLIS (see below). As explained below, the commencement of the priority period conferred by the search is governed by the method of application used. **9–019**

(1) *Paper searches* A paper search should be made in Form OS1 where the protectable disposition is of the whole of the registered estate, or in Form OS2 where it is of part only of the registered estate.

No plan need accompany Form OS2 if the part affected is a numbered plot on an estate plan approved by Land Registry relating to a developing estate (see para.21–003), provided that the plot number(s) and the date of Land Registry's approval are stated on Form OS2. Where there is no approved estate plan, Form OS2 must be accompanied by a plan, in duplicate, which should be drawn to a suitable scale (generally not less than 1/1250 for urban areas or 1/2500 for rural areas) and, when necessary, containing sufficient figured dimensions to define the part affected and to tie it to the existing physical features (such as road junctions, fences or walls) shown by firm black lines on the title plan of the disponor's registered title. The plan should be a copy of the plan intended to be bound up in the protectable disposition.

The application must be delivered to the proper office. Official search certificates are always despatched from Land Registry using first class post or the document exchange.

(2) *Fax searches* A credit account holder (see para.1–013) may apply for an official certificate of search with priority by fax. The application should be made in Form OS1 (search of whole) or Form OS2 (search of part).

For a search of part where there is no approved estate plan (see above) any plan which accompanies the application must adequately depict the extent to be searched on a single A4-sized plan, be referred to in panel 6, show the extent of the land to be searched by thick black edging, hatching or stippling and be sent in "fine mode" where possible.

The search form should be completed in black print or black ink.

The application must be faxed to the fax number specified for that purpose at the proper office.

Official search certificates will not be faxed to the applicant even where the application was lodged by fax.

(3) *Telephone searches* An application for an official certificate of search of whole with priority may be made by telephone by a credit account holder (see para.1–013). Land Registry will ask for the following information:

(a) the credit account key number and name and address of the account holder;

(b) the name and address to which the result is to be despatched if different from (a);

(c) the title number;

(d) the name of the registered proprietor;

(e) the administrative area and postcode (only if there is doubt that the correct title number has been given);

(f) the search from date (see para.9–020);

(g) the account holder's reference and, if different, the reference of the person to whom the result is to be despatched;

(h) the name of the applicant;

(i) whether a purchase, charge or lease is sought to be protected; and

(j) a name and telephone number to phone back, in case of need.

The caller may request as many searches as they wish within any one call.

Telephone requests may be made between 8.30am and 6.30pm Monday to Friday (other than public holidays) and between 8.30am and 1pm on Saturdays other than a Christmas Day. The call must be made to 0844 892 0307 (for registered titles within England) or 0844 892 0308 (for registered titles within Wales) and not to the proper office.

(4) *Oral searches* Anyone who is, or who acts for, a "purchaser" as defined in r.131 (see para.9–017) may apply for an official certificate of search with priority orally at the Customer Information Centre of any Land Registry office. The search must be in respect of the whole of the land in any registered title; searches of part cannot be requested in this way.

Land Registry will require the same information as set out at (3) above in respect of telephone searches. The applicant may request as many searches as they wish within any one visit.

Oral requests for searches by personal attendance at one of Land Registry's offices can only be made between 8.30am and 6pm Monday to Friday (other than public holidays).

(5) ***Land Registry Direct and NLIS searches*** Customers using Land Registry Direct or the NLIS (see para.1–027) can use the facility to order certain searches direct computer to computer.

The Land Registry Direct service is available between 7am and 10pm Monday to Friday (other than public holidays) and between 7am and 5pm on Saturdays other than a Christmas Day.

The "search from date"

Application for an official search with priority must be from a **9–020** date (the "search from date") which is the date shown on an official copy of the register of the individual registered title as the date on which the entries shown on that official copy were subsisting. A time is also printed on the official copy but this need not be quoted on an application for an official search.

In the case of an application using Land Registry Direct, the search can be made from the date stated at the time of an access by remote terminal to the register of the individual registered title as the date on which the entries accessed were subsisting.

The date on which a land or charge certificate was last officially examined with the register cannot be used as a "search from date".

The result of search

Whichever method of lodging an application for an official **9–021** search is used, an official search certificate can always be obtained in paper form, although applicants using Land Registry Direct or the NLIS may be able to request the certificate to be issued in electronic form (see below).

In a case where:

(1) a search is made by telephone, orally or through Land Registry Direct or the NLIS;

(2) there have been no entries made in the register since the search from date; and

(3) there are no pending applications or unexpired searches with priority on the day list,

an immediate and guaranteed result of search will be given by the same means as the search was made. Where a search does not produce an immediate "clear" result, Land Registry will, in the case of a search lodged orally or by telephone, usually give the applicant such details as it can of the adverse entries or pending applications or unexpired searches. Such information is not guaranteed and applicants are advised to wait for the official search certificate itself. In the case of a search lodged through Land Registry Direct, a message will be issued to inform the applicant of the situation; the applicant may then view the register and day list to obtain further details pending receipt of the official search certificate.

Except where a Land Registry Direct or NLIS applicant has been able to apply for an official search certificate to be issued in electronic form, an official certificate of search will be issued by first class post or document exchange in paper form (including cases where an immediate result has already been given as above). Search results are not issued by fax.

The certificate will contain details of:

(a) The date and time at which the priority period of the search commences and expires.

(b) A statement, where applicable, that there have been no adverse entries since the search from date. This means that no adverse entries have been made in the register and that there are no pending applications or unexpired priority searches noted on the day list.

Or:

(c) Details of any relevant adverse entries made in the register on or after the search from date. This will usually be by reference to an official copy of the register issued with the certificate, enabling any changes to be identified by comparing this official copy with the existing one already held by the applicant. Details of any entries made in the register and subsequently cancelled during the period searched may not be given.

(d) Notice of the entry of any relevant pending application or proposal by the registrar to alter the register affecting the title entered on the day list.

(e) Notice of the entry on the day list of any relevant official search the priority period of which has not expired.

If the extent of the property to which the search relates is not wholly comprised within the registered title, the official search certificate will be limited to the extent which falls within the title. The details of the limitation and the reason for it will normally be included with the official search certificate, but the applicant should not seek to rely on this as a means of "confirming" the registered proprietor's title and should instead rely on a proper investigation of that title (see para.11–005).

As more than one version of a register can be prepared in the course of the same day, the result of search will be given from one second past midnight on the "search from" date.

Accuracy of an official search certificate is guaranteed and indemnity may be payable as a result of any mistake in an official search (s.103 and para.1(1)(c) of Sch.8 to the Act—see Chapter 24).

The priority period

The period of priority begins when the official search application is deemed to be delivered. It will be deemed to be delivered at the time and on the date notice of it is entered on the day list (see paras 1–010 and 1–011). **9–022**

Notice of a search application delivered in documentary form or by fax to the proper office before noon on one business day will normally be entered on the day list on the same day. Where an application is received after noon, notice of it will normally be entered on the day list the same day or the following business day. Notice of a search application delivered by telephone, orally or by Land Registry Direct or the NLIS will normally be entered on the day list immediately after it is delivered unless it is lodged through Land Registry Direct or the NLIS on a day that is not a business day, when it will be entered on the day list on the next business day.

The priority period ends at midnight marking the end of the 30th business day after the day on which the search was deemed to be delivered, regardless of how the original application was made. "Business day" is defined in r.217 as "a day when the Land Registry is open to the public under rule 216". The 30 business day priority period will be extended to 36 business days under r.131 if the registrar in future gives notice under r.216(2) that Land Registry will be open on Saturdays.

The effect of priority

An official search certificate with priority confers priority upon an application to register the protectable disposition (see para.9–017), over applications relating to other registrable dispositions and other matters which were not entered on the day list prior to that search and are not themselves protected by an earlier official search with priority. **9–023**

If the protected application is dependent upon an earlier registrable disposition, that earlier disposition will also benefit from the protection conferred by the official search certificate if it is also lodged within the priority period of that search and is, in due course, completed by registration (r.151).

Thus, for example, where the disposition is a transfer for valuable consideration and the purchaser is obtaining a mortgage loan, it is not normally necessary to lodge two searches. An official search certificate obtained on behalf of the chargee will provide protection for both the chargee and the purchaser, as the registration of the charge is dependent on the registration of the transfer.

An application protected by an official search with priority will have priority over an application protected by another official search with priority, in respect of the same registered estate or charge, where the first search is deemed to have been delivered before the second one (see para.9–024).

If the completion of the protectable disposition is delayed to an extent likely to preclude the delivery of the application for registration within the priority period, a second application for an official search may be made, whether the priority period under the first official search certificate is still subsisting or has expired. However, the second official search certificate will **not** operate to extend the priority afforded by the first. It will only provide a separate priority period, which will not provide priority over any application lodged before its priority period commences.

Any entry made in the register during the priority period conferred by an official search will be postponed to a subsequent application to register the protectable disposition to which the priority period relates, unless the earlier entry was itself protected by an official search with a priority period ranking ahead of the one relating to the subsequent application (s.72(2) and (3)).

For this reason, where an official search with priority has not yet expired and has priority over an application on the day list, the registrar will not normally complete that application until the priority period of the search has expired (s.72(5)).

Points on the operation of priority periods

9–024 Two or more official certificates of search relating to the same registered estate or charge may be in operation at the same time. Rule 153 provides for the determination of priorities between concurrent searches in situations where priority is not clear, and in cases of doubt reference should be made to that rule.

Rule 154 provides that where an official search has been made in respect of a particular title and an application relating to that title is deemed to have been delivered at the same time as the expiry of the priority period relating to that search, the time of delivery of the application shall be deemed to be within that priority period.

Sub-dispositions and re-dispositions

On some occasions, it may be that there is a sub-disposition or an immediate re-disposition by a "purchaser" in favour of a third party, e.g. a sub-sale. Consideration then needs to be given as to how the purchaser is to deduce their title to the third party and how that third party may make an application for an official search to protect their own disposition. **9–025**

In the case of a sub- or re-disposition of whole, for example where the registered proprietor (R) transfers the whole of the registered estate to a purchaser (P) and, before that transfer is completed by registration, P contracts to sell the whole of the registered estate to a sub-purchaser (S), P will not at that stage be able to provide S with an official copy of the register showing P as proprietor. However, S can verify P's title by obtaining an official copy of the title showing R as proprietor and a copy of the transfer to P, supplemented by an application for an official search without priority (see para.9–032) using Form OS3, which should reveal the pending application for registration of the transfer to P. Immediately prior to the completion of the sub-sale, S should apply for an official search of whole with priority using Form OS1, which will confer a priority period for an application to register the transfer to S.

In the case of a sub- or re-disposition of part in such a scenario, where P instead contracts to sell only part of the registered estate being transferred to them by R, a similar procedure can be adopted. However in this instance, the application for an official search by S should be made using Form OS1 in respect of the new title number allotted to the transfer of part to P, rather than in respect of the existing registered title of R. If the application to register the transfer of part to P should fail to be completed for some reason, S's official search against the new title will also fail and in that situation, S should apply using Form OS2 for an official search of part in respect of R's registered title.

These procedures can be adapted for a chargee who proposes to lend to a sub-purchaser whose transfer has not yet been registered or where either of the two transactions is by way of lease.

Official search with priority in respect of an estate the subject of a pending application for first registration

Purpose

9–026 Rule 147(2) provides that where there is a pending application for first registration, the "purchaser" of a protectable disposition (see para.9–017) which relates to that pending application may apply for an official search with priority in relation to that pending application.

The purpose of the search is to enable a purchaser of a registrable estate which is the subject of a pending first registration application to confirm that the estate is, in fact, the subject of such an application lodged by a named applicant and received on a stated date, and to ascertain whether or not any applications affecting the estate have been received since that date. Provided the pending first registration application is subsequently completed, the purchaser is able to ensure (if they apply to register their disposition within the priority period conferred by the search) that they will be unaffected by an entry made between the date of the search certificate and the registration of their protectable disposition.

Who may apply?

9–027 These official searches are available only to a "purchaser" as defined in r.131 of a "protectable disposition" as also defined in r.131 (see para.9–017), which relates to a pending first registration application. The same considerations therefore apply as in the case of existing registered titles, as discussed above.

The application

9–028 The same methods of application are available as set out above in relation to searches against existing registered titles. Searches against the whole of the registrable estate comprised in a pending first registration application can be delivered as paper searches, by fax, by telephone, orally and through Land Registry Direct or the NLIS. Searches of part of the registrable estate comprised in a pending first registration can only be made as paper searches or through the NLIS. In all cases the procedures set out above in relation to searches against existing registered titles should be followed.

Official search certificates are always despatched from Land Registry using first class mail or document exchange.

The same provisions apply in relation to the deemed time of delivery and issue of the official search certificate as are set out above in relation to searches against existing registered titles, except that in some cases there may be a small delay if it is necessary for Land Registry to obtain the papers relating to the pending first registration application, which may be at any stage in the course of registration, in order to complete the official search certificate.

The result of search

Where a search has been lodged by telephone, orally or through Land Registry Direct or the NLIS, an immediate search result may be given in certain circumstances (as discussed above in relation to searches against existing registered titles—see para.9–021), but where that is not possible, basic details of any pending applications or unexpired official searches with priority may be provided. **9–029**

The official search certificate will enable the purchaser to satisfy themselves that the estate searched is the subject of a pending first registration application, and will state by whom the application was made and on what date the application was received. The certificate will state whether or not any applications have been received since that date which are pending and may affect the property (other than an application to designate a document as an exempt information document—see para.9–013), and will disclose particulars of any other official search with unexpired priority.

The certificate will not contain details of any entries that may be made in the register of title arising from the deeds or other evidence of title produced with the application for first registration. This includes charges or any other application(s) contained within the application for first registration. The issue of an official search certificate does not affect the position in this regard and a warning notice to this effect is issued with the certificate.

The accuracy of the official search certificate is guaranteed and indemnity may be payable as a result of any mistake in an official search (s.103 and para.1(1)(c) of Sch.8 to the Act—see Chapter 24).

Priority conferred by the search

The priority period conferred by an official search with priority of a pending first registration application is the same as that given by an official search with priority of an existing registered title (see para.9–022). **9–030**

The same priority protection is conferred as that in relation to an official search of an existing registered title (see para.9–023).

It should be noted that until the pending first registration application has actually been completed, no guarantee is given that any registered title will be granted or, if granted, that it will be of the class of title sought. Also, no information will be provided as to the entries which may eventually be made in the register. It is for the purchaser to satisfy themselves by enquiry of the applicant for first registration that the title lodged is in order and to identify the entries which are likely to be made. Should it be necessary, Land Registry will usually be prepared to return documents lodged with an application for first registration temporarily to the applicant who originally lodged them, but the application for first registration will not proceed until they are relodged.

Occasionally, sub-dispositions or re-dispositions may occur where an estate is the subject to a pending application for first registration. In the scenarios described in para.9–025, if R is the applicant for first registration, a registered title will not exist and therefore S will not be able to obtain an official copy of the registered title. To satisfy themselves as to the validity of P's title, S should obtain and examine copies of R's documents of title (which P should have obtained in connection with the disposition to P) and a copy of the disposition to P.

If, just before completion of the disposition to S, the first registration application has not been completed, S should apply for an official search with priority of whole or part (as appropriate) of the pending application for first registration. S will then secure a priority period for the application for registration of the disposition to S. However, if the first registration has by then been completed by registration, S should follow the procedure described in para.9–025, as appropriate.

Withdrawal of official search with priority

9–031 Under r.150 a person who has made an application for an official search with priority of a registered title or in relation to a pending first registration application can withdraw that official search by application to the registrar. There is no prescribed form. Once withdrawn, the priority period conferred by the search ceases to have effect.

Such an application cannot be made if an application for an entry in the register in respect of the protectable disposition protected by the search has been made and completed.

Official searches without priority

9–032 A person may at any time apply in Form OS3 for an official search without priority of the register. This form of official search is available to a person who is not a "purchaser" (see para.9–017); for example, to a mortgagee who intends to protect the mortgage in the register by entry of a notice under s.32 (see Chapters 14 and 16). Such a search can only be made in respect of a registered title; it cannot be used to search against a pending first registration.

The application can be made as a paper search or by fax in the case of a search of whole or part. It must be sent to the proper office. The position with regard to plans for a search of part is as stated above for official searches in Form OS2 (see para.9–019).

If the application is in order, a certificate of the result of the search will be issued. This will show, if they affect the estate in respect of which the application was made, details of:

(1) any adverse entries made in the register since the search from date (see para.9–020);

(2) any applications or proposal by the registrar to alter the register (other than an application to designate a document an exempt information document—see para.9–013) pending but not completed; and

(3) any other applications for an official search (Pt.3 of Sch.6 to the Rules).

The accuracy of the certificate is guaranteed but it will not confer on the applicant priority for the registration of any disposition.

Any credit account holder (see para.1–013) can apply for a search of whole without priority by telephone.

A search of whole may be made orally or using Land Registry Direct. A search of whole or part may be made using the NLIS.

Official search by mortgagee in Form HR3

The procedure whereby the proprietor of a registered charge or a mortgagee of registered land may search the register to enable them to comply with the provisions of s.56(3) of the Family Law Act 1996 is discussed in para.17–013. **9–033**

Fees on searches

Fees on searches are payable in accordance with the Fee Order. **9–034**

Outline applications

9–035 Outline applications can be lodged under r.54 to reserve periods of priority for applications which cannot be protected by an official search. This is discussed in paras 10–030 to 10–033.

Searches in the Land Charges Department

9–036 A Land Charges search is not normally necessary in relation to a registered estate. However, such a search needs to be made in respect of an estate which is currently unregistered, even though it may become subject to compulsory first registration as a result of a disposition (see para.5–005).

Such a search may sometimes be relevant even where the estate is already registered. For example, where an estate is registered with a class of title less than absolute or a "protective" entry appears in the register in respect of the possibility of there being undisclosed restrictive covenants, a Land Charges search may be relevant in relation to the pre-registration title or, in the case of a qualified title, in relation to the specified qualification, as though the title were unregistered (see para.5–017).

Also, an application to cancel a notice in respect of a restrictive covenant, on the basis that it was void for want of registration as a Land Charge, would need to be accompanied by a Land Charges search (see para.8–004).

A "bankruptcy only" Land Charges search may be appropriate where a conveyancer is acting for a purchaser of a registered estate who is purchasing with the aid of a mortgage and this will normally be required under the mortgage instructions from a mortgage lender.

Searches in the Companies Registry

9–037 A search in the Companies Registry is not normally necessary in relation to a registered estate. However, such a search may still be relevant for the purposes of checking that a company which is shown as the registered proprietor has not been dissolved, or that the company purporting to sell the property is that shown in the register (i.e. that the company registration number and/or other details correspond).

Local land charge searches

Searches in the registers of local land charges maintained by local authorities should be made in relation to a registered estate in the same way as in relation to an unregistered estate. A local land charge is an interest which overrides under both Sch.1 and Sch.3 to the Act (see paras 5–018 and 10–028). **9–038**

Practical points

- Remember that an official search is necessary to update official copies of the register and to confer a priority period upon a protectable disposition,
- Ensure that the application for registration is lodged within the priority period of a protecting official search,
- Be aware of the fact that the priority period of an official search cannot be "extended" by a further search,
- Take account of any new register entries and pending applications revealed by an official search,
- Remember to make a fresh official search with priority in the name of the new intending chargee, where a purchaser changes mortgage lenders shortly before completion of a purchase of a registered estate.

Chapter 10

Dispositions Generally

Dispositions authorised by the Act

A registered proprietor of a registered estate or a registered charge has "owner's powers" as conferred by the Act, enabling them to effect a disposition in relation to that estate or charge. Section 23 of the Act sets out the owner's powers of disposition. **10–001**

(1) Owner's powers in relation to a registered estate consist of:

- (a) power to make a disposition of any kind permitted by the general law, other than a mortgage by demise or sub-demise; and
- (b) power to charge the estate at law with the payment of money (s.23(1)).

(2) Owner's powers in relation to a registered charge consist of:

- (a) power to make a disposition of any kind permitted by the general law, other than a legal sub-mortgage; and
- (b) power to charge at law with the payment of money indebtedness secured by the registered charge (s.23(2)).

These owner's powers can be exercised by the registered proprietor of a registered estate or a registered charge, or by someone entitled to be registered as the proprietor (s.24). Thus a transferee, under a valid transfer which is a registrable disposition, may immediately charge or re-transfer the registered estate even though the transfer has not yet been completed by registration and they have not yet been registered as proprietor.

The Act confers protection upon disponees by providing that register is conclusive as to the registered proprietor's powers of disposition, so that the proprietor's right to exercise owner's powers is taken to be free from any limitation other than one reflected by an entry in the register or imposed by or under the Act (s.26). A disponee can therefore rely upon the register to show whether there are any limitations on the powers of disposition of the registered proprietor. Even if the registered proprietor's powers are restricted by statute (other than the Act) a disponee can assume that there are no limitations on the proprietor's powers unless there is an entry in the register reflecting the limitation, e.g. a restriction.

In consequence, the title of a disponee cannot be questioned due to an absence of power on the part of the registered proprietor, where that is not reflected by an entry in the register. However, although the disposition may be valid in favour of the disponee, a registered proprietor may themselves still be liable if the disposition is unlawful (s.23(3)), e.g. where a transfer has been made by a trustee in breach of trust.

Owner's powers include the power to effect not only registrable dispositions, but also dispositions which create legal interests which cannot be registered (e.g. most leases granted for a term of seven years or less from the date of the grant) and dispositions which create equitable interests (e.g. equitable easements or a trust of land).

The exercise of owner's powers in respect of a registrable disposition must comply with the requirements as to form and content set out in the Rules (s.25(1)) and be completed by registration in accordance with the registration requirements contained in Sch.2 to the Act.

Transfers, leases, charges and other specific dispositions relating to registered land are discussed under the relevant chapters of this book; this chapter contains additional guidance on general aspects of the registration of transfers and other dispositions.

Dispositions which are required to be registered

10–002 Section 27 sets out the dispositions which are required to be completed by registration. In the case of a registered estate these are:

(1) a transfer;
(2) where the registered estate is an estate in land, the grant of a term of years absolute:

(a) for a term of more than seven years from the date of the grant; or
(b) to take effect in possession after the end of the period of three months beginning with the date of the grant; or
(c) under which the right to possession is discontinuous; or
(d) in pursuance of Pt. 5 of the Housing Act 1985 (right to buy); or
(e) in circumstances where s.171A of the Housing Act 1985 applies (disposal of land which leads to a person no longer being a secure tenant);

(3) where the registered estate is a franchise or manor, the grant of a lease;

(4) the express grant or reservation of an interest of a kind falling within s.1(2)(a) of the Law of Property Act 1925 (easements and profits à prendre in gross or appurtenant to an estate), other than one capable of being registered under the Commons Registration Act 1965 or a grant as a result of the operation of s.62 of the Law of Property Act 1925;

(5) the express grant or reservation of an interest of a kind falling within s.1(2)(b) (a rent charge in possession issuing out of or charged on land being either perpetual or for a term of years absolute) or s.1(2)(e) (a right of entry exercisable over or in respect of a legal term of years absolute, or annexed, for any purpose to a legal rent charge) of the Law of Property Act 1925; and

(6) the grant of a legal charge (other than the creation of a legal charge which is a local land charge).

In the case of a registered charge, the dispositions which are required to be registered are:

(i) a transfer; and

(ii) the grant of a sub-charge.

Section 27 applies to dispositions by operation of law as it applies to other dispositions, but with the exception of a transfer on the death or bankruptcy of an individual proprietor and a transfer on the dissolution of a corporate proprietor (s.27(5)).

If a disposition of a registered estate or registered charge is required to be completed by registration, it does not operate at law until the relevant registration requirements are met; until then, it does not become void, but it operates only in equity. Schedule 2 to the Act sets out the relevant registration requirements—there are different registration requirements for different types of interest. The registration requirements for specific dispositions are dealt with under the relevant chapters of this book.

If the relevant registration requirements have not been met due to a mistake made by Land Registry, the disposition still does not operate at law, but there may be grounds for a claim for indemnity against Land Registry (s.103 and Sch.8 to the Act—see Chapter 24).

Effect of registration

10–003 Under s.28, the "basic rule of priority" is that the priority of an interest affecting a registered estate or charge is not affected by a disposition of the estate or charge, regardless of whether the interest or disposition is registered. This basic rule is, however, subject to a significant variation in relation to registrable dispositions.

Section 29 provides that if a registrable disposition of a registered estate is made for valuable consideration, completion of the disposition by registration has the effect of postponing to the interest under the disposition any interest affecting the estate immediately before the disposition, whose priority is not protected at the time of registration.

For the purposes of s.29 the priority of an interest is "protected" if the interest:

(1) is a registered charge or the subject of a notice in the register; or

(2) falls within any of the paragraphs of Sch.3 to the Act as an overriding interest (see para.10–028); or

(3) appears from the register to be excepted from the effect of registration, e.g. an undisclosed mortgage subsisting at the time of first registration where the registered estate is registered with a possessory class of title (see para.5–012).

In addition, in the case of a disposition of a leasehold estate, the priority of an interest is protected if its burden is incident to the estate, e.g. tenants' covenants contained in the registered lease.

"Valuable consideration" for this purpose does not include marriage consideration or a nominal consideration in money (s.132).

Section 30 contains similar provisions in relation to a registrable disposition of a registered charge for valuable consideration.

Production of land or charge certificates

As indicated in para.1–017, the Act makes no provision for land certificates and charge certificates and any existing certificates ceased to have effect from October 13, 2003. There is no longer any requirement to lodge such a certificate when applying for registration of a disposition or the making of an entry in the register. Any land or charge certificate lodged will be destroyed. **10–004**

Also, there is no requirement to lodge the Title Information Document which is issued as a matter of practice on completion of certain types of application (see para.1–018).

Application forms

Schedule 1 to the Rules contains various prescribed application forms. Under r.13, Form AP1 ("Application to change the register") is used as the "default" form, for use in any application for which no other application form is prescribed. It need not be used for applications to remove from the register the name of a deceased joint proprietor, or for applications made under r.14 (electronic applications) or r.54 (outline applications—see para.10–033). **10–005**

In particular, Form AP1 should be used for applications for registration of dispositions of the whole or part of the estate comprised in a registered title.

If it is desired that the application be expedited, a written request should be made and/or an endorsement made on the application form, "PLEASE EXPEDITE".

The information which should be supplied, as indicated in the numbered panels in Form AP1, includes the following:

Panel 3 Confirmation of whether the application affects the whole or part of the land in the title(s) should be given.

Panel 4 There must be listed in their correct priority the applications being made. Thus in the case of a typical purchase of a registered residential property, the discharge of the vendor's registered charge should appear before the transfer to the applicant and any new charge (see also para.1–015 as to Land Registry's "early completion" policy). Details of the appropriate fees payable and method of payment should also be entered.

Panel 5 A list of the documents lodged should be set out in panel 5 in the same order as the applications to which they relate, originals and copies being treated as separate items. If the original and a copy of a document are supplied, Land Registry will assume that the applicant wishes the original returned. If a certified copy of a document is not supplied, Land Registry may retain (and ultimately destroy) the original. Therefore, if the applicant wishes the original to be returned, a certified copy should be supplied (r.203).

Panel 6 The full name(s) of the applicant(s). Where the application is lodged by a conveyancer, this should be the name of the client not the conveyancer. Where the applicant is a UK company or a UK limited liability partnership, or an overseas company (see paras 10–010 to 10–012), the relevant details should be inserted.

Panel 7 The key number (if any), name, address, reference, e-mail address or DX box number and telephone and fax numbers of the person or firm lodging the application and to whom any requisitions by Land Registry, including requests for unpaid fees, are to be sent and documents returned.

Panel 8 Details of any third party to whom the applicant wishes Land Registry to send notification of completion of the application.

Panel 9 The address(es) for service (including post code) for entry in the register of any new or existing proprietor(s) of the registered estate. Particular care should be exercised in completing this panel. If this address becomes out of date, but is not altered in the register, there is a risk that official notices sent by Land Registry might not reach the registered proprietor. In the case of a purchaser who on completion of the purchase moves to the property being registered, the address to be entered on the register will usually be the full postal address of that property. However, where the property is being purchased for rental purposes, this is not likely to be appropriate and an alternative address should be provided. A proprietor may have up to three addresses, including the address of their conveyancer, entered in the register (r.198). One address for service must be a postal address, but it can be inside or outside the United Kingdom. Where the registrar sends a notice, the time period for responding to the notice is determined by reference to the date of issue of the notice, not the date it is deemed to have been received. A person providing an overseas address should bear in mind that notice periods are not extended for overseas addresses and there is a risk that they may not receive the notice in time to respond. Up to two additional addresses for service may be provided, which can include a document exchange box number and/or an electronic address.

Panel 10 The name and address(es) for service (including post code) for entry in the register of any new charge to be entered in the register, unless an MD reference is printed on the charge. The remarks above regarding panel 9 in relation to the address for service apply also to this panel. Where the chargee is a UK company or limited liability partnership or an overseas company, the relevant details should be inserted.

Panel 11 Section 71 and r.57 provide that subject to certain exceptions, an applicant for registration of a registerable disposition must provide information to the registrar about overriding interests falling within Sch.3 to the Act which are within the actual knowledge of the applicant or their conveyancer and affect the estate to which the application relates (see para.10–028). Panel 11 should be completed accordingly and, if appropriate, the application accompanied by Form DI containing the relevant details (see para.10–029).

Panel 12 Confirmation of identity, which requires completion of either panel 13 (if a conveyancer is acting) or panel 14 (if a conveyancer is not acting), where the application is to register a transfer or lease (whether or not for valuable consideration) or charge, surrender of a lease, or a discharge of a charge in paper form DS1 or DS3. Confirmation of identity is not required for registration of an assent nor for only entering a notice in respect of a lease or charge, nor where the value of the estate is certified as being less than £5,000. It is important that, where required, the confirmation of identity is provided, otherwise Land Registry will reject the application.

Panel 13 Confirmation of identity where a conveyancer is acting; the relevant details should be inserted, as discussed above.

Panel 14 Confirmation of identity where a conveyancer is not acting; the relevant details should be inserted, as discussed above.

Panel 15 Form AP1 should be signed by the applicant or their conveyancer.

No covering letter is necessary. The fees payable in accordance with the Fee Order should accompany the application.

Associated dispositions

10–006 Where several associated dispositions relating to a particular registered title are delivered for registration together, the application forms may be numbered consecutively (e.g. when there are five applications: 1/5, 2/5, 3/5, 4/5 and 5/5), so that Land Registry staff will readily identify that they should be dealt with together and in the order indicated. The appropriate number should be endorsed prominently at the top of the first page of each form.

Form of dispositions: approval of draft instruments

10–007 Section 25(1) provides that a registrable disposition of a registered estate or registered charge only has effect if it complies with the requirements in the Rules as to form and content. Most types of application and disposition have a prescribed form required under the Rules and r.206(1) requires that the prescribed form must be used.

Schedule 1 to the Rules contains numerous prescribed forms of application and disposition ("Sch.1 forms").

Schedule 3 to the Rules contains a small number of miscellaneous forms which must be used in all matters to which they refer ("Sch.3 forms"), but which can be adapted with the registrar's consent.

Schedule 9 to the Rules contains approved forms of execution of Sch.1 and Sch.3 forms, which can be adapted with the registrar's consent.

Specific forms are referred to under the relevant headings elsewhere in this book. Further information is contained in para.1–012 and a list of forms is contained in Appendix II.

The registrar's approval of a draft document may be sought:

(1) when it is desired to adapt a Sch.3 form for a particular matter (r.206(2)); or

(2) when it is a document for which no form is prescribed (r.212); or

(3) when it is desired to make an application for which there is a prescribed Sch.1 or Sch.3 form, but the applicant wishes to rely on an alternative document instead (r.209).

Care should be taken that the draft document conforms generally to the Act and the Rules and that, where appropriate, it refers to any relevant title number(s) and clearly identifies the registered estate or charge to which it relates. The draft (with plan if any) and a copy should be sent to the proper office. No fee is currently payable.

Approval will be limited to matters of form; the person lodging the document for registration will be responsible for ensuring that it carries out the intention of the parties and for all other matters of substance, due execution, etc.

The special procedure for the approval of draft instruments in connection with developing estates is discussed in para.21–004.

Deeds and their execution

General

With a few exceptions (including assents and certain leases for a term not exceeding three years), a legal interest in land cannot be conveyed or created other than by deed (s.52(1) of the Law of Property Act 1925). **10–008**

Under s.1 of the Law of Property (Miscellaneous Provisions) Act 1989 ("the 1989 Act"), to be a deed a document must:

(1) be in writing;

(2) make clear on its face that it is intended to be a deed by the person making it or, as the case may be, the parties to it (which can be done by the document describing itself as a deed or expressing itself to be executed as a deed or otherwise); and

(3) be validly executed as a deed by the person making it or, as the case may be, one or more of the parties to it.

Execution of deeds by individuals

Three elements are required: signature, attestation and delivery. **10–009**

(1) Signature: to be validly executed as a deed by an individual, they must sign the document.

(2) Attestation by a witness: the individual must sign in the presence of a witness who attests the signature, or it must be signed at the direction of the individual and in their presence and in the presence of two witnesses who each attest the signature (s.1(3)(a) of the 1989 Act).

(3) Delivery: the document must be "delivered as a deed" by each person executing it or by a person authorised to deliver it on their behalf (s.1(3)(b) of the 1989 Act). Delivery requires that the person expressly or impliedly acknowledges, by words or conduct, an intention to be bound by its provisions. In practice, Land Registry will assume that a document has been delivered as a deed unless there is some indication to the contrary. So if, for example, the words of execution have been modified to provide that delivery has not taken place, or that delivery is not to be presumed until some condition has been fulfilled, evidence will be required that delivery has subsequently taken place.

In transfers of registered land and other deeds whose form is prescribed by the Rules, the attestation clause in Form A or B in Sch.9 to the Rules must be used when an individual executes the deed.

A signature in foreign characters still constitutes a signature complying with the requirements for a valid deed. However, where any instrument is executed in foreign (ie non-Roman) characters, such as Arabic or Chinese characters, Land Registry will require either:

(a) the words of execution to be expanded to confirm that the signatory understands English or has familiarised themselves with its contents e.g. by having had it read to them out in their native language; or

(b) a separate certificate to that effect given by a conveyancer acting for the signatory.

Execution of deeds by UK companies

10–010 On April 6, 2008 s.44 of the Companies Act 2006 came into force and applies to deeds executed on or after that date by a UK company (i.e. one registered in England and Wales, Scotland or Northern Ireland under the Companies Acts or in Northern Ireland under the Companies (Northern Ireland) Order 1986).

(1) ***Execution by a company under its common seal*** Where this form of execution is adopted, the common seal will normally be affixed to the deed in the presence of the company secretary and one director, or two directors, who attest the sealing by countersigning the deed and describing themselves by their respective offices. If this is done, a purchaser is (from September 15, 2005) protected by s.74(1) of the Law of Property Act 1925 which provides that, in favour of a "purchaser" (as defined in s.205(1)(xxi) of that Act), an instrument executed in this manner shall be deemed to have been duly executed.

In transfers of registered land and other deeds whose form is prescribed, the attestation clause in Form C in Sch.9 to the Rules must be used when a company executes a deed under its common seal.

Most companies have articles of association that authorise the affixing of the company seal to a deed in the presence of people other than a director and the secretary. The protection provided by s.74(1) above is limited to cases where the seal is affixed in the presence of a director and the secretary or two directors. Where a deed is executed by a company affixing its seal in the presence of persons other than a director and the secretary or two directors, Land Registry may therefore call for evidence that the persons attesting the affixing of the seal are duly authorised by the company's articles to do so. Where their authority also depends upon a decision by the directors of the company, a certified copy of the board resolution may also be required.

Prior to October 1, 2009 similar provisions were contained in s.36(A)(2) of the Companies Act 1985.

(2) ***Execution by a company otherwise than under a common seal*** A different method of execution can be used by a company which either has no seal or chooses not to use it. Section 44(2)(a) and (3) of the Companies Act 2006 provides that a document is validly executed by a company if it is signed on its behalf by two "authorised signatories", being every director of the company and (in the case of a private company with a secretary or a public company) the secretary, or any joint secretary, of the company.

In transfers of registered land and other deeds whose form is prescribed, the attestation clause in Form D(i) in Sch.9 to the Rules must be used when a company executes a deed in this way.

In addition, for deeds executed on or after April 6, 2008, s.44(2)(b) of the Companies Act 2006 provides that a company may execute a document by a single director, if that signature is witnessed and attested. In transfers of registered land and other deeds whose form is prescribed, the attestation clause in Form

D(ii) in Sch.9 to the Rules must be used when a company executes the deed in this way.

Section 44(4) and (5) of the Companies Act 2006 provides that a document signed in accordance with s.44(2) of that Act and expressed, in whatever words, to be executed by the company has the same effect as if executed under the common seal of the company and that in favour of a "purchaser" (as defined in s.44(5) of that Act), a document is deemed to have been duly executed by a company if it purports to be signed in accordance with s.44(2) of that Act.

For deeds executed before April 6, 2008, s.36(A)(4) of the Companies Act 1985 provided that a document signed by a director and secretary of a company, or by two directors of a company and expressed (in whatever form of words) to be executed by the company had the same effect as if executed under the common seal of the company. Also, s.36(A)(6) of the Companies Act 1985 provided that, in favour of a "purchaser" (as defined in that sub-section), a document should be deemed to have been duly executed by a company if it purported to be signed by a director an the secretary of the company, or by two directors of the company.

(3) *Delivery* A deed which has been executed by a company must also be delivered (see para.10–009) in order to be effective. In practice, Land Registry will assume that a document has been delivered as a deed unless there is some indication to the contrary.

Execution of deeds by limited liability partnerships

10–011 A UK limited liability partnership is a body corporate, with a legal personality separate from that of its members, formed by being incorporated under the Limited Liability Partnerships Act 2000 or the Limited Liability Partnerships Act (Northern Ireland) 2002. In transfers of registered land and other deeds whose form is prescribed, the attestation clause in Form F(i) or F(ii) of Sch.9 to the Rules must be used when a limited liability partnership executes a deed. If instead a limited liability partnership uses a seal, Land Registry can accept this provided the attestation clause is in similar form to Form C in Sch.9 to the Rules, but with two members witnessing the affixing of the seal.

Execution of deeds by overseas companies

10–012 For deeds executed on or after April 6, 2008, "overseas companies" are those incorporated outside the United Kingdom (i.e. England and Wales, Scotland and Northern Ireland).

For deeds executed on or after October 1, 2009 the Overseas Companies (Execution of Documents and Registration of Charges) Regulations 2009 provide that a foreign corporation can execute a deed using one of the following three methods.

(1) *Execution under common seal* An overseas company possessing a common seal may execute a deed using that seal. The points made in para.10–010 in relation to a UK company apply if a deed is executed in this way.

(2) *Execution in a manner permitted by the local law* A deed can be executed in any manner permitted by the laws of the territory in which the company is incorporated for the execution of documents by such a company. If this method is used, Land Registry will require evidence (e.g. a letter from a qualified lawyer practising in or familiar with the laws of the territory of incorporation) to establish that the manner of execution used is effective according to the laws of the territory of incorporation. Any documentation in a language other than English or Welsh will need to be accompanied by a certified translation.

(3) *Execution by signature of authorised person(s)* A deed may be signed by a person who, in accordance with laws of the territory in which the company is incorporated, is acting under the express or implied authority of the company and expressed (in whatever form of words) to be executed by the company. A deed executed in this way has the same effect as it would have in relation to a company incorporated in England and Wales or Northern Ireland if executed under the common seal of a company so incorporated (see para.10–010). In transfers of registered land and other deeds whose form is prescribed, the attestation clause in Form E in Sch.9 to the Rules must be used when a foreign corporation executes a deed in this way.

Prior to October 1, 2009 similar provisions were contained in the Foreign Companies (Execution of Documents) Regulations 1994.

Execution of deeds following appointment of an administrator, receiver or liquidator

See Chapter 20. **10–013**

Execution of deeds by trustees of charities

See para.18–025. **10–014**

Execution by attorney

General points

A power of attorney is a deed by which one person (the donor) gives another person (the attorney) power to act on their behalf. It may be granted for either general purposes or for a specific **10–015** purpose. If it is for a specific purpose, it should be ensured that it contains clear authority to enter into the disposition, as powers of attorney are interpreted strictly.

Any deed lodged for registration that has been executed under a power of attorney must be accompanied by one of the following (r.61):

(1) a certificate by a conveyancer in Form 1 in Sch.3 to the Rules; or

(2) the original power; or

(3) a certified copy of the power in accordance with s.3 of the Powers of Attorney Act 1971.

Land Registry will retain the evidence lodged in its files. If, therefore, the applicant wishes to keep the original they should lodge a certified copy with the application (r.203).

The different types of power of attorney are as follows.

General powers under s.10 of the Powers of Attorney Act 1971 ("the 1971 Act")

10–016 The 1971 Act provides a short form of general power of attorney that can be used by a sole beneficial owner of land. A general power of attorney under the 1971 Act must follow the form set out in Sch.1 to the 1971 Act or be in a form to the like effect and expressed to be made under the 1971 Act.

The donor must execute the power as a deed. It confers upon the attorney authority to do anything that the donor can lawfully do by an attorney. However, powers in that form dated before March 1, 2000 are not appropriate for dealing with land of which the donor is a joint proprietor. Those dated after February 29, 2000 may only be used by a joint proprietor if certain conditions are satisfied under s.1 of the Trustee Delegation Act 1999 (see para.10–021). The death, bankruptcy or mental incapacity of the donor will automatically revoke the power. The donor may also revoke it at any time.

Other general and specific powers

10–017 As an alternative to the form set out in the 1971 Act, the donor of a power of attorney may use any form of wording, giving the attorney either general authority to act or limited powers, e.g. in connection with a particular transaction or in relation only to a specified property. The donor must execute the power as a deed.

Such a power may be used on behalf of a donor who is a joint proprietor only if certain conditions are satisfied under s.1 of the Trustee Delegation Act 1999 (see para.10–021).

Unless it is a security power (see para.10–018) the donor may revoke such a power and the death, bankruptcy or mental incapacity of the donor will automatically revoke it.

Security powers

A security power is a power of attorney that is expressed to be irrevocable and is given to secure: **10–018**

(1) a proprietary interest of the attorney; or

(2) the performance of an obligation owed to the attorney.

While the attorney retains the interest or until the obligation is discharged, the donor can only revoke the power with the attorney's consent and the death, bankruptcy or mental incapacity of the donor does not revoke it.

Enduring powers of attorney

The Enduring but are now subject to the provisions of Sch.4 to the Mental Capacity Act 2005, and in consequence no new enduring powers can be created after September 30, 2007. Enduring powers created before October 1, 2007 will continue to have effect, but are now subject to the provisions of Sch.4 to the Mental Capacity Act 2005 (see para.10–020). An enduring power must be in one of the prescribed forms according to the date of execution of the power. **10–019**

Enduring powers dated after February 29, 2000 may be used by a donor who is a joint proprietor if certain conditions are satisfied under s.1 of the Trustee Delegation Act 1999 (see para.10–021).

There were transitional provisions for enduring powers dated before March 1, 2000 under which such powers could be used by a donor who was a joint proprietor until March 1, 2001.

From March 1, 2001 an enduring power dated before that date can only be used by a donor who is a joint proprietor if:

(1) the donor has a beneficial interest in the property and there is no indication in the power that the donor did not intend the attorney to exercise trustee functions; or

(2) the power is registered with the Court of Protection following an application to the Court before March 1, 2001; or

(3) an application made to the Court before March 1, 2001 for registration of the power has not been finally refused.

Enduring powers of attorney continue to be effective even after the donor has lost capacity, provided the power has been registered with the Court of Protection or the Public Guardian, as appropriate. Otherwise the attorney cannot use it to act on behalf of the donor if the donor lacks capacity.

If two or more attorneys are appointed jointly, they must all execute a deed on behalf of the donor. If they are appointed jointly and severally, only one need execute it.

If an enduring power of attorney has been registered at the Court of Protection or with the Office of the Public Guardian and any order or direction has been made by the court under para.16 of Sch.4 to the Mental Capacity Act 2005 with respect to the power or to the donor or to the attorney, the order or direction, or an official copy or certified copy of it, must be lodged with the application (r.61(2)).

Lasting powers of attorney

10–020 Lasting powers of attorney were introduced by the Mental Capacity Act 2005 and replaced enduring powers (see para.10–019) as the primary way for a donor to choose an attorney (or "decision maker") to act in the event of loss of mental capacity. In addition to a "property and affairs" lasting power, donors are able to appoint an attorney to make decisions about their own welfare using a "personal welfare" lasting power for a time when they lack capacity to make such decisions themselves.

Part 1 of Sch.1 to the Lasting Powers of Attorney, Enduring Powers of Attorney and Public Guardian Regulations 2007 prescribes the form which must be used for a "property and affairs" lasting power of attorney and it must be executed in accordance with reg.9.

A lasting power may only be used once it has been registered with the Office of the Public Guardian.

If two or more attorneys are appointed jointly, they must all execute a deed on behalf of the donor. If they are appointed jointly and severally, only one need execute it.

If a lasting power of attorney has been registered with the Office of the Public Guardian and any order or direction has been made by the court under ss.22 or 23 of the Mental Capacity Act 2005 with respect to the power or to the donor or attorney, the order or direction, or an official or certified copy of it, must be lodged with the application (r.61(2)).

Powers of attorney by joint proprietors and other trustees

10–021 Trustees holding property upon trust (which includes joint owners who are holding on trust for themselves as beneficial joint tenants or tenants in common—see para.18–001) can only delegate their duties and powers when they have authority to do so. However, several statutory provisions now allow for delegation.

It should be borne in mind that where overreaching is necessary (see paras 2–021 and 18–001), the attorney must act with at least one other person (unless the donor is a trust corporation) so as to ensure there is a valid receipt by at least two trustees. If a transfer is lodged which has been executed by only one person, both as proprietor and as attorney for the other proprietor or as attorney for all the proprietors, Land Registry will return it for execution by the donor(s). If the transfer is not re-executed, Land Registry will enter a restriction in Form A in the register to reflect the fact that overreaching has not been effected and that there may therefore be beneficial interests that continue to subsist.

(1) ***Section 25 of the Trustee Act 1925*** Under this section, a trustee can delegate the exercise of their powers for a maximum of 12 months from the start of the delegation or, if there is no provision for when the delegation starts, for 12 months from the execution of the power by the trustee. The power must be in the form set out in s.25(6) of the Trustee Act 1925 or in a form to the like effect and expressed to be made under s.25 of that Act.

(2) ***Section 1 of the Trustee Delegation Act 1999*** This section allows a power of attorney to be used in relation to trust property after March 1, 2000 if there is no indication in the power that the donor does not intend the attorney to exercise trustee functions and, at the time the power of attorney is used, the donor has a beneficial interest in the property. This delegation is not limited in duration. This applies to general powers, certain enduring powers and lasting powers (see above).

A signed statement by the attorney made within three months of the date of the disposition will be conclusive evidence of the donor having had a beneficial interest at that time. The statement can be included within the transfer or other disposition or it may be made separately as long as it is dated within three months of the date of the disposition.

If such a statement cannot be produced, Land Registry will consider other evidence e.g. a statutory declaration or statement of truth, confirming that the donor had a beneficial interest at the relevant time.

In the absence of satisfactory evidence of the donor's beneficial interest, the disposition will need to be executed by the donor of the power.

(3) ***Section 9 of the Trusts of Land and Appointment of Trustees Act 1996 ("TLATA")*** All the trustees of a trust of land may jointly delegate their functions to a beneficiary or beneficiaries who are of full age and beneficially entitled to an interest in possession. The delegation may be for any period or indefinite.

However, these beneficiary attorneys are not treated as trustees for the purposes of receiving capital money, so that the trustees themselves will need to join in any disposition under which capital money arises in order to effect overreaching (s.9(7) of TLATA). This type of power will therefore only be appropriate when no capital money is passing, e.g. on the grant of a lease without payment of a premium.

Statutory protection is given to a third party who in good faith deals with an attorney to whom
trustee powers were delegated as a beneficiary, but who in fact was not a beneficiary to whom the trustee functions could be delegated. The attorney is presumed to have been a person to whom the trustee functions could be delegated unless the third party had knowledge that they were not such a person (s.9(2) of TLATA).

In consequence, where a beneficiary has executed a deed under a power of attorney, Land Registry may require a statutory declaration or statement of truth from the disponee to confirm that they acted in good faith and had no knowledge at the time of completion of the disposition that the attorney was not a person to whom the functions of the trustees in relation to the land could be delegated. Alternatively, the disponee's conveyancer can provide a certificate to the effect that at the time of completion their client had no such knowledge (r.63 and Forms 2 and 3 of Sch.3 to the Rules).

Gifts and dispositions at undervalue by an attorney

10–022 An attorney owes a fiduciary duty to the donor. In general therefore, an attorney cannot use the power to confer a benefit on themselves or others to the detriment of the donor. Where an application for registration of such a disposition is lodged, Land Registry's approach will depend upon the type of power used.

In the case of a general power (see paras 10–016 and 10–017), Land Registry will regard the disposition as within the authority of the attorney even though, potentially, it could be set aside as being in breach of fiduciary duty. This is because the disposition is voidable rather than void, but the registrar will usually serve notice upon the donor as a precaution.

In the case of an enduring power or lasting power (see paras 10–019 and 10–020), there are considerable limitations upon gifts being made; Land Registry will therefore reject applications to register such dispositions unless the disposition is re-executed in person by the donor or satisfactory evidence of authority to make the gift is lodged, e.g. if an enduring power is registered and the disposition has been approved by the court under para.16 of Sch.4 to the Mental Capacity Act 2005.

Where it is claimed, in relation to a disposition by an attorney under an enduring or lasting power granted by a joint proprietor, that there is no element of gift because the donor had no beneficial interest in the property, this may cause a consequential problem in relation to powers granted by a joint proprietor (see para.10–021).

Powers more than 12 months old—evidence of non-revocation

A purchaser from a person who has dealt with an attorney is **10–023** entitled to assume that the power of attorney has not been revoked if the transaction in question took place within 12 months of the date when the power came into question. Although under r.62, Land Registry may require evidence of non-revocation if the power of attorney is more than 12 months old, such evidence will not normally be required.

On the rare occasions when the registrar does require evidence of non-revocation, this must be in Form 2 in Sch.3 to the Rules, being either a statutory declaration or statement of truth made by the person dealing with the attorney or a certificate by that person's conveyancer.

As powers of attorney under s.25 of the Trustee Act 1925 can only operate for 12 months (see para.10–021), evidence of non-revocation is unnecessary for such powers.

Execution of deeds by an attorney

There is no prescribed attestation clause, but Land Registry has **10–024** published forms of execution which are acceptable for land registration purposes.

Powers of attorney given to receivers in debentures

See Chapter 20. **10–025**

Correction of mistakes in an application or accompanying document

Clerical and other errors (rule 130)

Rule 130 allows for an alteration to be made by the registrar for **10–026** the purpose of correcting a mistake in any application or accompanying document. The alteration has effect as if made by the applicant or other interested party or parties in all circumstances, if it is a case of a mistake of a clerical or like nature. In the case of any other mistake it only has this effect if the applicant and any other interested party has requested or consented to the alteration.

Rule 130 does not relate to an alteration of the register itself.

The decision of whether to make the alteration is at the discretion of the registrar and he may refuse where, for example, a deed of rectification or a replacement document would be more appropriate.

Alteration and variation of deeds

Where a need arises to alter a deed in order to correct a mistake after it has been executed but before an application to register it has been made, the deed may be altered and the alterations authenticated by the signatures of the parties to the deed.

If it is not practicable to delay lodging an application for registration until after the deed has been altered, e.g. if the priority period of a protecting official search (see para.9–022) is about to expire, the application may be lodged and a request made for the return of the deed by Land Registry to enable the alteration to be made. Such a request may also be made if an application has been lodged before the need to alter the deed becomes apparent. However, this will only be appropriate where the mistake in the deed does not render it substantially defective for registration purposes until it has been altered.

Land Registry may reject an application where a deed is substantially defective, or in other cases it may itself requisition for a deed to be altered, e.g. by the insertion of the relevant wording in a blank space in a deed.

Where a deed effecting a registrable disposition has already been completed by registration but contains a mistake which the parties wish to correct, a further deed, such as a deed of variation, will be required. However, where the further deed itself effects a registrable disposition, that deed will need to be in the prescribed form where appropriate (s.25—see paras 1–012 and 10–007). For example, where a transfer which has been completed by registration included too much land in error, a transfer of the additional land back to the transferor will need to be in the prescribed form within Sch.1 to the Rules, such as Form TR1 or TP1.

For a variation of a lease see paras 12–024 to 12–026 and for a variation of a charge, see para.14–018.

Electronic lodgement of applications to change the register

10–027 Certain applications to change the register can be lodged electronically. This includes, for example, a change of name of a registered proprietor or other person referred to in the register by marriage or deed poll; a change of address for service of the registered proprietor; and entry of a restriction or a unilateral notice. Limitations may apply in individual circumstances.

Only conveyancers (as defined by r.217) who use Land Registry Direct can use this service. Instead of supplying some form of documentary proof for such types of alteration of the register, where the application is lodged electronically the conveyancer must certify that they have seen or hold the appropriate evidence. Once the "e-application" is delivered, Land Registry makes the necessary changes in the register. Once completed, the conveyancer receives an acknowledgment through the post or document exchange as usual. Other users must lodge a paper application in the usual way, accompanied by the appropriate documentary evidence.

Unregistered interests which override registered dispositions

Schedule 3 to the Act lists those interests which override registered dispositions notwithstanding the fact that they are not mentioned in the register. These are as follows: **10–028**

(1) A leasehold estate in land granted for a term not exceeding seven years from the date of the grant, except for a lease in respect of which the tenant is under a duty to apply for first registration or which constitutes a registrable disposition.

(2) An interest belonging at the time of the disposition to a person in actual occupation so far as relating to the land of which they are in actual occupation, except for:

- (a) an interest under a settlement under the Settled Land Act 1925;
- (b) an interest of a person of whom enquiry was made before the disposition and who failed to disclose the right when they could reasonably have been expected to do so;
- (c) an interest of a person whose occupation would not have been obvious on a reasonably careful inspection of the land at the time of the disposition and which the person to whom the disposition is made did not know about at the time of the disposition; and
- (d) a leasehold estate granted to take effect in possession more than three months from the date of the grant, but which has not taken effect in possession at the time of the disposition.

Judicial decisions under s.70 of the Land Registration Act 1925 illustrate the importance of the overriding interests of persons in actual occupation—these are referred to in para.5–019. It is the interest, not the occupation, which has overriding status. If a person is in occupation of part of the land, the interest only has overriding status in relation to that part. Certain types of interest can never have overriding status under this paragraph:

(i) An interest under a settlement under the Settled Land Act 1925. However, an interest under a trust of land can have overriding status, if it otherwise qualifies, although it is still subject to overreaching (see paras 2–021 and 18–001).

(ii) A pending land action, a writ or order affecting land issued or made by a court for the purpose of enforcing a judgment or recognisance, an order appointing a receiver or sequestrator, or a deed of arrangement.

(iii) A spouse or civil partner's right of occupation under the Family Law Act 1996.

(iv) Rights of tenants arising from a relevant notice under the Leasehold Reform Act 1967.

(v) A disposition in exercise of the Preserved Right to Buy.

(vi) Rights under an access order made under the Access to Neighbouring Land Act 1992.

(vii) Rights of tenants under the Leasehold Reform, Housing and Urban Development Act 1992.

(viii) Rights arising from a request to a landlord for the grant of an overriding lease under the Landlord & Tenant (Covenants) Act 1995.

(3) A legal easement or profit à prendre, except for one which is not registered under the Commons Registration Act 1965, which at the time of the disposition is not within the actual knowledge of the person to whom the disposition is made and would not have been obvious on a reasonably careful inspection of the land over which the easement or profit is exercisable (unless the person entitled to the easement or profit proves that it has been exercised in the period of one year ending with the day of the disposition). Paragraph 10 of Sch.12 to the Act provided that for a period of three years from October 13, 2003, any legal easement or profit that was not registered would override a registered disposition and that this exception would not have effect.

(4) A customary right.

(5) A public right.

(6) A local land charge.

(7) An interest in any coal or coal mine, the rights attached to any such interest and the rights of any person under ss.38, 49 or 51 of the Coal Industry Act 1994.

(8) In the case of land to which title was registered before 1898, rights to mines and minerals (and incidental rights) created before 1898.

(9) In the case of land to which title was registered between 1898 and 1925 inclusive, rights to mines and minerals (and incidental rights) created before the date of registration of the title.

(10) A franchise.

(11) A manorial right.

(12) A right to rent which was reserved to the Crown on the granting of any freehold estate (whether or not the right is still vested in the Crown).

(13) A non-statutory right in respect of an embankment or sea or river wall.

(14) A right to payment in lieu of tithe.

(15) A right in respect of the repair of a church chancel.

At the end of a period of 10 years beginning on October 13, 2003, (10) to (15) above will cease to be interests that override registered dispositions (s.117(1)). No fee is payable for an application, if lodged before the expiry of that period, for a caution against first registration or entry of a notice in a registered title in respect of any such interests (s.117(2)).

Paragraph 8 of Sch.12 to the Act inserts a further paragraph into Sch.3 and provides that the interest of a person in receipt of rents and profits from the land upon the coming into force of Sch.3 on October 13, 2003 has overriding status over a disposition, except where the person was asked prior to the disposition but failed to disclose the right when he could reasonably have been expected to do so. The continuing overriding status only subsists whilst that person continues to be in receipt of those rents and profits.

Paragraph 9 of Sch.12 to the Act provides that easements which had overriding status by virtue of para.10 of Sch.12 to the Act, but which would not under Sch.3 of the Act e.g. certain equitable easements, will retain that status indefinitely.

Paragraph 11 of Sch.12 to the Act provided that for a period of three years from October 13, 2003, where an adverse possessor was entitled to be registered as proprietor of a registered estate because of their adverse possession under s.75 of the Land Registration Act 1925 (see para.7–007), that right had overriding status.

Paragraph 12 of Sch.12 to the Act provides that leases granted prior to October 13, 2003 for a term of less than 21 years retain the overriding status they enjoyed by virtue of s.70(1)(k) of the Land Registration Act 1925.

Under para.13 of Sch.12 to the Act, certain local land charges which had overriding status by virtue of s.70(1)(i) of the Land Registration Act 1925, will retain that status indefinitely.

Duty to disclose unregistered interests which override registered dispositions

10–029 Section 71 and r.57 impose a duty on the applicant for registration of a registrable disposition of a registered estate to provide information to the registrar about any of the interests that override first registration which:

(1) are within the actual knowledge of the applicant; and

(2) affect the estate to which the application relates.

Such information must be provided with the application in Form DI.

There is no requirement to provide information about:

(a) interests that cannot be protected by a notice (see s.33 and para.16–003);

(b) public rights;

(c) leases granted for a term not exceeding seven years from the date of the grant, not being a lease in respect of which the tenant is under a duty to apply for first registration or which constitutes a registrable disposition, when at the time of the application the term granted by the lease has one year or less to run;

(d) local land charges;

(e) any interest apparent from the deeds and documents accompanying an application for first registration.

The applicant must provide any documentary evidence of the existence of the overriding interest which is in their control.

Form AP1 requires the applicant or their conveyancer to certify either that Form DI accompanies the application or that the application is not one to register a registrable disposition or that it is but no disclosable interests affect (see also para.10–005).

Once an interest has been disclosed, the registrar may make an appropriate entry in the register and if he does the interest will then cease to be overriding (s.29(3)).

Outline applications

Outline applications can be lodged under r.54 to "reserve" periods of priority within which applications may be made for registration of rights, interests or matters that cannot be protected by an official search with priority (see para.9–017), e.g. a registrable disposition not for value or entry of a restriction. **10–030**

Limitations on use

The application in respect of a right, interest or matter for which a reserved period is sought must: **10–031**

(1) not be protectable by an official search with priority under r.147;

(2) exist at the time the outline application is lodged;

(3) relate to the whole of the registered title, or pending first registration, and not with part only of that title or pending first registration;

(4) not be an application for first registration, or for a caution against first registration or in respect of the cautions register or an application under Part 13 of the Rules (e.g. an application for official copies or an application relating to exempt information documents); and

(5) be in respect of one right, interest or matter only. If a reserved period for more than one right, interest or matter is required, a separate outline application for each must be lodged, even if they are subsequently contained within one application for registration.

Reserved period

The "reserved period" granted by a valid outline application commences at the date and time it is entered on the day list (see paras 1–010 and 1–011) and expires at 12 noon on the fourth **10–032** business day following the day that the outline application was taken to be made (r.54(9)).

When an outline application is lodged, the applicant will be given the date and time when the reserved period commences and expires and an official reference number.

For the outline application to be effective, the applicant must within the reserved period lodge the supporting papers, using the correct application form, at the proper office or at the office specified for delivery of applications of the nature specified in the outline application in a written arrangement made between the registrar and the applicant or their conveyancer. The application will then be registered with effect from the date and time of the outline application.

The outline application will be subject to any official searches with priority, other outline applications or any pending applications already entered on the day list at the time it is lodged.

If the applicant does not lodge their application for registration of the right, interest or matter before the expiry of the reserved period, it will be treated as a fresh application and will receive priority from the date and time it is entered on the day list. The outline application must be cancelled by the registrar (r.54(6) and (7)).

Application

10–033 Outline applications can only be made during the currency of a notice given by the registrar under Sch.2 to the Rules and in accordance with the limitations contained in the notice. There is no paper form for an outline application and it may be made orally at the Customer Information Centre of any Land Registry Office or through the NLIS (see para.1–027). Credit account holders can apply through Land Registry Telephone Services or through Land Registry Direct.

The applicant must provide the following information when lodging an outline application:

(1) Credit account key number, if appropriate.
(2) Name, address and reference of the person lodging the application.
(3) Title number of the registered title or that allocated to a pending first registration application.
(4) Name of the registered proprietor(s) or applicant(s) for first registration (if more than one person, the name of one of them will suffice). These will be used, where possible, to try and validate that the application is being lodged against the correct title. If the name(s) do not agree, the applicant will be given the option of either continuing or abandoning their application.

(5) Name of the applicant for whose application a reserved period is being sought.

(6) Nature of the application being protected.

(7) Name and address of the person or firm lodging the application.

(8) When requested, the administrative area and postcode (if known) in which the property falls.

A fee in accordance with the Fee Order is payable.

Restrictions

A disposition of a registered estate may be "caught" by the terms of an existing restriction in the register. A person entering into such a disposition should therefore ensure that it will be possible to complete the disposition by registration where necessary, by complying with the restriction or applying for it to be withdrawn, cancelled, modified or disapplied as the case may be. **10–034**

As a result of a disposition of a registered estate, it may be necessary for application to be made for entry of a new restriction in the register.

Restrictions are discussed further in Chapter 16.

Requisitions from Land Registry

Requisitions from Land Registry should be dealt with as expeditiously as possible and in accordance with the specified time limits for reply. Delay or failure to respond satisfactorily to requisitions may result in the cancellation of the application (see para.1–014). **10–035**

Foreign law

In general, the law relating to land is the law of the state in which the land is situated, i.e. the "lex situs". In relation to registered estates under the Act, "foreign law" is that of any country outside England and Wales; this therefore includes the law of Scotland, Northern Ireland, the Channel Islands and the Isle of Man. **10–036**

Issues of foreign law may sometimes arise, e.g. in relation to a foreign power of attorney, divorce or bankruptcy. Any such issue will be considered by the registrar on an individual basis. For example, in the case of a foreign power of attorney, the registrar will consider whether the power is valid for land registration purposes and authorises the execution of the disposition in question. For execution in foreign characters, see para.10–009.

Practical points

- Ensure a registrable disposition is completed by registration and that application is made within the priority period of any protecting official search with priority,
- Consider the basic and special rules of priority where necessary,
- Ensure Form AP1 is completed correctly,
- Ensure a power of attorney authorises the disposition and, where appropriate, that it can be used by a donor who is a joint proprietor,
- Ensure the correct address(es) for service are provided with the application for registration and are kept up to date subsequently,
- Consider the effect of any restriction in the register and how this may affect registration of a disposition,
- Take account of any other entries in the register, such as a unilateral notice or caution against dealings and take any necessary steps in respect of them, where appropriate,
- Check for the existence of interests which override and ensure any such interests are disclosed in Form DI where appropriate,
- Consider making an outline application where a matter is urgent and cannot be protected by an official search with priority.

Chapter 11

Transfers

Introduction

This chapter deals with transfers on sale but, where appropriate, the same principles will apply to transfers not on sale. The chapter assumes that both the vendor and the purchaser will each be represented by a conveyancer. **11–001**

Sale of a registered estate

Contract

A contract for the sale of a registered estate should specify the relevant details relating to the registered title(s) affected. A plan will usually be necessary on a sale of part of the estate in a registered title (see para.11–011). **11–002**

Application may be made to protect the contract in the register (provided that it relates to the legal estate) by entry of an agreed notice or unilateral notice (s.34) and also, where appropriate, by a a restriction (see Chapter 16); this will be particularly relevant where there is likely to be any significant delay before completion.

Deduction of title

Section 110 of the Land Registration Act 1925 contained specific provisions as to the evidence of title to be supplied by a vendor to a purchaser of registered land. However, although para.2 of Sch.10 to the Act allows for rules to be made as to the evidence of title which must be provided by a vendor under a contract for the transfer, or other disposition, for valuable consideration of a registered estate or charge, no such rules have currently been made. An intending purchaser of a registered estate is, therefore, entitled to such evidence of his **11–003** intending vendor's title as the contract for sale provides. However, an intending purchaser can obtain an official copy of the register and title plan of the vendor's title and use the official search procedure. Inspection of the register, official copies and official searches are discussed in Chapter 9.

The deduction of title by a vendor to a purchaser is therefore a generally matter of negotiation and contract, but on a sale of a registered estate the vendor will normally provide the purchaser with:

(1) a copy of the subsisting entries in the register;

(2) copies or abstracts of any documents referred to in the register which affect the estate being sold, except those relating to incumbrances to be discharged on or before completion; and

(3) a copy of the title plan (or, where the disposition affects part of the estate in a title, a certificate of official inspection of the title plan instead—see para.9–010).

The preferred method of providing these copies is to obtain from Land Registry an official copy of the register and of any document and title plan required—see Chapter 9 for further details. Official copies do not require verification, since s.67(1) provides that such copies shall be admissible in evidence to the same extent as the originals.

The vendor will also normally provide the purchaser with such copies, abstracts and evidence (if any) as the purchaser would have been entitled to if the land had been unregistered, in respect of:

(a) any subsisting rights and interests as to which the register is not conclusive; and

(b) any matters excepted from the effect of registration.

Examples of (a) would be a right of way which benefits the registered estate being sold but which is not the subject of an entry in the register; or an easement acquired over the registered estate being sold which is not the subject of a notice in the register but may be binding as an overriding interest (see para.10–028). An example of (b) would be a defect in the title which had led to the grant of a qualified class of title on first registration (see para.5–012).

Home Information Packs ("HIPs")

11–004 Under Part 5 of the Housing Act 2004 and the Home Information Pack (No.2) Regulations 2007, in the majority of cases the vendor of a residential property (being a single dwellinghouse) has to supply a copy of a HIP on request within 14 days. The HIP must be available on day one of marketing the property.

Some of the contents of a HIP, e.g. official copies of the register and title plan, may need to be obtained from the Land Registry (see Chapter 9).

Investigation of title

If official copies have been supplied, no verification of them is necessary (s.67(1)). **11–005**

The purchaser or their conveyancer must consider all subsisting entries in the register and ensure that any restriction limiting the vendor's powers of disposition will be complied with. Also, that such action (if any) as may be appropriate will be taken in regard to other entries; for example that a registered charge will be discharged, or that a caution will be withdrawn, on or before completion. Requisitions on title may be made as necessary in this regard.

The prescribed form of transfer in Sch.1 to the Rules must be used (see para.11–009) and a draft for approval by the vendor will normally be prepared by the purchaser or their conveyancer, unless in straightforward cases this is agreed to be unnecessary.

Except as discussed in paras 9–036 and 9–037, there is no need to make a Land Charges search or a search in the Companies Registry when investigating a title registered with absolute title, but the usual searches in local land charges registers and other searches and inquiries will need to be made as appropriate (see para.9–038).

The purchaser should consider making inquiries as to the existence of any overriding interests which may be binding upon them when they complete their purchase of the registered title, notwithstanding that there is no entry in the register in respect of them and which they themselves may need to disclose to Land Registry when making their application for registration of the transfer (s.29, r.57 and Sch.3 to the Act—see paras 10–028 and 10–029).

Official search of the register

Immediately before completion of their purchase, the purchaser must find out whether any adverse entry has been made in the register since the date of the official copy of the register (or, if appropriate, the date given as the subsisting entries date at the time of access by remote terminal using Land Registry Direct—see para.9–009). **11–006**

This information is obtained by making an application for an official search of the register with priority, as explained in Chapter 9.

In addition to disclosing any changes to the register and any pending applications on the day list, the official certificate of search confers priority upon an application to register the transfer, if that application is delivered to the proper office and entered on the day list within the priority period conferred by the search. These matters are discussed more fully in Chapter 9.

Completion

11–007 On completion of a purchase, the purchaser's conveyancer must obtain the executed transfer from the vendor's conveyancer, together with any necessary undertaking in respect of any subsisting registered charges from which the land transferred is to be discharged. Discharges of registered charges are discussed in para.14–019.

Where Form DS1 cannot be handed over at completion or the discharge is to be via an END, and the purchaser's conveyancer receives a suitable form of undertaking from the vendor's conveyancer, it is unnecessary to defer lodging the application for registration until the Form DS1 is received or confirmation is received from the lender that an END has been sent to Land Registry.

If the priority secured by obtaining the official certificate of search of the register might otherwise be lost, the application may be lodged at once; however Land Registry's "early completion" policy may then apply (see para.1–015).

If the registered estate is being transferred subject to the charge, the transfer will need to be handed over, with the chargee being a party to the transfer.

If the transfer is of part of the registered estate and only the part transferred is being discharged from the registered charge, the purchaser's conveyancer must obtain from the vendor's conveyancer a discharge in Form DS3 or a suitable undertaking to forward this when received from the chargee. An END cannot currently be used to discharge part of the land in a title from a charge.

After completion: registration of the transfer

11–008 Section 27 and Sch.2 to the Act provide that for a transfer to operate at law, it must be completed by registration and the transferee or his successor in title must be entered in the register as proprietor. Until it is completed by registration, the transfer will therefore take effect only in equity.

The application to register the transfer should be delivered to the proper office within the priority period conferred by the official search of the register (see para.9–023).

The application (which will commonly be delivered together with applications to register a discharge of an existing registered charge and register a new charge created by the purchaser), should be made in Form AP1 (see para.10–005). The appropriate SDLT evidence must accompany the application (see para.1–016).

In the case of a transfer of part, under r.72 the registrar must:

(1) make an entry in the transferor's title as to the removal of the land or estate comprised in that transfer, or create a new edition of that title; and

(2) where appropriate, make entries in the relevant individual registers in respect of any rights, restrictive covenants, provisions or other matters created by the transfer which are capable of being so entered. However, the registrar need make no such entries where the relevant title numbers have not been given in panel 2 of the Form AP1, unless separate application is made in respect of them.

A fee in accordance with the Fee Order is payable. A statement in writing, signed by the applicant or their conveyancer, of the full open market value (free from any charge of the land), must be supplied in the case of a transfer otherwise than for monetary consideration.

Forms of transfer

The Rules prescribe various forms of transfer for use according **11–009**
to the circumstances, as set out in Sch.1 to the Rules—see paras 1–012 and 10–007). Rule 58 states that a transfer must be in Form TP1, TP2, TR1, TR2, TR5, AS1 or AS3, as appropriate. Rule 59 prescribes the forms of transfer which must be used to effect a transfer by way of exchange and deals with the need for a receipt for equality money and suitable additional wording in the transfer. Rule 60 covers transfers of leasehold land where the rent is being apportioned or the land is being exonerated (see para.12–022). Schedule 1 forms are listed in Appendix II to this book.

Covenants, implied covenants and easements

These are discussed in Chapter 8. **11–010**

Transfer of part: requirement for a plan

Rule 213 provides that a transfer of part of the land in a **11–011**
registered title must have attached to it a plan clearly identifying the land dealt with. The only exception to this is when the land

dealt with is clearly identified on the title plan of the registered title, e.g. by being edged and lettered in blue, when it may instead be described by reference to that title plan rather than by attaching a new plan.

Where a plan is attached the transferor must sign the plan. Ideally the plan should be based on the title plan of the transferor's title or be capable, in the case of developing estates, of being associated with it. If the land transferred is not physically defined other than by surveyors' pegs, the boundaries shown on the plan should be tied to permanent features by accurate measurements. See Chapter 21 as to transfers of plots on registered developing estates generally.

Mines and minerals

11–012 Mines and minerals are "land" for the purposes of the Act (s.132(1)) and are rebuttably presumed to be included in the registered title of a registered estate in the surface land; this is in accordance with the common law position regarding mines and minerals where the surface land is unregistered.

However, para.2 of Sched.8 to the Act provides that no indemnity is payable in respect of mines and minerals unless there is a specific note in the register that title to them is included. Such a note can be entered as a result of a specific application on first registration or a subsequent application in Form AP1 and will only be made where evidence of title to the mines and minerals sufficient to satisfy the registrar that those mines and minerals are included in the registered estate is lodged (r.71). The form of the note will be:

> "NOTE: For the purposes of paragraph 2 of Schedule 8 to the Land Registration Act 2002 [*details of mines and minerals*] are included in this title."

Where a note cannot be made on the register that the title to the registered estate includes mines and minerals, but the description of the registered estate makes reference to mines and minerals, the registrar may make the following entry (r.70):

> "NOTE: The description of the registered estate is an entry made under rule 5(a) of the Land Registration Rules 2003 and is not a note to which paragraph 2 of Schedule 8 to the Land Registration Act 2002 refers that the registered estate includes the mines or minerals. The mines and minerals under the land are only included in the registration to the extent that they were included in [*title number*]."

Such an entry may be used, for example, where a transfer of part of a registered estate is expressed to include the mines and minerals, but the register of the transferor's title does not include a note for the purposes of para.2 of Sch.8 to the Act. The registrar will therefore wish to ensure that any reference to mines and minerals in the description in the transferee's property register is not a note for the purposes of para.2 of Sch.8.

Where a transfer of mines and minerals is granted out of a registered title to mines and minerals, or to surface land, which contains a note regarding the inclusion of those mines and minerals, the new title will be registered with the same class of title as the existing class of title. Where there is no such note, the new title will be registered with the same class of title as the existing class of title but with the entry referred to above being made in the register.

See paras 5–018 and 10–028 as to interests in mines and minerals which take effect as an overriding interest under Schs 1 and 3 to the Act.

Transfers to two or more transferees

The Sch.1 forms of transfer (see para.11–009) contain a panel entitled "Declaration of trust" for completion where there is more than one transferee. The appropriate box should be completed depending upon whether the transferees are to hold the registered estate on trust for themselves as joint tenants beneficially, or as tenants in common in equal shares, or upon some other trust. See Chapter 18 as to trusts generally. **11–013**

Completion of the declaration in the transfer and execution of the transfer by the transferees should not be overlooked, as it is important that the transferees consider and make an appropriate declaration as to the trusts upon which the land or estate will be held by them. This was emphasized by the House of Lords in the leading case of *Stack v Dowden* [2007] UKHL 17 (see para.5–007). A declaration of trust in a separate document may be executed if desired.

If the registrar enters two or more persons in the register as the proprietor of a registered estate in land, he is obliged, under s.44 and r.95, to enter a restriction in Form A. This is to ensure that interests which are capable of being overreached on a disposition of the estate are overreached (see also paras 5–007 and 18–002). If it is not clear from the application that the transferees are holding on trust for themselves as beneficial joint tenants, the registrar will enter the restriction by default.

In the case of other types of registered estate, r.94(2A) provides that where two or more persons apply to be registered as proprietors of an estate which is a rentcharge, profit à prendre in gross, franchise or manor, they must also apply for entry of a restriction in Form A if a sole (surviving) proprietor will not be able to give a valid receipt for capital money.

Fees on transfers to give effect to dealings with undivided shares

11–014 The Fee Order contains express provisions as to the fee payable on the registration of a transfer for the purpose of giving effect to a disposition of a share in a registered estate or registered charge.

Subject to certain exceptions, if the disposition of a share is for monetary consideration (as defined in the Fee Order) the fee is payable on the amount of the consideration.

If the disposition of a share is otherwise than for monetary consideration, the fee is payable on the value of that share.

The value of the estate is the open market value, free of any charge at the date of the application. A statement of such value, signed by the applicant or their conveyancer, should accompany the application.

Particular parties to transfers

Corporations

11–015 Where a UK company (i.e. one registered in England, Wales, Scotland or Northern Ireland under the Companies Acts or in Northern Ireland under the Companies (Northern Ireland) Order 1986), or a UK limited liability partnership (i.e. one incorporated in the United Kingdom under the Limited Liability Partnerships Act 2000 or the Limited Liability Partnerships Act (Northern Ireland) 2002) applies to be registered, the application must state its registered number including any prefix. No evidence of its powers to hold, sell or otherwise deal with land will normally be required.

Where a corporation or body of trustees holding on charitable, ecclesiastical or public trusts (other than a non-exempt charity) applies to be registered as proprietor of a registered estate or charge, the application must be accompanied by the document creating the trust (r.182). See also Chapter 18 as to charities generally.

If the applicant is a corporate body, but is not either:

(1) a UK company; or

(2) a UK limited liability partnership; or

(3) the trustee of a public, ecclesiastical or charitable trust (other than a non exempt charity),

evidence of the extent of its powers to hold and sell, mortgage, lease, and otherwise deal with land, and, in the case of a charge, to lend money on mortgage must be lodged (r.183(1)). The evidence must include the document(s) constituting the corporation, or a certified copy, and any further evidence the registrar may require (r.183(2)). If the evidence is in a language other than English or Welsh, a certified translation must be provided.

Alternatively a certificate in Form 7 (for a corporation incorporated outside the United Kingdom) may be given by a qualified lawyer practising in the territory of incorporation or in Form 8 (for a corporation incorporated within the United Kingdom) may be given by the applicant's conveyancer. Form 7 and Form 8 are contained in Sch.3 to the Rules.

These provisions enable the registrar to be satisfied that the applicant has the necessary power to hold, sell and otherwise deal with the registered estate (or to lend money on mortgage, in the case of a charge) and to enter any appropriate restriction(s) in the register.

In the absence of any restriction in the register, no evidence of a corporation's power to transfer land or otherwise deal with land of which it is the registered proprietor is required. See para.9–037 as to whether a purchaser of registered land from a company should make a search in the Companies Registry.

Trustees and charities

These are considered in Chapter 18. **11–016**

Personal representatives

Transfers by personal representatives are discussed in Chapter 19. **11–017**

Compulsory purchase and statutory vesting

These are discussed in para.5–020 in relation to unregistered land. **11–018**

In relation to a registered estate, the compulsory purchase or statutory vesting will need to be completed by registration in order to take effect at law, including situations where there is a vesting by operation of law (s.27(5)).

In the case of a transfer by virtue of a court order, an application for registration should be made accompanied by the court order (rr.127(2) or 161(2)).

Practical points
• Ensure the correct Sch.1 form is used for a disposition of a registered estate, • Ensure that a transfer is completed by registration in order to take effect at law and that the application for registration is made within the priority period of any protecting official search with priority, • Provide confirmation of the trusts upon which joint proprietors are to hold the registered estate, to avoid unnecessary entry of a restriction in Form A by default and/or unnecessary problems in the future, • Ensure the correct address(es) for service are provided on registration and kept up to date subsequently, • Remember to deal with any additional title(s) where necessary, e.g. the freehold title when transferring a leasehold title, or a separate registered title for a garage or parking space, • Ensure that any additional title numbers are included in panel 2 of Form AP1, to ensure that relevant entries will be made in those titles where necessary, • Consider the effect of any restriction in the register and how this may affect registration of a transfer.

Chapter 12

Leases

Leases of registered land

The landlord's title and power to grant the lease

Section 44 of the Law of Property Act 1925 contained limitations upon the right of an intended tenant (or assignee) to call for evidence of title to a freehold or leasehold reversion. However, those provisions were amended by para.2 of Sch.11 to the Act, so that they no longer apply to the grant of a lease which will trigger compulsory first registration (see para.5–003) or which is a lease derived out of registered land. **12–001**

Paragraph 2 of Sch.10 to the Act allows for rules to be made as to the evidence of title which must be provided by the landlord under an agreement for a lease of a registered estate, but no such rules have currently been made. An intending tenant of a registered estate is, therefore, entitled to such evidence of their intending landlord's title as the agreement for lease provides. However, an intending tenant can obtain an official copy of the register and title plan of the landlord's title and of any superior title and use the official search procedure. Inspection of the register, official copies and official searches are discussed in Chapter 9.

By virtue of the "owner's powers" conferred by s.23(1) (see para.10–001), a proprietor of a registered estate has full power to lease their estate (or to sub-lease it if it is a leasehold estate). Under s.26, a person's right to exercise owner's powers are, in favour of a tenant, taken to be free from any limitation affecting the validity of the lease, subject to any entry to the contrary in the register or any limitation imposed by or under the Act. For example, a restriction in the landlord's title may have to be complied with, or a registered chargee's consent obtained.

Where an existing lease is registered with less than absolute class of leasehold title, the significance of this is discussed in para.5–012.

Agreement for lease

12–002 An agreement for a lease of registered land may be protected as an estate contract by entry of a notice and, where appropriate, a restriction in the register of the intended landlord's title (see Chapter 16).

Form of lease

12–003 No form of lease was prescribed by the Rules as originally made. However, in 2006 the Rules were amended by the introduction of provisions relating to "prescribed clauses leases". Most registrable dispositions consisting of a lease of a registered estate in land must be now be in the form of a prescribed clauses lease—see para.12–004. Where a lease of a registered estate is not required to be in the form of a prescribed clauses lease, it may be in any form provided that it refers to the landlord's title number (r.212) and, if it is a lease of part of the registered estate, it must normally have attached to it a plan enabling the demised premises to be identified on the title plan of the landlord's title, unless it is already identified on that title plan (r.213). The route of any easements rights must similarly be clearly identified.

See Chapter 10 as to the execution of the lease and para.11–011 as to the signature of any plan. Usually, in the case of a lease, the landlord will sign the plan to the lease and the tenant will sign the plan to the counterpart.

Prescribed clauses leases

12–004 As from June 19, 2006 use of a prescribed clauses lease has (with certain limited exceptions) been compulsory for any lease granted out of a registered estate in land which is a registrable disposition under s.27(2)(b) required to be completed by registration (r.58A(1)).

A prescribed clauses lease is defined by r.58A(4) as a lease granted out of a registered estate in land on or after June 19, 2006 which is a registrable disposition required to be completed by registration under s.27(2)(b) and which is not granted in a form **expressly** required:

(1) by an agreement entered into before June 19, 2006;

(2) by an order of the court;

(3) by or under an enactment;

(4) by a necessary consent or licence for the grant of a lease given before June 19, 2006.

A lease by virtue of a variation of a lease which is a deemed surrender and re-grant is not a prescribed clauses lease; this exemption does not apply where a deed expressly provides for the surrender of an existing lease and the grant of a new lease in substitution.

A prescribed clauses lease must begin with the required wording (see below) or that wording must appear immediately after any front sheet. "Front sheet" means a front cover sheet, or a contents or index sheet at the beginning of the lease, or a front cover sheet and contents or index sheet where the contents or index sheet is immediately after the front cover sheet.

"Required wording" means the wording in clauses LR1 to LR14 of Sch.1A to the Rules completed in accordance with the instructions in that schedule as appropriate for the particular lease. These clauses are set out in Appendix IV of this book.

The prescribed clauses are therefore a standard set of clauses that must appear at the beginning of all such leases, containing relevant details which will assist in the registration of the lease. It is important that these clauses are correctly completed, as Land Registry will prepare the register entries to complete registration of the lease from the information provided in the clauses. Also, if a clause is not completed this may result in any entry not being made (see para.12–008). The remainder of the lease can be in whatever form the parties require, subject to the points discussed in para.12–003.

Official copies and searches

The usual searches and inquiries (including a local land charges search—see para.9–038) are necessary. Official copies of the landlord's registered title and any superior registered title may be obtained from Land Registry as discussed in Chapter 9. **12–005**

An official search of the register of the landlord's title should be obtained as also discussed in Chapter 9. See paras 9–036 and 9–037 as to making a Land Charges search or a search at the Companies Registry against a landlord in certain cases.

Consent to grant of lease

The tenant should obtain any consents that the register of the landlord's title shows to be necessary, e.g. from a registered chargee, or under the terms of a striction. If these are not lodged, the registrar may make a protective entry in the register to reflect this (see para.5–012). **12–006**

Registration

In the case of a registered estate in land, s.27(2)(b) provides that the grant of a lease for a term of years absolute is a registrable disposition which is required to be completed by registration where: **12–007**

(1) it is granted for a term of more than seven years from the date of the lease; or

(2) whatever the length of the term, it will take effect in possession more than three months beginning with the date of the lease; or

(3) the right to possession is discontinuous, e.g. a timeshare lease; or

(4) the lease is a right to buy lease granted pursuant to Pt 5 of the Housing Act 1985 or a lease where the right to buy is preserved under s.171A of the Housing Act 1985.

This is the position whether the registered estate in land out of which the lease is granted is freehold or leasehold.

An application for substantive registration of the title to the lease must be made in Form AP1. The form and its completion are discussed in para.10–005. The application should be accompanied by the original lease and, if the applicant wishes the original to be returned, a certified copy (r.203), together with the appropriate SDLT evidence (see para.1–016).

If the lease is of a registered estate in land granted to two or more persons and it contains either no details or conflicting details as to whether a restriction in Form A is required, the registrar will enter a restriction by default (see para.11–013). If the lease is a prescribed clauses lease, a declaration of trust is contained in clause LR14.

Under para.3 of Pt.1 of Sch.2 to the Act, the registration requirements are that the tenant, or their successor in title, must be registered as proprietor of the lease and a notice of the lease entered in the landlord's title.

In the case of a registered estate which is a franchise or manor, s.27(2)(c) provides that the grant of a lease is a registrable disposition which is required to be completed by registration. Under paras 4 and 5 of Pt.1 of Sch.2 to the Act, the registration requirements are that the tenant, or their successor in title, must be registered as proprietor of the lease (if it is for a term of more than seven years from the date of the lease) and a notice of the lease entered in the landlord's title.

In the case of a registered estate which is a profit à prendre in gross (see para.8–023), the grant of a lease is a registrable disposition regardless of the length of the term (s.27(2)(d)). Under paras 6 and 7 of Pt.1 of Sch.2 to the Act, the registration requirements are that the tenant, or their successor in title, must be registered as proprietor of the lease (if it is for a term of more than seven years from the date of the lease) and a notice of the lease entered in the landlord's title.

Register entries on registration of the lease

12–008 Rule 72A specifies certain entries which the registrar is obliged to make on registration of a lease granted out of a registered estate in land on or after June 19, 2006 which is required to be registered under s.27(2)(b). Rule 72A also specifies situations where the registrar is required to make no entry. This applies both to prescribed clauses leases and other leases.

Under r.72A(2), on completion of such a lease by registration the registrar must (where appropriate) make entries in the relevant individual register in respect of interests contained in the lease which are of the nature referred to in clauses LR9 (rights of acquisition etc.), LR10 (restrictive covenants by the landlord in respect of other land), LR11 (easements granted or reserved) and LR 12 (estate rentcharge). The requirement to make an entry in respect of an interest referred to in clause LR12 is satisfied by entry, where appropriate, of notice of the interest created.

Under r.72A(3), where the lease is a prescribed clauses lease and contains a prohibition or restriction on disposing of the lease of the nature referred to in clause LR8 or it contains interests of the nature referred to in clauses LR9, LR10, LR11 and LR12, but the prohibition or restriction or the interests are not specified or referred to in those clauses, or the lease does not contain the required wording in respect of them, then the registrar need take no action in respect of them unless a separate application is made. Rule 6(2) which requires the registrar to make an entry on registration in respect of a prohibition or restriction on disposing of a lease is amended accordingly.

Under r.72A(4), the registrar need not make entries in respect of interests of the nature referred to in clauses LR9, LR10 or LR11 or a standard form of restriction set out in clause LR13 where:

(1) in the case of a prescribed clauses lease, the title numbers of the individual registers have not been given in clause LR2.2; or

(2) in any other case, the title numbers of the individual registers required by clause LR2.2 have not been given in panel 2 of the Form AP1 lodged for the purpose of completing the lease by registration,

unless a separate application is made in respect of the interests or restriction.

Under r.72A(5), where a separate application is made in Form AP1 in respect of either a prohibition or restriction on disposal of the lease or the grant or reservation of an easement, the Form AP1 must specify the particular clause, schedule or paragraph of a schedule, where the prohibition or restriction or easement is contained in the lease.

Under r.58A(3), if it appears to the registrar that a lease is not a prescribed clauses lease, then the required wording is not necessary and r.72A(3) shall not apply to that lease, even though the lease would otherwise be a prescribed clauses lease.

Rule 92 relaxes the requirement for a Form RX1 to be lodged (see para.16–023), where application for the entry of a standard restriction is made in clause LR13 of a "relevant lease" which is defined as:

(a) a prescribed clauses lease; or

(b) any other lease which complies with the requirements as to form and content of a prescribed clauses lease and which either is required to be completed by registration under s.27(2)(b) or is the subject of an application for first registration of the title to it.

Under r.72B, on completion of the lease by registration, the registrar must enter a notice or other appropriate entry in respect of any interest which, at the time of registration, is the subject of a notice in the landlord's registered title and which the registrar considers may affect the registered lease.

Under r.77, where a right of re-entry is derived in a grant of a lease and the lease is a registrable disposition which is completed by registration, that is also sufficient to complete the grant of the right of re-entry (being itself a registrable disposition under s.27(2)(e)) by registration, without any specific entry being made in relation to it in the register.

Leasehold interests incapable of substantive registration

12–009 There are certain cases in which leasehold interests created out of registered land are incapable of substantive registration. These are:

(1) a lease granted for a term of seven years or less except for those mentioned at para.12–007;

(2) a lease for which a rent or premium is payable where the term commences more than 21 years from the date of the lease and the lease is void by virtue of s.149(3) of the Law of Property Act 1925;

(3) leases with no certain start date, so that the lease is not for a term of years certain;

(4) leases where the landlord and tenant are the same person and therefore of no effect (see *Rye v Rye* [1962] A.C. 496); and

(5) Public–private partnership ("PPP") leases (s.90).

Noting of leases

On substantive registration of a lease, the registrar will enter a notice of the lease in the landlord's registered title (see para.12–007). **12–010**

Where a lease granted out of a registered estate in land is not capable of substantive registration, the burden of it will be an overriding interest not requiring protection in the register, under Sch.3 to the Act (see para.10–028). An application may nevertheless be made for entry of a notice in the landlord's registered title provided the lease is granted for a term of more than three years (ss.33(b) and 34). The application should be in Form AN1 (for entry of an agreed notice) or Form UN1 (for entry of a unilateral notice)—see paras 16–005 and 16–008. A PPP lease cannot be noted (s.90).

Leases of unregistered land

A lease granted out of unregistered land is not required to contain the prescribed clauses which are required wording for a prescribed clauses lease (see para.12–004), but these clauses can be used voluntarily if desired. If the prescribed clauses are used, application for entry of a standard restriction may be made in clause LR13 rather than by using Form RX1 (r.92—see paras 12–008 and 16–023). **12–011**

Rule 72A (see para.12–008) does not apply to such leases.

Such a lease may be subject to compulsory first registration upon its grant or assignment or may be the subject of a voluntary application for first registration (see paras 5–002 and 5–003).

The registrar will enter a notice of the burden of an unregistered lease if it is disclosed on an application for first registration of the landlord's reversionary title, provided it is capable of being noted (see paras 5–013 and 12–010).

If the landlord's title is registered and no notice of the lease appears in the register, the registrar must when completing an application for first registration of the lease enter a notice of the lease in the landlord's title (r.37—see also para.5–013).

Where a lease granted out of unregistered land is not subject to compulsory first registration, the burden of it will be an overriding interest not requiring protection in the register, under Sch.3 to the Act (see para.10–028). An application may nevertheless be made for entry of a notice in the landlord's registered title provided the lease is granted for a term of more than three years (ss.33(b) and 34). The application should be in Form AN1 (for entry of an agreed notice) or Form UN1 (for entry of a unilateral notice)—see paras 16–005 and 16–008. A PPP lease cannot be noted (s.90).

Mines and minerals

12–012 Where a lease of mines and minerals is a registrable disposition and is granted out of an absolute registered title where there is a note in the title regarding the inclusion of those mines and minerals within the landlord's registered title, an absolute leasehold title can be granted. Where there is no such note and the landlord is registered with an absolute title, then an absolute leasehold title can still be granted but with the following entry being made after the description of the registered estate (r.70):

> "NOTE: The description of the registered estate is an entry made under rule 5(a) of the Land Registration Rules 2003 and is not a note to which paragraph 2 of Schedule 8 to the Land Registration Act 2002 refers that the registered estate includes the mines or minerals under the land. The mines and minerals under the land are only included in the registration to the extent that they were included in [*title number of the landlord's title*]."

The purpose of this note is discussed in para.11–012.

In those cases where the landlord is registered with a qualified or possessory title, a good leasehold title will be registered.

Easements and restrictive covenants in leases

12–013 From June 19, 2006 the register heading of a registered leasehold estate states that:

> "This register describes the land and estate comprised in the title."

This is supplemented by the following entry in the property register:

> "Unless otherwise mentioned the title includes any legal easements granted by the registered lease(s)but is subject to any rights that it reserves, so far as those easements and rights exist and benefit or affect the registered land."

Where a lease is lodged for registration, the registrar will where appropriate make an entry in the register in respect of easements granted and/or reserved by the lease. Where necessary, the entry will include any note qualifying or excluding an easement. The benefit of an equitable easement cannot be registered in the registered leasehold title, but the burden of it can be the subject of a notice in any registered burdened title.

Easements granted

In the case of a prescribed clauses lease, r.72A(3) applies and the registrar need only consider any easements granted that are referred to in clause LR11.1 (see para.12–008). **12–014**

If the lease is not a prescribed clauses lease, the registrar will consider any easements granted in the lease and make the appropriate entry in the register.

Where the easement is granted over other land within the landlord's registered title out of which the lease is granted, a notice of the easements will appear in the register by virtue of the standard entry made in the landlord's title on registration of the lease:

> "The parts of the land affected thereby are subject to the leases set out in the schedule of leases hereto. The leases grant and reserve easements as therein mentioned."

If the easement is granted over land within other registered titles, the title numbers must be stated in clause LR2.2 (in the case of a prescribed clauses lease) or panel 2 of Form AP1 (in the case of other leases), otherwise r.72A(4) applies and the registrar need make no entry in those other titles (see para.12–008). In that event, unless a separate application is made against each registered title comprising the burdened land, the easements will not have been completed by registration for the purposes of s.27 (see para.8–014) and the registrar will not be able to register the benefit of the easement in the registered leasehold title.

If the easement is granted over unregistered burdened land, any legal easement will bind any subsequent purchaser and the burden of it will take effect as an overriding interest on first registration (para.3 of Sch.1 to the Act—see para.5–018). Satisfactory evidence of the grantor's unregistered title will need to be lodged before the benefit of the easement could be registered in the registered leasehold title.

Easements reserved

The entry in the property register of a registered leasehold title **12–015**
referred to in para.12–013, also refers to easements reserved. Thus there is a notice entered in the register of the leasehold

title in respect of any easements reserved in the registered lease. If the lease contains no beneficial easements (or these are not being registered because clause LR11.1 has not been completed correctly—see para.12–008) an entry will be made in the charges register of the leasehold title in respect of the easements reserved by the lease.

In the case of a prescribed clauses lease, r.72A(3) applies and the registrar need only consider any easements reserved (or granted for the benefit of land owned by a third party) in the lease which are referred to in clause LR11.2 unless separate application is made (see para.12–008).

If the lease is not a prescribed clauses lease, the registrar will consider any easements reserved (or granted for the benefit of land owned by a third party) in the lease and make the appropriate entries in the register.

If the easements are reserved for the benefit of other land within the landlord's registered reversionary title, the easement is included in that title by virtue of the standard entry in the register of that registered title referred to above.

If the easement is reserved for the benefit of land in other registered titles, the title numbers must be stated in clause LR2.2 (in the case of a prescribed clauses lease) or panel 2 of Form AP1 (in the case of other leases), otherwise r.72A(4) applies and the registrar need make no entry in those other titles unless separate application is made (see para.12–008).

Where the benefiting land is unregistered, the benefit of the easement will subsist for the benefit of that land. On first registration of the benefiting estate, the estate will vest in the proprietor together with the benefit of the easement (ss.11(3) and 12(3)—see para.5–017).

Easements in unregistered leases

12–016 Easements may be granted or reserved in "unregistered leases", being leases:

(1) the grant of which is not a registrable disposition;

(2) the grant or assignment of which does not trigger compulsory first registration; and

(3) that are not the subject of voluntary first registration.

12–017 **(1) *Easements granted*** Where the burdened land is registered, the grant of such easements is a registrable disposition which must be completed by registration (see para.8–014), even if the lease itself will not be substantively registered or the subject of a notice in the register of the landlord's title. An application should therefore be made in Form AP1 to complete the grant of the easement by registration.

Where the lease itself *is* capable of being noted, details of it may be provided in a Form DI accompanying the application, and the registrar will normally then enter a notice in the register in respect of the lease at the same time.

If the easement is granted over unregistered burdened land, there is no register entry to be made; any legal easement will bind any subsequent purchaser and the burden of it will take effect as an overriding interest on first registration of the burdened estate (para.3 of Sch.1 to the Act—see para.5–018).

(2) *Easements reserved* As the burdened leasehold land is unregistered, the reservation is not a registrable disposition. Any legal easement will bind any subsequent purchaser and the burden of it will take effect as an overriding interest on first registration of the burdened estate (para.3 of Sch.1 to the Act—see para.5–018). **12–018**

Application can however be made in Form AP1 for the benefit of a legal easement to be registered in the register of any registered benefitting title (r.73A(1)(a)).

Equitable easements in leases

An easement may be equitable rather than legal, e.g. if the lease is merely in writing but not by deed, any easement granted or reserved within it can only be equitable. The effect of this is that: **12–019**

(1) Where the burdened land is registered, the grant or reservation of such an easement is not a registrable disposition which is required to be completed by registration, although it is capable of being noted.
(2) The benefit of such an easement cannot be registered in the register of any registered benefitting title.
(3) Where an easement is granted or reserved and the burdened land is unregistered, that easement will need to be protected by way of a Class D(iii) Land Charge.

Restrictive covenants in leases

A restrictive covenant made between a landlord and tenant so far as relating to the demised premises will be "incident to the estate" and cannot be the subject of a notice in the register (s.33(c)). A restrictive covenant relating to another registered estate may be protected by application for entry of a notice of the burden of the covenants in the register of the title(s) affected (see paras 16–005 and 16–008). **12–020**

Options and rights of pre-emption in leases of registered land

Where a lease granted out of a registered estate contains an option or a right of pre-emption granted by the landlord, the burden of that option or right should be protected by the entry **12–021** of a notice in the register of the landlord's title. Such an entry may be made when notice of the lease is entered on the landlord's title on completion of the lease by registration (see para.12–008). However, if no such entry is made or if a lease is not capable of substantive registration and takes effect as an overriding interest (see paras 10–028 and 12–009) a separate application to protect the option or right in the register of the landlord's title by means of entry of a notice and, where appropriate, a restriction, should be made (see Chapter 16).

Apportionment of or exoneration from rent

12–022 Under r.60(1) a transfer of a registered leasehold title containing a legal apportionment of, or exoneration from, the rent reserved by the lease must include the following statement in the additional provisions panel, with any necessary alterations and additions:

> "Liability for the payment of [*if applicable* the previously apportioned rent of £(*amount*) being part of] the rent reserved by the registered lease is apportioned between the Transferor and the Transferee as follows:
> £(*amount*) shall be payable out of the Property and the balance shall be payable out of the land remaining in title number (*title number of retained land*) or
> the whole of that rent shall be payable out of the Property and none of it shall be payable out of the land remaining in title number (*title number of retained land*) or
> the whole of that rent shall be payable out of the land remaining in title number (*title number of retained land*) and none of it shall be payable out of the Property".

Modification of implied indemnity covenants

12–023 Under para.20 of Sch.12 to the Act, certain indemnity covenants are implied in a transfer of a registered leasehold estate which is an "old tenancy", i.e. one that is not a new tenancy for the purposes of s.1 of the Landlord and Tenant (Covenants) Act 1995.

Under r.60(2) and (3), those implied covenants are modified in respect of a transfer of part of a registered leasehold estate where that part is, without the landlord's consent, expressed to be either exonerated from the whole rent, or to be subject to or charged with the entire rent, as the case may be.

Variation of leases

Deeds of variation in general

An application to register a deed of variation of a registered lease should normally be made in Form AP1 accompanied by sufficient evidence to show that the variation has effect at law and the alteration to the register should therefore be made (r.129). The application should be accompanied by: **12–024**

(1) the deed of variation; and

(2) the consent required from any chargee or under any restriction; or

(3) where the landlord's title is unregistered, evidence of that title; and

(4) any other evidence to show that the variation has effect at law.

If satisfied that the variation has effect at law, the registrar will make an entry relating to the deed in the property register of the tenant's title, together with a notice in the landlord's title (if registered).

It may be appropriate in some cases to apply for a notice in either Form AN1 (for an agreed notice), or Form UN1 (for a unilateral notice) in respect of a deed of variation (see paras 16–005 and 16–008) even when the lease is substantively registered, if sufficient evidence cannot be provided to satisfy the registrar that the variation takes effect at law under r.129.

If notice of an unregistered lease is entered in a landlord's title, an application may be made to enter a notice (see Chapter 16) in respect of a variation of the lease. Such an application can be in Form AN1 for entry of an agreed notice, if the deed of variation can be provided and the lease is already protected by an agreed notice. However, it may sometimes be appropriate to make an application in Form UN1 for entry of a unilateral notice, for example if the lease is already protected by way of unilateral notice and the lease or/and the deed of variation cannot be provided.

If the deed of variation contains easements which are a registrable disposition under s.27, these will not operate at law until completed by registration (see para.8–014).

Similar comments apply to a deed of rectification, where a lease is rectified so as to give effect to the original intention of the parties, e.g. by the addition of covenants which were omitted from the lease by mistake.

Deeds of variation varying the term

12–025 If a tenant takes a new lease of the same property before the existing lease has expired then the original lease is treated as surrendered immediately before the new lease. As the term of a lease cannot be altered by means of a deed of variation, Land Registry will treat any deed purporting to vary the term of a registered lease as being a new lease which will, therefore, have the effect of surrendering the original lease.

The proper application in such a case will be for closure of the title to the original lease and registration of the new lease (if as varied, it is a registrable disposition—see para.12–007). The deed of variation, in such a case, does not have to be in the form of a prescribed clauses lease (see para.12–004).

As an alternative to use of a deed of variation, an extension of a lease may be granted (see para.12–027).

Deeds of variation varying the extent

12–026 A deed of variation which reduces the extent of the premises demised by a lease will be treated as a surrender of the part in question. Surrenders of leases are discussed in paras 12–037 and 12–038.

As the extent of the premises demised by a lease cannot be increased by means of a deed of variation, Land Registry will treat any deed purporting to increase the extent of the demised premises in a registered lease as being a new lease which will, therefore, have the effect of surrendering the original lease.

The proper application in such a case will be for closure of the title to the original lease and registration of the new lease (if as varied, it is a registrable disposition—see para.12–007). The deed of variation, in such a case, does not have to be in the form of a prescribed clauses lease (see para.12–004).

As an alternative to use of a deed of variation, a supplemental lease may be granted or the existing lease surrendered and replaced with a new lease of the combined extent. A prescribed clauses lease should be used where necessary and application made to register the lease and any surrender.

Extension of leases

12–027 Aside from the grant of an extended lease under the provisions of the Leasehold Reform Act or the Leasehold Reform, Housing and Urban Development Act 1993 (see paras 12–045 and

12–058), an existing lease may be extended by the grant of a new lease, to either:

(1) take immediate effect; or
(2) commence on a future date.

Where the new lease takes immediate effect

In this case, the tenant is deemed to have surrendered their existing lease immediately before the new lease commences. This applies irrespective of the intention of the parties, because the new lease is inconsistent with the existing lease and therefore the tenant is estopped from denying that the existing lease has come to an end. **12–028**

The surrender of the existing lease must be effected in the register (see paras 12–037 and 12–038) and the new lease registered in its place.

Before completing the new lease, the tenant should contact any chargee of the existing lease to ascertain their requirements. The chargee may prefer either to release their existing charge and take a fresh charge over the new leasehold estate, or to use a deed of substituted security.

However, if the new lease is made *expressly subject* to the existing lease, the registrar will accept that surrender of the existing lease does not occur, as the new lease (as a lease of the landlord's reversionary interest), is not inconsistent with the existing lease. In this event, the existing leasehold title, if registered, will not be closed. When registering such a new lease, the registrar will have regard to the possibility that any chargee of the existing lease has an interest in the new lease and will, where appropriate make an entry in the register of the new leasehold estate to the effect that the extended lease is subject to such rights as may be subsisting in favour of the persons interested in a charge of the existing lease.

Where the new lease commences on a future date

The new lease may, when granted at a rent or for a premium, commence at any time up to 21 years from the date of the grant (see s.149(3), of the Law of Property Act 1925). Therefore, if the existing lease has less than 21 years to run, the new lease may be granted to commence on its expiry. However, if the existing lease has more than 21 years to run, it will have to be shortened, either by a separate deed of variation, or by suitable wording in the new lease, so that the existing lease determines just before the commencement of the new lease. **12–029**

Where an extension is effected by means of a deed of variation, see para.12–025.

Determination of leases

Background

12–030 There are various ways in which a leasehold estate in land may come to an end:

(1) merger;

(2) surrender by deed;

(3) surrender by operation of law;

(4) disclaimer;

(5) effluxion of time;

(6) forfeiture;

(7) determination by notice;

(8) frustration.

The determination may affect one or more registered titles, depending upon whether the leasehold estate and/or the landlord's reversionary estate are registered.

A lease may also come to an end upon enlargement—see para.12–044.

Applications in general

12–031 In addition to any documents that may be specified in the sections set out below relating to the particular method by which the lease has been determined, the following documents will be required, depending upon whether the leasehold estate and/or the landlord's reversionary estate are registered.

(1) **Both interests registered** An application in Form AP1 may be made to close a registered leasehold title on determination and cancel the notice of that lease on the registered reversionary title, accompanied by the original lease and/or counterpart lease, if in the applicant's possession.

(2) **Cancellation of notice of an unregistered lease—landlord's reversionary estate registered** An application in Form CN1 may be made for cancellation of the noted lease in the landlord's title if the applicant is able to lodge appropriate documentary evidence to prove that the unregistered leasehold estate has determined. Evidence of title to the determining leasehold estate as listed on Form DL (in duplicate) should be lodged, together

with a current Land Charges search against the name of the tenant and with any entries accounted for.

If the lease is noted by way of a unilateral notice, an application either to remove or cancel the unilateral notice must be made in Form UN2 or Form UN4 respectively (see paras 16–010 and 16–011).

(3) **Closure of registered leasehold title—landlord's reversionary estate unregistered** An application in Form AP1 may be made to close the registered leasehold title, accompanied by the original lease and/or counterpart lease, if in the applicant's possession and an examined abstract or epitome of the landlord's unregistered title.

Incumbrances affecting the determined lease

Any incumbrances affecting the leasehold estate being determined will need to be considered and any necessary action taken in respect of them, as follows. **12–032**

(1) If a lease is determined by notice, effluxion of time, forfeiture or frustration, all incumbrances will normally end automatically with the determination of the lease.

(2) If a lease is being determined by merger, surrender or disclaimer, all incumbrances affecting the leasehold estate which is being determined must be dealt with as appropriate. Where an incumbrance consists of a registered charge, it may be possible to deal with the matter by way of a deed of substituted security, and an application made to register it against a registered reversionary title, where appropriate.

(3) Where a lease has been determined by notice, effluxion of time, forfeiture or frustration, any inferior leases (such as any underleases derived from that lease) will also determine. Where a lease has been determined by disclaimer, see also Chapter 20. In other cases, any inferior leases will continue to subsist and may affect the reversionary estate, in which case they will be noted against any registered reversionary title.

(4) Where a leasehold estate is registered with a possessory leasehold class of title, it will not be possible to determine that registered leasehold title unless the applicant also lodges Form UT1, or the title is otherwise capable of being upgraded to absolute leasehold title (see Chapter 22). This reflects the fact that such a lease may be subject to other unregistered interests which might prevent determination.

Fees

12–033 The application should be accompanied by a fee in accordance with the Fee Order.

Notices

12–034 The registrar will where appropriate serve notice of the application on any person appearing to be affected by it.

Methods of determination

12–035 The applicant will need to consider which method of determination applies to the lease which is being determined. The main aspects are as follows.

12–036 **(1) *Merger*** Merger occurs where a leasehold estate, together with the reversionary estate, come into the same ownership and are held in the same capacity, so that the lease is absorbed by the reversionary estate and thus determined. There must also be an intention to merge the estates.

As regards any benefiting easements affecting the leasehold estate, it needs to be considered whether the reversionary estate has the benefit of an equivalent easement where necessary and if not, whether the two estates should continue to be held separately and the lease not determined.

In this regard, the Court of Appeal in *Wall v Collins* [2007] EWCA Civ 444 held that an easement must be appurtenant to a dominant tenement, but not necessarily to a particular interest in that dominant tenement. In consequence, when a lease is extinguished on merger, the tenant may not automatically lose any benefiting easements granted for the benefit of the leasehold estate and those easements may continue to exist and to be exercisable by the occupier of the dominant tenement for the period for which they were granted.

12–037 **(2) *Surrender by deed*** When a tenant surrenders their lease to their immediate landlord, who accepts the surrender, their lease is absorbed by the reversionary estate and thus determined. A deed effecting a surrender of a leasehold estate must contain wording which clearly shows that the tenant is surrendering the lease. Also, the landlord must consent to the surrender.

The application must be accompanied by the original deed of surrender and, as it will normally be a land transaction, the appropriate SDLT evidence (see para.1–016). Evidence of the landlord's consent to the surrender (if they have not executed the deed) must also be lodged.

12–038 **(3) *Surrender by operation of law*** Sometimes a surrender of a lease does not take place by deed but is effected by operation of law, i.e. as a result of the actions of both of the parties. For example, where the tenant gives up possession of the premises to the landlord, who then grants a new lease of the premises to a third party with the tenant's consent.

The application must be accompanied by satisfactory evidence of the acts which imply surrender (r.161(1)). This will normally consist of a statutory declaration or statement of truth made by a suitable person with full knowledge of the facts, together with any other available evidence relating to the surrender, e.g. a receipt for money paid for the surrender. Confirmation must be given that no deed of surrender was entered into.

A surrender by operation of law is a land transaction for SDLT purposes and by virtue of s.128 of the Finance Act 2000 any document evidencing the surrender, including consents, statutory declarations, statements of truth or Land Registry application forms, will represent an instrument of surrender. The appropriate SDLT evidence should therefore be lodged (see para.1–016).

(4) *Disclaimer* When a person becomes bankrupt or a company becomes insolvent, either a trustee in bankruptcy or a liquidator respectively may, by giving the prescribed notice, disclaim certain onerous property, including leases. This has the effect of determining the leases (see also Chapter 20). **13–039**

The application must be accompanied by:

(a) Satisfactory evidence of either bankruptcy or liquidation (see Chapter 20); and
(b) an official copy of the notice of disclaimer; and either
    (i) a certificate by the trustee in bankruptcy or liquidator that they have power to make the disclaimer, have served the prescribed notices and are not aware of any application to the court for a vesting order having been made within a period of 14 days from the day on which the last copy notice of disclaimer was served; or
    (ii) a certified copy of any court order directing that the disclaimer should take effect.

(5) *Effluxion of time* A lease for a fixed term will automatically determine when the fixed term expires, unless it is prolonged by virtue of the provisions of either the Landlord and Tenant Act 1954 or the Local Government and Housing Act 1989. **12–040**

The application must therefore be accompanied by confirmation that neither of those Acts affect the lease or that it has determined in accordance with their provisions.

If the tenant has an option to renew the lease, satisfactory evidence that the option has not been, and cannot now be, exercised must also be lodged.

12–041 **(6) *Forfeiture*** A lease containing a proviso for re-entry or "forfeiture clause" may enable a landlord to forfeit the lease by taking court proceedings or by peaceable re-entry, either because the tenant has not paid the rent or has breached some other covenant(s) in the lease.

An interested person may apply to the court for relief from forfeiture. However, this is not in itself a valid ground for objection to an application based upon determination on forfeiture.

If the forfeiture is based on a court order, the application must be accompanied by:

(a) the claim form, indicating the reason for the forfeiture;

(b) a certified copy of the court order directing the forfeiture of the lease; and

(c) the sheriff's return, or a statutory declaration or statement of truth, proving the facts which are stated to amount to re-entry on a stated date.

If the forfeiture is based on peaceable re-entry, the application must be accompanied by evidence in the form of a statutory declaration or statement of truth by a suitable person with full knowledge of the facts, proving the facts which, it is claimed, amount to a lawful re-entry on a specified date.

If the forfeiture is for non-payment of rent, the statutory declaration or statement of truth must establish whether a formal demand was required and, if so, whether it was made. Confirmation of the amount of rent arrears and that this was sufficient to trigger the proviso for re-entry must also be provided.

If the forfeiture is for if the forfeiture is for breach of covenant other than non-payment of rent, the statutory declaration or statement of truth must establish:

(a) That the landlord served the requisite notice under s.146(1) of the Law of Property Act 1925 upon the tenant on a stated date. If the leasehold estate is not registered, satisfactory evidence that the person served was the tenant must be lodged.

(b) In the case of a breach of a repairing covenant, that the service of the notice was known to the tenant, or to a sub-tenant where the tenant has only a nominal reversion, or to the person who last paid the rent due under the lease, either on their own behalf or as agent for the tenant or sub-tenant, and that a time reasonably sufficient to enable the repairs to be executed had subsequently elapsed—see s.18(2) of the Landlord and Tenant Act 1927.

(c) In the case of a breach of a repairing covenant contained in a lease of which three years or more remained unexpired at the date of the notice served under s.146 of the Law of Property Act 1925, that the notice contained the required statement that the tenant was entitled to serve a counter-notice claiming the benefit of the Leasehold Property (Repairs) Act 1938 and did not do so.

(d) That the tenant failed to comply with the notice served under s.146 of the Law of Property Act 1925.

If the demised premises are let as a dwelling, the only lawful method of enforcing a right of re-entry while anyone is lawfully residing there is by obtaining a court order (s.2 of the Protection from Eviction Act 1977). Therefore, if the demised premises comprise a dwelling, the statutory declaration or statement of truth must establish either that no one was residing in the premises or any part of them, or if someone was, that they were not lawfully residing there.

If the lease is a residential lease, the statutory declaration or statement of truth must establish that the following provisions either do not apply or have been complied with:

(i) Section 81 of the Housing Act 1996, which limits the landlord's right to forfeit a residential lease where there are arrears of service charges which are disputed by the tenant.

(ii) Section 166 of the Commonhold and Leasehold Reform Act 2002, which provides that a tenant under a long lease of a dwelling is not liable to make a payment of rent under the lease unless the landlord has given the tenant a notice relating to the payment and the date on which they are liable to make the payment is specified in the notice.

(iii) Section 167 of the Commonhold and Leasehold Reform Act 2002, which provides that a landlord under a long lease of a dwelling may not forfeit the lease for failure by the tenant to pay rent, service charge or administration charges unless the amount exceeds a prescribed sum (currently £350), or has been unpaid for a period in excess of a prescribed period (currently three years).

(iv) Section 168 of the Commonhold and Leasehold Reform Act 2002, which provides that a landlord under a long lease of a dwelling may not serve a notice under s.146 of the Law of Property Act 1925 for breach of covenant by the tenant unless the tenant has admitted the breach, or a period of 14 days has elapsed after a Leasehold

Valuation Tribunal or court has determined that the breach has occurred.

12–042 **(7) *Notice*** A lease for a fixed term may contain an option, usually called a "break clause", allowing either one or both parties to the lease to determine the lease before the expiry of the fixed term. The option is usually only exercisable by written notice.

The application must be accompanied by evidence of the determination of the lease by notice in accordance with the terms of the lease, such as a copy of the receipted notice, or a statutory declaration or statement of truth by the applicant, or a certificate by the applicant's conveyancer confirming the relevant facts.

12–043 **(8) *Frustration*** A lease may be determined under the doctrine of frustration, i.e. the occurrence of an unforeseen event that makes performance of the lease impracticable. Such cases will be rare and any application will be considered on its individual facts.

This situation should be distinguished from the determination of a lease by notice (see para.12–042) on the occurrence of an event (such as the damage of the premises by fire beyond so as to be beyond repair) referred to in a "frustration clause" in the lease.

Enlargement

12–044 A tenant who holds the residue of a long lease of land may, under certain conditions, "enlarge" it into a freehold. This is usually achieved by either the execution of a deed poll, or endorsement on one of the unregistered title deeds relating to an unregistered lease.

On enlargement, the land remains subject to the same trusts and covenants that affected the original lease.

To be capable of enlargement, the lease must satisfy all of the following requirements (s.153 of the Law of Property Act 1925):

(a) the unexpired residue of the term of the lease must have at least 200 years left to run;

(b) the original term must have been for at least 300 years;

(c) there must be no trust or right of redemption in favour of the freeholder or other reversioner;

(d) there must be no rent, or merely a peppercorn or other rent having no money value, or any rent must have ceased to be payable;

(e) there must be no right of re-entry for condition broken; and

(f) the lease must not be a sub-lease out of a lease which is itself incapable of enlargement.

A rent of no more than £1 a year, which has not been collected or paid for 20 years or more, is deemed to have ceased to be payable—evidence of this by way of statutory declaration or statement of truth should be lodged if this provision is relied on.

The application should be made in either:

(i) Form FR1 if the lease being enlarged is unregistered (whether or not there is an existing registered freehold title). No additional fee is payable on first registration, in respect of the enlargement itself.

(ii) Form AP1—if the lease being enlarged is substantively registered.

The application should be accompanied by the documentation effecting the enlargement (see above) and evidence as to non-payment of rent, if applicable.

The original lease or, if it is not available, full evidence of its contents must be lodged otherwise the registrar may only be in able to grant a qualified freehold class of title (see para.5–012), to reflect the possibility that the lease may not be capable of being enlarged.

Leasehold Reform Act 1967 ("the 1967 Act")

Background

The 1967 Act confers on a tenant of a house for the last two years under a long tenancy at a low rent the right to acquire either: **12–045**

(1) the freehold on enfranchisement; or

(2) an extended lease of the house and premises expiring 50 years after the date on which the existing term is due to expire (s.1 of the 1967 Act).

The low rent requirement in respect of the right to enfranchise (but not the right to an extended lease) has been abolished in relation to a long tenancy granted in England on or after September 7, 2009 unless arising from a written agreement for lease entered into prior to that date.

"House" does not include flats in a horizontally divided building and "premises" includes any garage, outhouse, garden, yard and appurtenances let with the house (s.2(1) to (3) of the 1967 Act).

"Long tenancy" means any tenancy originally granted for a term exceeding 21 years whether or not it is determinable by notice or re-entry (s.3 of the 1967 Act).

There are further conditions and exceptions that apply in particular circumstances.

A tenant who wishes to enfranchise or to have an extended lease may find out whether their landlord's or any superior landlord's title is registered by means of a search of the index map (see para.3–015) and, if it is, the tenant may apply for official copies of the registers and of documents referred to on the registers as described in Chapter 9.

Protecting the tenant's claim (s.5(5) of the 1967 Act)

12–046 The rights of a tenant arising from a notice under the 1967 Act do not take effect as an overriding interest under Schs 1 and 3 to the Act (see paras 5–018 and 10–028). However, when a tenant has given their landlord notice of their wish to enfranchise or to acquire an extended lease, they can protect their claim as if it were an estate contract by the entry of a notice in the register of the landlord's reversionary title (see paras 16–005 and 16–008).

Assignment of the rights under the 1967 Act of a tenant who has served notice of their wish to enfranchise or to acquire an extended lease

12–047 The assignment of such rights should not be included in a transfer of a registered leasehold estate but should instead be effected by a separate instrument "off the register".

No entry of such an assignment will be made in the register, but if the rights are already protected in the register by a unilateral notice, the assignee should apply in Form UN3 to be registered as the new beneficiary of the notice (see para.16–009).

Enfranchisement

12–048 The transfer or conveyance should include a statement confirming that it is made under the provisions of the 1967 Act; this will enable Land Registry to identify it as such and make relevant entries (see para.12–049).

The appropriate application should be made for registration of the transfer, if the title is already registered (see paras 10–005 and 11–008), or for the first registration of the title, if it is not (see paras 5–006 and 5–007). Any necessary request for merger should be included in the application (see para.12–036).

Where a deed of substituted security transferring a legal charge on a merged lease to the freehold estate is lodged, the charge will normally be registered against the tenant's freehold title. If the charge is only to be noted, Form AN1 (for an agreed notice) or Form UN1 (for a unilateral notice) should be lodged (see paras 16–005 and 16–008).

Rights and burdens under section 10 of the 1967 Act

Section 10(2) of the 1967 Act provides that the benefit and burden of certain rights that affect the leasehold interest shall automatically continue on enfranchisement, but without prejudice to any rights that may be expressly granted or reserved. **12–049**

The rights passing under s.10(2) take effect so far as the landlord is capable of granting them and consist of rights of support, rights of access of light and air and rights to the passage, use or maintenance of the usual common services, such as water, drainage, electricity etc.

If the registrar is aware that a conveyance or transfer has been made under the 1967 Act, appropriate entries will be made in the register as to the benefit and burden of rights passing under s.10(2). If the conveyance or transfer expressly excludes or restricts any of the benefitting rights, this will be reflected in the entry.

If the conveyance or transfer includes new easements or restrictive covenants under s.10(3) or (4) of the 1967 Act, entries will be made in the register in respect of these.

The applicant should ensure that where the reversionary title over which the easement is granted is registered in the name of the landlord but under a different title number to that of the house, application is also made against the burdened title (see para.12–008), or that where the title is unregistered satisfactory evidence of title is lodged.

In some instances rights originally granted or reserved affecting the leasehold interest will, by virtue of s.10 of the 1967 Act, now affect the freehold estate. If reference to the deed which granted or reserved those rights is required to be made in the register, this should be expressly requested and the original deed, or a certified copy or examined abstract of it, should be lodged.

Discharge of charges on the landlord's registered or unregistered reversionary title

12–050 The chargee may have expressly discharged the charge or released the land from it. If not, and the tenant claims that they have paid to the landlord's chargee enough money to discharge the house from the charge, a verified copy of the chargee's (appropriately worded) receipt must be lodged. Alternatively, if sufficient money to discharge or release the house from the charge has been paid into court by the tenant under s.13 of the 1967 Act, there must be lodged a verified copy of the affidavit the tenant will have made for that purpose, and a verified copy of the court's official receipt.

If there has been an express discharge or release, or if, on the receipt of the appropriate evidence of payment to the chargee or into court the registrar is satisfied that the tenant may be registered as the freehold proprietor free from the charge, no entry of it will appear in the register of the tenant's freehold title. In appropriate cases, the registrar may serve notice upon the chargee explaining the nature of the transaction and inviting them to consent. If in response to the notice the chargee provides arguable grounds for objection, the application cannot proceed until the objection is disposed of either by agreement or following reference to the Adjudicator (see Chapter 23).

In the case of a floating charge created by a landlord, a certificate by the solicitor, secretary or other responsible officer of the landlord company or of the debenture holder that the charge had not crystallised at the date of the conveyance or transfer on enfranchisement will be accepted as sufficient evidence for the registration of the tenant's freehold title free from the charge.

Rentcharge on the landlord's title

12–051 The house may be released or exonerated from a rentcharge by the rentcharge owner. Alternatively, sufficient money may be paid into court under s.11(4) of the 1967 Act, in which case evidence of such payment should be lodged in the form of a verified copy of the tenant's or landlord's affidavit and a verified copy of the court's receipt.

Extended lease

12–052 As an alternative to enfranchisement, a tenant may instead acquire an extended lease under s.14 of the 1967 Act. Where the tenant holds under a sub-lease, there are complicated provisions in Sch.1 to the 1967 Act to determine which landlord is to act as reversioner on behalf of all the landlords where there are sub-leases.

The lease should include a statement confirming that it is made under the provisions of the 1967 Act. An appropriate application to register the title to the extended lease should be made (see para.12–007) and include, when appropriate, an application to give effect in the register to the surrender of the tenant's existing lease, which is taken to have been surrendered by operation of law on the grant of the new extended lease (see para.12–038).

If the landlord's title is unregistered, an examined abstract or epitome of their title and a current Land Charges search (with any entries accounted for) should be obtained and lodged with the application, to facilitate the grant of an absolute leasehold title.

The consent of the landlord's mortgagee (and any other person interested in the mortgage) should be lodged where the existing lease:

(1) was granted on or after January 1, 1968;

(2) was made subsequent to the date of the landlord's mortgage; and

(3) would not have been binding on the persons interested in the mortgage (i.e. it was outside the mortgagor's leasing powers and they did not concur in it).

Where any necessary consent is not lodged, a protective entry will be made in the property register of the new title (see para.5–012).

When the applicant's title to their existing lease is unregistered, an application for first registration of the extended lease should be accompanied by satisfactory evidence of the applicant's title to the existing lease. This is necessary so that appropriate entries can be made in the register of the applicant's title to the extended lease as to any rights of a mortgagee of the existing lease.

If the extended lease incorporates the terms of an unregistered existing lease, a certified copy or examined abstract of the existing lease should be lodged for filing in Land Registry.

If an interest is protected in the register of a registered existing lease but does not affect the new extended lease, application should be lodged as appropriate for the withdrawal or cancellation of the existing entry in respect of it. If the interest affects the extended lease, an application to protect it by means of a suitable entry in the register of the new title should accompany the application to register the extended lease (see Chapter 16).

A fee in accordance with the Fee Order is payable.

The normal considerations governing the grant of absolute or good leasehold class of title (see para.5–012) apply.

Where the extended lease is being granted under the 1967 Act rather than the 1993 Act (see para.12–058), a mortgage secured on the existing lease does not transfer automatically to the extended lease and should, therefore, either be discharged and replaced, or transferred to the extended lease by using a deed of substituted security.

Where the existing lease is registered, any chargees of the applicant's existing lease should be contacted prior to completion of the extended lease and the necessary arrangements made. If the mortgage is discharged then the appropriate form of discharge should be lodged with the application for registration (see para.14–019). If a deed of substituted security is used, the deed should be lodged. Any new mortgage (with a certified copy, if the applicant wishes the original to be returned—r.203) should be lodged with the application for registration.

Where the existing lease is unregistered, if the mortgage is discharged then the discharged mortgage and evidence of discharge should be lodged with the application for registration. If a deed of substituted security is used, the mortgage and the deed should be lodged. Any new mortgage (with a certified copy, if the applicant wishes the original to be returned—r.203) should be lodged with the application for registration.

If the mortgagee's cooperation cannot be secured, the registrar will endeavour to serve notice on them, and any other person appearing to be interested in the mortgage, giving relevant details of the applicant and the nature of the application.

If there is no response to the notice, the application will be completed and a protective entry will be made to the effect that the extended lease is subject to such rights as may be subsisting in favour of the persons interested in a charge of the existing lease. The entry will not be a registration of the charge, but will take effect as a notice which will protect the priority of the charge in the register.

If, in response to the notice, the mortgagee lodges the original mortgage, it will either be registered or a notice entered in respect of it, as appropriate.

Landlord and Tenant Act 1987 ("the 1987 Act")

Background

12–053 The 1987 Act gives certain rights to tenants of flats as against their landlord that continue to exist in addition to the provisions of the 1993 Act (see para.12–058). These are set out below.

Tenant's right of first refusal to purchase the reversion

A landlord of a building containing flats must not dispose or contract to dispose of an interest in those premises unless they have served a notice of their intention on the tenants giving them collectively a right of first refusal (ss.1(1), 4A and 5(1) of the 1987 Act). The 1987 Act contains detailed definitions and prescribed procedures in this regard. **12–054**

As any offer and any acceptance are deemed to be "subject to contract", there is at that stage no interest capable of being protected in the register. However, once a contract has been entered into, the tenants can protect their interest by applying for entry of a notice in the landlord's title (see paras 16–005 and 16–008).

Where a landlord has disposed of an interest in the premises in contravention of the tenants' right of first refusal, the tenants have additional rights such as, where applicable, the right to take the benefit of the contract or to compel the purchaser to sell to them. The notice by which the right is exercised does not itself give an interest that can be protected in the register, but when a binding contract has been entered into in pursuance of the tenant's rights, their interest may, in the case of registered land, be protected by entry of a notice in the landlord's title (see paras 16–005 and 16–008).

Appointment of manager

A tenant of a building containing flats may apply to a leasehold valuation tribunal for the appointment of a manager if the landlord has failed to manage the premises in accordance with their obligations or the service charges are unreasonable (s.21 of the 1987 Act). It may, in the case of registered land, be possible to protect such an application as a pending land action by entry of a notice in the landlord's title (see para.16–037). **12–055**

The leasehold valuation tribunal may then, if it thinks fit, make an order appointing a manager to carry out functions in connection with management or functions of a receiver. Any such order may, in the case of registered land, be protected by entry of a suitable non-standard restriction in the register of the landlord's title (see para.16–023).

Compulsory acquisition by tenants of their landlord's interest

Where a landlord of a building containing flats is in breach of their obligations to their tenants with regard to the maintenance or management of the premises, the court may, on the application of the tenants, make an acquisition order (ss.25, 28 and 29 of the 1987 Act). If granted, the order will provide for the **12–056** tenant's nominee to be entitled to acquire the landlord's interest in the premises on such terms as may be agreed, or, failing agreement, on such terms as a leasehold valuation tribunal may determine (ss.30 and 31 of the 1987 Act).

An application for an acquisition order may be protected, in the case of registered land, as a pending land action by entry of a notice in the landlord's title (see para.16–037).

When an acquisition order has been made, it may, in the case of registered land, be protected by the entry of a notice in the landlord's title (see paras 16–005 and 16–008).

A person who has applied for an acquisition order under s.28 of the 1987 Act may apply for entry of a restriction in Form N and a person who has obtained an acquisition order may apply for entry of a restriction in Form L or N (r.93(o) and (n)—see para.16–023).

Following the acquisition, the appropriate application for registration should be made, i.e. in Form FR1 for first registration of title (see paras 5–006 and 5–007) or in Form AP1 for registration of the nominee as proprietor of an existing registered title (see paras 10–005 and 11–008).

Where the landlord cannot be found, s.33 of the 1987 Act enables the court to order the vesting of the landlord's interest in a nominated person and for the payment of the purchase money into court. Following the vesting, the appropriate application to register the vesting may be made as above, accompanied by the court order and court receipt for the purchase money.

Variation of leases

12–057 Any party to a long lease of a flat may apply to a leasehold valuation tribunal for an order varying the lease on the grounds that the lease fails to make satisfactory provision with respect to repair, maintenance, the provision of services, insurance, the recovery of expenses or the computation of service charges (s.35 of the 1987 Act).

The leasehold valuation tribunal may then make an appropriate order that will be binding on the parties to the lease and any other persons concerned (ss.38 and 39 of the 1987 Act). The entry of the variation order in the register of the titles affected will be dealt with in the same way as a deed of variation (see para.12–024).

Leasehold Reform, Housing and Urban Development Act 1993 ("the 1993 Act")

Background

12–058 The 1993 Act gives qualifying tenants of flats either:

(1) a collective right to buy the freehold of the block ("collective enfranchisement") if the flats are contained in premises that satisfy certain conditions; or

(2) an individual right to a new lease expiring 90 years after the termination of an existing lease.

Exercise of right to collective enfranchisement

The right of collective enfranchisement conferred by the 1993 Act enables qualifying tenants of flats the right to have the freehold of the premises in which the flats are contained acquired on their behalf by an "RTE" company of which they are the members, whether or not the landlord wishes to sell. A person is a "qualifying tenant" if they are a tenant under a long lease for a term exceeding 21 years whether or not it is determinable by notice or re-entry. **12–059**

The initial notice served by the tenants on the landlord is not an overriding interest under Schs 1 and 3 to the Act (see paras 5–018 and 10–028), but may be protected in the register of the landlord's title as if it were an estate contract by the entry of a notice (s.97(1) of the 1993 Act—see paras 16–005 and 16–008).

The transfer or conveyance will be in favour of the RTE company. The 1993 Act does not contain any provision for the grant or reservation of statutory easements, unlike the 1967 Act (see para.12–049), and so the parties must include any necessary easements in the conveyance or transfer.

It is a requirement that the conveyance or transfer under the 1993 Act must contain a statement in the following terms:

> "This conveyance [or transfer] is executed for the purposes of Chapter I of Part I of the Leasehold Reform, Housing and Urban Development Act 1993."

Once completed, the transfer or conveyance should be the subject of the appropriate application in Form FR1 (see paras 5–006 and 5–007) or Form AP1 (see paras 10–005 and 11–008 to 11–013), depending upon whether the title to the freehold estate is currently unregistered or registered.

Unless the landlord and the RTE company agree otherwise, the conveyance or transfer discharges the land from any mortgage or charge and it is the duty of the RTE company to apply the consideration payable, in the first instance, in or towards the redemption of any such mortgage or charge and, if there are more than one, then according to their priorities (s.35 and para.2 of Sch.8 to the 1993 Act).

Where the freehold estate is to be discharged from a mortgage or charge and any difficulty arises in ascertaining how much is payable or in making a payment, e.g. because the chargee cannot be found or refuses to accept payment, the RTE company may pay into court an amount calculated in accordance with the provisions of para.4 of Sch.8 to the 1993 Act.

The application for registration must be accompanied by the normal evidence of discharge (e.g. in Form DS1—see para.14–019) or by a statutory declaration or statement of truth establishing that the RTE company has applied a sufficient part of the purchase money in discharge of the mortgage or charge direct to the chargee or into court. The registrar may serve notice of the application upon the chargee, if he considers it necessary.

If such evidence is not lodged the registrar will assume that the mortgage or charge is subsisting.

The transfer or conveyance will normally take effect subject to any existing rentcharge affecting the freehold estate. The landlord may either procure a release of the rentcharge from the rentcharge owner, or require, subject to the reasonable consent of the tenant, that the land be exonerated or the rentcharge apportioned.

The 1993 Act gives power to the court to make vesting orders where the terms of acquisition are in dispute, or there is a failure to enter into a contract, or the landlord fails to give a counter-notice or cannot be found or identified.

Application may be made for such an order, or for an application to the court for such an order, to be protected by entry of a notice (see paras 16–005 and 16–008). Also, a person who has applied for such an order may apply for entry of a restriction in Form N and a person who has obtained such an order may apply for a restriction in Form L or N (r.93(q) and (o)—see para.16–023).

Grant of a new lease

12–060 A qualifying tenant of a flat for the last two years is entitled, on payment of a premium, to take a new lease for a term expiring 90 years after the end of the existing lease at a peppercorn rent. If the immediate landlord does not have sufficient interest to grant such a lease, the new lease must be granted by the nearest landlord whose lease is sufficient.

A notice served by a tenant exercising their rights is not an overriding interest under Schs 1 and 3 to the Act, but it may be protected as if it were an estate contract by entry of a notice (s.97(1) of the 1993 Act and see paras 16–005 and 16–008). The benefit of service of notice is assignable. If the benefit assigned is already protected by an agreed notice, no further action by the assignee is necessary to protect their position. If the benefit assigned is already protected by a unilateral notice, the assignee should apply to be registered as beneficiary of the notice in Form UN3 (see para.16–009).

The new lease, which takes effect in substitution for the existing lease, is to be on the same terms as the existing lease but with such modifications as may be required or appropriate. The lease must (r.196) contain a statement in the following terms:

> "This lease is granted under section 56 of the Leasehold Reform, Housing and Urban Development Act 1993."

Where the lease is a prescribed clauses lease (see para.12–004) this statement must be referred to in clause LR5.1.

On completion of the new lease, application for registration of the lease should be made in Form FR1 (see paras 5–006 and 5–007) or Form AP1 (see paras 10–005 and 11–008), depending upon whether the reversionary title is unregistered or registered. If necessary, application should also be made to give effect to the deemed surrender of the existing lease, if registered, which will have taken place by operation of law (see para.12–038).

The consent of the landlord's mortgagee (and any other person interested in the mortgage) should be lodged where the existing lease:

(1) was granted on or after November 1, 1993;

(2) was made subsequent to the date of the landlord's mortgage; and

(3) would not have been binding on the persons interested in the mortgage (ie it was outside the mortgagor's leasing powers and they did not concur in it).

Where any necessary consent is not lodged, a protective entry will be made in the property register of the new title (see para.5–012).

If the existing lease is subject to a mortgage or charge immediately before surrender, on the grant of a new lease the mortgage or charge will attach to the new lease (s.58(4) of the 1993 Act). The application for registration should therefore include an application in respect of the registration of an existing mortgage or charge against the title of the new lease.

If the charge is to be protected by entry of a notice only, application should be made in either Form AN1 or Form UN1 (see paras 16–005 and 16–008), as appropriate. The registrar will serve notice on a chargee before closing the existing lease title, if registered.

Any other entries in the register of the existing leasehold title, if registered, must be considered and the appropriate steps taken.

The court has power to make vesting orders where the terms of acquisition are in dispute or there is failure to enter into a lease, or where the landlord fails to give a counter-notice or cannot be found or identified. See para.12–059 as to the protection of such an order and an application for such an order.

Estate Management Scheme under the 1967 Act

12–061 In certain circumstances on enfranchisement (see para.12–045), s.19 of the 1967 Act provides for the retention of management powers by the landlord for the general benefit of the neighbourhood, exercised by means of a scheme authorised by the Secretary of State and approved by the High Court. To be effective, such a scheme must be registered as a local land charge. Rights under local land charges, unless and until registered or protected in the register of title, take effect as overriding interests under Schs 1 and 3 to the Act (see paras 5–018 and 10–028).

Notice of such a scheme will not therefore normally be entered in a registered title and in addition, given the nature of the scheme, entry of a notice would not be appropriate. An exception to this would be where a scheme imposes a statutory charge, in which case this may be the subject of a notice in the register, although such a charge would have to be registered before it could be realised (s.55).

Right to manage ("RTM") companies

12–062 Part 2 of Chapter 1 of the Commonhold and Leasehold Reform Act 2002 came into force on September 30, 2003 and makes provision for the management functions of the landlord (and certain third parties) to be exercisable by an RTM company in place of the landlord. An RTM company is a special company limited by guarantee, the membership of which is restricted to qualifying tenants (generally a tenant under a long lease).

Land Registry takes the view that applications to protect an RTM company by way of entry of an agreed notice or unilateral notice (in the case of a registered estate), or registration of a caution against first registration (in the case of an unregistered estate) under the Act are not appropriate, because the RTM is not an adverse right affecting the landlord's title.

Rule 79A does, however, now allow for application to be made in Form AP1 for an entry to be made in the proprietorship register to record the acquisition of the RTM by an RTM company. Such an application must be accompanied by evidence to satisfy the registrar that:

(1) the applicant is an RTM company;

(2) the right to manage is in relation to the premises comprised in the registered estate;

(3) the registered proprietor of the registered estate is the landlord under a lease of the whole or part of the registered estate; and

(4) the right to manage the premises has been acquired, and remains exercisable, by the RTM company.

Such evidence may be provided by way of a conveyancer's certificate. If the registrar is so satisfied, he must make the appropriate entry in the proprietorship register.

The entry does not guarantee that the RTM has been acquired or that, if acquired, it remains exercisable, but it does highlight to those proposing to deal with the landlord's title that there is a RTM company which claims to have acquired the RTM in respect of the premises concerned.

Practical points

- Ensure that a lease is in the form of a prescribed clauses lease where required and that all the relevant clauses are completed as necessary,
- Ensure a lease which is a registrable disposition is completed by registration in order to take effect at law,
- Bear in mind the effect of a variation of a lease which extends the term or the extent demised i.e. that this may take effect as a deemed surrender and re-grant,
- Ensure that all relevant title numbers are inserted in clause LR2.2 of a prescribed clauses lease or in panel 2 of Form AP1, where necessary,
- Ensure the relevant evidence is lodged in support of an application for determination of a lease,
- Ensure the relevant statements are included in a lease or transfer under the 1967 Act or 1993 Act,
- Ensure that rights under the 1967 Act or the 1993 Act are protected by entry of a notice and/or restriction where appropriate and any necessary action taken in respect of any existing charges.

Chapter 13

Commonhold

What is commonhold?

Commonhold is a form of freehold ownership of properties which share common parts. It was introduced by Pt.1 of the Commonhold and Leasehold Reform Act 2002 which came into force on September 27, 2004. Until it was introduced such properties were normally held as leasehold because positive covenants to maintain common parts were enforceable under a lease, but not where the land was owned freehold. **13–001**

Commonhold must be registered at Land Registry in accordance with the Commonhold (Land Registration) Rules 2004 and can only be created out of a freehold estate in land registered with absolute title. It must consist of a minimum of two residential, commercial or industrial units which share common parts. It cannot be:

(1) a flying freehold;

(2) agricultural land; or

(3) a title which could in certain circumstances revert to someone other than the registered proprietor.

Unit-holders in a commonhold development own the freehold of their own unit and are members of a commonhold association, which owns and manages the common parts.

A commonhold unit is each property in the commonhold, as defined in the commonhold community statement (see para.13–003). It may be a flat and a garage or a flat may be defined as one unit and a garage as another. Common parts are all parts of the commonhold which are not a unit.

A commonhold can be created either where there are no unit-holders and a new development is planned or where freeholders or leaseholders agree to convert an existing development into a commonhold.

An application to register commonhold land can be made by two or more persons who are the registered proprietors of different registered titles, if all the land is included in a single commonhold community statement and an individual unit does not straddle more than one title.

If the title is not yet registered, an application for first registration can be accompanied by an application to register the commonhold.

The commonhold association

13–002 A commonhold association is a private company limited by guarantee incorporated under the Companies Act 1985 or the Companies Act 2006. The members of the company are the unit holders with each unit being represented by one member.

The two documents which govern a commonhold are the memorandum and articles of association (or, as from October 1, 2009, the articles of association) of the commonhold association and the commonhold community statement. The form and contents of those two documents is prescribed by the Commonhold Regulations 2004.

The memorandum and articles (or articles) define the powers of the association and contain the rules, e.g. as to voting rights and meetings, under which it operates.

Neither document can be designated as an exempt information document (r.3(3)(c) of the Commonhold (Land Registration) Rules 2004—see para.9–013).

The commonhold community statement

13–003 The commonhold community statement:

(1) defines the extent of the commonhold and the extent of the units;

(2) sets out the framework for the commonhold including the regulations for the use and maintenance of the units and the rights and duties of the association and the unit holders; and

(3) describes how management decisions will be taken.

The plan to the commonhold community statement

The commonhold community statement will define the extent of the commonhold and the extent of each unit in the commonhold by reference to a plan. **13–004**

To meet the technical requirements and specifications required by Land Registry the plan must:

(1) be on paper no larger than A0 size;

(2) clearly show the scale and orientation; and

(3) be drawn to the scale quoted.

The preferred scale is 1/500, although 1/1250 may be accepted if details of the layout including individual plot boundaries are clear.

Plans which bear a statement of disclaimer intended to comply with the Property Misdescriptions Act 1991 are not acceptable, nor are plans marked "For identification only" or with a similar phrase.

The plan must show:

(a) the boundaries of the commonhold land in relation to the boundaries of the freeholder's registered title and the boundaries of the commonhold units in relation to the boundaries of the commonhold land;

(b) the extents of the commonhold units using a colour and number reference (if two or more floors of a block of units are co-extensive and the layout and extents of the units are identical on each floor, a plan of one floor showing the number and floor level for each unit will be acceptable);

(c) the extent of the commonhold land using a colour reference distinct from the colour used to define the commonhold units; and

(d) any access drives and pathways which form unit boundaries.

Where more than one plan is used it must be made clear which define the extents of the commonhold and units and which are for another purpose.

Land Registry will approve the plan in advance if requested to do so. The whole of the commonhold community statement must be lodged although only the plan will be approved. There is currently no fee for this service.

Applying to register a commonhold

13–005 An application to register a freehold estate in commonhold land must be made in Form CM1. Application can either be for registration without unit-holders, when it is a new development, or with unit-holders when an existing leasehold or freehold development is being converted to commonhold.

The applicant must lodge the following documents with the Form CM1:

(1) certified copies of the community association's current certificate of incorporation and memorandum and articles (or articles) of association;

(2) two certified copies of the commonhold community statement;

(3) consent to registration in Form CON1 from interest holders listed in para.13–006 or, in appropriate circumstances, a court order dispensing with consent. A consent relating to an unregistered interest or to an interest the subject only of a notice, caution or restriction, must be accompanied by evidence (which can be a conveyancer's certificate) that the person whose consent has been lodged is the person entitled to that interest at the time the consent was given;

(4) a certificate given by the directors of the community association confirming that the memorandum and articles (or articles) comply with the Commonhold Regulations 2004, that the commonhold community statement satisfies the requirements of the Commonhold and Leasehold Reform Act 2002; that the land is not land which cannot become commonhold land (see para.13–001); and that the community association has not traded and has not incurred any liability which has not been discharged;

(5) a statement of truth given by the applicant listing all necessary consents that have been obtained or the court orders dispensing with consent; and confirming that a restriction in the register does not protect an interest in respect of which the consent of the holder is required, or if it does protect such an interest, that the appropriate consent has been obtained; that there are no other consents required by s.3 of the Commonhold and Leasehold Reform Act 2002 and the Commonhold Regulations 2004; that no consent has lapsed or been withdrawn; and that if a consent is subject to conditions, all conditions have been fully satisfied.

Where the application involves the extinguishment of a charge of part of a unit, that is the subject of an entry in the register of title, the statement of truth must:

(a) identify the charge to be extinguished;
(b) identify the registered title of the owner of the charge;
(c) give the name and address of the owner of the charge; and
(d) confirm that the consent of the owner of the charge has been obtained;

(6) when the application is for a registration with unit-holders:

(a) a statement in Form COV. This statement contains the request by the applicant that s.9 of the Commonhold and Leasehold Reform Act 2002 ("Registration with unit holders") should apply to the application; and a list of the commonhold units, giving the name and address of the proposed initial unit-holder or joint unit-holders for each unit;
(b) evidence of the discharge of all charges registered on the existing leasehold titles (which, if registered, will be closed). If the appropriate lender is taking a charge on the new commonhold unit, a new charge or a deed of substituted security must also be lodged.

Fees in accordance with the Fee Order are payable.

Consents to registration

Registration of land as commonhold land requires consent in Form CON1 from the following: **13–006**

(1) the registered proprietor of the freehold estate in the whole or part of the land;
(2) the registered proprietor of a leasehold estate in the whole or part of the land granted for a term of more than 21 years;
(3) the estate owner of any unregistered freehold estate in the whole or part of the land;
(4) the estate owner of any unregistered leasehold estate in the whole or part of the land granted for a term of more than 21 years;

(5) the proprietor of a charge protected by an entry in the register over the whole or part of the land;

(6) the owner of any mortgage, charge or lien for securing money or money's worth over the whole or part of any unregistered land;

(7) the holder of a lease granted for a term of not more than 21 years which will be extinguished under ss.7(3)(d) or 9(3)(f) of the Commonhold and Leasehold Reform Act 2002. Such consent is not required if the tenant is entitled to the grant of a new lease of the same premises, on the same terms, at the same rent, for a term equivalent to the unexpired term of the extinguished lease, which does not contain any provision which would create a term of more than 21 years, and the tenant has protected their entitlement to the grant of a new lease by registering a notice in the register of the freehold title or a Land Charge against the name of the estate owner of the freehold title.

A court may dispense with the need for consent if, after all reasonable efforts have been made to ascertain their identity, the person required to give consent cannot be identified; or if, after all reasonable efforts have been made to trace them, that person cannot be traced; or if that person has been sent a request for consent but, after all reasonable efforts to obtain a response, they have not responded.

Consent is deemed to have been given by the applicant for registration and anyone deriving title from the applicant.

Where a consent relates to an unregistered interest or is the subject only of a notice, caution or restriction in the register, evidence (which may be in the form of a conveyancer's certificate) must also be lodged to show that the person giving the consent is the person entitled to the interest at the time the consent was given.

Consent is binding on the successor in title to the person who gave it, but it will lapse if no application is made within twelve months of the date it was given, or such shorter period as is imposed by a condition. Consent cannot be withdrawn after the application has been submitted to Land Registry.

Registration

Registration without unit-holders

13–007 ***The transitional period*** This relates only to applications without unit-holders and is the period between when the freehold is registered as a freehold in commonhold land and when a person other than the applicant becomes entitled to be registered as the proprietor of the freehold estate in one or more, but not all, of the commonhold units.

During the transitional period, the common parts will be registered in one title and each individual unit will be registered in its own separate title. All titles (i.e. common parts and units) will be registered in the name of the applicant and will have the following entry in the property register:

> "The freehold estate in the land is registered as a freehold estate in commonhold land under Part 1 of the Commonhold and Leasehold Reform Act 2002."

The following entry will also be made in the property register but it will be cancelled without application at the end of the transitional period when the common parts title is vested in the community association:

> "The rights and duties conferred and imposed by the commonhold community statement will not come into force until the end of the transitional period referred to in section 8(1) of the Commonhold and Leasehold Reform Act 2002."

The common parts title will also have the following entry:

> "This title comprises the common parts of the commonhold defined by the commonhold community statement. The land in this title has the benefit of and is subject to the rights and duties conferred and imposed by the commonhold community statement.
> NOTE 1: Version [. . .] of the commonhold community statement is dated [. . .]
> NOTE 2: Version [. . .] of the [memorandum and] articles of association of the commonhold association is dated [. . .]
> NOTE 3: Copies filed."

The unit titles will have a similar entry except that they will refer to the copies of the commonhold community statement and memorandum and articles of association being filed under the common parts title.

The common parts title also has either of the following entries:

> "The commonhold units described in the commonhold community statement referred to below have been removed from this title."
>
> or
>
> "The commonhold units within the parts tinted green on the title plan and described in the commonhold community statement referred to below have been removed from this title."

The following restriction in Form CA is entered in the common parts title:

> "No charge by the proprietor of the registered estate is to be registered other than a legal mortgage which is accompanied by a certificate by a conveyancer or a director or secretary of the commonhold association that the creation of the mortgage was approved by a resolution complying with section 29(2) of the Commonhold and Leasehold Reform Act 2002."

The following restriction in Form CB is entered in the unit titles:

> "No disposition by the proprietor of the registered estate (other than a transfer or charge of the whole of the land in the title) is to be registered without a certificate by a conveyancer or a director or secretary of the commonhold association that the disposition is authorised by and made in accordance with the provisions of the Commonhold and Leasehold Reform Act 2002 or the regulations made under that Act."

All entries on the pre-commonhold title, e.g. charges, cautions, notices etc. are carried forward to both the common parts and unit titles unless evidence of their discharge, cancellation or withdrawal accompanies the application.

13–008 ***Commonhold land ceasing to be registered as commonhold during the transitional period*** A registered proprietor may decide, after registering land as commonhold without unit-holders, that they no longer want to create a commonhold development. During the transitional period (i.e. before any of the units have been sold), they may apply in Form

CM2 for the land to cease to be registered as commonhold. A fee in accordance with the Fee Order is payable. The consent provisions apply to such an application in the same way that they applied to the original application. Consents, from all those people whose interest subsists at the time of the application, must therefore be lodged in Form CON2 and the application must be accompanied by a statement of truth (as discussed in paras 13–005 and 13–006). When such an application is completed, the commonhold entries will be removed and the titles will revert to ordinary freehold but, unless the applicant requests amalgamation, the individual titles will be retained.

13–009

After the transitional period The transitional period ends when a person other than the applicant becomes entitled to be registered as the proprietor of one or more, but not all, of the commonhold units. Land Registry then registers the unit(s) which have been transferred in that person's name (removing the entry relating to the transitional period) and registers the common parts in the name of the community association. Entries relating to charges on the common parts and notice of any leases, which have been extinguished under the statutory provisions, will be cancelled.

All other units will remain registered in the original applicant's name until they are sold.

Registration with unit-holders

This involves an existing freehold and/or leasehold development **13–010** where the owners/tenants wish it to become a commonhold. When an application is lodged, Land Registry will register the common parts in the name of the community association and the units in the names of the unit-holders listed in the Form COV (see para.13–005). Entries will be made in common parts and unit titles as set out in para.13–007, although the entry relating to the transitional period will not be made. Entries relating to charges and noted leases on the common parts title will be cancelled as they will have been extinguished under the statutory provisions.

If it was a leasehold development, the existing leasehold titles under which the units were formerly registered will be closed. Evidence of the discharge of all charges on the leasehold titles must be lodged and if the mortgage lender is taking a charge on the new commonhold unit, a new charge or a deed of substituted security must be lodged.

Changes to the commonhold community statement and memorandum and articles (or articles) of the community association

13–011 A commonhold community statement may be altered to change the wording or to change the extent of the commonhold. The memorandum and articles (or articles) may also be altered. The amendment or alteration has no effect until the amended commonhold community statement or altered memorandum and articles (or articles) is registered.

An application must be made in Form CM3 accompanied by:

(1) a certified copy of the new version of the memorandum and articles (or articles) or two certified copies of the new version of the commonhold community statement;

(2) the consent of the unit-holder and their chargee (if any) if the extent of a unit has been changed or a court order dispensing with consent;

(3) the consent of the chargee of any unit title from which land has been added to the common parts title; and

(4) a certificate by the directors of the community association that the amended commonhold community statement satisfies the requirements of the Commonhold and Leasehold Reform Act 2002 or that the altered memorandum and articles (or articles) complies with the Commonhold Regulations 2004.

When an application is made to amend the commonhold community statement, the amendments must be summarised in panel 10 of Form CM3. Where the extent of the units and/or the common parts is amended, the amendments must be reflected on a new plan attached to the commonhold community statement which complies with the requirements set out in para.13–004. Even where the extent of the units and/or the common parts remain unchanged, a plan must be attached to the commonhold community statement because an amended commonhold community statement cannot refer to an earlier commonhold community statement.

If the amendment of the commonhold community statement removes land from a unit over which there is a charge, the charge will be extinguished in respect of the land which has been removed. If it adds land to a unit, the charge will be extended so as to relate to the land which is added. The Commonhold Regulations 2004 prescribes that notice must be served on Land Registry when this happens. This notice must be in Form COE and must be included with the application to register the amended commonhold community statement.

If land is added to a commonhold development, application must be made in Form CM4 accompanied by:

(a) consent in Form CON1 from those interest holders listed in para.13–006, or a court order dispensing with such consent;

(b) a statement of truth as referred to in para.13–005;

(c) an application in Form CM3 to register the commonhold community statement which has been amended to include the added land; and

(d) a certificate by the directors of the community association confirming that the land is not land which cannot be commonhold land (see para.13–001) and that the application was approved by a unanimous resolution.

Fees in accordance with the Fee Order are payable on these applications.

Surrender of a development right

A commonhold community statement may confer rights, called "development rights", on the developer of a commonhold which allow them to complete the work on the development, advertise the sale of the units, add land to or remove land from a development and/or appoint and remove directors of the community association. These rights can be surrendered by the developer. **13–012**

If the developer surrenders any such rights, they must notify Land Registry by lodging a notice in Form SR1, with an application in Form AP1 against the common parts title. Land Registry will then file a copy of the SR1 with the common parts title and enter a note in the property register of that title referring to the filed notice, and send a notice to the community association informing it that rights have been surrendered.

A fee in accordance with the Fee Order is payable.

Transfers of part of unit and common parts titles

If the community association transfers part of the common parts title or a unit-holder transfers part of a unit, two applications must be lodged together—in Form AP1 to register the transfer **13–013** of the land transferred and in Form CM3 to register the commonhold community statement which will have been amended to reflect the change in extent of the common parts and/or units. The only exception is when land which forms part of a unit is added to the common parts. This can be effected by transfer or solely by an amendment to the commonhold community statement, but an amended commonhold community statement is always required.

A fee in accordance with the Fee Order is payable on the registration of the transfer, but no fee is payable to register the amended commonhold community statement, as it accompanies the transfer.

Application to register a successor community association

13–014 Where a community association has been wound up by the court and a succession order has been made under s.51 of the Commonhold and Leasehold Reform Act 2002, an application to register the successor community association must be made in Form CM6 accompanied by:

(1) the succession order—this may make provision as to the treatment of any charge over all or part of the common parts or require the registrar to take action of a specified kind;

(2) the winding-up order; and

(3) a certified copy of the memorandum and articles (or articles) of association of the successor community association.

If any charge is to be discharged over the common parts, or any part of the common parts, the usual evidence of discharge must be lodged (see para.14–019).

No fee is currently payable to give effect to the court order.

Winding up or dissolution of a community association

Voluntary winding up

13–015 When a commonhold is voluntarily wound up under ss.43–49 of the Commonhold and Leasehold Reform Act 2002, a termination application in Form CM5 must be lodged accompanied by:

(1) a termination statement specifying the community association's proposals for the transfer of the land and how its assets will be distributed;

(2) evidence of the liquidator's appointment;

(3) notification that the liquidator is content with the termination statement, or a copy of the court order which determines the terms of the termination statement; and

(4) a fee in accordance with the Fee Order.

The community association will then be registered as the proprietor of all the commonhold units and the commonhold entries will be removed from all the titles. The liquidator will then dispose of all the titles in accordance with the terms of the termination statement.

Winding up by the court

If the court has made a winding-up order and has not made a succession order in respect of the community association, an application must be made to terminate the commonhold registration in Form CM5 accompanied by: **13–016**

(1) notification by the liquidator that the court has made a winding-up order and has not made a succession order;

(2) any directions giving the liquidator supplementary powers;

(3) any notice of the liquidator vacating his office after the final meeting of the commonhold association;

(4) any notice of completion of winding up;

(5) any application made to the Companies Registry that there are insufficient assets; or of an early dissolution or of completion of winding up;

(6) any other matter which in the liquidator's opinion is relevant to Land Registry; and

(7) a fee in accordance with the Fee Order.

Land Registry will remove the commonhold entries from the common parts and all the unit titles. The titles will then be ordinary freehold titles and unit-holders will not be able to rely on the rights contained in the commonhold community statement and will need to make arrangements with the liquidator, or whoever to whom the common parts are transferred, to ensure that new deeds are completed granting them any necessary rights etc.

If the court makes a winding-up order and a succession order, application should be made as discussed in para.13–014.

Termination by court order

13–017 Where a commonhold is registered in error the court may make an order under s.6(6)(c) of the Commonhold and Leasehold Reform Act 2002, or, where the commonhold community statement or the memorandum and articles (or articles) of association are incorrect, under s.40(3)(d) of that Act. The order may be that the land in relation to which a commonhold association exercises functions will cease to be commonhold land and the order may provide for alteration of the register.

When such an order is made, the court has the powers under s.55 of the Commonhold and Leasehold Reform Act 2002 which it would have if it were making a winding-up order in respect of the commonhold association. A person appointed as liquidator by virtue of such an order has the powers and duties of a liquidator following the making of a winding-up order by the court in respect of a commonhold association. But the order of the court may require the liquidator to exercise their functions in a particular way; impose additional rights or duties on the liquidator; and/or modify or remove a right or duty of the liquidator.

Following such an order an application must be made in Form AP1 accompanied by the court order to which Land Registry will then give effect. There is no fee currently payable.

If the court grants a declaration that a freehold estate should not have been registered as a freehold estate in commonhold land, then, under s.6(6)(g) of the Commonhold and Leasehold Reform Act 2002, the court may by order apply, disapply or modify a provision of Sch.8 to the Act.

Where a commonhold is registered in error, the register may not be altered by the registrar under Sch.4 (s.6(2) of the Commonhold and Leasehold Reform Act 2002).

Stamp duty land tax

13–018 Most transactions under the Commonhold and Leasehold Reform Act 2002 are land transactions and, where appropriate, the appropriate SDLT evidence should be lodged with an application (see para.1–016). However, certain transactions, such as the vesting of the common parts in the community association at the end of the transitional period, are not land transactions and such evidence will not then be required.

Practical points

- Check that the estate is capable of being the subject of a commonhold,
- Ensure all necessary documentation is lodged with an application for registration of a commonhold,
- Remember to take the necessary action in respect of subsequent changes to a commonhold.

Chapter 14

Charges

Charges subsisting at the time of first registration

In the case of an unregistered estate in land, the creation of a protected first legal mortgage may be a "trigger" for first registration (see para.5–003). **14–001**

Where a charge or mortgage subsists at the time of first registration, it must be disclosed in the application for first registration. The charge will be registered under r.22 (in the case of a protected first legal mortgage) or under r.34 (in the case of a subsequent legal charge).

Where a charge or mortgage has been created contemporaneously with the purchase of the property which has "triggered" first registration, under r.38 this will need to be completed by registration as a "dealing" taking place prior to completion of the first registration. In such a case, the charge should be lodged for registration with the application for first registration of the estate and it will be registered on completion of the first registration; under r.38(2) the registration of the charge has effect from the time of the making of the application for first registration.

If a charge accompanies an application for first registration in Form FR1, no separate application or fee for its registration will be necessary.

Charges of registered estates

Power to create

By virtue of s.23, a registered proprietor has "owner's powers" (see para.10–001) enabling them to deal with a registered estate or a registered charge in any way permitted by the general law, **14–002** save that a proprietor of a registered estate cannot create a mortgage by demise or sub-demise and a proprietor of a registered charge cannot create a legal sub-mortgage.

Section 23(1)(b) provides that a proprietor of a registered estate may charge the estate at law with the payment of money. Section 23(2)(b) provides that a registered chargee may charge at law with the payment of money indebtedness secured by the registered charge.

These owner's powers may be exercised by the registered proprietor or someone entitled to be registered as the proprietor.

Save for a limitation imposed by or under the Act, a chargee can assume that there are no limitations on the registered proprietor's powers unless there is an entry on the register, e.g. a restriction, reflecting any limitation.

Form

14–003 Schedule 1 to the Rules contains a prescribed form of charge of registered land, being Form CH1. Agreed terms, e.g. as to express covenants for the payment of secured moneys and interest, further advances and default events, can be inserted in the general provisions panel. By virtue of r.103, use of this form is not compulsory.

Many lenders have their own standard form of charge. Where Form CH1 is not used, care should be taken to ensure that the form used charges the estate in accordance with both the general law and s.23. It must also clearly describe the estate being charged by reference to the title number (if the charge is of the whole of the estate in a title) or, where part of the estate in a title is to be charged, a suitable plan signed by the chargor and enabling the part charged to be clearly identified on the title plan must be attached to it, unless the part charged can be clearly identified by reference to the title plan (r.213).

See para.1–023 as to the development of electronic charges in form "e-CSF".

Approval of standard forms of charge

14–004 Land Registry has a facility to approve standard forms of charge (not being in Form CH1) and major lenders are encouraged to apply for such approval. An approved form of charge is given a unique "MD reference", which assists in the processing of an application to register the charge. Re-approval is necessary if changes are made to the approved form. Application is made in Form ACD and no fee is currently payable.

Use of an approved form of charge avoids the need to lodge Form RX1 (see para.16–023) and/or Form CH2 (see para.14–010) where the charge (or any incorporated conditions) contains an application to enter a standard restriction and/or notice of an obligation to make further advances. The Commercial Arrangements Section, Land Registry, 32 Lincoln's Inn Fields, London, WC2A 3PH, DX No. 1098 London/Chancery Lane WC2 can advise on how to obtain approval.

Completion by registration

The grant of a legal charge over a registered estate, and the transfer of a registered charge or grant of a sub-charge, are registrable dispositions which must be completed by registration in accordance with s.27. Until this is done the disposition does not operate at law. In the case of the grant of a legal charge over a registered estate, application for registration should be made in Form AP1 together with: **14–005**

(1) the charge and a certified copy (if the applicant wishes the original to be returned (r.203));

(2) any certificate or consent necessary to comply with any restriction in the register of the chargor's title;

(3) Form CH2 in respect of an application to note an obligation to make further advances, if appropriate (see para.14–010), unless the charge is in Form CH1 or an approved form (see paras 14–003 and 14–004) and contains such an application;

(4) Form RX1 in respect of an application for a restriction, unless the charge is in Form CH1 or an approved form (see paras 14–003 and 14–004) and contains an application for a standard restriction;

(5) the fee payable in accordance with the Fee Order. No fee is currently payable if the charge is lodged for registration at the same time as (or before completion of) certain types of application where a fee has already been paid.

In addition, special evidence may be required in relation to particular kinds of chargors and chargees, e.g. charities (see Chapter 18).

If the Land Registry needs to see an incorporated document in order to complete the registration, a copy will be requested.

The need to deliver the application for the registration of the charge to the proper office within the priority period of any official search with priority (see para.9–023) must be borne in mind.

On completion of registration, if the charge is to secure further advances (see para.14–009), the register entries will show this; and if the chargee is under an obligation to make further advances and application is made (see para.14–010) this will also be shown.

If the application to register the charge is being made at the same time as another application affecting the title (e.g. to register a transfer), a single Form AP1 will cover both dealings. General points on completing Form AP1 are discussed in para.10–005. Particular points relating to charges by and to companies are discussed below.

On a charge of part of a registered estate, under r.72 the registrar must:

(a) make an entry in the chargor's title as to the removal of the estate comprised in that charge (where the charged part is registered under a separate title from the uncharged part), or a new edition of that title created; and

(b) where appropriate, make entries in the relevant individual registers in respect of any rights, restrictive covenants, provisions or other matters created by the charge which are capable of being so entered. However, the registrar need make no such entries where the relevant title numbers have not been given in panel 2 of the Form AP1, unless separate application is made in respect of them.

Charges by companies incorporated in the UK under the Companies Acts, limited liability partnerships and overseas companies

14–006 In the case of a UK company (i.e. one registered in England and Wales, Scotland or Northern Ireland under the Companies Acts or in Northern Ireland under the Companies (Northern Ireland) Order 1986) or a UK limited liability partnership (i.e. one incorporated in England and Wales or Scotland under the Limited Liability Partnerships Act 2000 or in Northern Ireland under the Limited Liability Partnerships Act (Northern Ireland) 2002), registration of the charge at the Companies Registry should precede an application for registration to Land Registry.

Prior to October 1, 2009, if a charge should have been registered at the Companies Registry under the Companies Act 1985 but there is no evidence that it has been so registered, a note will be made in the register that it is subject to s.395 of the Companies Act 1985 in the case of a company incorporated in England and Wales (or an equivalent entry in the case of a company incorporated in Scotland or in Northern Ireland). The position is similar in relation to limited liability partnerships incorporated in England and Wales, Scotland or Northern Ireland, by virtue of Regulations which applied the relevant provisions of the Companies Act 1985 to such partnerships.

As from October 1, 2009, r.111 provides that when making an application for registration of a charge created by a UK company or a UK limited liability partnership, the applicant must produce to the registrar the appropriate certificate that the charge has been registered at the Companies Registry. If the certificate is not produced, the registrar must enter a note in the register stating that no evidence of registration of the charge in accordance with s.860 or s.878 of the Companies Act 2006 (as appropriate) has been lodged.

As from October 1, 2009, r.111A provides that an application for registration of a charge created by an overseas company (i.e. one incorporated outside the UK), must be accompanied by evidence to satisfy the registrar that the charge has been registered in the Companies Registry under Pt.3 of the Overseas Companies (Execution of Documents and Registration of Charges) Regulations 2009, or the charge must include a statement that the charge, when created, did not require to be so registered. In default of this, the registrar must enter a note in the register to the effect that no evidence has been lodged either that the charge has been so registered or that such registration was not required.

It is important to bear in mind that registration of a charge of registered land at the Companies Registry is not sufficient protection. It should also be completed by registration in accordance with s.27, if it is to take effect at law and be protected in the register.

A fixed legal charge or mortgage of registered land in a debenture (see para.14–025) can be registered as a registered charge. If the original debenture and a certified copy are lodged, the copy will be filed and the original deed will be returned.

A fixed equitable charge or floating charge in a debenture may be capable of protection by entry of a notice in the register (see para.14–025).

Charges to companies incorporated in the UK under the Companies Acts, limited liability partnerships and overseas companies

If a UK company or a UK limited liability partnership (see para.14–006), is to be registered as the proprietor of a charge no evidence of its incorporation, objects and powers need generally **14–007** be provided. However, its registration number should always be provided.

In the case of an overseas company or limited liability partnership, i.e. one incorporated outside the UK, evidence of its power to lend money on mortgage must be lodged (r.183—see para.11–015).

Priorities

14–008 Section 48 provides that registered charges upon the same registered estate, or upon the same registered charge, rank as between themselves in the order shown in the register. Rule 101 states that, except as shown by an entry in the individual register to the contrary, the order in which registered charges are entered in an individual register shows the order in which the registered charges rank as between themselves. This means that where the identifying entry in respect of a registered charge ("the prior charge") appears in the charges register before that of another registered charge, the prior charge ranks in priority before the other charge. This general rule does not apply where there is an entry to the contrary in the register, e.g. where:

(1) priority has been altered under r.102 (see below); or
(2) a statutory charge has overriding priority under s.50 (see para.14–012).

Rule 102 provides a mechanism whereby the priority of registered charges can be altered. Application must be made in Form AP1 by or with the consent of the proprietor or person entitled to be registered as proprietor of any registered charge whose priority is adversely affected by the alteration. No such consent is required from a person who has executed the instrument which alters the priority of the charges. The registrar may accept a conveyancer's certificate that they hold any necessary consents. If the application is in order the registrar must make an entry in the register in such terms as he considers appropriate to give effect to the application.

Rule 116A provides that the registrar may, on application, make an entry in the register referring to an agreement which it is claimed relates to the priorities between a registered charge and a charge which is the subject of a notice in the register.

Further advances

14–009 Under s.49 there are four ways in which an existing registered chargee can make further advances and obtain priority for those further advances over later charges:

(1) If they make a further advance when they have not received from a subsequent chargee notice of the creation of the subsequent charge (s.49(1)). The onus is no longer on the registrar to notify an existing chargee of the creation of a further charge as it was under s.30 of the Land Registration Act 1925. There are no prescribed methods of giving such notice, but notice is treated as received at the time it ought to have been received in accordance with r.107. It is advisable for a subsequent chargee to use one of the methods referred to in r.107 in view of the certainty which this provides.

(2) If they make a further advance in pursuance of an obligation and at the time of creation of the subsequent charge the obligation was entered in the register (s.49(3)—see para.14–010).

(3) If they make a further advance where the parties to the prior charge have agreed to a maximum amount for which the charge is security and at the time of creation of the subsequent charge the agreement was entered in the register (s. 49(4)—see para.14–011).

(4) If they reach agreement with the subsequent chargee (s.49(6)).

Obligation to make further advances

Rule 108 provides that the proprietor of a registered charge or a **14–010**
person entitled to be registered as the proprietor of a registered charge who, under the terms of the charge is under an obligation to make further advances, may apply to the registrar for such an obligation to be entered in the register. Application must be made in Form CH2, unless the application is contained in panel 8 of Form CH1 or in an approved form of charge (see paras 14–003 and 14–004). The registrar will make an appropriate entry in the register.

When the proprietor of a registered charge is under an obligation to make a further advance which is noted in the register, a subsequent registered charge takes effect subject to any further advance made in pursuance of the obligation (s.49(3)—see para.14–009).

No fee will normally be payable because the application will usually accompany the application for registration of the charge. However, if, unusually, the application is lodged on its own a fee in accordance with the Fee Order is payable.

Agreement of maximum amount of security

14–011 Rule 109 provides that where the parties to a legal charge which is a registered charge or a registrable disposition have agreed a maximum amount for which the charge is security, the proprietor of the charge or person applying to be the proprietor can apply to the registrar for such agreement to be entered in the register. Application must be made in Form CH3 (even if the maximum amount is stated in the charge itself and the charge is in Form CH1 or an approved form—see paras 14–003 and 14–004). The registrar will make an appropriate entry in the register.

When there is such an entry in the register, priority is given to further advances, up to the sum agreed, over any charge created after the agreement is noted (s.49(4)—see para.14–009).

Overriding statutory charges

14–012 Section 50 provides that if the registrar enters a person in the register as the proprietor of a charge which is created by or under any enactment and has effect to postpone a charge which at the time of registration of the statutory charge is entered in the register or is the basis of an entry in the register, he must give notice of the creation of the statutory charge in accordance with the Rules. The relevant rules are r.105 which deals with applications to register statutory charges and r.106 which deals with service of notice.

An example of a statutory charge would be a charge imposed by a local authority for expenses incurred in repairing or improving a dwellinghouse.

Application for registration must be made in Form SC. The applicant must state the statute under which priority is claimed and the registered charges over which the statutory charge has priority. If the registrar is satisfied that the statutory charge has the priority claimed, he must make an entry showing that priority in the charges register. If the registrar is not so satisfied, but considers that the applicant has an arguable case, he may make an entry to the effect that the specified priority is claimed.

In either case the registrar will give notice of the entry to the registered proprietor of the registered charge (and to any person who appears to the registrar to be entitled to a charge protected by a notice, if that person's name and address for service is set out in the register) entered in the charges register at the time of registration of the statutory charge.

If the registrar has made an entry regarding a claim to such priority, the proprietor of either that statutory charge or of a charge which would, but for that entry, be shown in the register as ranking in priority or having equal priority to the statutory charge, may apply for the entry to be removed or replaced by one showing that the charge has the priority claimed. Notice of such an application will be served on the proprietors of the other affected charge(s). If a valid objection is received which cannot be disposed of by agreement, the matter must be referred to the Adjudicator (see Chapter 23).

Powers of the proprietor of the land

Subject to any express contrary intention, the proprietor of the land whilst in possession has the powers of leasing and accepting surrenders of leases given by ss.99 and 100 of the Law of Property Act 1925, as varied by the charge or any instrument varying it. All other dispositions by the proprietor of the land made without the concurrence of the proprietor of the charge take effect subject to the charge. The proprietor of the land can transfer their equity of redemption without the consent of the registered chargee provided that there is no contrary provision in the registered charge reflected by an entry in the register, e.g. a restriction. **14–013**

Powers of the proprietor of the charge

The effect of s.51 is that, on completion by registration, a charge created by means of a registrable disposition has effect, even if it would not otherwise do so, as a charge by deed by way of legal mortgage. This is the effect of the "fact of registration" in relation to a registered charge under the Act. **14–014**

Section 52 confers protection upon a disponee by providing that, subject to any entry in the register to the contrary, the proprietor of a registered charge has all the powers of disposition conferred by law on the owner of a legal mortgage (see para.10–001). If nothing to the contrary appears in the register, the chargee is therefore taken to have all the powers of disposition of a legal mortgagee under the Law of Property Act 1925, so the title of a disponee cannot be questioned. However, this does not prevent a claim being brought by the chargor against the chargee if they have acted unlawfully.

A registered proprietor of a sub-charge has the same powers as the sub-chargor (s.53).

A registered chargee will have a number of methods of enforcing their security, the most common being a transfer in the exercise of the chargee's power of sale. Such a transfer should be in Form TR2 (for a transfer of whole) or TP2 (for a transfer of part), which should be lodged for registration in the normal way (see Chapter 11), together with a fee in accordance with the Fee Order. By virtue of s.52, a purchaser can assume (unless the register indicates otherwise) that the chargee has a power of sale and that it has arisen and become exercisable.

A transfer by a chargee in exercise of their power of sale is subject to any charges which have priority over the chargee's charge (for which a discharge will therefore be required if it is to be removed from the register), but otherwise the purchaser will take free of any other legal or equitable charges, which will be cancelled automatically upon registration of the transfer.

A foreclosure order is obtained in the same way as if the land were unregistered. The order absolute, or a conveyancer's certificate that they hold it or an office copy of it, should be lodged with Form AP1 together with a fee in accordance with the Fee Order, so that the proprietor of the charge can be registered as proprietor of the land, subject to any prior charges (r.112).

Chargees' duty regarding proceeds of sale

14–015 Section 105 of the Law of Property Act 1925 provides that money received on a sale by a mortgagee is held by the mortgagee on trust to pay:

(1) all expenses incidental to the sale;
(2) the principal sum, interest and costs due under their own charge; and
(3) the surplus (if any) to any subsequent chargee and thereafter to the mortgagor.

Under s.54 (of the Act), a mortgagee in these circumstances is deemed to have notice of anything in the register immediately before the disposition on sale. This means that such a mortgagee will need to consult the register when discharging their duty under s.105 above.

Transfer of a charge

14–016 A transfer of a charge is required to be in Form TR4 (for a transfer of a charge or portfolio of charges) or AS2 (for an assent of a charge) as appropriate (r.116). An application for registration should be made in Form AP1. A fee in accordance with the Fee Order is payable.

Consolidation of a charge

A chargee who has a right of consolidation in relation to a registered charge may apply in Form CC for an entry in respect of that right to be made in the register (r.110). **14–017**

Variation of the terms of a registered charge

Rule 113 provides that an application to register an instrument varying the terms of a registered charge must be made by, or with the consent of: **14–018**

(1) the proprietor of the registered charge and the proprietor of the estate charged; and
(2) the proprietor, or a person entitled to be registered as proprietor, of every other registered charge of equal or inferior priority, and of every registered sub-charge of a registered charge, that is prejudicially affected by the variation.

No such consent is required from a person who has executed the instrument nor where the terms of their charge or sub-charge do not require that consent. The registrar may accept a conveyancer's certificate that they hold any necessary consents.

A variation that effects a reduction in the interest rate or capital debt under the charge is not likely to prejudicially affect a charge (or sub-charge of a charge) of equal or inferior priority; however an increase in the interest rate or capital debt or the creation of an obligation to make further advances, for example, is likely to do so.

Application for registration of the variation should be made in Form AP1 accompanied by the original instrument and a copy of it (if the applicant wishes the original to be returned (r.203)). A fee in accordance with the Fee Order is payable. If the registrar is satisfied that the proprietor of any other registered charge, and of any registered sub-charge of that registered charge, of equal or inferior priority to the varied charge that is prejudicially affected by the variation is bound by it, he shall make a note of the variation in the register.

If not so satisfied, the registrar may make an entry that an instrument has been entered into which is expressed to vary the terms of the registered charge.

Discharge of a registered charge

14–019 Rule 114 provides that (subject to r.115, which deals with electronic discharges and releases), a discharge of a registered charge must be in Form DS1 and a release of part of the registered title from a registered charge must be in Form DS3. Form DS1 or Form DS3 must be executed as a deed or authenticated in such other manner as the registrar may approve. However, under r.114(4), the registrar is entitled to accept and act upon any other proof of satisfaction of a charge which he may regard as sufficient.

Details of the appropriate methods of execution are referred to in Chapter 10.

Prior approval of the proposed method of execution of a significant number of discharges of registered charges may be obtained by approaching the Commercial Arrangements Section of Land Registry at the address referred to in para.14–004.

An application to register a discharge in Form DS1 must be made in Form AP1 or DS2. An application to register a release in Form DS3 must be made in Form AP1.

No fee is currently payable for the registration of a discharge of a registered charge.

If the discharged charge affects also an unregistered interest, e.g. a policy of insurance, or unregistered land, and the original deed will be required after registration of the discharge, a special request for its return should be made.

Rule 115 provides for discharges and releases of registered charges in electronic form. During the currency of a notice given by the registrar under Sch.2 to the Rules ("Notices publicising arrangements for electronic delivery of applications and other matters") and subject to and in accordance with the limitations contained in such a notice, notification of the discharge of a registered charge may be delivered to the registrar in electronic form. The release of part of a registered charge in electronic form is not currently permitted.

The electronic notification of discharge ("END") method involves an electronic element, although it must still be combined with a paper application to cancel the charge from the register. An increasing number of major lending institutions now use this system. The chargee (using the information provided by the chargor in Form END1) transmits an electronic message to Land Registry authorising discharge of the registered charge and no Form DS1 needs to be lodged. But the END does not in itself cause the charge to be cancelled and a formal application must still be made in Form AP1 or DS2 (or Form DS2E if supplied by the chargee), referring to the use of the END system.

The electronic discharge ("ED") method is now being used by a number of major lending institutions. An ED differs from an END in that it cancels the charge entries automatically and, in most cases, immediately. No DS1 and no formal paper application to discharge the charge is therefore required and the process is completely automated. The introduction of EDs is a step towards e-conveyancing (see para.1–023) and is intended to overcome some of the delays and other difficulties with the DS1 and END methods of discharge.

EDs have recently been supplemented by the introduction of e-DS1s, which is an electronic form of discharge submitted through the Land Registry portal. The e-DS1 acts as both the evidence of discharge and the application to cancel the charge from the register. Currently, the e-DS1 service is designed for corporate chargees and their agents only.

Discharges are also discussed in para.11–007. See also para.1–015 as to Land Registry's "early completion" policy in respect of the discharge of registered charges.

Generally, any restriction that specifically relates to the charge being discharged will be cancelled automatically when the charge is discharged. However, if a restriction in favour of the chargee does not specifically refer to the charge being discharged, a separate withdrawal of that restriction in Form RX4 must be lodged (see para.16–027) otherwise the restriction will remain in the register.

Public sector housing: discount charge

The discount charge

Sales under the right to buy provisions of the Housing Act 1985 (and earlier Acts) and voluntary sales under the 1985 Act and under the Housing Associations Act 1985 may allow or have allowed a discount. If so, the transfer, charge or lease (including a "shared ownership" lease) must contain a covenant to repay the discount in the event of a further disposal within the statutory period. The statutory period is normally either three or five years. **14–020**

"Disposal" includes a conveyance of the freehold or the assignment of the lease or the grant of a lease for more than 21 years. It also includes the grant of an option to transfer or grant a lease of the property but not a mortgage. Certain disposals, including some inter-family transfers, vestings under a will or on intestacy, disposals on compulsory purchase and disposals of part of the garden or other land occupied with the dwelling-house, are exempt from the repayment requirement.

The liability under the discount covenant is a charge on the property which takes effect as a charge by way of legal mortgage or a noted charge, depending on the type of discount covenant. The charge is protected by an entry in the charges register.

Priority

14–021 The discount charge has priority immediately after any legal charge in favour of the vendor to secure an outstanding part of the purchase price or after any legal charge in favour of the Housing Corporation, building societies, friendly societies, the major banks, the Post Office and certain insurance and loan companies to secure an advance for the purposes of the purchase.

The question of priority is disregarded in the register when the entry is made. In practice the entry of the discount charge is made in the charges register before the entry of any legal charge.

The discount charge is overreached on a sale by one of the corporations or companies specified above pursuant to their power of sale in a charge having priority to the discount charge.

Postponement

14–022 A formal deed is not necessary and a discount charge may be postponed to an advance or further advance made by one of the corporations or companies referred to above, by means of a written notice signed on behalf of the body having the benefit of the discount charge ("the discount chargee"). Any such postponement will be noted in the register on production of the signed notice of postponement.

Cancellation of entry of a discount charge

14–023 Where a disposal takes place **within** the statutory discount charge period and the discount is repaid, application should be made to cancel the entry of a discount charge. There is no prescribed form of discharge, but whatever evidence is lodged will need to satisfactorily show the discount chargee's concurrence with the application for the removal of the entry.

The evidence may be:

(1) a discharge e.g. in Form DS1 with suitable amendments; or

(2) Form CN1 accompanied by a release or a request in writing for cancellation.

The document should be executed by the discount chargee or its solicitor, except in the case of a local authority, where it may be signed by the chief executive or some other authorised official.

On an application **after** the statutory discount charge period has expired, the notice will be cancelled:

(a) only with the concurrence of the discount chargee as above, if there is evidence of a disposal within the statutory discount charge period which may have led to the discount becoming repayable; or

(b) in certain other cases without the discount chargee's concurrence but (in some instances) only after service of notice by the registrar on the discount chargee.

A discount charge in a shared ownership lease will never be cancelled automatically and evidence of discharge or release will always be required.

No fee is currently payable for cancellation of the notice of a discount charge.

Equitable charges

Where a charge takes effect in equity only, consideration should be given to the need to apply for the interest to be protected in the register by entry of a notice or a restriction (see Chapter 16). **14–024**

When an equitable charge protected by a notice has been repaid and cancellation of the notice is desired, an appropriate application must be made as follows:

(1) An application to cancel a notice (other than a unilateral notice) must be made in Form CN1, accompanied by sufficient evidence that the charge has been discharged as follows:

(a) Discharges of fixed equitable charges:

(i) a form DS1 or form DS3; or

(ii) an endorsed receipt on the instrument of charge; or

(iii) a letter from the chargee addressed to Land Registry, confirming that the charge has been satisfied and including where appropriate confirmation that there has been no assignment of the benefit of the charge. If an assignment has been made, the normal conveyancing evidence of devolution of title must be lodged.

(b) Discharges of floating charges:

(i) a copy of a declaration of satisfaction in Companies Registry Form 403A stamped as "registered"; or

(ii) a letter from the Companies Registry confirming that the charge has been satisfied; or

(iii) a letter from the chargee addressed to Land Registry confirming that the charge has been satisfied and including (where appropriate) confirmation that there has been no assignment of the benefit of the charge. If an assignment has been made, the normal conveyancing evidence of devolution of title must be lodged; or

(iv) where a subsequent transfer on sale of the estate has been lodged for registration, a certificate signed by the solicitor, licensed conveyancer or secretary of the chargor company that none of the events which would cause the charge to become fixed occurred before the date of the transfer.

(2) An application to remove or cancel the entry of a unilateral notice must be made in:

(i) Form UN2—where the application is for removal by the registered beneficiary under r.85 (see para.16–010); or

(ii) Form UN4—where the application is for cancellation by the registered proprietor under r.86 (see para.16–011).

Evidence of discharge is not required in either of these situations.

Debentures

14–025 These are used by companies to secure money raised by way of loan. A debenture may create a legal charge or an equitable charge; if equitable, it may be in the form of a fixed equitable charge or a floating charge.

A legal charge of registered land created by a debenture can be registered as a registered charge (see para.14–005).

If a company has created a debenture containing a fixed equitable or a floating charge on its assets, the existence of the charge must be disclosed when the company makes an application for the first registration of its title to an estate affected by the debenture. A certified copy of the debenture must be lodged with the application if the applicant wishes the original to be returned (r.203). A notice of the charge will be entered in the register, and the copy of the debenture will be filed (r.35).

Where a company that has created a debenture acquires a registered estate or a registered charge, or where a company that is already the proprietor of a registered estate or a registered charge creates a debenture, no entry will be made in the register to protect any charge created by the debenture (whether registered in the Companies Registry or not) in the absence of a specific application. Such an application, as regards any equitable charge created by the debenture, would normally be for the entry of a notice and/or a restriction (see Chapter 16).

A purchaser taking a transfer of registered land from a company registered with absolute title or good leasehold title is not concerned to search that company's file at the Companies Registry in respect of debentures. If any had been created before the company became registered proprietor of the estate, a notice should appear in the register and if the company had created a debenture and then acquired a registered estate, or had become proprietor of a registered estate and then created a debenture, a purchaser of the registered land would not be concerned with any charge created by the debenture unless it was registered or protected in the register (see paras 2–019 and 10–003).

Where a company is the proprietor of a registered estate and a notice of a fixed equitable charge by the company appears in the register, any application to register a lease by the company with absolute leasehold title must be accompanied by the consent of the chargee, otherwise a protective entry may be made in the register (see paras 5–012 and 12–006).

For a discharge of a fixed equitable charge, see para.14–024.

Where a notice of a floating charge appears in the register and a transfer on sale of the estate by the chargor company is being registered, a certificate by the conveyancer or secretary of the chargor company that none of the events which would cause the charge to become fixed has occurred will normally be accepted by the registrar as sufficient evidence for the cancellation of the notice. A certificate to like effect from the chargee or their conveyancer would also usually be accepted. Alternatively, a copy of a declaration of satisfaction from the Companies Registry stamped "registered" or a letter to Land Registry from the Companies Registry confirming the charge has been satisfied can be lodged instead.

Where a lease by the chargor company is being registered with absolute leasehold title the consent of the chargee under the floating charge will be required, otherwise a protective entry may be made in the register (see paras 5–012 and 12–006).

Unexpired notices of (intended) deposit

14–026 Since April 3, 1995, it has not been possible to apply for registration of a new notice of (intended) deposit. However there are some registered titles where such entries still subsist.

By virtue of the transitional provisions in the Act, any notice of (intended) deposit entered in the register before April 3, 1995, shall, until cancelled, continue to operate as a caution against dealings under s.54 of the 1925 Act, as it has since April 3, 1995. Part 16 of the Rules contains transitional provisions regarding cautions against dealings. Anyone who has entered such a notice will have to consider their position in the light of *United Bank of Kuwait Plc v Sahib* [1995] 2 W.L.R. 94 in which it was held that s.2 of the Law of Property Act 1925 prevents the creation of a lien by mere deposit of deeds and documents including a land or charge certificate. The effect of a caution against dealings is considered in Chapter 16 (see paras 16–013 to 16–017).

When there is to be a transfer of part of the registered estate in a title, or when a lease or rentcharge is to be granted out of a registered estate, a depositee usually provides a letter of consent which can then be sent to Land Registry together with the application to register the transfer or grant. When necessary, the consent must refer to a plan enabling the estate to which it relates to be identified on the title plan. A depositee's consent to a disposition may be by way of a letter or it may be endorsed by way of reply on a notice sent by the registrar to the depositee. Consent may be given by the depositee or their personal representative or by their conveyancer.

A transfer of whole should be accompanied by a withdrawal of the notice of (intended) deposit.

A notice of (intended) deposit can be "warned off" in the same way as a caution against dealings (see para.16–016).

Land Registry will accept the following evidence to cancel a notice of (intended) deposit entry:

(1) an application in Form 86 to the Land Registration Rules 1925, provided it is dated before October 13, 2003; or

(2) the duplicate part of the original application Forms 85A, 85B or 85C for entry of the notice (under the Land Registration Rules 1925), provided it is dated before October 13, 2003; or

(3) a withdrawal in Form WCT by the chargee in whose favour the notice was made; or

(4) an application in Form CCD by the proprietor of the registered estate or registered charge to which the notice relates, provided it is shown that the notice does not protect a valid interest, or that the interest has come to an end.

Consent to withdrawal may be given by the depositee or their personal representative or by their conveyancer. No fee is currently payable.

Practical points

- Consider the effect of any restriction in the register and how this may affect registration of a charge,
- Ensure that a charge which is a registrable disposition is completed by registration in order to take effect at law and that the application for registration is lodged within the priority period of any protecting official search with priority,
- Ensure that charges by UK companies and UK limited liability partnerships are registered in the Companies Registry as appropriate,
- Lodge the appropriate form of discharge or release in respect of an equitable charge where necessary,
- Bear in mind the effect of a notice of (intended) deposit where this appears in the register.

Chapter 15

Rentcharges

Introduction

A rentcharge is any sum of money charged on land payable annually or periodically, other than rent reserved by a lease or interest charged under a mortgage. Rentcharges are sometimes described in deeds as rent charges, chief rents, quit rents, fee farm rents or some other similar term. A rentcharge is usually perpetual, but can be granted for a term of years so that it is terminable. The land affected by a rentcharge can be either freehold or leasehold (in which case the rentcharge will always be terminable because the lease itself will eventually come to an end). 15–001

A rentcharge is usually created by way of a conveyance or transfer, where the vendor of the land reserves an annual rent, payable to them and their successors in title and charged upon the land sold. In modern times, most new rentcharges created are "estate rentcharges" (see para.15–002). A rentcharge is capable of being bought and sold or charged.

A rentcharge may be capable of being substantively registered with its own title and the burden of it may be the subject of a notice in the register of registered land affected by it (see below).

The Rentcharges Act 1977 ("the 1977 Act")

The 1977 Act made a number of important changes to the law relating to rentcharges. It prohibits the creation, and provides for the extinguishment, apportionment and redemption, of certain rentcharges and limits the scope for the creation of new rentcharges. Its main provisions, including ss.1, 2 and 3 referred to below, came into operation on August 22, 1977. 15–002

Section 1 of the 1977 Act defines a rentcharge as "any annual or other periodic sum charged on or issuing out of land except (i) rent reserved by a lease or tenancy or (ii) any sum payable by way of interest". "Land" for this purpose has the same meaning as in s.205(1) of the Law of Property Act 1925.

Section 2 of the 1977 Act prohibits the creation of any rentcharge, whether at law or in equity, after the coming into force of the section, except the following classes of rentcharge specified in s.2(3):

(1) a rentcharge created under statute in connection with improvements or other works on land;

(2) certain rentcharges created in a case where para.3 of Sch.1 to the Trusts of Land and Appointment of Trustees Act 1996 ("trust in case of family charge") applies to the land on which the rent is charged or would apply but for that land being settled land or subject to a trust of land;

(3) a rentcharge arising out of an order of a court; or

(4) an estate rentcharge.

Section 2(4) and (5) of the 1977 Act define an "estate rentcharge" as being a rentcharge of either:

(a) a nominal amount for the purpose of making covenants to be performed by the owner of the land affected by the rentcharge enforceable by the rent owner against the owner for the time being of the land; or

(b) a reasonable amount to meet, or contribute towards, the cost of the performance by the rent owner of covenants for the provision of services, the carrying out of maintenance or repairs, the effecting of insurance or the making of any payment by them for the benefit of the land affected by the rentcharge or for the benefit of that and other land.

On developing estates (see Chapter 21) where estate rentcharges are being created in transfers of individual plots, these may sometimes be in the form of two reserved rentcharges; one for a nominal amount to secure the performance of positive covenants and the other for a variable sum to secure the payment of a service charge.

Under the transitional provisions contained in s.17 of the 1977 Act rentcharges created pursuant to agreements entered into before July 22, 1977 are excluded from the prohibition of s.2.

Section 3 of the 1977 Act, referred to in more detail in para.15–011, provides (subject to exceptions) for the extinguishment of rentcharges after a period of 60 years. Sections 4 to 10 deal with apportionment and redemption (see para.15–010).

First registration of rentcharges

Rentcharges capable of being registered

A rentcharge is capable of registration under s.3 of the Act if it is a legal rentcharge, i.e. a rentcharge in possession issuing out of or charged on a legal freehold or leasehold estate in land and being either perpetual or for a term of years absolute of which more than seven years are unexpired and either: 15–003

(1) it is based on a deed dated before August 22, 1977; or

(2) it is based on a deed dated on or after August 22, 1977, and its creation is not prohibited by s.2 of the 1977 Act.

The fact that a rentcharge is subject to extinguishment in accordance with the provisions of the 1977 Act does not of itself prevent it from being "perpetual" or for a term of years "absolute" for the purposes of registration.

Rentcharges that subsist as equitable interests only, e.g. because of the mode of their creation or because they are informally apportioned parts of a legal or equitable rentcharge, cannot be registered but they can be protected in the register by means of a notice (see para.15–007).

Rentcharges created out of unregistered land

A legal rentcharge created out of unregistered land is not compulsorily registrable on creation nor does it ever become compulsorily registrable on sale or transfer. If capable of registration (see para.15–003) it may be voluntarily registered at any time. This was also the case under the Land Registration Act 1925. 15–004

Where a conveyance of unregistered land lodged for first registration also creates a rentcharge, the rentcharge will be the subject of a notice in the new registered title to the land without a specific application, regardless of whether the rentcharge is it itself capable of substantive registration. However, Land Registry will take no steps to register a rentcharge substantively unless a specific application for first registration of the rentcharge is lodged.

An application for first registration of a rentcharge must be made in Form FR1, accompanied by the original or duplicate deed creating the rentcharge, satisfactory evidence of title to the rentcharge and the conveyance, assignment or assent to the applicant. A fee in accordance with the Fee Order is payable.

Land Registry will not enter a restriction in Form A in the register unless a specific application is made. This is so even when two or more persons are being registered as proprietors of a rentcharge, because it is not an estate in land (s.44(1)).

Registration of rentcharges created out of registered land

15–005 A legal rentcharge created out of registered land is a registrable disposition which must be completed by registration (s.27).

(1) In the case of a rentcharge granted in fee simple or for a term of more than seven years, the grantee must be registered as proprietor of the rentcharge and a notice of the rentcharge must be entered in the register of the title out of which it was created.

(2) In the case of a rentcharge granted for a term of less than seven years, a notice of the rentcharge must be entered in the register of the title out of which it was created. (s.27 and paras 6 and 7 of Pt 1 of Sch.2 to the Act).

A legal rentcharge may be created as a disposition of registered land in one of two ways:

(a) it may be the subject of a deed of grant by the proprietor of the land; or

(b) it may be granted in a transfer or lease of registered land by the transferee or tenant to the transferor or landlord, charged upon the land transferred or demised. Typically, this will be the case where there is a transfer or lease of a plot on a developing estate, where an estate rentcharge is imposed on each plot (see para.15–002).

In both cases an application for the registration of the rentcharge should be made in Form AP1.

In the case of (b) a single Form AP1 can cover both registration of the land and registration of the rentcharge if desired. The registrar is not obliged to substantively register the rentcharge unless specific application is made in the Form AP1 (rr.72(6) and 72C(4)). The rentcharge cannot be registered until the transfer or lease itself has been completed by registration and therefore taken effect at law.

If a legal rentcharge is granted out of leasehold land registered with good leasehold title, and more than a qualified title to the rentcharge is desired, satisfactory evidence must be produced to show that the lease (and any superior lease) was validly granted.

Every deed creating a rentcharge out of registered land must contain a reference to the title number of that land (r.212(3)) and particulars, by plan if necessary, to enable the land charged to be identified on the title plan of the grantor's title (r.213).

A fee in accordance with the Fee Order is payable.

If completed by registration, the rentcharge will be substantively registered under its own individual title (where it is capable of substantive registration) and/or a notice of the burden will be entered in the register of title of the land charged.

If not completed by registration, the rentcharge will take effect in equity only, although the burden will still be capable of being protected by a notice in the register of the title to the land charged (see para.15–007).

A right of re-entry relating to a rentcharge created out of registered land on or after October 13, 2003 must itself be completed by registration if it is to take effect at law (s.27(e)). In the case of such a right created in a lease for a term of years absolute which is itself a registrable disposition, r.77 provides that completion by registration of the lease will be sufficient to meet the registration requirements for the right of re-entry and no additional entry will need to be made in respect of it.

Rentcharges which cannot be registered

Rentcharges subsisting as equitable interests only cannot be registered but the burden of such rentcharges should be protected in the register of the title to the land out of which they were created, where that land is registered. **15–006**

When an equitable rentcharge is created out of registered land, a notice of the burden of the rentcharge should be entered in the register of the title to the land charged.

If an equitable rentcharge is created by the transferee in a transfer of registered land, a notice of the burden will be entered in the register of the transferee's title as a matter of course when the transfer is registered (rr.72(4) and 72C(2)).

If an equitable rentcharge is created by the tenant in a prescribed clauses lease (see para.12–004) and the requisite details are inserted in clause LR12, a notice of the burden will be entered in the register of the tenant's title as a matter of course when the lease is registered (r.72A(2) and (3)). If created in a non-prescribed clauses lease, a notice of the burden will be entered in the register of the tenant's title as a matter of course when the lease is registered (r.72C(2)). (See also para.12–008).

In any other case of an equitable rentcharge created out of registered land, a separate application should be made to enter a notice of the rentcharge in the register of the title of the land charged (see para.15–007 and Chapter 16).

Entry of notice of rentcharge

15–007 When land is first registered, a notice of the burden of any subsisting rentcharge, whether legal or equitable, charged on the land and appearing in the title will be entered in the charges register of the title to the land charged (r.35), together with details of any apportionments and exonerations (see para.15–010).

On the completion by registration of a legal rentcharge created out of registered land, a notice of the burden of the rentcharge will be entered in the register of the title to the land charged, in accordance with the registration requirements (see para.15–005).

If a rentcharge is a registerable disposition under s.27 but is not completed by registration, it takes effect in equity only, but the burden of it will still be capable of being protected by entry of a notice in the register of the title to the land charged. In the case of a rentcharge granted in a transfer or lease, the registrar will enter such a notice as a matter of course when registering the transfer or lease itself (rr.72(4), 72A(2) and 72C(2)).

On the creation out of registered land of a rentcharge which cannot be registered, a specific application for the entry of a notice of the rentcharge in the register of the title to the land out of which the rentcharge issues will be necessary (see Chapter 16).

Dealings with registered rentcharges

15–008 A registered rentcharge can be transferred, leased or charged in the same way and subject to the same rules as a registered estate in land, so far as the nature of a rentcharge permits. The guidance appearing elsewhere in this book, whilst primarily relating to registered estates in land, also applies generally to registered rentcharges. However, a rentcharge owner cannot create easements or restrictive covenants.

Any transfer of a rentcharge should provide for the express assignment of the benefit of the grantor's covenant to pay the rent, because such a covenant does not run at law with the rentcharge so as to enable the rentcharge owner to sue under it.

Dispositions of rentcharges have the same SDLT requirements as other dispositions of registered land, as a rentcharge is for this purpose "land" (see para.1–016).

Transfer of registered estate subject to a rentcharge

Under r.69 where the covenants set out in Pt VII (Covenants Implied in a Conveyance for Valuable Consideration, other than a Mortgage, of the Entirety of Land Affected by a Rentcharge) or Pt VIII (Covenants Implied in a Conveyance for Valuable Consideration, other than a Mortgage, of Part of Land Affected by a Rentcharge, Subject to a Part (not Legally Apportioned) of that Rentcharge) of Sch.2 to the Law of Property Act 1925 are included in a transfer, the references to "the grantees", "the conveyance" and "the conveying parties" shall be treated as references to the transferees, the transfer and the transferors respectively. **15–009**

Rule 69(2) and (3) contains provisions modifying the covenants in Pt VIII of Sch.2 to the Law of Property Act 1925 when they are included in certain transfers of parts of registered land affected by rentcharges to which s.77(1)(B) of the Law of Property Act 1925 does not apply.

Rule 69(4) provides that on a transfer of a registered title subject to a rentcharge:

(1) any covenant implied by ss.77(1)(A) or (B) of the Law of Property Act 1925 may be modified or negatived; and

(2) any covenant included in the transfer may be modified,

by adding suitable words to the transfer.

Apportionment and redemption of rentcharges

Apportionment is the division of a rentcharge. A formally apportioned rentcharge can be dealt with separately in its own right. **15–010**

Exoneration is the release of part of the land charged from any liability for payment.

An apportionment or an exoneration may each be formal or informal. There are two types of formal apportionment. The most common is by a ministerial order (or certificate of apportionment) given by the secretary of state. The other is a deed made between all the relevant parties. To be formal (and to have full effect at law), all the owners of the land affected by the rentcharge and the rentcharge owner must join in the deed.

An informal apportionment or exoneration arises where not all the relevant parties join in the deed; this often occurs where there is a transfer or lease of part of the land in a registered title and the rentcharge owner is not a party to the apportionment or exoneration.

A registered title which relates to an estate in land or to a rentcharge may be affected by a ministerial order apportioning a rentcharge or by a ministerial certificate that a rentcharge has been redeemed. If it is not known whether the title to the land or rentcharge is registered, a search of the index map may be made in Form SIM (see para.3–015). A fee calculated in accordance with the Fee Order is payable.

An application should be made for effect to be given to the order or the certificate in the registered title(s) affected; but where an apportionment is made conditional on the redemption of the rentcharge, the application should not be made until after the redemption has taken place.

The application should be made in Form AP1, referring to "Apportionment of rentcharge" or "Redemption of rentcharge" as the case may be. It should be supported by:

(1) an official copy of the order and/or an official copy of the certificate of redemption as appropriate; and
(2) a fee in accordance with the Fee Order.

No fee is payable if the application is accompanied by an application upon which a scale fee is payable, e.g. where the order or certificate has been obtained in anticipation of a sale of the registered land or rentcharge and the application for the registration of the order or certificate is lodged with the application for the registration of the transfer on sale of the land or rentcharge.

Where a rentcharge has been formally exonerated, this acts as an extinguishment of the rentcharge (see para.15–011).

Extinguishment of rentcharges

15–011 Section 3(1) of the 1977 Act provides that, subject to certain exceptions, every rentcharge shall (if it has not then ceased to have effect) be extinguished at the expiry of the period of 60 years beginning with:

(1) the passing of the 1977 Act (i.e. July 22, 1977); or

(2) the date on which the rentcharge first became payable,

whichever is later.

The section will not extinguish any rentcharge payable wholly or partly in lieu of tithes or of a kind referred to in s.2(3) of the 1977 Act (disregarding s.2(5) which relates to estate rentcharges—see para.15–002). Variable rentcharges are also excluded from extinguishment under s.3(1) of the 1977 Act, but where a variable rentcharge ceases to be variable s.3(1) will apply as if the date on which the rentcharge first became payable was the date on which it ceased to be variable.

Apart from extinguishment under the 1977 Act, a rentcharge may also be determined or extinguished by a number of other means, including;

(a) merger;

(b) a deed of release whereby the rentcharge owner releases the rentcharge to the owner of the land charged;

(c) re-entry after an order of the court, where the rentcharge owner has obtained possession of the land charged by order of the court;

(d) a certificate of redemption given by the secretary of state (see para.15–010);

(e) effluxion of time, in the case of a terminable rentcharge;

(f) adverse possession where, by virtue of non-payment of the rent, the rentcharge has become statute barred (see para.7–017);

(g) cessation of the estate in the land charged, e.g. on forfeiture of a leasehold estate subject to a terminable rentcharge; and

(h) informal letter or receipt from the rentcharge owner.

An application following the extinguishment of a rentcharge, other than by ministerial certificate (see para.15–010), should be made supported by appropriate evidence of extinguishment and documents. The application should be made in Form AP1 (where both the land and the rentcharge are registered, or only the rentcharge is registered) or in Form CN1 for cancellation of an agreed notice (see para.16–006) or Form UN4 for cancellation of a unilateral notice (see para.16–011) (where only the land charged is registered). A fee in accordance with the Fee Order is payable, unless the application is accompanied by an application upon which a scale fee is payable, when no fee is payable.

Adverse possession of a rentcharge

15–012 See para.7–017.

Practical points

- Be aware of the limitations on the creation of new rentcharges,
- Check the requirements for the creation of an estate rentcharge where necessary,
- Lodge the relevant evidence with any application for apportionment, redemption or extinguishment of a rentcharge.

Chapter 16

Protection of Third Party Rights

Introduction

Unless it takes effect as an interest which overrides under Sch.3 to the Act (see para.10–028) or is excepted from the effect of registration (see para.10–003), the burden of a third party right or interest affecting a registered estate may need to be protected in the register. Under the Act, this protection may take the form of entry of a notice and/or a restriction. **16–001**

A notice entered in the register in respect of a third party interest will protect its priority against that of a subsequent registrable disposition for value for the purposes of the special rule of priority under s.29. A restriction, by preventing the registration of a subsequent registrable disposition for value, will prevent the priority of a third party interest from being postponed as a result of the special rule of priority under s.29. See paras 2–019, 2–020 and 10–003 as to the rules of priority relating to registered estates.

Neither a notice nor a restriction guarantees the validity of the interest that it seeks to protect.

Section 77 imposes a duty not to apply for a notice or restriction without reasonable cause. The duty is owed to any person who suffers damage as a consequence of its breach, such as the registered proprietor or a registered chargee, who may therefore have a right of action for breach of statutory duty against anyone who unreasonably applies for entry of a notice or restriction.

Previous law

Under the Land Registration Act 1925 there were four methods of protecting third party interests in the register: **16–002**

(1) notices;

(2) restrictions;

(3) inhibitions; and

(4) cautions against dealings.

Any such entries made prior to October 13, 2003, will continue in force under the transitional provisions contained in the Act, so that:

(a) notices entered under the Land Registration Act 1925 are treated as agreed notices;

(b) restrictions entered under the Land Registration Act 1925 are generally treated as restrictions entered under the Act;

(c) inhibitions are treated as restrictions for the purposes of the Act (see para.16–029); and

(d) cautions against dealings continue to have effect under the Act and the Rules contain provisions specifically dealing with such cautions (see paras 16–013 to 16–017).

Notices

16–003 A notice is an entry in the register in respect of the burden of an interest affecting the registered estate or registered charge against which it is entered. The fact that a notice is entered in the register does not necessarily mean that the interest is valid, but does mean that if it is valid its priority is protected for the purposes of priority under ss.29 and 30 (s.32).

Matters typically protected by a notice are contracts for sale and agreements for lease, adverse easements, leases, rentcharges, restrictive covenants, and home rights. Also protected in this way are orders of a court, including charging orders made under the Charging Orders Act 1979 affecting the registered estate itself (see paras 16–020 and 16–033 as to the position if the charging order is on a beneficial interest under a trust of land).

In many cases a notice is entered by the registrar as a matter of course, without the need for a separate application, as part of the registration process; these are referred to as a "registrar's notice" and take effect as an agreed notice. For example, on first registration a notice of the burden of existing adverse easements and restrictive covenants will be entered in the register of the new title (s.14 and r.35). Also, a notice of newly created easements and restrictive covenants in a transfer of a registered estate will be entered in the register of the burdened title(s) as appropriate (rr.72(4) and 72C(2)). On the registration of a lease granted out of a registered estate, a notice of the lease will be entered in the register of the landlord's title (s.38 and Sch.2 to the Act) and similarly on first registration of either a leasehold estate where the reversion is registered (r.37(3)) or of the reversion (r.35) a notice of the lease will be entered in the register of the landlord's title.

Also where the registrar is satisfied that the registered land is subject to an interest which overrides under Sch.1 to the Act (see para.5–018) and which is capable of being the subject of a notice (see below) he may enter notice of that interest (s.37) without an application being made. If the registrar enters a notice under s.37 he must give notice to the registered proprietor, unless they applied for or consented to the entry of the notice. The registrar must also give notice to any person who appears to him to be entitled to the interest protected by the notice, or whom the registrar otherwise considers appropriate, unless that person applied for or consented to the entry of the notice, or that person's name and address for service are not set out in the register in which the notice is entered (r.89).

Where an interest which overrides under Sch.1 or Sch.3 of the Act is disclosed by an applicant under either r.28 (on an application for first registration—see para.5–008) or r.57 (on an application to register a registrable disposition—see para.10–029), the registrar may enter a notice in the register in respect of it. An interest will cease to be an overriding interest on becoming the subject of a notice in the register and it will not regain its overriding status if the notice is subsequently removed from the register (s.29(3)).

By virtue of s.33 a notice cannot be entered to protect:

(1) interests under a trust of land or a settlement under the Settled Land Act 1925;

(2) a lease granted for three years or less which is not required to be registered;

(3) a restrictive covenant between a landlord and tenant so far as it affects the demised premises (see para.12–020);

(4) an interest which is capable of being registered under the Commons Registration Act 1965 (see para.8–023); and

(5) an interest in any coal or a coal mine, the rights attached to any such interest and the rights of any person under ss.38, 49 or 51 of the Coal Industry Act 1994.

Under s.90(4) no notice may be entered in respect of an interest under a public–private partnership lease; such an interest is deemed to be an interest which overrides under Schs.1 and 3 to the Act (s.90(5)).

Agreed notices

16–004 The registrar may only approve an application for an agreed notice if (s.34):

(1) it is made by or with the consent of the registered proprietor or by a person entitled to be registered as such; or

(2) if the registrar is satisfied that the applicant has a valid claim to the interest to which the notice relates.

Rule 80 provides that an application for entry of a notice must be for the entry of an agreed notice where the application is for:

(a) a home rights notice (see Chapter 17);

(b) an inheritance tax notice (see para.19–010);

(c) a notice in respect of an order under the Access to Neighbouring Land Act 1992;

(d) a notice of a variation of a lease under s.38 of the Landlord and Tenant Act 1987 (including any variation as modified by an order under s.39(4) of that Act); or

(e) a notice in respect of a public or customary right.

Application for the entry of an agreed notice

16–005 An application for the entry of an agreed notice, unless it relates to home rights (see Chapter 17), must be made in Form AN1 accompanied by (r.81):

(1) the order or document (if any) which created the claimed interest or (if none) such other details of the interest as are required to satisfy the registrar as to the nature of the applicant's claim;

(2) the appropriate SDLT evidence where applicable (see para.1–016);

(3) any evidence required to satisfy the registrar that the claim to the interest is valid;

(4) if appropriate, evidence of the right to be registered or of consent (see para.16–004); and

(5) a fee in accordance with the Fee Order.

The entry of the agreed notice must be in the charges register and it must give details of the interest protected and identify the registered estate or registered charge affected and, if it only affects part of the land in the title, it must identify that part (r.84(2)).

Application to cancel an agreed notice

An application to cancel an agreed notice, unless it relates to home rights (see para.17–009), must be made in Form CN1 accompanied by evidence to satisfy the registrar that the interest has determined (r.87). Where appropriate, this should include evidence of devolution to prove either determination of the interest and/or the right of the applicant to apply for the notice to be cancelled. **16–006**

No fee is currently payable unless the application relates to the determination of an unregistered lease or rentcharge.

If satisfied that the interest protected has come to an end, the registrar must cancel the notice or make an entry in the register that the interest has come to an end. If the interest protected by the notice has come to an end only in part, the registrar must make an appropriate entry.

If the registrar is not satisfied that the interest protected by the notice has come to an end, details of the circumstances in which the applicant claims the interest has determined may be entered in the register.

Unilateral notices

A unilateral notice may be entered in the register without the consent of the registered proprietor of the registered estate or registered charge which it affects. **16–007**

The entry must state that it is a unilateral notice and identify who is entitled to the benefit of the notice (s.35(2)). It must also identify the registered estate or registered charge affected and give such details of the interest protected as the registrar considers appropriate (r.84(5)). If it only affects part of the land in the title it must identify that part (r.84(2)).

Application for the entry of a unilateral notice (sections 34 and 35 and rule 83)

An application for the entry of a unilateral notice must be made in Form UN1. This form incorporates a declaration to be given by the applicant or certificate to be given by their conveyancer in **16–008** which must be set out the nature of the interest claimed. Provided the declaration or certificate discloses an interest of a type which is capable of being the subject of a notice (see para.16–003) the notice will be entered in the charges register; no evidence to satisfy the registrar as to the validity of the claimed interest is required.

A fee in accordance with the Fee Order is payable.

No notice is normally served prior to completion of the application. However, the registrar must, subject to the exceptions mentioned below, serve notice of the entry of a unilateral notice on the registered proprietor of the registered estate or registered charge to which it relates and on any person who appears to the registrar to be entitled to the interest protected by the notice or on whom the registrar considers it appropriate to serve notice (s.35(1) and r.89).

The registrar is not obliged to give notice to a registered proprietor or other person if they applied for entry of the notice or consented to the entry being made. Nor is the registrar obliged to serve notice on any person (not being the registered proprietor) if that person's address for service does not appear in the register of the title in which the entry is to be made (r.89(2) and (3)).

Application to be registered as beneficiary of an existing unilateral notice (rule 88)

16–009 An application to be registered as beneficiary of an existing unilateral notice must be made in Form UN3. The application must be supported by such evidence as is necessary to satisfy the registrar of the applicant's title to the interest which is the subject of the unilateral notice. Unless the existing registered beneficiary has signed the Form UN3 or otherwise consented or the application is by their personal representative, the registrar must serve notice on that registered beneficiary before proceeding. If the application is completed, details of the applicant will be entered in place of the existing registered beneficiary or jointly with that registered beneficiary as the case may be.

A fee in accordance with the Fee Order is payable.

Application to remove a unilateral notice (rule 85)

16–010 An application to remove a unilateral notice must be made in Form UN2. The application may be made by the registered beneficiary or, where appropriate, by their personal representative or trustee in bankruptcy. Where someone other than the registered beneficiary applies, they must lodge evidence of their entitlement to apply.

No fee is currently payable.

Application to cancel a unilateral notice (section 36 and rule 86)

An application to cancel a unilateral notice must be made in Form UN4 by the registered proprietor, or by someone entitled to be registered as proprietor, of the registered estate or registered charge to which the notice relates. The application may be made at any time and the applicant does not need to provide grounds for the application. If the applicant is a person entitled to be registered they must produce evidence, or a certificate by a conveyancer, that they are so entitled. **16–011**

No fee is currently payable.

Notice of such an application must be served on the registered beneficiary allowing 15 business days for objection. This 15-day period can be extended to a period of up to 30 business days if the beneficiary applies (within the original 15-day period) for an extension and the registrar, after consulting the applicant if he thinks it appropriate, agrees to allow such extension as he thinks appropriate, which need not be the same as that requested. Where there are two or more persons shown as the beneficiary of a notice, each one may object.

If the registered beneficiary or a person entitled to be registered as beneficiary does not object within the notice period, the unilateral notice must be cancelled (s.36(3)). Even if an objection is lodged the registrar may decide that it is groundless and cancel the notice (s.73(6)). If the objection is not held to be groundless and cannot be disposed of by agreement, the matter must be referred to the Adjudicator (see Chapter 23).

Variation to an interest which is the subject of a notice

Where an interest that has been protected by a notice in the register is varied, the priority of the interest, as varied, may be protected by applying either: **16–012**

(1) to cancel the existing notice (or in the case of a unilateral notice, by applying to remove it) and applying for entry of a new notice in respect of the interest as varied; or

(2) for an additional notice in respect of the variation.

The registrar will not normally agree to alter an existing notice to reflect a variation in the interest protected, because the date of entry of that notice as originally entered will be relevant for priority purposes (see para.16–001).

Cautions against dealings

A caution against dealings is an entry in the register in respect of a claim to an interest in a registered estate or registered charge, entered under s.54 of the Land Registration Act 1925. **16–013**

Although it has not been possible to enter any new caution against dealings since October 13, 2003, any such caution entered pursuant to an application lodged before that date continues to have effect under the transitional provisions contained in the Act. Paragraph 2(3) of Sch.12 to the Act provides that ss.55 and 56 of the Land Registration Act 1925 shall continue to have effect in relation to such cautions; it will be some years before all such cautions are withdrawn or cancelled.

It should be noted that, although the term "cautioner" includes their personal representative (r.218), unlike a unilateral notice, the benefit of a caution cannot be transferred. If the interest protected by the caution has been assigned, the person now entitled to the interest should register a notice or restriction as appropriate and procure the withdrawal of the caution (see para.16–015).

A cautioner against dealings is liable in damages to anyone injured as a result of their lodging a caution without reasonable cause (s.56(3) of the Land Registration Act 1925 and para.2(3) of Sch.12 to the Act).

The effect of a caution against dealings

16–014 If a caution against dealings appears in the register, the registrar cannot, without the cautioner's consent in writing signed by the cautioner or his conveyancer (r.219)), register any dealing with the land or charge affected until notice has been served on the cautioner. As to service of such notice see para.16–016.

Unlike a notice in the register, a caution against dealings does not in itself protect the priority of the interest which it protects nor does it give notice of the nature of the interest (see *Clark v Chief Land Registrar* [1993] 2 W.L.R. 141). Instead, the caution affords the cautioner the opportunity to object to the registration of a dealing with the registered estate or registered charge and/or to seek to protect the priority of the cautioner's interest in the register.

It is important to note that a caution against dealings against a registered estate will not affect dispositions by the proprietor of a registered charge which is registered against that estate; this is because such a caution will only affect dispositions by the registered proprietor and not by a registered chargee. On registration of a transfer of the land by a registered chargee in exercise of their power of sale, any caution against dealings against the registered estate will therefore be cancelled automatically without the cautioner being given the opportunity to object.

Also, it should be noted that a caution against dealings entered by a person claiming an equitable interest, e.g. in the proceeds of sale, will not be allowed to prevent the registration of a disposition by which the protected interest would be overreached (i.e. under ss.2 and 27 of the Law of Property Act 1925—see paras 2–021 and 18–001).

Withdrawal of a caution against dealings

A caution against dealings may be withdrawn by the cautioner at any time by lodging Form WCT signed by the cautioner or their conveyancer. No fee is currently payable. **16–015**

A cautioner is not permitted to apply for a notice or a restriction in respect of the claimed interest protected by the caution unless they also apply to withdraw the caution (para.17 of Sch.12 to the Act).

Cancellation of a caution against dealings

A caution against dealings can be cancelled following service of notice by the registrar: **16–016**

(1) under s.55(1) of the Land Registration Act 1925 on receipt of an application to register a dealing with the registered estate or registered charge to which the caution relates; or

(2) pursuant to an application for cancellation (or "warning-off") in Form CCD lodged by the registered proprietor, or by someone who, but for the caution, would be entitled to be registered as proprietor, of the registered estate or charge to which the caution relates (r.223). If the applicant is a person who, but for the caution, would be entitled to be registered they must produce evidence that they are so entitled. No fee is currently payable.

The notice must warn the cautioner that the caution will cease to have any effect after the expiration of a period of 15 business days (or such longer period as the registrar directs under r.218) unless the registrar makes an order to the contrary (r.221(4)).

Cautioner showing cause (r.221)

Before the expiration of the notice period the cautioner can "show cause" (i.e. an arguable case) why the registrar should not give effect to the application which led to the service of notice. To show cause the cautioner must lodge a written statement setting out grounds relied upon, signed by the cautioner or their conveyancer, showing a fairly arguable case why the registrar should not give effect to the application. **16–017**

If the registrar is satisfied, by reading the written submission and making whatever other enquiries he thinks necessary, that the cautioner has shown cause, he must order that the caution is to continue until withdrawn or otherwise disposed of (r.221(4)).

When such an order has been made the registrar must give notice of it to the applicant and to the cautioner. The cautioner is then treated as having objected to the application under s.73. If the objection cannot be disposed of by agreement, the matter must be referred to the Adjudicator (see Chapter 23).

In the case of a notice served as a result of an application to register a disposition of the registered estate or registered charge to which the caution relates, the cautioner may object to the application being completed, or may (where the application would not result in the cautioner's interest being defeated) consent to the application being completed subject to the caution remaining in the register.

If the registrar is not satisfied that the cautioner has shown cause and does not therefore make an order under r.221(4), he must cancel the caution in the register.

If the application that led to the service of the notice is cancelled, withdrawn or otherwise does not proceed, the registrar must make an order that the caution will continue to have effect, unless he has already done so or the caution has already been cancelled (r.221(6)).

Restrictions

16–018 A restriction is an entry in the register regulating the circumstances in which a disposition of a registered estate or registered charge may be the subject of an entry in the register. It therefore represents a limitation on the exercise of the "owner's powers" contained in s.23, for the purposes of ss.26 and 52 of the Act (see para.10–001). A restriction may prohibit, in relation to a registered estate or registered charge:

(1) the making of an entry in respect of any disposition or of a disposition of a particular kind specified in the restriction;

(2) the making of an entry:

  (a) indefinitely;
  (b) for a specified period; or
  (c) until a specified event which may, for example, be the giving of notice, the obtaining of consent or the making of an order of the court or of the registrar (s.40).

Effect of a restriction (section 41)

16–019 If a restriction is entered in the register, no entry in respect of a disposition to which it applies may be made in the register except in accordance with the terms of that restriction, unless the registrar by order disapplies or modifies the restriction in relation to a specific disposition or types of disposition (see para.16–025).

A restriction affecting a registered estate may also affect a charge that is subsequently registered, if its wording is sufficiently wide to catch dispositions by both a registered proprietor and a registered chargee; it will not, however, affect a charge which was registered prior to the entry of the restriction.

A restriction affecting a registered charge will not catch dispositions by the proprietor of the registered estate and a separate restriction in that regard would be necessary. Nor will it affect a charge which was registered prior to the entry of the restriction.

Entry of a restriction by the registrar or the court (sections 42, 44 and 46)

(1) *Restrictions entered at the registrar's discretion* Section 42(1) contains a general power enabling the registrar to enter a restriction if it appears to him that it is necessary or desirable to do so for the purpose of: **16–020**

(a) preventing invalidity or unlawfulness in relation to dispositions of a registered estate or charge;

(b) securing that interests which are capable of being overreached on a disposition of a registered estate or charge are overreached; or

(c) protecting a right or claim in relation to a registered estate or charge.

The registrar may enter a restriction for one of these purposes whether or not an application has been made. The relevant proprietor will be notified when a restriction is entered without an application having been made. See para.16–023 as to applications to enter a restriction.

There are certain limitations on the registrar's power to enter a restriction for the purposes of s.42(1)(a), (b) or (c) above:

(i) A restriction may not be entered to protect the priority of an interest that is or could be
protected by a notice (s.42(2)). However, a restriction might still be necessary or desirable for one of the other permitted purposes set out in s.42(1)(a) or (b) (e.g. to prevent an unlawful breach of a provision in a contract that has been protected by a notice) and may therefore be entered in addition to a notice.

(ii) a right or claim may only be protected under s.42(1)(c) if it relates to a registered estate or registered charge, i.e. a legal estate. This does not therefore include rights or claims that relate only to a beneficial interest in an estate or charge under a trust of land, which can generally be the subject of a restriction for the purposes of s.42(1)(a) or (b). In most cases, a restriction in Form A will be appropriate, to ensure that overreaching takes place on a disposition that gives rise to capital monies. A specific exception to this is a charging order affecting a beneficial interest under a trust, which may nevertheless be protected by a restriction entered under s.42(1)(c), LRA 2002, such as a restriction in Form K (s.42(4) and r.93(k)—see para.16–033).

16–021 **(2) *Obligation on the registrar to enter a restriction*** The registrar is obliged to enter a restriction in certain circumstances, e.g. a restriction in Form A when entering two or more persons as joint proprietors of a registered estate in land and the survivor will not be able to give a valid receipt for capital money (s.44(1)—see paras 5–007 and 11–013).

Rule 95 specifies the forms of restriction that the registrar is obliged to enter under various statutory provisions.

16–022 **(3) *The court's power to order the entry of a restriction*** The court may make an order requiring the registrar to enter a restriction if it appears necessary or desirable to do so for the purposes of protecting a right or claim in relation to a registered estate or registered charge (s.46). This may be a standard or non-standard restriction, e.g. a restriction in Form AA where a freezing order has been made by the court.

Although the order may be addressed directly to the registrar, a formal application for the restriction to be entered should be made, as the registrar may not otherwise be aware of the order. The application should be made in Form AP1 not RX1 (r.92(8)) and should be accompanied by a fee in accordance with the Fee Order.

The order may include a direction that the restriction is to have overriding priority, e.g. over that conferred by any official search with priority that is pending when the application for the restriction is made (s.46(3)). The restriction will then be entered immediately even if there is an unexpired priority period arising from an official search to protect the priority of a disposition that has not yet been lodged.

Such a direction may be appropriate if, for example, there is a risk that a person other than a bona fide purchaser may apply for an official search with priority before the restriction can be entered, so that they can register a disposition of the property without being caught by the terms of the restriction.

Application to enter a restriction (section 43 and rule 92)

A person may apply for entry of a restriction if they: **16–023**

(1) are the registered proprietor or a person entitled to be registered as such; or

(2) have the consent of the registered proprietor or of a person entitled to be registered as such;

(3) are a person who has a sufficient interest in the entry of the restriction (s.43(1)). Rule 93 contains a detailed, but not exhaustive, list of persons regarded as having such an interest.

Rule 94 prescribes certain circumstances where a person *must* apply for entry of a restriction, e.g. the registered proprietor must apply for entry of a restriction in Form A where a registered estate, other than on a registrable disposition, becomes subject to a trust of land and the proprietor or survivor of joint proprietors will not be able to give a valid receipt for capital money.

An application for entry of a restriction must, subject to certain exceptions, be made in Form RX1. The exceptions are where an application to enter a standard form restriction is made in:

(a) the additional provisions panel of any of the following forms: TP1, TP2, TR1, TR2, TR4, TR5, AS1, AS2, AS3 and panel 9 of Form CH1;

(b) Form SEV for entry of a restriction in Form A following the severance of a beneficial joint tenancy by agreement or notice;

(c) an electronic legal charge;

(d) an approved form of charge (see para.14–004);

(e) a lease containing clauses LR1 to LR14 of Sch.1A to the Rules (see paras 12–004 and 12–008), where the restriction application is inserted in clause LR13. If clause LR13 is not completed, any application to register a restriction contained within the body of the lease will be ignored. Also, where the restriction is to be entered against titles other than the landlord's or that created by the registration of the lease, it will only be registered if the relevant title numbers are inserted in clause LR2.2 or panel 2 of Form AP1 unless separate application is made (r.72A(4));

(f) pursuance of an order of the court made under s.46 (see para.16–022).

The application must be accompanied by:

(i) full details of the restriction applied for;

(ii) an address for service for anyone named in a standard form restriction whose address is required by that restriction or whose consent or certificate is required or to whom notice must be given by the registrar or another person;

(iii) where the application is made with the consent of the relevant proprietor or someone entitled to be registered as such, either the consent, or a conveyancer's certificate confirming that they hold the relevant consent;

(iv) where the application is made by or with the consent of someone entitled to be registered as the relevant proprietor, either evidence of their entitlement, or a conveyancer's certificate confirming that they are satisfied that person is entitled to be registered and that they hold original documentary evidence of that entitlement or that there is a pending application to register that person as proprietor at Land Registry;

(v) where the application is not made by or with the consent of the relevant proprietor, evidence of the applicant's interest in the making of the application. Details of the nature of the interest and of how that interest arose must be given either as a statement by the applicant in panel 12 or as a conveyancer's certificate in panel 13 of Form RX1. Where it is available, documentary evidence of the interest should be lodged with the application;

(vi) a fee in accordance with the Fee Order.

An application for entry of a restriction under s.43 will be "notifiable" and the registrar must give notice of it to the relevant proprietor before completing the application, unless it is either:

(a) made by or with the consent of the relevant proprietor or someone entitled to be registered as such;

(b) one of the compulsory applications listed in r.94; or

(c) applied for to reflect a limitation under a court order or an order of the registrar (or an undertaking given in place of such an order) (s.45).

The notice will give the relevant proprietor 15 business days to object to the application. If a valid objection is made within that period which cannot be resolved by agreement, the matter will have to be referred to the Adjudicator (see Chapter 23).

Form of restriction

Schedule 4 to the Rules contains standard forms of restriction and these are set out in Appendix III of this book. Certain standard forms of restriction are obligatory in the circumstances set out in rr.94 and 95. Some of the more commonly used standard forms are referred to in the chapters of this book to which they are relevant. **16–024**

Examples of standard forms are:

(1) Form A (restriction on dispositions by a sole proprietor);
(2) Form L (disposition by registered proprietor of registered estate or proprietor of charge—certificate required);
(3) Form N (disposition by registered proprietor of registered estate or proprietor of charge—consent required);
(4) Form P (disposition by registered proprietor of registered estate or proprietor of charge—consent of proprietor of specified charge or certificate required).

Certain of the standard forms contain variables and r.91A allows certain amendments to the standard forms. Other than that, the amendment of a standard form will result in a restriction being non-standard.

Use of the standard forms of restriction is recommended if at all possible. If no standard form is suitable application may be made to enter a non-standard form of restriction, but the registrar may only accept it if (s.43(3)):

(a) its terms are reasonable; and
(b) applying the restriction would be straightforward and would not place an unreasonable burden on the registrar.

Standard forms of restriction do not prevent the entry of a notice of a disposition and a non-standard restriction will not be accepted if its wording seeks to do so. The fee under the Fee Order for the entry of a non-standard restriction is double that payable for the entry of a standard restriction. Care should therefore be taken when completing Form RX1 not to alter the wording of a standard form so as to inadvertently change it to a non-standard form.

Application to disapply or modify a restriction (section 41 and rule 96)

An application for an order of the registrar to disapply or modify a restriction must be made in Form RX2 and state whether it is for disapplication or modification of the restriction. **16–025**

Details of any modification requested must be given. The application must give details of the disposition or types of disposition that will be affected by the order. The applicant must explain why they have sufficient interest to apply and why the order is required and should be made. The registrar may serve notice or make further enquiries before making an order. If an order is made it must, if appropriate, be noted in the register.

A fee in accordance with the Fee Order is payable.

Application to cancel a restriction (rule 97)

16–026 An application to cancel a restriction must be made in Form RX3 accompanied by evidence to satisfy the registrar that the restriction is no longer required. If the registrar is satisfied with the evidence he must cancel the restriction.

No fee is currently payable.

When registering a disposition of a registered estate, the registrar must cancel a restriction entered for the purpose of protecting an interest, right or claim arising under a trust of land if he is satisfied that the registered estate is no longer subject to that trust of land (r.99). Thus the registrar will, for example, automatically cancel a restriction in Form A where the beneficial interests under the trust of land have clearly been overreached on a transfer on sale (see para.2–021).

Application to withdraw a restriction (section 47 and rule 98)

16–027 An application to withdraw a restriction must be made in Form RX4 accompanied by the required consent as specified in r.98, or a certificate by a conveyancer that they hold such consent. Such consents include, for example, the consent of a person specified in the restriction as a person whose consent or certificate is required under the terms of that restriction, or the consent of any person who appears to the registrar to have an interest in the restriction.

No fee is currently payable.

In general, a "voluntary" restriction (i.e. one applied for voluntarily rather than entered in pursuance of an obligation under the Act) cannot be cancelled as a matter of course when a disposition is registered, even where the terms of the restriction have been complied with and the disposition is a transfer on sale, for example. Therefore, if it is intended that the restriction should not remain in the register following the registration of the disposition, an express withdrawal should normally be obtained.

Obligatory restrictions entered in pursuance of an obligation under the Act (such as a restriction in Form A) and those entered pursuant to an order of the registrar or of the court cannot be withdrawn and must be the subject of an application for cancellation where appropriate (see para.19–006).

Compliance with a restriction

An application must, where necessary, comply with the terms of a restriction before it can be completed. 16–028

Rule 91B contains provisions relating to a certificate or consent by a corporation required under the terms of a restriction.

Restrictions entered under the Land Registration Act 1925 may prevent the registration or noting of a disposition. Under the Act, the registrar will not interpret this as preventing the entry of a unilateral notice in respect of an interest.

Inhibitions

Although it has not been possible to enter a new inhibition since October 13, 2003, an inhibition entered before that date will continue to have effect and will be treated as a restriction for the purposes of the Act. Inhibitions prohibit, wholly or partially, the exercise of a proprietor's powers of disposition. Inhibitions, other than bankruptcy inhibitions (see Chapter 20), are very uncommon. An application to cancel an inhibition must be made to the court if the inhibition was originally entered pursuant to an order of the court; otherwise it must be made to the registrar. 16–029

No fee is currently payable for cancellation.

Local land charges

Rights under local land charges affecting registered land are interests which override both first registration and registered dispositions (Schs 1 and 3 to the Act—see paras 5–018 and 10–028). 16–030

If a local land charge affecting registered land is a legal charge or a legal mortgage and is to be realised, it must be registered as a registered charge (s.55).

Searches in the registers of local land charges maintained by local authorities must be made in relation to registered land just as for unregistered land.

Examples of protection of third party interests

The following are examples of some of the most common types of third party interest affecting a registered estate or registered charge, with details of how they may be protected in the register. 16–031

Interests under a trust of land

16–032 An interest under a trust of land, for land registration purposes, means the interest of a person under such a trust who stands only one "step" away from the legal estate. Thus, where A and B are holding the legal estate upon trust for C for life and D in remainder thereafter, both C and D have an interest under a trust of land.

An interest under a trust of land may arise formally, by way of an express declaration of trust in writing, or informally as a result of an implied, resulting or constructive trust.

An interest under a trust of land cannot be protected by entry of an agreed notice or unilateral notice (s.33(a)(i)). It may, however, be protected by entry of a restriction. An application may therefore be made for entry of a restriction in Form A, if such a restriction does not already appear in the register. A restriction in Form A reflects the existence of a trust of land and ensures that overreaching is effected on a disposition for value of the registered estate (see paras 2–021 and 18–001).

Where the interest has arisen by virtue of an express declaration of trust and the trust deed contains a provision requiring the consent of a beneficiary to any disposition of the registered estate, application for entry of an appropriate restriction, such as one in Form N, may be made. This would not, however, be appropriate where the trust deed contained no such provision or the trust had arisen informally.

When required, application may also be made for entry of a restriction in Form II, the purpose of which is to ensure that the person named in the restriction receives notice of the disposition, thereby giving them the opportunity of pursuing the proceeds of sale where appropriate.

The interest of a person who is two or more "steps" away from the legal estate is for land registration purposes referred to as a "derivative interest" and does not represent an interest under a trust of land for those purposes. Thus, where P and Q are holding the legal estate upon trust for R and S and S is in turn holding their share on trust for T, R will have an interest under a trust of land but T will have only a derivative interest.

Another example would be where X and Y hold the legal estate upon trust for themselves as beneficial tenants in common and Y charges their beneficial share to Z. Z has a charge on an interest under a trust of land, so their charge represents a derivative interest.

A person with a derivative interest may apply for entry of a restriction in Form A, if such a restriction does not already appear in the register. They will not normally be entitled to apply for entry of any other form of restriction (including one in Form II) because:

(1) they cannot apply under s.42(1)(a) on the basis that the restriction might prevent the trustees from misapplying the proceeds of sale following a disposition which overreaches the beneficial interests, as that subsection is concerned only with preventing unlawfulness or invalid dispositions of registered estates and not with subsequent dealings with the proceeds of sale; and

(2) a derivative interest is not a right or claim in relation to a registered estate or registered charge within s.42(1)(c), as it is a right or claim in relation to the beneficial interest under the trust of land and not in relation to the registered estate or registered charge.

There are certain exceptions to this, e.g. a charging order against a beneficial share (see para.16–033).

Charging orders **16–033**

(1) An interim or final charging order against the legal estate, i.e. one made against a sole proprietor who is the sole legal and beneficial owner or against joint proprietors expressly as "trustees", may be protected by entry of an agreed notice or a unilateral notice. An application to the court for such a charging order may be similarly protected.

(2) An interim or final charging order against a beneficial interest, i.e. one made against the equitable share of a joint proprietor, cannot be protected by entry of a notice, but may be protected by entry of a restriction in Form K. This is an exception to the general rule concerning derivative interests (see paras 16–020 and 16–032). Separate charging orders made against joint proprietors in the same court proceedings will not be treated as charging the legal estate and separate applications for a restriction in Form K would instead need to be made. Application for entry of a restriction in Form A may also be made, if such a restriction does not already appear in the register. An application to the court for such a charging order cannot be protected in the register.

Bankruptcy
See Chapter 20. **16–034**

Contracts for sale, option agreements and rights of pre-emption
Where these relate to the legal estate, they may be protected by **16–035**
entry of an agreed notice or unilateral notice. If the agreement

contains a provision limiting the proprietor's powers of disposition, application may be made for entry of an appropriate restriction, e.g. in Form L, to reflect this.

16–036 *Equitable charges*

(1) An equitable charge against the legal estate may be protected by entry of an agreed notice or unilateral notice. This may be relevant where, for example, a second charge is created and a restriction in the register entered by the prior registered chargee prevents the second charge being completed by registration and taking effect at law.

(2) An equitable charge against a beneficial interest cannot be protected by entry of a notice as it is a derivative interest (see para.16–032) and does not fall within the exception applicable to charging orders mentioned above. Application for entry of a restriction in Form A may be made, if such a restriction does not already appear in the register, but no other restriction can be applied for.

Pending land actions, writs and orders, deeds of arrangement

16–037 By virtue of s.87(1), a pending land action, a writ or order affecting land or made for the purpose of enforcing a judgment, an order appointing a receiver or sequestrator, and a deed of arrangement are all deemed to be an interest affecting an estate or charge for the purposes of the Act.

A pending land action, writ or order affecting land, or made for the purpose of enforcing a judgment, may be protected by entry of an agreed notice or unilateral notice and/or a restriction. Forms of restriction appropriate to certain types of order are specified in r.93. The form of the restriction will depend on the nature of the pending land action or the nature of the writ or order. A writ or order relating to an undivided share under a trust of land is not an interest affecting land for this purpose. Where the order has the effect of creating a trust of land the interest cannot be protected by the entry of a notice, but may be protected by a restriction, normally in Form A.

An order appointing a receiver or sequestrator, and a deed of arrangement may not be protected by entry of a notice, but may be protected by entry of a restriction (s.87(2)).

Prevention of forgery

16–038 Where it is believed that there is the possibility of an attempt to register a forged disposition, application may be made for entry of a restriction in Form LL. This provides an element of protection against forgery by requiring a conveyancer's certificate to be lodged with an application, certifying that they are satisfied that the person who executed the document submitted for registration as disponor is the same person as the proprietor.

Where it is considered that there is a higher risk of fraud, application may be made under s.43 for entry of a non-standard restriction in the following form: "No disposition of the registered estate by the registered proprietor is to be registered."

This form of restriction is intended to effectively "freeze" the register, so that no disposition by the proprietor could be registered until the restriction was cancelled under r.97 or disapplied by the registrar under s.41(2) (see paras 16–025 and 16–026). Such a restriction would not, however, prevent a disposition by a registered chargee in exercise of its power of sale.

Practical points

- Be aware of the difference between legal and equitable interests and how these may be protected in the register,
- Be aware of the nature and effect of a notice and the distinction between an agreed notice and a unilateral notice,
- Ensure that an interest affecting a registered estate is where necessary protected in the correct manner,
- Be aware of the nature and effect of a caution against dealings,
- Ensure that all panels of an application form are completed correctly and the relevant information provided,
- Distinguish between charging orders as to those which affect the legal estate and those which affect only a beneficial interest and use the appropriate method of protection of such charging orders in the register.

Chapter 17

Home Rights

Definitions

In this chapter: 17–001

"home" means the dwelling house constituting the matrimonial or civil rights home to which the home rights attach;

"home rights" means the rights of occupation of the home conferred upon a spouse or civil partner by s.30 of the Family Law Act 1996;

"the spouse or civil partner" means the person whose home rights are protected or in need of protection; and

"the owning spouse or civil partner" means the other spouse or civil partner, being the owner of the home.

The Civil Partnership Act 2004 created a new legal relationship of civil partnership, which two people of the same sex can form by signing a registration document. It also provides same sex couples who form a civil partnership with parity of treatment, in a wide range of legal matters, with those opposite sex couples who enter into a civil marriage. Section 82 and Sch.9 to the 2004 Act amended the Family Law Act 1996 to extend to civil partners the same rights of occupation of their home as apply to a matrimonial home. The Rules were amended to take account of the provisions of the Civil Partnership Act 2004, so that a "matrimonial home rights notice" became a "home rights notice".

Family Law Act 1996 ("the 1996 Act")

Home rights under the 1996 Act constitute a charge on the home (s.31 of the 1996 Act) which, if the home is held under a registered title, should be protected by the entry of an agreed 17–002 notice (r.80(a)). Such a notice is referred to in the Rules as a "home rights notice" (r.217).

Prior to February 14, 1983, such a charge could also be protected by the entry of a caution against dealings (see para.16–013).

Even if the spouse or civil partner is in actual occupation of the home, their home rights are not an overriding interest (s.31(10)(b) of the 1996 Act).

The home rights charge arises on whichever is the latest of:

(1) the date when the owning spouse or civil partner acquires the home;

(2) the date of the marriage or civil partnership;

(3) January 1, 1968 (being the date of commencement of the Matrimonial Homes Act 1967).

Where the owning spouse or civil partner is not the registered proprietor (or sole registered proprietor) of the home, but is entitled to occupy the home by virtue of a beneficial interest under a trust, the spouse or civil partner may still be entitled to home rights which are capable of protection against the trustees' registered title. However, this will only be the case where the property is held on trust for:

(a) the owning spouse or civil partner only; or

(b) the owning spouse or civil partner and the spouse or civil partner only (s.31(4) and (5) of the 1996 Act).

No protection under the 1996 Act is necessary when the matrimonial home is held jointly, both legally and beneficially, by both the spouses or civil partners.

The registration of a Class F Land Charge is relevant only to unregistered land and will confer no protection in relation to registered land.

The protection of a home rights notice (registered land) or a Class F Land Charge (unregistered land) is only available in respect of one home at any one time (see para.17–007).

Is the home registered?

17–003 If it is not known whether the title to the home is registered, an application for an official search of the index map should be made in Form SIM (see para.3–015). The top of the form should be endorsed: "This search is being made solely for the purposes of the Family Law Act 1996. Please reveal details of any registered lease". Provided that the applicant makes it clear that the search is required for the purposes of the 1996 Act, even if no plan of the property is available where one would normally be required, Land Registry will endeavour to identify the property and avoid raising any point which might otherwise arise as to the precise boundaries of the property.

The certificate of the result of the search will reveal what registered estates or interests (if any) exist in the land, including particulars of any registered lease. If any doubt remains as to whether or not the registered title is owned by the owning spouse or civil partner, an official copy of the register can be obtained by lodging Form OC1 (see para.9–006).

Application for a home rights notice

The application should be made in Form HR1 (r.82(1)). If the court has made an order by virtue of s.33(5) of the 1996 Act (see para.17–006) either an office copy of the order must accompany the application or a conveyancer's certificate that they hold an office copy of it (r.82(3)). No fee is currently payable. The priority of the application may be reserved by lodging an outline application (see paras 10–030 to 10–033). **17–004**

The registrar will serve notice of the application upon the registered proprietor.

Rights continued by order of the court

Home rights will only continue so long as the marriage or civil partnership subsists, unless the court directs otherwise during the subsistence of the marriage by means of an order under s.33(5) of the 1996 Act. If the court makes such an order and those home rights have not already been protected in the register, an application for a home rights notice should be made. **17–005**

If the court makes such an order, and the home rights have already been protected in the register, an application for renewal of the registration in respect of home rights should be made (see para.17–006).

Renewal of registration in respect of home rights

If the court makes an order under s.33(5) of the 1996 Act directing that the home rights shall not be brought to an end by the termination of the marriage or civil partnership, whether by **17–006** death or otherwise, and those rights have already been protected in the register by means of a home rights notice or (prior to February 14, 1983) by a caution against dealings, an application should be made for the renewal, by way of entry of a home rights notice, of the registration of the existing notice or the caution so that the making of the order can be protected in the register.

The application should be made in Form HR2 (r.82(2)) either accompanied by an office copy of the order or a conveyancer's certificate that they hold an office copy of it. The renewal will be effected in the register by the entry of a home rights notice referring to the order. It will not affect the priority of the original home rights charge (para.4(5) of Sch.4 to the 1996 Act). No fee is currently payable. The priority of the application may be reserved by lodging an outline application (see paras 10–030 to 10–033).

The registrar will serve notice of the application for renewal upon the registered proprietor.

Change of home

17–007 A spouse or civil partner can have protection in relation to only one home at any one time, whether the protection is by way of a home rights notice or a caution against dealings in respect of a registered home or a Class F Land Charge in respect of an unregistered home. Accordingly, any subsisting registration must be disclosed in Form HR1, and it will be cancelled when the new charge is registered (para.2 of Sch.4 to the 1996 Act).

Cessation of home rights

17–008 A spouse's or civil partner's home rights may be brought to an end in the following ways:

(1) by the death of either spouse or civil partner (s.31(8)(a) of the1996 Act), but subject to the power of the court to make an order under s.33(5) of the1996 Act;

(2) by the ending of the marriage or civil partnership otherwise than by death (s.31(8)(b) of the 1996 Act), but subject to the power of the court to make an order under s.33(5) of the 1996 Act;

(3) by an order of the court (para.4(1)(c) of Sch. 4 to the 1996 Act); or

(4) by the spouse or civil partner voluntarily releasing the home rights in writing (para.5(1) of Sch.4 to the 1996 Act).

Cancellation of a home rights notice

An application to cancel a home rights notice must be made in Form HR4 (r.87A), accompanied by the evidence required by para.4 of Sch.4 to the 1996 Act. That evidence will normally be: **17–009**

(1) the death certificate or other sufficient evidence of death of either spouse or civil partner (but see also (5) below); or

(2) an office copy of a decree absolute of divorce or nullity (if a decree of divorce by an overseas court is lodged, additional evidence, e.g. as to residence, domicile or nationality, may be required and, if the decree is not in English, a notarially certified translation should be provided) (but see also (5) below); or

(3) an office copy of an order of the court terminating the home rights; or

(4) a written release of the home rights by the spouse or civil partner; and

(5) where the supporting evidence is evidence of the husband's death or a copy of a decree absolute produced in accordance with (1) or (2) above and the court has made an order under s.33(5) of the 1996 Act and that order is referred to on the register, satisfactory evidence that the order has ceased to have effect.

No fee is currently payable.

Cancellation of a caution against dealings

An application to cancel a caution against dealings protecting home rights may be made in one of the following ways: **17–010**

(1) by application for cancellation in Form CCD (r.223) by the registered proprietor or a person who, but for the caution, would be entitled to be registered as proprietor (see para.16–016); or

(2) by withdrawal of the caution in Form WCT (r.222) signed by the spouse or civil partner (or by their personal representative where appropriate) or by their conveyancer (see para.16–015).

(3) by letter, accompanied by the appropriate evidence confirming one of the events described in (1), (2) or (3) in para.17–009. If the court has made an order under s.33(5) of the 1996 Act which is referred to in the register, the applicant must also supply satisfactory evidence that this order has ceased to have effect.

No fee is currently payable.

Rights of occupation of a bankrupt's spouse or civil partner

17–011 A spouse or civil partner cannot acquire home rights in the period between the presentation of a bankruptcy petition and the vesting of the bankrupt's property in a trustee (s.336(1) of the Insolvency Act 1986). Any rights of occupation existing prior to the bankruptcy petition continue to subsist notwithstanding the bankruptcy (s.336(2) of the Insolvency Act 1986).

The trustee in bankruptcy may apply to the bankruptcy court at any time for an order to restrict or terminate the home rights. In making an order the court must have regard to all the circumstances of the case except the needs of the bankrupt. Where such an application is made more than one year after the date on which the bankrupt's property vested in a trustee, the court has to assume that the interests of the creditors are paramount unless there are exceptional circumstances (s.336(4) and (5) of the Insolvency Act 1986). An office copy of the court order should accompany any application for cancellation based upon it.

Bankruptcy is discussed further in Chapter 20.

Rights of occupation of a bankrupt

17–012 Whether or not their spouse or civil partner has rights of occupation, a bankrupt who:

(1) is entitled to occupy a dwelling-house by virtue of a beneficial estate or interest;

(2) at some time occupied that dwelling-house with children under 18; and

(3) provided a home for those children under 18 at the time of the bankruptcy petition and at the time of the bankruptcy order,

has rights of occupation against their trustee in bankruptcy under the 1996 Act.

If they are in occupation, they have a right not to be evicted or excluded without leave of the bankruptcy court. If they are not in occupation, they have a right, with leave of the bankruptcy court, to enter into occupation (s.337 of the Insolvency Act 1986).

The bankrupt's rights are a charge which has the same priority as an equitable interest created immediately before the commencement of the bankruptcy (s.337(2)(b) of the Insolvency Act 1986). Where a bankrupt has such rights, these may be protected by entry of an agreed notice under the 1996 Act notwithstanding the fact that the bankrupt is shown in the register as the registered proprietor. In the application in Form HR1 the applicant should state that they are applying pursuant to the provisions of s.337 of the Insolvency Act 1986 and that the property is vested in their (named) trustee in bankruptcy.

To restrict or terminate these rights, the trustee in bankruptcy must apply to the bankruptcy court, which must have regard to the same matters mentioned in para.17–011 (s.337(4), (5) and (6) of the 1986 Act). An office copy should accompany any application for cancellation based upon such an order.

Bankruptcy is discussed further in Chapter 20.

Search by a mortgagee

A mortgagee of a dwelling-house who brings an action to enforce their security is obliged, under s.56 of the 1996 Act, to serve notice of the action on a spouse whose rights of occupation are protected at the relevant time by notice or caution. A mortgagee of registered land that consists of or includes all or part of a dwelling house may apply in Form HR3 or by telephone or electronically (r.158) for an official certificate of the result of a search. This will reveal if there is a home rights notice or a matrimonial home rights caution registered, or a pending application for entry of a home rights notice on the day list. The search will confer priority for a period of 15 days (s.56(5) of the 1996 Act). **17–013**

A fee in accordance with the Fee Order is payable.

Practical points

- Remember that a home rights notice can be entered only in respect of one home at any one time,
- Where there is a change of home, remember to apply for a home rights notice in respect of the new home in place of a home rights notice against the previous home,
- Carry out a search of the index map if it is not known whether the title to the home is registered,
- Remember to apply for renewal of a home rights notice if the court has made an order under s.33(5) of the 1996 Act.

Chapter 18

Trusts, Charities and Settled Land

Trusts of land

Nature of a trust of land

The Trusts of Land and Appointment of Trustees Act 1996 ("TLATA") reformed the law relating to trusts of land and the appointment of trustees. It defines a "trust of land" as any trust of property which consists of or includes land, except for settled land (as defined in the Settled Land Act 1925) and land to which the Universities and Colleges Estates Act 1925 applies (s.1 of TLATA). **18–001**

This definition includes both a trust created before the commencement of TLATA and also any description of trust, so that it includes an express, implied, constructive or resulting trust as well as a trust for sale and a bare trust. "Land" for this purpose includes an undivided share in land.

Where a sole owner of land holds both the legal title to the land, i.e. the legal estate *and* the underlying equitable or beneficial interest, the legal estate and equitable interest are merged and there is no trust of land. The essential characteristic of a trust of land is that the legal estate to the land is separated from the equitable interest, with the legal estate being vested in the trustee(s) and the equitable interest being vested in the beneficiary or beneficiaries.

A trust of land may:

(1) be expressly created in writing (s.53(1)(b) of the Law of Property Act 1925);

(2) be a "bare trust" arising where the trustee is merely the nominee for a beneficiary of full age;

(3) arise by operation of law either:

(a) as an implied, resulting or constructive trust, e.g. where the proprietor has purchased the land using funds provided by a third party; or
(b) as a statutory trust, e.g. the statutory trust automatically imposed by ss.34 and 36 of the Law of Property Act 1925 where two or more persons own land jointly, so that they hold the legal estate on a trust of land even if they are holding the equitable interest on trust for themselves.

A trust of land may therefore exist where the trustees are holding on trust for themselves only, for themselves and a third party or for a third party only.

The property reforms introduced by the Law of Property Act 1925 were intended to simplify unregistered conveyancing. In consequence, the legal estate can never be severed and can only be held by two or more persons as beneficial joint tenants (ss.1(6) and 34 of the Law of Property Act 1925). This means that if one joint owner dies, the legal estate will pass by "survivorship" and vest automatically in the surviving joint owner(s), regardless of the devolution of the equitable interest (see para.19–001).

However, the equitable interest may, where there are two or more beneficiaries, be held as between themselves as beneficial joint tenants or tenants in common. In the case of a beneficial joint tenancy, the whole equitable interest is held equally and the right of "survivorship" applies so that, if one joint tenant dies, their interest passes automatically to the survivor(s). In the case of a beneficial tenancy in common, the equitable interest may be held in either equal or unequal undivided shares and the right of "survivorship" does not apply, so that, if one tenant in common dies, their share passes under the terms of their will or intestacy. A tenant in common may also assign or dispose of their share during their lifetime (see also paras 2–023, and 19–001).

Since 1926, a purchaser of land (which for this purpose includes a mortgagee—see s.205(1)(xxi) of the Law of Property Act 1925) need only be concerned with the legal estate, the devolution of which on death is clear, and does not need to investigate or be concerned with the equitable interest provided that, where necessary, "overreaching" is effected.

Overreaching occurs where there is a disposition of land, which is subject to a trust of land, and capital money arises, e.g. on a sale of the property. It is the mechanism under which the capital money is paid to not less than two trustees (or to a sole personal representative acting as such) or to a trust corporation, so that the equitable interests of the beneficiaries under the trust are transferred to the capital monies, e.g. the proceeds of sale, leaving the purchaser to take free of those interests (ss.2 and 27 of the Law of Property Act 1925—see also para.2–021).

If there is only a sole trustee of land held on a trust of land, that trustee (unless they are a trust corporation or a sole personal representative acting as such) will therefore need to appoint a co-trustee to act jointly with them in respect of a sale of the land, so that there is a valid receipt for the capital money by not less than two trustees and overreaching is effected.

Only certain equitable interests can be overreached, being those which relate to an equitable interest under a trust of land rather than to the legal estate, e.g. an equitable share in land, or an equitable charge on an equitable share in land, such as a charging order on the beneficial share of one of joint owners of land (see also paras 16–032 and 16–033).

Other equitable interests cannot be overreached, where they relate to the legal estate, e.g. a restrictive covenant, equitable easement or equitable charge on the legal estate. Legal estates and interests cannot be overreached, e.g. a leasehold estate in land or a legal easement.

In the case of unregistered land which was held jointly by two or more persons on trust for themselves as beneficial joint tenants, where the number of joint tenants has reduced to one the trust of land will have come to an end. As an alternative to deducing the equitable title or appointing a co-trustee, the Law of Property (Joint Tenants) Act 1964 provided that the survivor of joint tenants is, in favour of a purchaser, deemed to be the sole beneficial beneficial owner if:

(i) they convey as beneficial owner, or the conveyance contains a statement that they are solely and beneficially interested in the property;

(ii) no memorandum of severance is endorsed on the conveyance that vested the legal estate in the joint tenants; and

(iii) no bankruptcy petition or order is registered as a Land Charge against any of the joint tenants.

Unfortunately, since July 1, 1995 the standard covenants for title have been imported by the phrase "with full title guarantee" rather than "beneficial owner" (see para.8–006), but the Law of Property (Joint Tenants) Act 1964 was not amended to reflect this. Consequently, care needs to be taken to include in a conveyance of unregistered land, where necessary, a statement that a sole surviving joint tenant is solely and beneficially interested.

Trusts of land and registered land

18–002 In relation to registered land, the register records the ownership of the legal estate, not the beneficial interests, and the registrar is not affected with notice of a trust (s.78). As far as possible, references to trusts should therefore be kept off the register.

A person dealing with a registered proprietor can assume that they have unlimited power to dispose of the registered estate or registered charge concerned, free from any limitation affecting the validity of the disposition, unless there is a restriction or other entry in the register limiting their powers, or a limitation imposed by or under the Act (s.26—see para.10–001). In the context of a trust of land, this means that, if two or more persons are registered as joint proprietors, a purchaser can safely acquire the legal estate from them, or from the survivor of them, unless there is a restriction or other entry to the contrary in the register.

In the case of a private trust, i.e. one not for charitable, ecclesiastical or public purposes, it is the duty of the trustees to apply for any necessary restriction(s), though a beneficiary may also apply (rr.93 and 94). The registrar is obliged to enter a restriction without application in only one circumstance, though he may do so in certain other cases if it appears to be necessary or desirable.

The registrar is obliged to enter a restriction when registering two or more persons as joint proprietors of a registered estate in land, whether on first registration or subsequently. A restriction in Form A must then be entered unless the registrar is satisfied that the applicants hold on trust for themselves as beneficial joint tenants and that the survivor of them can therefore give a valid receipt for capital money (s.44(1) and r.95(2)(a)—see paras 5–007 and 11–013). The purpose of this is to reflect the existence of a trust of land and ensure that overreaching is effected on a disposition for value of the land. The restriction will not catch a disposition where no capital money arises, e.g. on the appointment of a new trustee.

In the case of other types of registered estate, r.94(2A) provides that where two or more persons apply to be registered as proprietors of an estate which is a rentcharge, profit à prendre in gross, franchise or manor, they must also apply for entry of a restriction in Form A if a sole (surviving) proprietor will not be able to give a valid receipt for capital money.

A disposition "off the register" of an individual share in the proceeds of sale of registered land may be followed by a transfer of the registered land so as to bring the registered ownership into line with the beneficial ownership, if desired.

The position on the death of a joint proprietor or the survivor of joint proprietors, and the cancellation of a restriction in Form A in certain circumstances, are discussed in Chapter 19.

Application to register trustees

There are no prescribed forms specifically for dispositions to or by trustees; the standard forms prescribed in Sch.1 to the Rules must be used where the title is already registered (see paras 1–012 and 10–007). In the case of the grant of a lease out of a registered estate, this should where necessary be in the form of a prescribed clauses lease (see para.12–004). The consideration panel in a Sch.1 form may be completed to the effect that the transfer is not for money or anything which has a monetary value. The declaration of trust panel can be completed to the effect that the trustees are to hold the property "on the trusts of a trust deed (*or as the case may be*) dated (. . .)". The trust deed should not usually accompany the application. **18–003**

As with unregistered land, the number of trustees of a private trust of registered land cannot exceed four; if more than four are named, only the first four named who are able and willing to act will be registered as proprietors. This limitation does not apply to charitable trusts (see para.18–010).

The basis upon which the applicants are holding the land on trust, i.e. for themselves as equitable joint tenants or tenants in common or otherwise upon trust, should be made clear in the appropriate panel of the transfer, assent or prescribed clauses lease or (where the application is for first registration) of Form FR1. In a new lease of land granted out of a registered title, an appropriate declaration should be included within the prescribed clauses (if used) or within a clause in the lease. If this is not done, the registrar may have to enter a restriction in Form A by default in pursuance of his obligation (see para.18–002).

The registrar will not enter a restriction in Form A in respect of a registered charge, because although a charge can be held on trust, the survivor of the registered chargees is always able to give a valid receipt for the money secured by it (s.56).

The trustee(s) should apply for any other restriction(s) necessary to ensure that the interests of the beneficiaries are protected and the trusts duly executed (see para.18–004). If any special restriction based on the terms of a trust deed is needed, the registrar may retain an original trust deed lodged with the application but will return the original if requested to do so and the application is accompanied by a certified copy of the deed (r.203).

Section 27(2) of the Law of Property Act 1925 does not affect the right of a sole personal representative acting as such to give a valid receipt for capital money. Therefore the registrar will not automatically enter a restriction in Form A when registering a personal representative as proprietor of a registered estate. However, any existing such restriction will remain in the register because, in that case, the personal representative will be succeeding the deceased as trustee of the trust (see Chapter 19).

For the same reason, the registrar will enter a restriction in Form A on first registration when registering the personal representative of a deceased proprietor who was a sole trustee or (unless the deceased was the survivor of beneficial joint tenants) the last surviving trustee.

A fee for registration of a transfer other than for monetary consideration is payable, in accordance with the Fee Order. No fee is currently payable in respect of the entry of a restriction in Form A. Fees in respect of additional restrictions are payable in accordance with the Fee Order.

Application for restriction(s)

18–004 Where necessary, an application should be made for the entry of any appropriate restriction(s) to be entered in the register of a registered estate which is subject to a trust of land.

In cases where a restriction in Form A is appropriate and it has not already been automatically entered by the registrar, application should be made for entry of the restriction.

A proprietor of a registered estate must apply for a restriction in Form A when either (r.94(1)):

(1) The estate becomes subject to a trust of land, other than on a registrable disposition, and the proprietor or the survivor of joint proprietors will not be able to give a valid receipt for capital money. For example, if the proprietor has executed a declaration of trust, or if a constructive trust has arisen.

(2) The estate is held on a trust of land and, as a result of a change in the trusts, the proprietor or the survivor of joint proprietors will not be able to give a valid receipt for capital money. For example, where a beneficial joint tenancy has been severed by notice.

An application by one of two or more trustees satisfies the requirement to apply (r.94(9)).

If a sole or last surviving trustee of land applies for first registration, or to register a disposition of a registered estate in their favour, they must at the same time apply for a restriction in Form A (r.94(2)). Section 44(1) only applies to the entry of joint proprietors and so the registrar is not obliged to enter a restriction in Form A automatically on registering a sole or last surviving trustee.

Section 44(1) also only applies to registered estates in land. It does not apply when two or more persons are registered as proprietors of a rentcharge, manor, franchise or profit à prendre in gross. Nevertheless, if the survivor of them will not be able to give a valid receipt for capital money, a restriction in Form A should be applied for (r.94(2A)).

Where a registered estate is held on a trust of land and a sole proprietor or survivor of joint proprietors (not being a trust corporation) will not be able to give a valid receipt for capital money, any person interested in the estate can apply for entry of a restriction in Form A (s.43(1)(c) and r.93(a)). Unless the consent of the registered proprietor(s) accompanies the application, the registrar will have to serve notice of the application upon them (s.45(1)). If a valid objection is received which cannot be disposed of by agreement, the matter must be referred to the Adjudicator (see Chapter 23).

Application should also be made by the trustees for entry of a restriction in Form B (r.94(4) and (5)), where:

(a) (in respect of a registered estate) a declaration of trust imposes limitations on the powers of the trustees under s.8 of TLATA; or

(b) (in respect of a registered estate) a change in the trusts on which it is held imposes or changes limitations on the powers of the trustees under s.8 of TLATA; or

(c) (on an application for first registration of a legal estate held on a trust of land) the powers of the trustees are limited by s.8 of TLATA.

This applies not only when the legal estate is held by trustees, but also when it is held by the personal representative of a sole or last surviving trustee (r.94(7)). An application by one of two or more trustees satisfies the requirement to apply (r.94(9)).

Where a registered estate is held on a trust of land and the powers of the trustees are limited by s.8 of TLATA, any person interested in the estate can apply for a restriction in Form B (s.43(1)(c) and r.93(c)). Unless the consent of the registered proprietors accompanies the application, the registrar will have to serve notice of the application upon them (s.45(1)). If a valid objection is received which cannot be disposed of by agreement, the matter must be referred to the Adjudicator (see Chapter 23).

Other forms of restriction, such as a restriction in Form N or Form Q, may be applied for voluntarily where appropriate.

See para.16–023 for further guidance on applications for entry of restrictions and Appendix III as to the wording of standard forms of restriction.

Dispositions by trustees

Any restriction(s) in the register will, where necessary, need to be complied with before a disposition by the trustees can be registered. **18–005**

In the case of a restriction in Form A, where capital money arises as a result of the disposition and a sole or sole surviving trustee cannot give a valid receipt, e.g. because they are not a trust corporation, at least one new co-trustee will need to be appointed to join in the disposition. The appointment may be effected within the form of disposition, such as a transfer, or by separate deed; however it will in either event give rise to an additional fee payable in accordance with the Fee Order.

In the case of a restriction in Form B, the appropriate certificate, statutory declaration, or statement of truth will need to be provided.

In certain circumstances, an existing restriction may be cancelled automatically following completion of a disposition by registration. Thus a restriction in Form A will be cancelled on registration of a transfer on sale by two or more trustees or a trust corporation (except where the transfer is to one or more of the existing proprietors) under r.99.

A restriction in Form B will be cancelled on registration of a transfer on sale by the trustees when the appropriate certificate, statutory declaration, or statement of truth has been provided.

In other cases, application may be made to cancel a restriction where appropriate. The application should be made in Form RX3, accompanied by evidence to satisfy the registrar the restriction is no longer required. If the registrar is so satisfied, he must cancel the restriction (r.97).

Such an application could be made where, for example, a restriction in Form A appears in the register, but a sole or sole surviving proprietor has become the sole owner, legally and beneficially. The application would need to be accompanied by the appropriate evidence (see para.19–006).

Appointment and discharge of trustees

18–006 It is important that the names and addresses for service of trustees in the register are kept up to date and that any change of trustees is reflected in the register. An appointment of a new trustee will not be effective to vest the registered title in the new and any continuing trustees until it has been completed by registration. There are a number of methods of effecting the appointment and discharge of trustees of land.

(1) If all outgoing trustees are willing to co-operate, the simplest method is for the existing registered proprietors to execute a transfer in the appropriate form, e.g. Form TR1 or TR5 to the new and any continuing trustees. None of the statements in the consideration panel should be completed; instead, the words "This transfer is made for the purpose of effecting an appointment of new

trustees" should be inserted in the additional provisions panel.

Such a transfer can be used in addition to a separate deed of appointment or discharge, or on its own, instead of a deed of appointment. If a deed of appointment is used as well, Land Registry will not usually need to see it, but words such as "This transfer is made pursuant to a deed of appointment of new trustees of even date" should be inserted in the additional provisions panel of the transfer. The transfer must be executed by all the current trustees, including any trustee who is retiring from the trust.

A transfer used purely to effect the appointment of new trustees does not require SDLT evidence (see para.1–016).

(2) Under s.40 of the Trustee Act 1925, most deeds of appointment or retirement automatically vest trust property in the new and any continuing trustees. The exception is where the land is held under a lease which contains a provision against alienation without consent; in that event the deed will not operate to vest the land unless the necessary consent has been obtained (and which should therefore be lodged with the application for registration). If the trust property includes a registered estate or registered charge, this transfer by operation of law must be completed by registration (s.27(5)).

An application should be made in Form AP1 accompanied by the deed of appointment and either a certificate from the conveyancer acting for the persons making the appointment confirming that they are entitled to do so, or such other evidence (e.g. a copy trust instrument or statutory declaration or statement of truth proving the relevant facts) to satisfy the registrar that the persons making the appointment are entitled to do so (r.161(3)).

Such a deed of appointment may be the best way to proceed where, for example, a trustee has been replaced under s.36(1) of the Trustee Act 1925 on the grounds that they have remained out of the United Kingdom for more than 12 months, or refuse or are unfit to act in the trust, or are incapable of doing so. A statutory declaration or statement of truth proving the relevant facts would in that event need to be lodged with the application.

The registrar may serve notice of the application upon the trustee(s) being replaced and, if a valid objection is received which cannot be disposed of by agreement, the matter must be referred to the Adjudicator (see Chapter 23).

(3) Under s.41 of the Trustee Act 1925 the court may by vesting order appoint a new trustee. Where it relates to a registered estate, such an order must be completed by registration (s.27(5)). Application should be made in Form AP1, enclosing an office copy of the court order (r.161(2)). The registrar may retain the order, but will return it if requested to do so and the application is accompanied by a certified copy of the order (r.203).

(4) In certain cases where trustees may be appointed or discharged by resolution of a meeting of the trustees or other persons, e.g. under ss.13 and 129 of the Trade Union and Labour Relations (Consolidation) Act 1992, a vesting declaration is implied by statute in the memorandum or written record of the resolution. If the trust property is a registered estate or a registered charge, this declaration has to be completed by registration (s.27(5)). In many cases the simplest option will be for the existing registered proprietors to execute a transfer to the new and any continuing trustees. Alternatively, application may be made in Form AP1 to register the implied vesting declaration itself; a certified copy of the memorandum or resolution and evidence of the provision under which it operates to vest the estate in the trustees should accompany the application (r.161(1)).

(5) When a trustee has died, an application to remove their name from the register, or an application to register a disposition by the remaining trustees, should be accompanied by evidence of the death (r.164—see Chapter 19).

In the case of (1) and (2) above, any restriction in Form A can be ignored (as capital money does not arise), but any other restrictions should be complied with as necessary.

In the case of unregistered land, the appointment of a new trustee may be a "trigger" for compulsory first registration (see para.5–003).

Fees in accordance with the Fee Order are payable.

Charities

Introduction

18–007 In addition to the requirements of the Act and the Rules, the requirements of the Charities Act 1993 should be borne in mind when making applications to register dispositions by or in favour of charities. The Charities Act 1993 was amended by the

Charities Act 2006 which effected numerous changes in relation to the law relating to charities generally.

Most charities are subject to the jurisdiction of the Charity Commission (previously "the Charity Commissioners") and are referred to as "non-exempt" charities, as opposed to the minority of charities, referred to as "exempt charities", which are covered by the Charities Act 1993 for some purposes, but are largely exempted from the jurisdiction of the Charity Commission. Exempt charities include certain universities and colleges and the board of trustees of certain museums, for example.

The trustees of non-exempt charities are generally allowed to sell, mortgage or otherwise dispose of the charity's land without an order of the court or of the Charity Commission, if they follow the correct procedures. These procedures are not binding on exempt charities, nor do they apply to certain specific transactions.

All dispositions of an estate **in favour of a charity** must contain an appropriate statement (see para.18–008) as to whether the charity is exempt or non-exempt and, if the latter, as to the restrictions on dispositions imposed by the Charities Act 1993.

All dispositions of a registered estate **by a charity** must contain an appropriate statement (see para.18–014). In the case of a non-exempt charity the disposition may also need to contain a certificate by the charity trustees (see para.18–015).

The statements enable the registrar:

(1) when registering a non-exempt charity or its trustees as proprietors of land, to enter an appropriate restriction; and

(2) when registering a disposition by a non-exempt charity, to be satisfied that the restriction has been complied with.

A transfer of a registered or unregistered estate on or in consequence of the appointment of a new charity trustee is not a "disposition" for the purposes of the Charities Act 1993. Therefore, none of the statements nor the certificate are required to be included in a deed that appoints a new trustee or is made in consequence of the appointment of a new charity trustee.

In the case of an unregistered estate, the appointment of a new charity trustee may "trigger" compulsory first registration (see para.5–003).

Dispositions to charities

A transfer, lease or other disposition of registered land to a charity and any conveyance or assignment or lease of unregistered land which "triggers" compulsory first registration must **18–008** (r.179) contain one of the following statements as required by s.37(5) of the Charities Act 1993, depending upon whether it is an exempt or a non-exempt charity:

> "The land transferred (*or as the case may be*) will, as a result of this transfer (*or as the case may be*), be held by (*or* in trust for) (*charity*), an exempt charity."

or

> "The land transferred [*or as the case may be*] will, as a result of this transfer [*or as the case may be*], be held by (*or* in trust for) (*charity*), a non-exempt charity and the restrictions on disposition imposed by section 36 of the Charities Act 1993 will apply to the land (subject to section 36(9) of that Act)."

The statements set out above are not required to be included in any charge in favour of a charity.

Where the charity trustees are incorporated as a body corporate under Part VII of the Charities Act 1993, any disposition in favour of the charity must describe the trustees as: "a body corporate under Part VII of the Charities Act 1993" and the application to register the disposition should be accompanied by a certified copy of the certificate granted by the Charity Commission under s.50 of the Charities Act 1993 (r.177). Where the charity is a body corporate incorporated under a statute or charter other than the Charities Act 1993 this should be stated.

Applications for registration by charities

18–009 In the case of an exempt charity the registrar does not have to enter a restriction. Application for an appropriate restriction must be made, if such a restriction is required because of limitations on the powers of the charity.

In the case of a non-exempt charity, the registrar is under an obligation to enter a restriction that reflects the powers of the charity as registered proprietor (r.176)

In the event of a voluntary application for first registration by a non-exempt charity, the conveyance or other instrument will not contain one of the above statements and therefore r.176 provides that the application must be accompanied by an application for entry of the appropriate restriction in Form E (see para.18–011). Application for a restriction must be made in Form RX1.

Application for the appropriate restriction must also be made where application is made to register a transfer which does not contain the necessary statement set out above or application is made under r.161 to register the vesting of a registered estate in a person other than the proprietor of that estate.

Where application is made for registration of the Official Custodian for Charities ("the Official Custodian") as proprietor, the application must include:

(1) a certified copy of an order of the court made under s.21(1) of the Charities Act 1993; or

(2) a certified copy of an order of the Charity Commission made under ss.16 or 18 of the Charities Act 1993 (r.178(1)).

In addition, where land is vested in the Official Custodian (other than by virtue of an order under s.18 of the Charities Act 1993) the address of the charity (if a corporation) or its trustees (if not a corporation) must be supplied for entry in the register (r.178(3)).

However, the address of the Official Custodian will be entered as the address for service if the land is vested in him by virtue of an order under s.18 of the 1993 Act and r.178(2) provides that the application must be accompanied by an application for a restriction in Form F (see para.18–011).

Where the disposition is in favour of an exempt charity, the document creating the charitable trust should be lodged (r.182). Otherwise no evidence of the charity's constitution or trusts should be lodged, save for where the charity is incorporated otherwise than under the Charities Act 1993 or under the Companies Acts, when such documentation (or a conveyancer's certificate in the appropriate Sch.3 form specified in r.183, being Form 7 or Form 8 as the case may be) should be lodged.

Entry of proprietor

The normal limit of no more than four trustees of a legal estate does not apply to charities. **18–010**

Where charity trustees are individuals the registrar will, if requested, enter the name of the charity as a description after the names and addresses of the trustees. If the charity trustees have been incorporated under Pt VII of the Charities Act 1993 this fact will be stated in the proprietorship entry as follows:

> "Proprietor: The Trustees of [*name of charity*] of [*address of charity*] incorporated under Part VII of the Charities Act 1993".

Where the charity is a corporation, the registrar will enter its name and address in the register, together with the company registration number if applicable.

Where an estate has been transferred to the Official Custodian the proprietorship entry will read:

"Proprietor: The Official Custodian for Charities on behalf of [*name of charity*] of [*address of charity*]."

In the past, the Land Registry registered the trustees of some unincorporated charities collectively as, for example, "The trustees of the charity known as [*name* of charity]". This practice has been discontinued. The Land Registry will accept a certificate from the secretary or conveyancer of the charity as to the identity of the present trustees where trustees are so registered. The names of all the individual trustees will be entered on the register at the next available opportunity.

Entry of restrictions

18–011 **(1) *Restrictions for non-exempt charities*** Under s.37 of the Charities Act 1993, the registrar is obliged to enter an appropriate restriction in the register when registering a disposition in favour of a non-exempt charity. The statement in the disposition to the charity (see para.18–008) will show if the charity is non-exempt. The appropriate restriction is in Form E as set out in Sch.4 to the Rules (r.176). See Appendix III for the wording of a standard restriction in Form E.

For the purposes of this restriction, the term "disposition" includes, for example, the grant and release of easements. Also, the term "registered" includes not only the making of an entry in the register but also the cancellation of such an entry.

(2) *Restriction where the Official Custodian is registered as proprietor* In addition to a restriction in Form E, when the Official Custodian is being registered as proprietor as a result of a vesting order made under s.18 of the Charities Act 1993 a further restriction in Form F is required (r.178). An application must be made in Form RX1 for entry of this restriction. See Appendix III for the wording of a standard restriction in Form F. A former version of this restriction referred to the Charity Commissioners rather than the Charity Commission.

(3) *Restrictions for exempt charities* An application to register an exempt charity as proprietor must be accompanied by a copy of the document creating the charitable trust (r.182(1)). If the trust document limits the power of the charity to deal with land, application should be made in Form RX1 for a restriction to be entered in the register reflecting the limitations.

(4) *Restriction in Form A* When registering charity trustees as joint proprietors, whether or not one of them is a trust corporation, the registrar will enter a restriction in Form A (see paras 18–001 to 18–006). In the case of a sole trustee or custodian trustee, application should be made for such a restriction, either in the transfer to the trustee or in Form RX1 (r.94(2)).

(5) *First registration of a non-exempt charity* When a non-exempt charity applies for first registration voluntarily under the provisions of s.3, or following an event that "triggers" compulsory registration under s.4 in circumstances where that event is not a "disposition" for the purposes of the Charities Act 1993, there will not be a disposition to the charity containing the statement referred to in para.18–008. In these circumstances, an application must be made in Form RX1 for the entry of a restriction in Form E (r.176(2)).

(6) *Other restrictions* Where there are any other limitations on the powers of a charity which is being registered as proprietor, application should be made in Form RX1 for entry of any appropriate restrictions in the register (see para.16–023).

Dispositions by charities

(1) *Exempt charities* **18–012**

A disposition by an exempt charity of registered land, or of unregistered land which "triggers" first registration (see para.5–003), is required to contain a statement about the land and the charity (ss.37(1) and 39(1) of the Charities Act 1993). The statement to be included depends on whether or not the disposition is a mortgage.

(a) The statement for dispositions other than mortgages is (r.180(1)(a)):

> "The land transferred (or as the case may be) is held by ((proprietors) in trust for) (charity), an exempt charity."

(b) The statement for mortgages (r.180(2)(a) is:

> "The land charged is held by (or in trust for) (charity), an exempt charity."

A disposition by an exempt charity lodged for registration which does not contain one of these statements will be returned to the applicant for the appropriate statement to be included.

(2) *Non-exempt charities*

Background Under s.36 of the Charities Act 1993, a **18–013**
non-exempt charity is required to go through certain procedural steps before disposing of land, such as taking advice from a qualified surveyor. Once these steps have been taken then,

provided that it has power under the trusts of the charity to make the disposal and the transaction is not in favour of a connected person (as defined in the Charities Act 1993), the charity can dispose of the land without an order of the Charity Commission or the court. In all other cases (subject to s.36(9) of the 1993 Act—see below) such an order is required.

Under s.38 of the Charities Act 1993 a non-exempt charity is normally required (subject to s.38(5)—see below), before mortgaging its land, to take certain procedural steps such as taking advice on whether the loan is necessary and its terms are reasonable.

Generally therefore, non-exempt charities are subject to restrictions on dispositions under s.36 and to restrictions on mortgaging under s.38 of the Charities Act 1993. However, dispositions falling within s.36(9)(a), (b) or (c) and mortgages falling within s.38(5) are not subject to those restrictions and so these will not need to be complied with nor will the consent of the Charity Commission or the court be required.

The categories of disposition covered by s.36(9)(a), (b) or (c) are:

(1) any disposition for which general or special authority is expressly given by a statutory provision or a legally established scheme (which must be lodged with any application relying on it);

(2) any disposition of an estate in land which:

 (a) is made to another charity otherwise than for the best price; and
 (b) is authorised to be made by the trusts of the disposing charity;

(3) any disposition by way of lease to a beneficiary under the trusts of the charity which:

 (a) is granted for less than the best rent that can be obtained; and
 (b) is intended to enable the demised premises to be occupied for the purposes of the charity; and
 (c) is in accordance with the trusts of the charity.

Under s.38(5), there is no restriction on mortgages for which general or special authority is expressly given by a statutory provision or a legally established scheme.

Where the charity's land is registered, the requirements of the Charities Act 1993 are reflected in the register by the entry of a restriction in Form E (see para.18–011), the effect of which is that no disposition by the proprietor of the land is to be registered if ss.36 or 38 of the Charities Act 1993 apply, without an appropriate certificate from the charity trustees being contained within the instrument effecting the disposition.

Providing any disposition by a non-exempt charity contains the relevant statement confirming whether or not the restrictions imposed by ss.36 or 38 apply (see para.18–014) and, if they do apply, also contains a certificate by the charity trustees confirming that those restrictions have been complied with (see para.18–015), the requirements of the restriction in Form E will be met and the disposition can be registered.

The statements required in the disposition A disposition by a non-exempt charity of registered land, or of unregistered land which "triggers" first registration, is required to contain a statement about the land and the charity (ss.37(1) and 39(1) of the Charities Act 1993). The appropriate statement to be included depends upon whether or not the disposition is a mortgage and whether or not the restrictions in ss.36 or 38 of the Charities Act 1993 apply. Rule180 specifies the alternative forms of statement to be included. **18–014**

The statements for dispositions other than mortgages are either:

(1) "The land transferred (or as the case may be) is held by ((proprietors) in trust for) (charity), a non-exempt charity, and this transfer (or as the case may be) is not one falling within paragraph (a), (b) or (c) of section 36(9) of the Charities Act 1993, so that the restrictions on disposition imposed by section 36 of that Act apply to the land" (r.180(1)(c)); or

(2) "The land transferred (or as the case may be) is held by ((proprietors) in trust for) (charity), a non-exempt charity, but this transfer (or as the case may be) is one falling within paragraph (a), (b) or (c) (as the case may be) of section 36(9) of the Charities Act 1993" (r.180(1)(b)).

The statements for mortgages are either:

(a) "The land charged is held by (or in trust for) (charity), a non-exempt charity, and this charge (or mortgage) is not one falling within section 38(5) of the Charities Act 1993, so that the restrictions imposed by section 38 of that Act apply" (r.180(2)(c)); or

(b) "The land charged is held by (or in trust for) (charity), a non-exempt charity, but this charge (or mortgage) is one falling within section 38(5) of the Charities Act 1993" (r.180(2)(b).

In addition, a mortgage by a non-exempt charity that "triggers" first registration (see para.5–003) should also contain the following statement:

> "The restrictions on disposition imposed by section 36 of the Charities Act 1993 also apply to the land (subject to section 36(9) of that Act)" (r.180(3)).

18–015 *The certificate required in the disposition* Where a restriction in Form E appears in the register of registered charity land, in addition to the appropriate statement referred to in para.18–014 the disposition must also contain a certificate where either:

(1) it is a disposition to which s.36 of the Charities Act 1993 applies; or

(2) it is a charge to which s.38 of the Charities Act 1993 applies.

There is no prescribed form of certificate, but it should normally reflect the appropriate statement in the deed effecting the disposition, depending upon whether the charity trustees have complied with the relevant provisions of the Charities Act 1993 (so far as applicable to the disposition) and whether the disposition is a charge. The alternative to complying with the provisions of the Charities Act 1993 is to obtain an order of the Charity Commission or the Court authorising the disposition.

Where the charity trustees have complied with s.36 of the Charities Act 1993 (which relates to dispositions other than charges), a suitable form of certificate would be:

> "[Description of charity trustees and capacity in which they certify] certify that they have power under its trusts to effect this disposition and that they have complied with the provisions of the said section 36 so far as applicable to this disposition."

Where the charity trustees have complied with s.38 of the Charities Act 1993 (which relates to mortgages) a suitable form of certificate would be:

> "[Description of charity trustees and capacity in which they certify] certify that they have power under its trusts to effect this charge and that they have obtained and considered such advice as is mentioned in section 38(2) of the said Act."

Where the disposition has been sanctioned by an order of the Charity Commission or the Court, a suitable form of certificate would be:

> "[Description of charity trustees and capacity in which they certify] certify that this disposition (or charge) has been sanctioned by an order of the Charity Commission (or the Court)."

Where a disposition or charge contains any such certificates, when a person acquires an interest in land estate for money or money's worth it shall be conclusively presumed that the facts are as stated in the certificate (ss.37(3) and 39(3) of the Charities Act 1993).

Who gives the certificate? The certificate must be given by the charity trustees (ss.37(2) and 39(2) of the Charities Act 1993). Therefore, if they are not also the registered proprietors, they will need to join in and execute the disposition or charge in order to give the certificate. The Charities Act 1993 defines "charity trustees" as the persons having the general control and management of the administration of the charity. **18–016**

Unregistered land Where unregistered land is held by or in trust for a charity, the owners' powers to dispose of it are restricted in much the same way as they would be if their title were registered. Therefore, when examining a title on first registration, Land Registry will apply the principles outlined above as if the appropriate restriction had applied. **18–017**

Land Registry will be able to determine if a certificate is appropriate because the requirement that the disposition contains statements about the land, the charity and the nature of the disposition also applies to conveyances, mortgages and leases of unregistered land.

A disposition of unregistered land by a non-exempt charity, to which s.36 or s.38 of the Charities Act 1993 applies, should therefore contain an appropriate certificate as described above.

When a certificate is not required A certificate will not be required where the disposition is one falling within s.36(9)(a), (b) and (c) of the Charities Act 1993 or where it is a charge falling within s.38(5) of that Act (see para.18–013), as will be confirmed by the appropriate statement in the deed or charge. **18–018**

Also, a certificate should not be included in a deed that is not a "disposition" for the purposes of s.36 of the Charities Act 1993, such as a deed that appoints a new trustee.

Complying with restrictions

18–019 ***Form A*** A restriction in Form A will be complied with where the disposition is by charity trustees as joint proprietors or by a trust corporation. However, if the proprietor is a sole trustee (other than a trust corporation) it will be necessary for an additional trustee to be appointed (see paras 18–001 to 18–006 above).

18–020 ***Form E*** This restriction will be complied with if the disposition contains the relevant statement and, if needed, a certificate as mentioned in paras 18–014 and 18–015.

18–021 ***Form F*** If a restriction in Form F appears in the register (see para.18–011) and the disposition has been executed in the name of and on behalf of the Official Custodian by the charity trustees, an order of the Charity Commission will be required to authorise the disposition (s.22(3) of the Charities Act 1993). If this is the case, the disposition should include a certificate stating that it has been sanctioned by an order of the Charity Commission or of the court, as appropriate.

The restriction does not apply to dispositions executed by the Official Custodian.

18–022 ***Other restrictions*** Any other restrictions appearing in the register will need to be complied with as necessary.

18–023 ***Dispositions of charity land registered before 1993 or between 1993 and 2003*** The registered title to the land of a non-exempt charity registered before 1993, or registered between 1993 and 2003, will be subject to old forms of restriction. On an application to register a disposition these restrictions will be treated as if they were in the relevant current form and the appropriate statement and certificate should be included in the disposition.

Cancellation of restrictions

18–024 A restriction in the register in Form A, Form E or Form F will be cancelled automatically where an application is made to register a transfer of the title by the proprietor provided:

(1) the restriction has been complied with; and

(2) the application is otherwise in order.

If a charity will remain as proprietor following registration of a disposition, such as a lease or a charge, the restriction(s) will remain in the register.

Execution by charities

Where the charity is a body corporate incorporated under the Companies Acts, it should execute a disposition in the form appropriate for a company (see paras 10–010 to 10–012). **18–025**

Where the charity consists of individual trustees, a disposition must normally be executed by them all. However, s.82 of the Charities Act 1993 allows charity trustees to delegate to no fewer than two of their number an authority to execute on behalf of all of them any deed giving effect to a transaction to which the trustees are a party. Land Registry will not require any evidence of delegation if the transfer, charge or other disposition states that it has been executed pursuant to s.82 and the disposition is for money or money's worth and there is no reason to doubt the good faith of the person in whose favour it is made. In the absence of a delegation under s.82 all the trustees must execute the deed.

If the charity trustees have been incorporated under Part VII of the Charities Act 1993, the body corporate can execute a disposition by affixing its common seal (if it has one) in the presence of appropriate officers of the charity. If the charity chooses not to use or does not have a common seal, two other methods of execution are provided by the Charities Act 1993. These are:

(1) by a majority of the individual charity trustees and expressed to be executed by the body (e.g. "This Transfer is executed by [*names of trustees*] being a majority of the incorporated trustees of [*name of the charity*] under the provisions of section 60(3)(a) of the Charities Act 1993")—Land Registry will require evidence that those executing are a majority; or

(2) pursuant to a general or limited authority conferred on any two or more trustees to execute in the name and on behalf of the body corporate (s.60(4) of the 1993 Act)—Land Registry will require evidence of the authority.

If charity land is registered in the name of the Official Custodian, he does not execute deeds personally. Instead, the charity trustee(s) have full power to execute a disposition where the Official Custodian is the registered proprietor, except where the estate has been vested in him under s.18 of the Charities Act 1993 and a restriction in Form F appears in the register (see para.18–011).

The charity trustee(s) must execute the disposition, for the purposes of giving the required certificate (see para.18–015), using one of the methods of execution outlined above.

Changes of charity trustees, etc.

18–026 Where a charity is registered as proprietor, application should be made to reflect any relevant changes to the charity in the register, as appropriate. For example, if there is a change in the individual charity trustees following an appointment and/or discharge, or a change in the name of the charity.

The general law relating to the appointment and discharge of trustees also applies to charities. In addition, s.83 of the Charities Act 1993 provides that a charity may, provided its trusts permit it, appoint and discharge trustees by resolution of a meeting of the charity trustees, members or other persons. A memorandum signed at the meeting is sufficient evidence of the resolution(s). To be effective to transfer the legal estate the memorandum must:

(1) be executed as a deed;

(2) be executed by the person presiding at the meeting or in some other manner directed by the meeting;

(3) be witnessed by two persons present at the meeting; and

(4) relate to land to which s.40 of the Trustee Act 1925 applies (see para.18–006).

An application to alter the register so as to register the current trustees must be accompanied by the original memorandum, evidence of the death of any trustee currently shown in the register who has died, and a certificate by a conveyancer acting for the charity that it has power to use the procedure set out in s.83.

Appointment of a new trustee may also be effected by a transfer (see Chapter 11). No statement or certificate is required in a transfer to appoint new trustees as it is not a sale, lease or other disposal by the charity.

Settled land

18–027 TLATA provided that no new strict settlements under the Settled Land Act 1925 could be created after the commencement of TLATA. As regards existing settlements, s.89 (of the Act) provides that rules may make provision in relation to the application of the Settled Land Act 1925 to registered land and this is dealt with in r.186 and Sch.7 to the Rules.

Settled land is registered in the name of the tenant for life, statutory owner or special personal representatives in whom the legal estate would be vested if the land were unregistered. The successive or other interests created by or arising under the settlement and capable of being overridden under the Settled Land Act 1925 or any other statute do not appear in the register. The rights of the persons beneficially interested in the land are, however, protected by restrictions entered in the proprietorship register. Three restrictions are prescribed by the Rules:

(1) Form G (for use where the tenant for life is the registered proprietor of settled land and there are trustees of the settlement).

(2) Form H (for use where statutory owners are the trustees of the settlement and the registered proprietors of settled land). NB: this restriction does not apply where the statutory owners are not the trustees of the settlement.

(3) Form I (for use where the tenant for life is the registered proprietor of settled land and there are no trustees of the settlement).

See Appendix III for the wording of these standard restrictions. The restrictions may be modified on application or as the registrar sees fit, according to the circumstances. Where one of the prescribed restrictions should have been entered in the register and has not been, any person who has an interest in the settled land can apply for such restriction (modified if appropriate) to be entered. The persons interested under the settlement may apply for any additional restriction(s) necessitated by the provisions of the settlement.

When a registered estate consists of settled land the proprietor or, if there is no proprietor, the personal representative(s) of a deceased proprietor must apply in Form RX1 for the entry of any appropriate restrictions, in addition to a restriction in Form G, H or I. The application must state that the restrictions are required for the protection of the beneficial interests and powers under the settlement.

Except in the instances referred to in para.8 of Sch.7 to the Rules (proprietor ceasing in his lifetime to be the tenant for life) and para.14 (discharge of registered land from beneficial interests and powers under a settlement) the restrictions bind the proprietor in their lifetime but do not affect dispositions by their personal representative(s).

Fees may be payable in respect of restrictions, in accordance with the Fee Order. See para.16–023 as to an application for entry of a restriction.

Schedule 7 to the Rules makes the following provision in relation to settled land.

First registration

18–028 An application for first registration of settled land must be accompanied by an application for entry of a restriction in Form G, H, or I as appropriate.

Transfer of land into settlement

18–029 When registered land is transferred into settlement, the transfer must include the appropriate provisions set out in para.4 of Sch.7 to the Rules. The application for registration of the transfer must be accompanied by an application for entry of the appropriate restriction.

Registered land brought into settlement

18–030 Where registered land is brought into a settlement and the existing registered proprietor is the tenant for life, the registered proprietor must make a declaration in Form 6 (contained in Sch.3 to the Rules) and apply for the entry of a restriction in Form G, modified if appropriate.

Registered land bought with capital money

18–031 Where registered land is bought with capital money the transfer must be in one of the Sch.1 forms prescribed by r.206 and include the appropriate provisions set out in para.6 of Sch.7 to the Rules. The application for registration must be accompanied by an application for the appropriate restriction.

Registration of statutory owner during a minority otherwise than on death

18–032 If a minor becomes entitled in possession to registered land otherwise than on a death (or will be so entitled on attaining full age) the statutory owner during the minority is entitled to have the land transferred to them and to be registered as proprietor. The transfer must be in Form TR1 and must not refer to the settlement. An application to register the transfer must be accompanied by an application for a restriction in Form H.

Registration of special personal representatives

18–033 Paragraph 11 of Sch.7 to the Rules deals with registration of special personal representatives where the land was settled before the death of the sole or last surviving joint registered proprietor and not by their will and the settlement continues after death.

Minority where settlement arises under a will or intestacy

During a minority, the personal representatives under a will or intestacy of a person who died before January 1, 1997 under which a settlement of registered land is created or arises, must be registered as proprietors and will have all the powers conferred by the Settled Land Act 1925 on a tenant for life and on the trustees of the settlement. **18–034**

When the minor becomes beneficially entitled to an estate in fee simple or a term of years absolute in registered land or would, if they were of full age, be or have the powers of a tenant for life, the personal representative(s) must (unless they are themselves the statutory owner) during the minority give effect in the register to the directions of the statutory owner. The statutory owner must direct the personal representatives to apply for a restriction in Form H.

The registrar is under no duty to call for any information regarding why an application is made, or the terms of the will or devolution under the intestacy, or the directions of the statutory owner. Instead the registrar can assume that the personal representative(s) are acting according to the directions given and that the directions were given and were correct.

A disponee dealing with the personal representatives who complies with the Form H restriction is not concerned to see or enquire whether any directions have been given by the statutory owner with regard to the disposition to them.

As changes take place under a settlement of registered land, the registered proprietor or his personal representatives must execute the instruments necessary to give effect to the changes in the register and must apply for any necessary changes in the restrictions appearing in the register. An appropriate prescribed form in Sch.1 to the Rules should be used, modified where necessary according to the facts, e.g. in accordance with para.12 of Sch.7 to the Rules where there is a transfer on the death of the tenant for life.

New trustees are appointed in the usual way (see para.18–006). Where, however, a restriction in Form G appears in the register, an application to modify the restriction by substituting the new names is necessary. This should be made in Form RX2 signed by any continuing trustees and the new trustees or their respective conveyancers. Deaths of trustees must be proved by death certificates. A fee in accordance with the Fee Order is payable.

When the settlement ends on the death of the tenant for life, an application to register a transfer by the personal representative(s) to the person(s) entitled must be accompanied by the grant of probate or letters of administration of the deceased proprietor (if the personal representative is not already registered) and Form RX3 for cancellation of the restriction relating to the settlement. A fee in accordance with the Fee Order is payable.

If the settlement ends because the tenant for life becomes absolutely entitled, free from all interests under the settlement, the trustees may release the land from the interests under the settlement by a deed of release. If this is lodged at Land Registry with a certified copy, together with an application in Form RX3 for the cancellation of any restriction relating to the settlement, the restriction will be cancelled. No fee is currently payable for the cancellation of a restriction.

Practical points

- Be aware of the significance of a trust of land and the practical effects of this, e.g. the need to comply with a restriction in Form A,
- Be aware of the need to ensure overreaching is effected on a disposition for value,
- Remember to provide confirmation of the trusts upon which joint proprietors are to hold the registered estate with an application where appropriate, to avoid unnecessary entry of a restriction in Form A by default and/or unnecessary problems in the future,
- Remember to apply for entry of any appropriate restrictions relating to a trust of land,
- Ensure a change of trustees is properly effected and any appropriate application made in relation to it,
- Ensure the correct statement is included within a disposition to a charity, where necessary,
- Ensure the correct statement and certificate are included within a disposition by a charity, where necessary,
- Ensure that any necessary details are included within a disposition relating to settled land and any restrictions applied for/complied with as necessary.

Chapter 19

Death

Devolution on death

It is important to consider the devolution of the legal estate and the equitable or beneficial interest as a result of the death of a proprietor of a registered estate. Where a sole or sole surviving proprietor dies, the legal estate will vest in their executor or administrator (s.1(1) of the Administration of Estates Act 1925). **19–001**

In the case of joint proprietors, the legal estate can only be held as joint tenants; it cannot be severed so as to be held as *legal* tenants in common (ss.1(6), 34 and 36 of the Law of Property Act 1925). This means the principle of "survivorship" applies, so that if one joint proprietor dies, the legal estate will automatically vest in the survivor(s) by operation of law regardless of what happens to the beneficial interest.

The equitable or beneficial interest, on the other hand, may be held as beneficial joint tenants or as beneficial tenants in common. The principle of survivorship applies to the share of a deceased joint tenant which will therefore automatically vest in the surviving joint tenant(s), but not that of a deceased tenant in common which will pass under their will or intestacy.

Death of sole or sole surviving proprietor

Noting the death in the register

On the death of the proprietor, the legal estate will have vested in their personal representative by operation of law (see para.19–001). As an interim measure, before any further action is taken in relation to the title, application may be made to note the death in the proprietorship register. This is not obligatory, but it helps to keep the register up to date and reduce the **19–002** possibility of fraud, particularly if there is likely to be some delay in obtaining a grant of representation.

The application should be made in Form AP1, citing "death of sole proprietor". There is currently no fee payable, but the application must be accompanied by evidence of the death in the form of the original or an office copy of the death certificate or grant of representation (if any). Alternatively, written confirmation of the fact of death in a certificate from a conveyancer may (except where the deceased died abroad) be provided.

On completion of the application, the registrar will enter a simple note of the death in the register. No change will be made to the address for service, even if requested, unless the personal representative applies to be registered as proprietor at the same time.

Once a grant of representation has been obtained, the personal representative may either apply to register themselves as proprietor, execute an assent of the registered estate in favour of the beneficiaries or transfer the property to a third party.

Registration of the personal representative

19–003 On the death of a sole or sole surviving proprietor, their personal representative may apply to be registered as proprietor in place of the deceased. The application should be made in Form AP1 citing "transfer by operation of law" or "registration of personal representatives" with a fee in accordance with the Fee Order and accompanied by:

(1) the original or an office copy of the grant of probate or letters of administration to the estate of the deceased; or

(2) a court order appointing the applicant as the deceased's personal representative; or

(3) a certificate from the conveyancer acting for the applicant that they hold the original or an office copy of the grant, letters of administration or court order (r.163(2)).

There are exceptions to this general rule. Where the register states that the deceased was the administrator of the estate of a deceased proprietor, a grant of letters of administration *de bonis non* to the estate of that deceased proprietor must be obtained, and the administrator *de bonis non* can then apply to be registered as proprietor. Similarly, when the register states that the deceased was the executor of a deceased proprietor, but the executor has died intestate, his administrator is not entitled to be registered in the deceased executor's place; a grant of letters of administration *de bonis non* to the estate of the original testator is necessary, and the administrator *de bonis non* can then apply to be registered as proprietor. These exceptions apply because the "chain of representation" does not apply in these circumstances.

A chain of representation arises where the executor of a deceased proprietor themselves dies without having completed the administration of the estate. If the executor has left a will appointing an executor, then on proving that will, that latter executor also automatically becomes executor of the deceased proprietor's estate as well. The chain of representation only applies to executors not administrators and if the chain of successive executorships is broken then a grant *de bonis non* to the deceased proprietor's estate would then be required. If an applicant relies upon a chain of representation, evidence of any additional grant of probate showing the chain will also need to be lodged, as well as the grant to the deceased proprietor's estate.

Although the personal representative is not obliged to become registered as proprietor before exercising their powers of disposition, a disadvantage of not doing so is that the register remains out of date longer than it would if they were registered as proprietor as soon as the grant of representation was made. Whilst the register is out of date, any notice sent by Land Registry and addressed to the deceased proprietor may go astray, to the detriment of the interests of the deceased's estate and the beneficiaries.

On completion of the application, the personal representative will be described in the register as "executor *or* executrix (*or* administrator *or* administratrix) of [name] deceased" and will have full powers of disposition, subject to any entry to the contrary in the register. They will however still be bound by any existing "joint proprietorship" restriction in Form A (previously Form 62 in the Land Registration Rules 1925) appearing in the register (see para.18–002).

This restriction will not be cancelled automatically by the registrar on the registration of the personal representative as proprietor in the place of a deceased proprietor, because the trust of land reflected by the restriction may not have come to an end. However, the personal representative may make an application for cancellation of the restriction if they are able to show that the deceased had become legally and beneficially entitled to the whole of the registered estate (see para.19–006).

A personal representative holding a registered estate on a trust of land created by the deceased's will, or on a trust of land arising under the laws intestacy which is subsequently varied, and whose powers have been limited by s.8 of TLATA, must apply for a restriction in Form C to reflect this in the register (r.94(3)). See also para.18–004 as to a restriction in Form B.

Assent by the personal representative

19–004 Where a beneficiary is entitled to a registered estate either under the will or intestacy of a deceased proprietor, the personal representative may execute an assent in their favour, whether or not the personal representative has themselves first been registered as proprietor in place of the deceased proprietor.

The assent must be in the appropriate form as prescribed by r.58, i.e. Form AS1 (assent of whole) or Form AS3 (assent of part), or by r.116, i.e. Form AS2 (assent of a charge).

An application to register such an assent should be made in Form AP1 citing "registration of assent" and be accompanied by:

(1) the assent;
(2) (unless the personal representative has already been registered as proprietor) the requisite evidence of appointment similar to that required by r.163(2) (r.162(1)—see para.19–003);
(3) the appropriate SDLT evidence (see para.1–016); and
(4) the fee payable in accordance with the Fee Order.

For settled land, reference should be made to Chapter 18.

Rule 162(2) places responsibility on the personal representative in relation to registered land forming part of the deceased's estate, by providing that the registrar shall not be under a duty to investigate the reasons a transfer of registered land by a personal representative of a deceased sole proprietor or last surviving joint proprietor is made nor to consider the contents of the will and, provided the terms of any restriction on the register are complied with, he must assume, whether he knows of the terms of the will or not, that the personal representative is acting correctly and within their powers. Provided any restriction in the register is complied with, the registrar will not therefore look beyond the assent and investigate whether it has been made in accordance with the will or intestacy.

The beneficiary will be registered subject to any existing entries in the register which are not cancelled or withdrawn, including any existing restrictions. The terms of any such restrictions (such as those of a "chargee" type restriction in Form P—see Appendix III) will, where necessary, need to be complied with before the assent can be completed by registration. Where a restriction in Form C (see para.19–003) appears in the register, the assent will not be caught by it and it will be automatically cancelled on registration of the assent.

A restriction in Form A will be entered where necessary; any other new restrictions required should be applied for as appropriate (see Chapter 16).

It should be noted that an "assent of a share" relating only to the beneficial share of a deceased proprietor does not effect a transfer of the legal estate. Such an assent should not be lodged for registration and, if a transfer of the legal estate is required, this should be in the prescribed form and application made to complete it by registration (see Chapter 11).

Transfer by the personal representative

The personal representative may deal with the registered estate in accordance with their powers in that capacity, subject to any entry to the contrary in the register, whether or not they have been registered as proprietor in place of the deceased. **19–005**

If a restriction in Form A appears in the register when the transfer is registered, it will be cancelled by the registrar if the transfer is by two or more personal representatives or a trust corporation, as the equitable interests under the trust of land will have been overreached (ss.2 and 27 of the Law of Property Act 1925—see paras 2–021 and 18–001).

However, if the transfer is by a sole personal representative (not being a trust corporation) of a sole surviving proprietor, the application will be caught by the restriction as if it were an application to register a transfer on sale by the deceased. Therefore, unless the registrar is satisfied that the equitable interests have been overreached, it will be necessary either to appoint a new co-trustee to act jointly with the personal representative and give a joint receipt for the purchase money, or for evidence of the equitable title to be lodged so as to satisfy the registrar that the trust of land has come to an end (see para.19–006). The reason for this is because although a sole personal representative *acting as such* can give a valid receipt for the purposes of overreaching, that will not apply where (as is the case in this situation) the personal representative is acting in a capacity of trustee under a trust of land.

Any other restrictions appearing in the register will also need to be complied with or cancelled or withdrawn, as appropriate. Thus, where a restriction in Form C appears in the register (see para.19–003), the appropriate certificate, statutory declaration or statement of truth will need to be provided; on registration of the transfer the restriction will then be automatically cancelled.

Whether the personal representative has been registered as proprietor or not, a transfer by them must be in the appropriate form as prescribed by r.58, i.e. Form TR1 (transfer of the whole of the land in a registered title), Form TR3 (transfer of charge), or Form TP1 (transfer of part), or by r.116, i.e. Form TR4 (transfer of a registered charge or portfolio of charges).

An application to register such a transfer should be made in Form AP1 accompanied by:

(1) the transfer;

(2) (unless the personal representative has already been registered as proprietor) the requisite evidence of appointment similar to that required by r.163(2) (r.162(1)—see para.19–003);

(4) the appropriate SDLT evidence (see para.1–016); and

(5) the fee payable in accordance with the Fee Order.

For settled land reference should be made to Chapter 18.

As with an assent, provided any restrictions in the register are complied with, the registrar will not look beyond the transfer and investigate whether it has been made in accordance with the will or intestacy (r.162(2)).

Death of a joint proprietor (not being the survivor of joint proprietors)

19–006 When one of two or more joint proprietors of a registered estate dies, the registered estate will vest by survivorship in the remaining proprietor(s) (see para.19–001), who should apply for the register to be altered by the removal of the name of the deceased.

Such an application must be accompanied by evidence of death (r.164), i.e. the original or an office copy of the death certificate or grant of representation (if any); alternatively, written confirmation of the fact of death in a certificate from a conveyancer may (except where the deceased died abroad) be provided. Form AP1 or Form DJP, citing "death of joint proprietor", can be used but this is not required (r.13(2)(a)). No fee is currently payable. Such an application can also be lodged electronically by conveyancers via Land Registry Direct; the conveyancer must certify that they have seen the appropriate evidence (see para.10–027).

On completion of the application, the surviving proprietor(s) can deal with the registered estate, subject to any entry in the register.

It is sometimes the case that a sole survivor of joint proprietors remains as proprietor of land with the restriction in Form A referred to above in the register. If they are a trustee for themselves and/or others, a new trustee can be appointed and registered as proprietor jointly with them as indicated in para.18–006. This appointment will not be caught by the restriction, which will remain in the register to reflect the fact the registered estate is still subject to a trust of land.

It may be, however, that the sole surviving joint proprietor has become legally and beneficially entitled to the whole of the estate and, if this is the case, they can apply for the cancellation of the restriction. The application should be made in Form RX3 and supported by evidence of the equitable title showing that the surviving proprietor can give a valid receipt for capital money arising on a disposition of the estate. Usually the registrar will accept a statutory declaration or statement of truth by the survivor, or a certificate by a conveyancer with personal knowledge of the facts, that:

(1) in stated circumstances, e.g. under the will of a deceased joint proprietor, the survivor has become legally and beneficially entitled to the whole of the registered estate;

(2) they have not incumbered their share in any way; and

(3) they have not received notice of any incumbrance of the share of any deceased proprietor.

The declaration, statement or certificate should be accompanied by any available documentary evidence, e.g. an assent relating to an undivided share. No fee is currently payable for the cancellation of the restriction.

The circumstances in which a restriction in Form A is entered in the register in relation to transfers of registered land is discussed in para.11–013. The same principles apply to first registrations as discussed in para.5–007.

First registration

Where a legal estate is currently unregistered, the vesting of that estate in the personal representative by operation of law will not "trigger" compulsory first registration (s.4(3)). However, an assent or conveyance of that estate may be a "trigger" for compulsory first registration, in which case the appropriate application should be made (see Chapter 5). Also, the personal representative may apply for voluntary first registration if desired, in which case the requisite evidence of their appointment (see para.19–003) must accompany the application. **19–007**

The registrar does not have the statutory protection conferred upon a "purchaser" under s.36(7) of the Administration of Estates Act 1925 nor does r.162(2) apply in relation to an application for first registration; the registrar may therefore investigate the will or intestacy if he considers it necessary in order to satisfy himself that the applicant is entitled to apply. In practice, this will not normally be necessary except where a liability for inheritance tax may arise (see para.19–010).

Inheritance tax: capital transfer tax: death duties

19–008 In some circumstances a registered estate may be subject to a liability for inheritance tax (formerly known as capital transfer tax) in respect of deaths occurring after March 12, 1975. This tax replaced death duties (in practice only estate duty) which applied in respect of deaths occurring on or before that date. The entry and/or removal of entries relating to inheritance tax or death duties may therefore need to be considered.

Liability for death duties

19–009 Where the proprietor of a registered estate died before March 13, 1975 and it appeared that the registered estate was subject to a charge for death duties, the registrar would make the following entry (known as a notice in Form 60) in the register:

> "Until the registration of a disposition in favour of a purchaser for money or money's worth, the land is liable to such death duties as may be payable or arise by reason of the death of A.B. of [*address*] who died on [*date*]."

The registrar will automatically cancel this entry upon the registration of a transfer of the registered estate on sale or other disposition for value. However, application to cancel this entry may be made at any time by lodging Form CN1 completed by the Commissioners of HM Revenue & Customs ("the Commissioners"). No fee is currently payable.

Liability for capital transfer tax/inheritance tax

19–010 When inheritance tax is due to the Commissioners, a statutory charge in their favour is imposed on the registered estate that is the subject of the gift. The registrar will not automatically make any entry in respect of this, but the Commissioners can, if they so wish, apply in Form AN1 to protect this charge by entering in the register an agreed notice (rr.80 and 81) in the following form:

> "Notice of an Inland Revenue charge (Reference number—) in respect of such tax as may arise ."

Section 31 of the Act provides that the effect of a disposition of a registered estate or charge on a charge under s.237 of the

Inheritance Tax Act 1984 is to be determined not in accordance with ss.28 to 30 of the Act (see Chapters 2A and 9), but in accordance with ss.237(6) and 238 of the Inheritance Tax Act 1984, under which a purchaser in good faith for money or money's worth takes free from the charge (in the absence of registration). A disposition of the registered estate therefore takes subject to a subsisting Inland Revenue charge unless:

(1) the disposition is in favour of a purchaser within the meaning of the Inheritance Tax Act 1984; and

(2) the charge is not, at the time of registration of the disposition, protected by a notice in the register.

Such a notice will not be cancelled by the registrar, even when registering a transfer on sale, without receipt of Form CN1 completed by the Commissioners. If the Commissioners have certified in the Form CN1 that the application for cancellation is only to take effect upon the registration of a disposition to a purchaser, then the registrar will cancel the entry only when the Form CN1 is accompanied by a proper application to register the transfer, or other specified disposition, in favour of the purchaser.

On an application for first registration not based on a disposition for value and where a gift has been made within eight years of the date of the application, where no charge is disclosed and no Class D(i) Land Charge is registered, consideration will be given by the registrar as to whether any liability to capital transfer tax or inheritance tax has arisen.

Where the value of the estate is above the inheritance tax threshold, a certified copy (or probate copy) of the will or a statutory declaration or statement of truth as to entitlement under an intestacy, together with any relevant deed of family arrangement or variation must be lodged in order to satisfy the registrar as to the applicant's entitlement to apply.

If it appears from the application that the property being registered may be subject to a charge for inheritance tax Land Registry will inform the applicant that it intends to make the following entry in the register:

> "Notice of the possibility of an Inland Revenue charge in respect of such inheritance tax as may arise as a result of the death of [name] who died on [date]."

However, if the applicant confirms in writing details of the surrounding circumstances of the case and that either no inheritance tax was ever payable, or that it has been paid in full, the entry will not be made. Alternatively, the applicant may supply a certificate of discharge from the Capital Taxes Office, or a letter from the Capital Taxes Office addressed to the registrar confirming the same.

Practical points

- Consider carrying out a search of the index of proprietors names against the name of the deceased in order to obtain details of registered estates of which they may have been proprietor, where this is unclear,
- Be aware of how the legal estate and the beneficial interest devolves on death,
- Remember that an assent of a share is not capable of registration and that a transfer or assent of the legal estate is required and must be completed by registration in order to transfer the legal estate,
- Remember to lodge the appropriate evidence of death or appointment of a personal representative, where necessary,
- Consider the effect of any restriction in the register and how this may affect registration of a transfer or assent,
- Be aware of Land Registry requirements and procedures in relation to inheritance tax.

Chapter 20

Insolvency

Introduction

This chapter relates to both personal insolvency (bankruptcy and individual voluntary arrangements) and corporate insolvency (liquidation, administration and receivership). The main statutory provisions relating to insolvency are contained in the Insolvency Act 1986 ("the 1986 Act") as amended by the Enterprise Act 2002, as supplemented by specific provisions in the Act and the Rules relating to insolvency. **20–001**

Bankruptcy

Introduction

The proprietor of a registered estate or charge may become bankrupt. The Act makes special provision for when this occurs. **20–002**

The bankruptcy process involves two stages:

(1) the presentation by a creditor of a bankruptcy petition to the court for a bankruptcy order;
and

(2) the making of a bankruptcy order by the court.

After the bankruptcy order is made a trustee in bankruptcy is appointed who will be either an authorised insolvency practitioner or the Official Receiver.

Previous law

Prior to October 13, 2003, under the Land Registration Act 1925 whenever a bankruptcy petition was presented, the court informed the Land Charges Department, and the petition was **20–003** then registered in the register of pending actions kept by that Department. Details of the registration were passed from the Land Charges Department to Land Registry, which then entered a "creditors' notice" against any title of a proprietor of any registered estate or registered charge which appeared to be affected.

Where it appeared that the title of the proprietor of a registered estate was affected, the creditors' notice was entered in the proprietorship register as follows:

> "CREDITORS' NOTICE entered under section 61(1) of the Land Registration Act 1925 to protect the rights of all creditors, as the title of the proprietor of the land appears to be affected by a petition in bankruptcy against [*name of debtor*], presented in the [*name*] Court (Court Reference Number . . .) (Land Charges Reference Number PA . . .)."

Where it appeared that the title of the proprietor of a registered charge was affected, the creditors' notice, in a similar form, was entered in the charges register.

When a bankruptcy order was registered in the register of writs and orders affecting land, as kept by the Land Charges Department, details were passed to Land Registry and a "bankruptcy inhibition" was entered against any title of a proprietor of any registered estate or registered charge which appeared to be affected.

Where it appeared that the title of the proprietor of a registered estate was affected, the bankruptcy inhibition was entered in the proprietorship register as follows:

> "BANKRUPTCY INHIBITION entered under section 61(3) of the Land Registration Act 1925, as the title of the proprietor of the land appears to be affected by a bankruptcy order made by the [name] Court (Court Reference Number. . .) against [*name of debtor*] (Land Charges Reference Number WO. . .).
>
> No disposition by the proprietor of the land or transmission is to be registered until the trustee in bankruptcy of the property of the bankrupt is registered."

Where it appeared that the title of the proprietor of a registered charge was affected, the bankruptcy inhibition, in a similar form, was entered in the charges register.

Entry of bankruptcy notice and/or bankruptcy restriction under the Act

20–004 The Act contains similar provisions to those in the Land Registration Act 1925 and (subject to the changes mentioned below) similar procedures now operate when a bankruptcy petition is presented or a bankruptcy order is made. Section 86 places an obligation on the registrar to make appropriate entries in the register in relation to bankruptcy petitions and orders after they have been registered under the Land Charges Act 1972, where it appears to him that a registered estate or charge is affected.

A creditors' notice is now designated a "bankruptcy notice". Rule 165 provides that a bankruptcy notice in relation to a registered estate must be entered in the proprietorship register and a bankruptcy notice in relation to a registered charge must be entered in the charges register. The form of the notice is as follows:

> "BANKRUPTCY NOTICE entered under section 86(2) of the Land Registration Act 2002 in respect of a pending action, as the title of the [proprietor of the registered estate] or [the proprietor of the charge dated . . . referred to above] appears to be affected by a petition in bankruptcy against [name of debtor], presented in the [name] Court (Court Reference Number . . .) (Land Charges Reference Number PA . . .)."

The Act does not permit the entry of any new inhibitions in the register (see para.16–030). As a result, the entry which is made following the making of a bankruptcy order is now a "bankruptcy restriction". Rule 166 provides that a bankruptcy restriction in relation to a registered estate must be entered in the proprietorship register and a bankruptcy restriction in relation to a registered charge must be entered in the charges register. The form of the restriction is as follows:

> "BANKRUPTCY RESTRICTION entered under section 86(4) of the Land Registration Act 2002, as the title of [the proprietor of the registered estate] or [the proprietor of the charge dated . . . referred to above] appears to be affected by a bankruptcy order made by the [name] Court (Court Reference Number . . .) against [name of debtor] (Land Charges Reference Number WO . . .).
>
> [No disposition of the registered estate] or [No disposition of the charge] is to be registered until the trustee in bankruptcy of the property of the bankrupt is registered as the proprietor of the [registered estate] *or* [charge]."

The registrar must give notice of the entry of a bankruptcy notice (r.165(2)) or bankruptcy restriction (r.166(2)) to the proprietor of the registered estate or registered charge to which it relates.

If any doubt arises as to the identity of the debtor or the bankrupt, the registrar will make such inquiries and serve such notices as he considers necessary or desirable before deciding whether to enter a bankruptcy notice or bankruptcy restriction.

Where there is doubt as to whether the debtor or bankrupt is the same person as the proprietor of the registered estate or charge in respect of which a notice or restriction has been entered, the registrar must, as soon as practicable, take such action as he considers necessary to resolve the doubt (r.167(2)).

Section 86(5) protects a disponee for value in good faith by providing that the title of the trustee in bankruptcy is void against a person to whom a registrable disposition is made, if it is for valuable consideration, the disponee is acting in good faith and at the time of the disposition no bankruptcy notice or bankruptcy restriction is in the register and the disponee has no notice of the bankruptcy petition or order. A disponee under a registrable disposition is not required to make any search under the Land Charges Act 1972 (s.86(7)).

Neither a bankruptcy notice nor a bankruptcy restriction will be entered in relation to a registered estate or registered charge where the debtor is one of two or more joint proprietors (see para.20–012).

Effect of bankruptcy notice and/or bankruptcy restriction

20–005 Where a bankruptcy notice (or creditors notice) appears in the register, an application to register a disposition by the registered proprietor after the entry of a bankruptcy notice, e.g. a transfer, can still be made but, unless it is clear the interest of the disponee has priority over the bankruptcy proceedings, the registration will be made subject to the bankruptcy notice by the entry of a note in the register along the following lines:

> "The registration of the proprietor is subject to the rights of all creditors of [transferor's name] (a former proprietor) protected by the Bankruptcy Notice(s) referred to above."

Where a bankruptcy restriction (or bankruptcy inhibition) appears in the register, no disposition (other than the registration of the trustee in bankruptcy) affecting the registered estate or charge can be completed by registration until the restriction is cancelled. The restriction may additionally have the effect of precluding the entry of notices to protect certain third party interests which consist of a disposition by the bankrupt.

The bankruptcy restriction does not prejudice dealings with, or in right of, interests or charges having priority over the registered estate or registered charge. Thus the proprietor of a registered charge, which was registered before a bankruptcy restriction (and any bankruptcy notice) was entered, could exercise their power of sale notwithstanding the entry of the bankruptcy restriction in the proprietorship register. However, the restriction would need to be considered on a disposition by a receiver appointed by the chargee as they would be acting as agent for the bankrupt/chargor, not the chargee.

Registration of the trustee in bankruptcy

All the property, including any registered estate or registered charge, owned by the bankrupt for their own benefit at the date of the bankruptcy order automatically vests without any formal transfer in the trustee in bankruptcy when his appointment takes effect (s.306 of the 1986 Act). Property held by the bankrupt on trust for any other person is excluded, whether or not they also hold it on trust for themselves—see para.20–012. **20–006**

This transfer by operation of law does not have to be completed by registration in order to take effect at law (s.27(5)(a)).

Rule 168 makes provision for registration of the trustee in bankruptcy as proprietor in place of the bankrupt. An application may be made by the trustee in bankruptcy in Form AP1 accompanied by:

(1) the bankruptcy order; and

(2) a certificate by the official receiver that the registered estate or registered charge is comprised in the bankrupt's estate; and

(3) a certificate by the Official Receiver that he is the trustee (where applicable) or, where the trustee is another person, the following evidence of their appointment:

   (a) their certificate of appointment as trustee by the meeting of the bankrupt's creditors; or
   (b) their certificate of appointment as trustee by the Secretary of State; or
   (c) the order of the court appointing them as trustee.

A fee in accordance with the Fee Order is payable, based upon a certificate as to the value of the registered estate or charge which should accompany the application.

On the registration of the trustee in bankruptcy as the proprietor of the bankrupt's registered estate or registered charge, the bankruptcy notice and bankruptcy restriction will be cancelled.

Similar provisions apply where an insolvency administration order is made in respect of a deceased proprietor.

Transfer by the trustee in bankruptcy

20–007 If they have been registered as proprietor in place of the bankrupt (see para.20–006), the trustee in bankruptcy may execute a transfer of the registered estate or registered charge.

Where the trustee wishes to transfer the registered estate or registered charge without having been registered as proprietor, the transfer must be lodged for registration accompanied by the same evidence of bankruptcy as would have been required for registration of the trustee, as mentioned at para.20–006 above. The bankruptcy notice and bankruptcy restriction will be cancelled when the transfer is registered.

Cancellation of a bankruptcy notice or bankruptcy restriction

20–008 A bankruptcy notice (or creditors notice) will not be cancelled on the production of an order of the court which simply authorises the cancellation of the registration of the bankruptcy petition as a pending action in the Land Charges Department. Similarly a bankruptcy restriction (or bankruptcy inhibition) will not be cancelled on the production of an order of the court which simply authorises the cancellation of the registration of the bankruptcy order at the Land Charges Department. Such an order does not re-vest property in a bankrupt which has automatically vested in the trustee in bankruptcy. Such property will remain vested in the trustee in bankruptcy, subject to the provisions for re-vesting of the bankrupt's home (see para.20–009).

Rule 167(1) provides that a bankruptcy notice or bankruptcy restriction will be cancelled if the registrar is satisfied that:

(1) the bankruptcy order has been annulled or rescinded; or

(2) the bankruptcy proceedings have been dismissed or withdrawn with the court's permission; or

(3) the bankruptcy proceedings do not affect or have ceased to affect the registered estate or registered charge in relation to which the bankruptcy notice or restriction has been entered in the register.

Neither an automatic discharge under the provisions of s.279 of the 1986 Act nor an order for discharge by the court under s.280 of the 1986 Act operates to re-vest the bankrupt's property. Production of evidence of discharge is not therefore sufficient to enable a bankruptcy notice or bankruptcy restriction to be cancelled, even if accompanied by the consent of the trustee or an order of the court under s.1(6) of the Land Charges Act 1972 ordering cancellation of Land Charge bankruptcy entries.

The application for cancellation should be made in Form AP1. Where made in the circumstances referred to at (1) and (2) above, it must be accompanied by an office copy of the relevant court order which must expressly authorise the cancellation of the pending action and/or the bankruptcy order at the Land Charges Department under the reference number set out in the bankruptcy notice and/or bankruptcy restriction.

Where application for cancellation is made in the circumstances referred to at (3) above, and the proprietor of a registered estate or registered charge is not affected by the bankruptcy proceedings and the entry was made recently, the registrar will normally remove it if the applicant provides a signed disclaimer (supplied by Land Registry) that they were not the subject of the bankruptcy proceedings. In some cases, particularly where the entry was made some years ago, the applicant may be required to supply a statutory declaration or statement of truth to similar effect. Production of a clear Land Charges search showing that the registration of the relevant bankruptcy petition and/or bankruptcy order is no longer subsisting is not sufficient without further evidence.

No fee is currently payable for the cancellation of a bankruptcy notice or bankruptcy restriction.

Re-vesting of bankrupt's home

Section 261 of the Enterprise Act 2002 introduced a new s.283A **20–009** into the 1986 Act, with effect from April 1, 2004. This applies where the bankrupt's estate includes an interest in a dwelling-house which, at the date of the bankruptcy order, was the sole or principal residence of either:

(1) the bankrupt;

(2) the bankrupt's spouse or civil partner; or

(3) a former spouse or former civil partner of the bankrupt.

The interest will automatically re-vest in the bankrupt (without any transfer, assignment or conveyance) three years after the date of the bankruptcy order, unless the trustee in bankruptcy takes action to deal with the interest in the meantime, for instance by selling it or applying for a possession order.

However, if the bankruptcy order was made before April 1, 2004 the period is three years from April 1, 2004.

The three-year period can be extended by order of the court, or if the bankrupt fails to inform the trustee in bankruptcy or the official receiver of their interest in the property. The three year period can also be reduced in certain circumstances. If the trustee in bankruptcy considers that:

(a) the continuing vesting of the property in the bankrupt's estate is of no benefit to the creditors; or

(b) the re-vesting in the bankrupt will facilitate a more efficient administration of the bankrupt's estate,

the trustee can send the bankrupt a notice to that effect. The property will then re-vest in the bankrupt one month after the date of the notice.

Where re-vesting occurs in respect of a registered estate or registered charge which had vested in the trustee in bankruptcy because the bankrupt was a sole proprietor, the trustee in bankruptcy must, within seven days, make whatever application to Land Registry is necessary to reflect the re-vesting in the register (rr.6237A and 6237B of the Insolvency Rules 1986). This will normally (where the trustee has not been registered as proprietor in place of the bankrupt) be an application in Form RX3 (see para.16–026) to cancel the bankruptcy restriction (or bankruptcy inhibition), accompanied by:

(i) a certificate by the trustee stating that the interest has re-vested in the bankrupt under s.283A(2) or 283A(4) of the 1986 Act or s.261(8) of the Enterprise Act 2002; and

(ii) (unless the applicant is the Official Receiver), evidence of the trustee's appointment as specified in para.20–006.

No fee is currently payable.

Any bankruptcy notice (or creditors' notice) which relates to the petition under which the bankruptcy order was made will be cancelled, but not any other bankruptcy notice (or creditors' notice) without the evidence specified in para.20–008.

If a re-vesting occurs in a case where the trustee in bankruptcy has been registered as proprietor, an application should be made in Form AP1 for alteration of the register under para.5(b) of Sch.4 to the Act, accompanied by a certificate by the trustee as above. No fee is currently payable.

If a re-vesting occurs in a case where the bankrupt is a joint registered proprietor, see para.20–012.

Charging order on bankrupt's home

20–010 Where a dwelling-house occupied by a bankrupt, or their spouse or former spouse, forms part of the bankrupt's estate and the trustee is unable to realise it, they can apply to the court for a charging order on the property. Any such order shall provide for the property to re-vest in the bankrupt subject to the charge and any prior charges (s.313 of the 1986 Act). Where such an order is made, an office copy or certified copy should be lodged so that the bankruptcy notice and/or bankruptcy restriction can be cancelled, any other entry necessary to reflect the vesting provisions can be made and a notice entered in respect of the charging order. Where the bankrupt is the sole registered proprietor and does not hold as trustee, the trustee in bankruptcy can apply for entry of an agreed notice or unilateral notice in respect of the court order (see paras 16–005 and 16–008).

Where the bankruptcy is of one of joint proprietors, application for entry of a restriction in Form K may be made instead (see Chapter 16 and Appendix III).

Rights of occupation of a bankrupt and of a bankrupt's spouse or civil partner

The effect of bankruptcy on a spouse or civil partner's statutory rights of occupation under the Family Law Act 1996 and the rights of occupation of a bankrupt who has occupied a dwelling-house with a person under 18 are considered in paras 17–011 and 17–012. **20–011**

Bankruptcy of a joint proprietor

When one of two or more joint proprietors is made bankrupt and a trustee in bankruptcy is appointed, the legal estate in the land or charge affected does not automatically vest in the trustee. Property held by a bankrupt on trust for another, whether or not the bankrupt also holds it on trust for themselves, does not form part of the bankrupt's estate. No bankruptcy entries will therefore be made in the register. Any subsequent transfer of the property needs to be executed by all the joint proprietors in the usual way and not by the trustee on behalf of the bankrupt proprietor. **20–012**

If the bankrupt is a beneficial joint tenant, the joint beneficial tenancy is automatically severed.

If the debtor has a beneficial interest in a registered estate or registered charge, their trustee in bankruptcy may apply for the entry of a restriction in Form J (see Chapter 16 and Appendix III). A restriction in Form J will not prevent registration of a disposition provided the terms of the restriction have been complied with, but it helps to ensure the trustee is given notice of the disposition so that they can pursue a share of any proceeds of a sale.

The trustee may also apply for entry of a restriction in Form A (see Chapter 16 and Appendix III), if this does not already appear in the register. Where re-vesting occurs in respect of the bankrupt's beneficial interest in a jointly owned property (see para.20–009), the trustee in bankruptcy must, within seven days, make whatever application is necessary to reflect the re-vesting in the register. This will normally be an application in Form

RX4 (see para.16–027) to withdraw a restriction in Form J, accompanied by:

(i) a certificate by the trustee stating that the interest has re-vested in the bankrupt under s.283A(2) or 283A(4) of the 1986 Act or s.261(8) of the Enterprise Act 2002; and

(ii) (unless the applicant is the trustee named in the Form J restriction or is the Official Receiver), evidence of their appointment as specified in paragraph 20–006.

No fee is currently payable.

Under the Land Registration Act 1925, the trustee in bankruptcy could apply for entry of a caution against dealings in such circumstances. Where this has occurred, the application will be in Form WCT to withdraw the caution against dealings (see para.16–015) in favour of the trustee in bankruptcy, accompanied by the same documents as those required for withdrawal of a restriction in Form J as above. No fee is currently payable.

The re-vesting will not "undo" the severance of a beneficial joint tenancy effected by the bankruptcy (see above) and therefore any restriction in Form A will not be automatically cancelled.

Individual voluntary arrangements

20–013 A voluntary arrangement with creditors (as an alternative to bankruptcy) consists of either a composition in satisfaction of debts or a scheme of arrangement of affairs. In either case it must be approved by a meeting of creditors (see Part VIII of the 1986 Act) and is implemented by the "supervisor" of the voluntary arrangement. The effect of a voluntary arrangement, if any, on the debtor's property depends upon its terms.

If the voluntary arrangement is simply an agreement to pay regular sums to the supervisor, then any registered estate or registered charge of the debtor will be unaffected and neither a notice nor a restriction can be applied for.

If the debtor is the sole proprietor of a registered estate or registered charge which they hold for their own benefit, and the arrangement creates an equitable charge, a contract for sale, option, or right of pre-emption in favour of the supervisor affecting that registered estate or registered charge, an application may be made in Form AN1 or Form UN1 for entry of an agreed notice or unilateral notice, in respect of the interest created (see paras 16–005 and 16–008).

If the debtor has a beneficial interest under a trust of land of a registered estate, and the arrangement creates an equitable charge, a contract for sale, option, or right of pre-emption in favour of the supervisor affecting that interest, the interest created cannot be protected by an agreed notice or unilateral notice (s.33(a)(i)).

If the effect of the arrangement is to create a trust and it affects a registered estate, then it may be possible to protect this by an application in Form RX1 for entry of a restriction in Form A (if this does not already appear in the register) and/or Form II depending upon the circumstances (see Chapter 16).

Liquidation

The liquidator of a company may apply for notice of their appointment to be entered in the register, but the company will remain the registered proprietor. Application must be specifically made for this as such an entry will not be made automatically. Rule 184(4) and (5) applies to such an application, which should be made in Form AP1 and accompanied by the order, appointment by the Secretary of State or resolution under which the liquidator was appointed and such other evidence as the registrar may require. The evidence required will depend upon the type of liquidation. **20–014**

(1) If the liquidation is by order of the court, a certified copy of the winding up order; and:
   - (a) a certified copy of the resolution passed at the creditors' meeting appointing the liquidator; or
   - (b) a certified copy of the resolution passed at the contributories' meeting appointing the liquidator and a certificate by the liquidator (or their conveyancer) that a meeting of the creditors was duly held at which either the appointment of the liquidator by the contributories' meeting was confirmed or no resolution nominating a liquidator was passed; or
   - (c) a certified copy of the order of the court appointing the liquidator; or
   - (d) a certified copy of the appointment by the Secretary of State of the liquidator.

(2) If the winding-up is a members' voluntary winding-up:
   - (a) a certificate by the secretary of the company (or their conveyancer) or by the liquidator (or their conveyancer) that a statutory declaration of solvency complying with the requirements of s.89 of

the 1986 Act has been filed with the Companies Registry; and

(b) a certified copy of the resolution passed by the general meeting of the company appointing the liquidator.

(3) If the winding-up is a creditors' voluntary winding-up, a certified copy of the resolution passed at the company's general meeting that the company be wound up and appointing a liquidator; and:

(a) a certified copy of a resolution passed at the creditors' meeting appointing the liquidator; or

(b) a certificate by the liquidator (appointed at the company's meeting) or their conveyancer that the meeting of the creditors was duly held in accordance with s.98(1) of the 1986 Act at which either the appointment of the liquidator by the company's meeting was confirmed or no resolution nominating a liquidator was passed.

A fee in accordance with the current Fee Order is payable, unless it accompanies an application to register the company as proprietor of the registered estate or registered charge.

When notice of the appointment is entered in the register, consideration should be given as to whether application should be made for any appropriate restriction to be entered.

If a transfer of a registered estate or registered charge by or in favour of a company in liquidation is lodged for registration (and notice of the appointment has not previously been entered, in the case of a disposition by the company), evidence as at (1), (2) or (3) above will be required. This will also apply in relation to an application for first registration.

A disposition by a company in liquidation should be executed by the liquidator either by affixing the company seal and signing the document to attest that the seal has been affixed in their presence or by signing the document as a deed in the name and on behalf of the company.

Liquidation of foreign companies

20–015 **(1) *Overseas liquidation*** The liquidation of a foreign company in its country of incorporation is recognised by English law. An application to register a disposition made by or on behalf of such a company must be made in Form AP1, accompanied by appropriate evidence of the liquidation and of its effect. Certified translations should be supplied of any documents not in English or Welsh.

(2) *Liquidation in United Kingdom* A foreign company that has been carrying on business in the United Kingdom may be wound up as an unregistered company under the 1986 Act even though it may already have been dissolved or otherwise ceased to exist, under the law of its country of incorporation. The winding up will be by order of the court and the evidence specified in paragraph 20–014 would need to be lodged.

Disclaimer

A liquidator can, under the 1986 Act, disclaim onerous property by giving the prescribed notice, even though they have already taken possession of the property, tried to dispose of it or otherwise exercised rights over it. The notice operates to determine the rights, interests and liabilities of the company in respect of the property. It does not, however, otherwise affect the rights or liabilities of any other person. **20–016**

The disclaimer may be in respect of a registered leasehold estate or, more rarely, in respect of a registered freehold estate.

An appropriate application may be made in Form AP1, accompanied by the relevant documentation. A fee in accordance with the Fee Order is payable.

Dissolution

On dissolution, all the property and rights of a company (other than property held on trust for another) are deemed to be bona vacantia and will belong to the Crown or to the Duchy of Lancaster or the Duke of Cornwall, as the case may be (s.1012 of the Companies Act 2006 as from October 1, 2006; previously s.654 of the Companies Act 1985). **20–017**

Under the Limited Liability Partnerships (Application of Companies Act 2006) Regulations 2009, s.1012 of the Companies Act 2006 is modified to apply to a limited liability partnership incorporated in England and Wales, Scotland, or Northern Ireland.

Rule 185 provides that where a company which is the proprietor of a registered estate or registered charge has been dissolved, the registrar may enter a note of that fact in the proprietorship register or charges register, as appropriate.

Administrators

Appointment

An administrator is a person appointed under s.8 and Sch.B1 to the 1986 Act to manage the affairs, business and property of a company. An administrator must be an insolvency practitioner and can be appointed by either: **20–018**

(1) an administration order made by the court;
(2) the holder of a qualifying floating charge; or
(3) the company or its directors.

A "qualifying floating charge" for this purpose is one which either:

(a) states that para.14 of Sch.B1 applies to it;
(b) authorises its holder to appoint an administrator; or
(c) authorises its holder to appoint a receiver who would be an administrative receiver.

A person "holds" a qualifying floating charge if they hold either:

(i) a qualifying floating charge which relates to the whole or substantially the whole of the company's property;
(ii) a number of qualifying floating charges which together relate to the whole, or substantially the whole, of the company's property; or
(iii) charges and other forms of security which together relate to the whole, or substantially the whole, of the company's property, and at least one of which is a qualifying floating charge.

Where the administrator is appointed by the court, the appointment takes effect at a time appointed by the order, or if no time is appointed, when the order is made.

Where the administrator is appointed by the holder of a floating charge or by the company or its directors, the appointment takes effect when the appointor files in court the appropriate notice of appointment accompanied by the prescribed documents.

While a company is in administration its property remains vested in it. The administrator acts as the agent of the company and has powers enabling them to do anything necessary or expedient for the management of the affairs, business and property of the company. This includes the powers specified in Sch.1 to the 1986 Act, which include power to sell and to grant or accept a surrender of a lease. A person dealing with the administrator in good faith and for value need not inquire whether the administrator is acting within their powers.

Effect of liquidation and receivership on administration

20–019 (1) An administrator cannot be appointed while a company is in liquidation, except by the court on the application of the liquidator or, in some circumstances, on the application of the holder of a qualifying floating charge. If the court appoints an administrator it will discharge any winding-up order (paras 8, 37 and 38 of Sch.B1 to the 1986 Act).

(2) A company that is in administration cannot normally be placed in liquidation (paras 40 and 42 of Sch.B1 to the 1986 Act).

(3) Where a company is in administrative receivership (see para.20–024) an administrator can be appointed only by the court, and only in the limited circumstances set out in para.39 of Sch.B1 to the 1986 Act. The appointment of an administrator automatically dismisses any administrative receiver of the company (para.41(1) of Sch.B1 to the 1986 Act).

An administrative receiver cannot be appointed while a company is in administration.

(4) The existence of a Law of Property Act receiver (see para.20–032) does not prevent an administrator being appointed, nor is such a receiver automatically dismissed if such an appointment occurs, although they must vacate office if required to do so by the administrator (para.41(2) of Sch.B1 to the 1986 Act).

Entry of appointment in the register

Under r.184 an application may be made by an administrator to **20–020** note their appointment in the register where the company is the proprietor of a registered estate or registered charge. The application should be made in Form AP1 accompanied by either:

(1) an office copy or certified copy of the order of the court appointing the administrator; or

(2) a sealed copy of the prescribed notice of appointment, as appropriate.

A fee in accordance with the Fee Order is payable.

The registrar will make the following entry in the proprietorship register:

> "(Date) By [an order of the Court made on] [a notice of appointment filed on] (date) [. . .] of (address) was appointed administrator of [. . . Limited]".

Although administration normally terminates automatically after one year, this period can be extended (see para.20–021). The registrar will not cancel the entry merely on grounds of the lapse of time without evidence that an appropriate notice has been registered with the Companies Registry.

Where the administration has come to an end, an application to cancel such an entry should be made in Form AP1, accompanied by either:

(a) an office copy or certified copy of a court order; or

(b) a certified copy of the prescribed notice registered with the Companies Registry.

There is currently no fee payable.

Dispositions by an administrator

20–021 An application to register a disposition by an administrator must (unless their appointment has already been noted in the register) be accompanied by evidence of their appointment in the form referred to in para.20–020.

The appointment of an administrator ceases to have effect after one year, unless it has been expressly extended. It can be extended only for a specific time and only by either:

(1) an order of the court; or

(2) (once only and for not more than six months) with the consent of all the secured creditors and a majority of the unsecured creditors of the company.

If a disposition is made by an administrator more than one year after the company went into administration, the applicant must therefore supply evidence that the administrator's appointment has been extended, in the form of either:

(a) an office copy or certified copy of an order of the court; or

(b) a certified copy of a prescribed notice of extension.

The administrator can dispose of the company's property free from any floating charge to which it is subject (para.70 of Sch.B1 to the 1986 Act) and an application to remove a notice of the floating charge from the register can then be made as follows:

(i) Where a floating charge has been protected in the register other than by way of a unilateral notice, the application should be made in Form CN1 (see para.16–006) signed by the administrator, with panel 12 clearly stating that the disposal is "pursuant to paragraph 70 of Schedule B1 to the Insolvency Act 1986".

(ii) Where a floating charge has been protected in the register by way of a unilateral notice, application may be made either in Form UN2 to remove it, or in Form UN4 to cancel it (see paras 16–010 and 16–011).

The administrator can dispose of the company's property free from any other charge with the authorisation of the court. In such a case an office copy or certified copy of the court order will need to accompany an application to register the disposition, so that any entry in the register relating to the charge can be cancelled.

Registration of a company in administration as proprietor

When, with the authorisation of the court, an administrator has disposed of a company's property free from a charge as described above, the chargee is entitled to their original security over any new estate the company acquires with the proceeds. Therefore, when registering a company that he is aware is subject to an administration order as proprietor of an estate, the registrar will make the following entry in the charges register: **20–022**

> "[Date] The registered estate is subject to such security or securities as may exist and affect the same by virtue of the provisions of paragraph 70(2) of Schedule B1 to the Insolvency Act, 1986."

Application in Form CN1 to cancel the entry may be made, if the administrator produces a certificate that no such securities affected the title or, where they did, that they have been discharged. No fee is currently payable.

Execution by an administrator

A company which is in administration may execute a deed either by affixing the company seal in the presence of the administrator, or by the administrator signing in the name and on behalf of the company. **20–023**

Administrative receivers

An administrative receiver is either: **20–024**

(1) a receiver or manager of the whole (or substantially the whole) of a company's property appointed by, or on behalf of, the holders of any debentures of the company secured by a charge which, as created, was a floating

charge, or such a charge and one or more other securities; or

(2) a person who would be such a receiver or manager but for the appointment of some other person as the receiver of part of the company's property (s.29(2) of the 1986 Act).

Appointment

20–025 An administrative receiver must be an insolvency practitioner appointed either by the court or under powers contained in a debenture.

In the case of a debenture created by deed, a statutory power arises when the mortgage money has become payable and the power of sale is exercisable (ss.101(1), 103 and 109 of the Law of Property Act 1925). This statutory power may be varied, extended or excluded by the debenture, which may contain an express power to appoint (ss.109(3) and 101(4) of the Law of Property Act 1925).

An important limitation, introduced by the Enterprise Act 2002, is that an administrative receiver cannot (subject to certain limited exceptions) be appointed by the holder of a debenture dated on or after September 15, 2003, notwithstanding any provision contained in the debenture (s.72A of the 1986 Act). The exceptions are set out in ss.72B to 72GA of the 1986 Act and include, for example, the circumstances where the company is a registered social landlord or is a project company of a project which is a public–private partnership.

Register entries on appointment

20–026 An entry in respect of the debenture under which the receiver is appointed should already appear in the register by virtue of it having been registered as a registered charge or protected by entry of a notice. As the property remains vested in the company, the receiver cannot registered as proprietor nor can a note of the receiver's appointment be entered in the register.

The receiver may, however, make an application for any necessary changes to the company's address for service in the register under r.198.

Powers of an administrative receiver

20–027 The powers given by the debenture to an administrative receiver are deemed to include the powers specified in Sch.1 to the 1986 Act, except in so far as they are inconsistent with the provisions of the debenture. The powers in Sch.1 include power to sell and to grant, or accept a surrender of, a lease.

Execution by an administrative receiver

20–028 An administrative receiver has a statutory power to use the company's seal and to execute any deed in the name and on behalf of the company (s.42(1) and Sch.1 to the 1986 Act).

The powers of execution in relation to Law of Property Act receivers (see para.20–036) will normally also be available to administrative receivers, but in practice the statutory power will normally be used.

Effect of liquidation on an administrative receiver's powers

An administrative receiver is the agent of the company. On liquidation this agency comes to an end, but the receiver continues to have power to act for the purposes of holding and disposing of the company's property and may use the company's name for that purpose (*Sowman v David Samuel Trust Ltd* [1978] 1 All E.R. 616). **20–029**

In a winding-up by the court, any disposition of the company's property after commencement of the winding-up is void unless sanctioned by an order of the court (s.127 of the 1986 Act). However, where a debenture has been created prior to the winding-up, any subsequent disposition by the debenture holder or receiver under powers contained in the debenture does not require an order of the court.

The 1986 Act makes provision for transactions at an undervalue, preferences, extortionate credit transactions and the avoidance of certain floating charges (ss.238 to 241 and 244 and 245) which may have the effect of invalidating the debenture wholly or in part. When making an application for registration of a disposition by a receiver, the applicant must therefore disclose any such challenge they are aware of and if there is any suggestion that the liquidator may be seeking to have the debenture avoided under these provisions, the registrar may serve notice upon them, giving them the opportunity to object. If a valid objection is received which cannot be disposed of by agreement, the matter will have to be referred to the Adjudicator (see Chapter 23).

If the debenture confers a power of attorney upon the receiver, this power is not a security power and it will be revoked by the winding-up of the company. However, the right to sell, or otherwise dispose of the company's property, will include the right to execute in the name and on behalf of the company and such a right will continue after winding-up commences (*Barrows v Chief Land Registrar, The Times,* October 20, 1977).

Release from mortgages and charges on a disposition by an administrative receiver

An administrative receiver is the agent of the company not of the debenture holder and therefore has no power to discharge the company's property from any mortgage or charge (including the debenture under which they were appointed), whether or not the mortgage or charge was created after the debenture. **20–030**

Consequently, on a sale of a property by an administrative receiver, the purchaser must where appropriate ensure that a release or discharge is obtained for all mortgages and charges including the debenture itself.

Evidence required on application for registration of a disposition by administrative receiver

20–031 An application to register a disposition by a receiver must be accompanied by:

(1) The debenture or a certified copy of it (if not already held by Land Registry), to enable the registrar to check that the debenture has been registered in the Companies Registry (see para.14–006), that it is properly executed and that it contains the appropriate provisions to allow the receiver to be appointed and to make the disposition.

(2) Evidence that the power of appointment of a receiver under the debenture has arisen. This may be in the form of a certificate by, or on behalf of, the chargee that the power of appointment under the debenture has arisen. If the debenture is dated on or after September 15, 2003, and the appointment is not made by the court, evidence that one of the exceptions in ss.72B to 72GA of the 1986 Act applies (see para.20–025) will also be required.

(3) The instrument of appointment of the receiver or a certified copy of it. If joint administrative receivers are appointed the appointment must state whether they can act jointly and severally.

(4) A release or discharge (where appropriate) from all registered or noted mortgages or charges, including the debenture under which the receiver was appointed.

(5) Evidence of non-revocation, where the receiver executes as attorney (see para.20–036).

(6) Details of any challenge to the validity of the debenture by a liquidator of the company, including the name and address of the liquidator.

Law of Property Act receivers ("LPA receivers")

20–032 An LPA receiver is a receiver appointed under the statutory powers of appointment conferred by ss.101(1), 103 and 109 of the Law of Property Act 1925 or under an express power contained in a debenture, who does not meet the requirements for an administrative receiver (see para.20–024).

Appointment

An LPA receiver can be appointed in the same circumstances and manner as an administrative receiver (see para.20–025). **20–033**

Register entries on appointment

The position is similar to that in relation to an administrative receiver (see para.20–026). **20–034**

Powers of an LPA receiver

An LPA receiver has only limited statutory powers (s.109, LPA 1925) and these powers are normally extended by the debenture. The statutory powers must be extended if the LPA receiver is to have power to dispose of the company's property. **20–035**

Execution by an LPA receiver

An LPA receiver has no statutory power to execute on behalf of the company. The debenture will normally include a power of attorney in favour of the receiver. Such a power is not a security power and will not survive liquidation (see para.20–029). **20–036**

If the receiver executes as attorney, even if the power is under 12 months old, the application for registration of the disposition will need to be accompanied by a statutory declaration or statement of truth confirming that the applicant did not, at the time of the completion of the transaction, know of any revocation of the power or know of the occurrence of any event (such as the winding-up of the company) which had the effect of revoking the power. A conveyancer's certificate to the like effect may be provided instead.

Usually the debenture will also give the receiver the right to sell or otherwise dispose of the company's property and this includes the power to execute in the name and on behalf of the company; such a power will survive liquidation (see para.20–029).

The deed can also, at the direction of the receiver, be sealed by the company using its common seal in the presence of the duly authorised officers of the company, or signed as a deed by a director and secretary or by two directors of the company.

The effect of liquidation on an LPA receiver's powers

The position is similar to that in relation to an administrative receiver (see para.20–029). **20–037**

Release from mortgages and charges on a disposition by an LPA receiver

The position is similar to that in relation to an administrative receiver (see para.20–030). **20–038**

Evidence required on application for registration of a disposition by LPA receiver

20–039 The position is similar to that in relation to an administrative receiver (see para.20–031).

Inspection of the register on insolvency

20–040 This is discussed in Chapter 9.

Practical points

- Be aware of the nature and effect of entries in the register relating to insolvency,
- Be aware of the provisions for re-vesting of the bankrupt's home, where relevant,
- Bear in mind the distinction between the bankruptcy of a sole proprietor and a joint proprietor,
- Remember to lodge the necessary evidence of company insolvency, where necessary,
- Be aware of the distinction between administrators, administrative receivers and LPA receivers,
- Bear in mind the limited scope for appointment of an administrative receiver on or after September 15, 2003,
- Ensure that documents are correctly executed in relation to a company which is insolvent.

Chapter 21

Developing Estates

Introduction

The land in a registered title may sometimes consist of development land which is intended to be developed for residential or commercial purposes and divided into plots or units which will be individually transferred or leased. Land Registry provides a number of services relating to such "developing estate" titles and developers are encouraged to utilise these services in order to minimize the scope for problems as the estate is being developed and to facilitate registration of subsequent transfers and leases. Those services are: **21–001**

(1) estate boundary approval;

(2) estate plan approval;

(3) approval of draft transfers and leases;

(4) pre- and post- registration services on plot sales.

These services are designed to complement each other, but may be used independently if preferred. The aim of these services is to ensure the early identification and resolution of registration problems so that the process of estate development and plot sales takes place as smoothly and effectively as possible. This is of benefit to all parties involved in the process.

There are currently no fees for any of these services. Further details of the services available and the procedures involved are set out below. This information relates equally to developments by way of transfers of plots and to those by way of long leases and commonhold developments (see Chapter 13). Where appropriate therefore, reference to an "estate plan" includes a plan showing a flat or maisonette development as well as a development consisting of individual houses.

Estate boundary approval

21–002 This service is for use *before* design of the estate layout. It ensures that the developer's initial site survey plan corresponds with the extent of the developer's registered title. Any discrepancies between the registered extent and the proposed or actual physical external boundaries can be identified and resolved. Advice can also be given on easements intended to be granted. The initial site survey plan showing the extent of the land included in the development should be sent in duplicate to the proper office. If it is satisfied that the external boundaries shown on the site survey plan agree with those shown on the title plan and the latest Ordnance Survey map, Land Registry will give estate boundary approval. Such approval cannot be given until the developer's title has been registered.

Estate plan approval

21–003 As early as possible before the first transfer or lease of part is likely to be lodged for registration, the developer or their conveyancer should send the estate plan in duplicate to the proper office, for approval of its use in connection with official searches of the register and official certificates of inspection of the title plan (see paras 9–010 and 21–010). Where the estate boundary approval service has been used, the estate plan should be based upon the same plan.

The estate plan should show the final layout of the proposed development and must show sufficient detail to enable it to be accurately related to the title plan of the developer's title and the surrounding boundary features. It must be drawn to a suitable scale, usually 1/500; its true scale and orientation must be shown and it must clearly and precisely define each plot or property and identify it by a plot number or other reference. Plans marked "For identification only" or with some similar phrase are not acceptable, nor are those bearing a statement of disclaimer intended to comply with the Property Misdescriptions Act 1991.

Where a property comprises more than one parcel (e.g. a house and separate garage), each parcel must be distinguished on the estate plan by means of a separate number. If two or more floors of a purpose-built block of flats are co-extensive and the layout of the flats on each floor is identical, it is usually sufficient to lodge the plan of a single floor, but this plan must show the reference numbers distinguishing each flat on each floor. Common areas should be identified. All buildings, drives and pathways should be shown in their correct positions. Land Registry is always willing to advise as to the plan to be used for any particular estate.

If approved, one copy of the plan will be retained by Land Registry. The other, marked as officially approved, will be returned to the developer or their conveyancer. The advantages of obtaining estate plan approval are that:

(1) negotiations for the sale of individual plots can proceed without an official copy of the title plan (see para.21–010);
(2) applications for official searches of the register and for official certificates of inspection of the title plan may describe the land being purchased by reference to the plot number(s) on the approved plan, so avoiding the need to provide separate plans (see paras 21–010 and 21–012); and
(3) the approved plan, or extracts from it, can form the basis of transfer or lease plans (see para.21–013), ensuring consistency throughout the transaction.

Much trouble can be avoided if, before contract, the developer and their builders and surveyors check the position of plot fences on the ground against the approved estate plan. The developer should notify Land Registry immediately of any change in the layout of the estate and should return the duplicate approved estate plan to Land Registry with a new estate plan for approval (in duplicate) showing the changes. Failure to do this will probably lead to the withdrawal of approval of the obsolete part of the plan and in turn to the cancellation of applications for official searches against individual plots, and may also lead to difficulties in the registration of transfers or leases based on the obsolete part of the estate plan.

Land Registry should be kept informed of the progress of the development periodically so that new surveys can be made as necessary.

Approval of draft transfers and leases

The appropriate form of transfer in Sch.1 to the Rules, such as Form TP1 or TP2, should be used for transfers of individual plots (see para.11–009). In the case of leases of individual plots, the lease will normally need to be in the form of a prescribed **21–004** clauses lease and contain the prescribed clauses set out in Sch.1A to the Rules (see para.12–004 and Appendix IV).

A draft of the proposed form of transfer or lease (with plan) for general use may be sent, in duplicate, to the proper office for approval. This will ensure consistency and help to avoid difficulties in connection with easements and the development generally. If the draft is approved, it should be used as the basis for all plot transfers or leases on the development.

Surveys

21–005 Land Registry plans are based on the Ordnance Survey map and in the case of developing estates, are normally drawn to a scale of 1/1250. Surveys of developing estates are made at frequent intervals and Land Registry's plans are then revised to show all new buildings, fences, roads and other physical features. The registration of transfers and leases is facilitated if Land Registry is notified, when the estate plan is lodged for approval, of the areas in which new roads are being laid out and development is proceeding. Land Registry should again be notified when more roads are being constructed and fences or other boundary structures are being erected.

Voluntary applications to enter notice of interests which override

21–006 Although the developer may have been under a duty to disclose any existing overriding interests when they were registered as proprietor of the land, it may be that further overriding interests may subsequently arise or come to light. If these affect more than one plot, then they will have to be disclosed with each application to register a transfer or lease of an individual plot.

There may therefore be an advantage in a developer applying voluntarily to enter a notice of the burden of any such overriding interests in the register where appropriate, before the development of the estate and sales of individual plots or flats commences. Application should be made to the proper office in Form AN1 (see para.16–005). A fee in accordance with the Fee Order is payable.

Official copies

21–007 When a developer requires official copies of the register (see para.21–009) or certificates of inspection of the title plan (see para.21–010) for issue to purchasers as part of the contract documentation, they should apply for these in batches as the development proceeds. This will avoid the disadvantages of using out of date official copies or certificates of inspection in the later stages of the development.

Checks and searches by purchasers

A purchaser and their conveyancer will need to be satisfied: **21–008**

(1) that the plot is in the developer's title and whether it is affected by any references on the title plan and register entries; and

(2) that the developer has title to grant or assign the benefit of any easements benefitting the plot; and

(3) (just prior to completion of the purchase) that the plot remains in the developer's title and that it is not subject to any adverse entry made in the register since the date of the official copy of the register of the developer's title nor adversely affected by any pending application against that title.

Official copies

A purchaser or their conveyancer will need to obtain and check **21–009** an official copy of the register of the developers title; this will normally be contained within the contract documentation provided by the developer, although a purchaser can apply for official copies themselves if necessary. Applications for official copies are discussed in Chapter 9. Under s.67, official copies are admissible in evidence to the same extent as the originals.

Official copies issued on developing estates, particularly leasehold developments, are frequently backdated. This is because an official copy must be dated prior to the earliest application which is currently pending against the title. In the case of a leasehold development, a notice of each lease must be entered in the developer's title in chronological order, according to the date of registration of each lease. However, at the pre-contract stage the purchaser and their conveyancer are only concerned to confirm that the plot is within the developer's title and need not therefore be concerned that the official copy of the register does not yet set out particulars of all transfers or leases of plots already sold.

The pre-completion official search made by the purchaser (see para.21–012) will bring the position up to date as far as the plot they are purchasing is concerned.

Proof that a plot is in the developer's title

21–010 Application should be made to the proper office in Form OC1 for a certificate of official inspection of the title plan in Form CI (see also para.9–010). A fee in accordance with the Fee Order is payable. This application may be made by the developer, or by the purchaser if the developer does not supply Form CI with the contract documentation.

An adequate verbal description of the property being purchased must be given in the application, as well as the plot number on the approved estate plan. In the case of a property which comprises more than one parcel, all relevant plot numbers must be quoted. If there is no approved estate plan or if there is but the applicant does not wish to rely upon it, the application must be accompanied by a plan (in duplicate) of a kind that would be appropriate to an application for an official search in Form OS2 (see para.9–019).

If the application is in order, the certificate in Form CI will be issued without delay. It will certify that the property is in the title and whether or not it is affected by any colour or other reference shown on the title plan and referred to in the entries in the register. The certificate's accuracy is guaranteed, but it confers no priority.

If they have this certificate, a purchaser does not need to inspect an official copy of the title plan of the developer's title for themselves, because they are given the information that they would obtain by such an inspection.

The use of certificates of official inspection of title plans is designed to save the delay and expense of numerous applications for official copies of the title plans of registered developing building estates.

It will still be a matter for the purchaser to check with the developer that the plot is or will be fenced on the ground in accordance with the estate layout plan.

Proof of title to easements

21–011 The purchaser will also need to satisfy themselves as to proof of the developer's title to grant any easements benefitting the plot, including both "standard" easements (such as general rights of way over estate roads and rights of drainage) and also any "non-standard" easements relating specifically to that plot.

If a draft transfer or lease for the estate has been approved (see para.21–004), Land Registry will supply a letter to the developer, which may be passed to purchasers, confirming that if easements are granted in the approved form they will be registered as appurtenant to the purchaser's title. This avoids the need to inspect the title plan to ensure that the developer has power to grant the easements.

If a draft transfer or lease for the estate has not been approved, the purchaser will need to satisfy themselves as to the developer's title to grant any easements. However, it is possible, when applying for Form CI, to ask Land Registry to confirm that the land over which the easements are granted is within the developer's title. In some cases, it may be possible for a developer to arrange with Land Registry to include confirmation in the Form CI certificates that a particular road, for example, over which rights of way are to be granted is within the developer's title.

Official searches

Just before completing their purchase, the purchaser will need to ascertain whether any adverse entry affecting their plot has been made in the register of the developer's title since the date of issue of the official copy. This is done by applying for an official search of the register in Form OS2 (see para.9–019). The search will confer priority upon the disposition which is protected by the search, provided the application to complete the disposition by registration is lodged within the priority period of the search. **21–012**

Sometimes a plot falls within more than one title owned by the developer, or the plot is served by an estate road or by other easements to be granted over land owned by the developer but comprised in another registered title. In such a case, a single Form OS2 may be used for a search against both titles. The printed wording must be appropriately modified and, in particular, if the official copies of the two registers were issued on different dates, both dates must be shown in the Form OS2.

It is unnecessary, however, to refer in the Form OS2 to easements and rights to be assigned or granted over land in the same title as the plot that is being transferred or leased, because the priority under the certificate of search will extend to those interests and rights.

Transfer and lease plans

Under r.213, where there are transfers or leases of individual plots forming part of the developer's title, each transfer or lease must normally be accompanied by a plan clearly identifying the plot concerned. Mere reference to plot numbers on the estate plan in a transfer of part or similar instrument is not sufficient. Transfer and lease plans may be drawn to any suitable scale. The scales most commonly used range between 1/500 and 1/1250, but the true scale and orientation must be shown. **21–013**

It is recommended that an extract from the approved estate plan (see para.21–003) is used for the transfer or lease plan, but if this is not done the transfer or lease plan should show not only the plot being dealt with but also sufficient adjacent details to enable its position to be ascertained on the developer's title plan. These details should include figured dimensions tying the position of the land to the nearest road, corner or other physical feature and also the dimensions of the land itself. A plan marked "For identification only" or similar phrase or bearing a statement of disclaimer intended to comply with the Property Misdescriptions Act 1991 is not acceptable.

In the case of a flat or maisonette, the transfer or lease must identify the precise position and extent of the parcel(s) that make up the premises in the building and the floor(s) on which they are situated. Care should be taken to ensure that "T" marks and other plan references mentioned in the body of the transfer or lease appear on the transfer or lease plan.

To comply with r.213, the transfer or lease plan must be signed by the developer. If the developer is a company or corporation the plan should be executed in the same way as the transfer or lease.

Discharges and consents

21–014 When the developer's title is subject to subsisting registered or noted charges, each plot being sold will need to be discharged from the charge (in the case of a transfer) or the subject of a consent from the chargee (in the case of a lease). Discharges are discussed in para.14–019.

In the case of a transfer, a discharge of part in Form DS3 must be accompanied by a suitable plan identifying the plot which is being discharged, which ideally should be an exact copy of the transfer plan. When a standard form of transfer, previously approved by Land Registry, is being used, the discharge need not refer to "standard" easements of the usual kind granted by the transfer. But if non-standard easements are granted which are specific to the particular plot, the discharge should specifically refer to them.

An application to cancel a noted charge in respect of a plot being transferred should, where the charge has been protected by an agreed notice (see para.16–004), be made in Form CN1 accompanied by satisfactory evidence of discharge (r.87(1)—see para.16–006). Where a noted charge has been protected by a unilateral notice (see para.16–007), application to withdraw the unilateral notice in respect of the plot should be made in Form

UN2 or application to cancel it in respect of the plot should be made in Form UN4 (see paras 16–010 and 16–011).

In the case of a lease, where the developer's title is subject to any legal charge, equitable fixed charge or floating charge in the register, the chargee's consent to the grant of the lease should be lodged.

Where the lease of a plot is a sub-lease and there is a note in the developer's title showing that the head lease contains prohibition against alientation without consent, that consent should be lodged. If any necessary consents are not lodged, this may affect the registration of the lease (see para.21–016).

Restrictions

An application for a **standard** restriction can be made either: **21–015**

(1) in the additional provisions panel of Form TP1 or TP2;

(2) in Form RX1; or

(3) by completing clause LR13 in a prescribed clauses lease (see para.12–004).

A **non-standard** restriction must be applied for in Form RX1.

Restrictions are discussed further in Chapter 16.

Applications to register transfers and leases

An application to register a transfer or lease of part of a registered title should be made in Form AP1, accompanied by the appropriate documentation and a fee in accordance with the Fee Order (see Chapters 10 and 11). **21–016**

When a developer registered with absolute title grants leases of part, the purchaser should apply for registration of their lease with absolute leasehold title and supply any necessary consents from a chargee and/or head landlord (see para.21–014). If this is not done, Land Registry may complete the application, but subject to a protective entry being made in the register (see paras 5–012 and 12–006).

Practical points

- Use the Land Registry services relating to developing estates, to minimize the scope for problems later on,
- Ensure a satisfactory plan is used both as an estate layout plan and as a plan in a transfer or lease of individual plots or flats,
- Ensure that boundary fences or other features are erected on the ground in accordance with an estate layout plan and/or transfer or lease plan,
- Consider making a voluntary application to enter notice of interests which override, where appropriate.

Chapter 22

Upgrading the Class of Title

Introduction

Although on completion of first registration a registered title will be granted a particular class of title (see para.5–012), it may subsequently be possible to apply for that title (where it is not absolute title) to be upgraded. This can arise where, for example, evidence of title that was not available on first registration can subsequently be produced. **22–001**

Section 62 of the Act gives the registrar power to upgrade title and r.124 provides details as to how an application for a title to be upgraded should be made. The only persons who can apply for a title to be upgraded are:

(1) the registered proprietor of the title to which the application relates;

(2) a person entitled to be registered as the proprietor of that title (such as the personal representatives of a deceased proprietor, or a purchaser who has taken a transfer of that title which remains to be completed by registration);

(3) the proprietor of a registered charge affecting that title; and

(4) a person interested in a registered title which derives from that title (such as the tenant of a registered lease derived out of a registered freehold title).

Upgrading possessory titles

Application may be made to upgrade a possessory title where either (in the case of a freehold or leasehold estate in land) the estate has been registered with possessory title for a period of at **22–002** least 12 years or (in the case of any estate) the registrar is satisfied as to the title. Thus:

(1) The registrar may upgrade a possessory title, in the case of freehold land to absolute or in the case of leasehold land to good leasehold, if the land has been registered with possessory title for at least 12 years and the registrar is satisfied that the proprietor is in possession (s.62(4) and (5)).

The applicant must state who is in physical possession of the land in the title and, if this is not the proprietor, they must demonstrate that the proprietor's relationship with the person in physical possession means that the proprietor is nevertheless to be treated as being in possession of the land. The meaning of "proprietor in possession" is defined in s.131 and includes not only cases where the land is physically in the proprietor's possession, but also where it is occupied by the tenant or licensee of the proprietor, for example (see para.24–003).

The Lord Chancellor may by order substitute a different period of years for the 12-year period (s.62(9)), but no such order has currently been made.

(2) Application may be made to upgrade a possessory title (whether or not relating to a registered estate in land) at any time after registration by providing additional evidence of title so as to overcome the defect which caused the possessory class of title to be granted in the first place. For example, where lost pre-registration title deeds subsequently come to light after first registration has taken place.

The registrar may upgrade a possessory freehold title to absolute freehold if satisfied as to the title to the estate (s.62(1)).

The registrar may upgrade a possessory leasehold title to good leasehold if satisfied as to the title to the estate (s.62(3)(a)) or to absolute leasehold if satisfied both as to the title to the estate and as to the superior title (s.62(3)(b)).

Documentary evidence to satisfy the registrar as to the title must accompany the application (r.124(2)). An application under s.62(3)(b) must also be accompanied by the evidence listed in r.124(3) to satisfy the registrar as to the superior title (r.124(4)—see para. 22–003).

Upgrading good leasehold to absolute leasehold

The registrar may upgrade a good leasehold title to absolute if he is satisfied as to the superior title (s.62(2)). It must be established that the landlord had power to grant the lease. An application must therefore be accompanied by (r.124(3)): **22–003**

(1) such documents as will satisfy the registrar as to any superior title which is not registered;

(2) where any superior title is registered with possessory, qualified or good leasehold title, such evidence as will satisfy the registrar that that title qualifies for upgrading to absolute title; and

(3) evidence of any consent to the grant of the lease required from any chargee of any superior title, and any superior landlord.

Since the effect of registration with an absolute title is to confer an absolute title to any easements granted in the lease, the title of the landlord to grant the easements should also be shown. Where the registrar is not satisfied on this point, an entry may be made in the register excluding the easement concerned from the registration.

Where good leasehold title was granted prior to June 19, 2006 because the consent of a superior landlord and/or the landlord's mortgagee was not lodged at the time of registration of the lease, application may be made to upgrade to absolute title if the consent can be produced. Alternatively, such an application can be made if accompanied by a covering letter requesting the upgrade to be made on the basis of the current Land Registry practice introduced on that date, which is to grant absolute title where the consent is not lodged, but to make protective entries in the register (see paras 5–012 and 12–006). An application on that basis will, however, result in the protective entries having to be made in the register of the upgraded title.

Upgrading qualified titles

The registrar may upgrade a qualified freehold title to absolute freehold if satisfied as to the title to the estate (s.62(1)). **22–004**

The registrar may upgrade a qualified leasehold title to good leasehold if satisfied as to the title to the estate (s.62(3)(a)) or to absolute leasehold if satisfied both as to the title to the estate and as to the superior title (s.62(3)(b)).

Documentary evidence to satisfy the registrar as to the title must accompany the application (r.124(2)). An application under s.62(3)(b) must also be accompanied by the evidence listed in r.124(3) to satisfy the registrar as to the superior title (r.124(4)—see para.22–003).

Inquiries before upgrading

22–005 Before approving an application for upgrading, the registrar may require the production of further documents or evidence, or serve such notices, as he considers necessary or desirable.

In deciding whether he is satisfied as to any title, the registrar must apply the same standards as those which apply under ss.9 and 10 on first registration (s.62(8)—see para.5–012).

Effect of upgrading of title

22–006 When title is upgraded to absolute, the proprietor no longer holds the estate subject to any estate, right or interest whose enforceability was preserved by virtue of the previous entry about the class of title (s.63(1)). The same is true where the title is upgraded to good leasehold save that the upgrading does not affect or prejudice the enforcement of any estate, right or interest affecting, or in derogation of, the title of the landlord to grant the lease (s.63(2)).

Application form and fees

22–007 All applications for upgrading of title must be made in Form UT1 (r.124(1)).

A fee in accordance with the Fee Order is payable, but no fee is currently payable where the application is accompanied by an application upon which a scale fee is payable or by a letter confirming that it is made on the sole basis that good leasehold title was granted because the consent of a superior landlord and/or the landlord's mortgagee was not lodged at the time of registration of the lease (see para.22–003).

The applicant must state the class of title to which they are applying for the title to be upgraded and also state in what capacity they are entitled to apply for upgrading of title.

If the applicant is entitled to be registered as the proprietor of the title to which the application relates evidence of that entitlement must accompany the application (r.124(5)).

If the applicant is interested in a registered title which derives from the title to which the application relates, details of that interest and (where the interest is not apparent from the register) evidence to satisfy the registrar of the applicant's interest must accompany the application (r.124(6)).

Confirmation is required that no claim adverse to the title of the proprietor has been made by virtue of an estate, right or interest whose enforceability is preserved by virtue of the existing entry about the class of title. If any adverse claim has been made upgrading cannot take place until it has been disposed of (s.62(6)). However, this confirmation is not necessary where the application is to upgrade a good leasehold title which was granted because the consent of a superior landlord and/or the landlord's mortgagee was not lodged at the time of registration of the lease (see para.22–003).

Practical points

- Check the class of title when entering into a disposition of a registered estate and, if this is less than absolute, consider whether it is capable of being upgraded,
- Ensure all necessary supporting evidence is lodged with an application to upgrade the class of title.

Chapter 23

Objections, Disputes and Adjudication

Introduction

Although the vast majority of applications to Land Registry are completed without becoming contentious, provision is needed to enable the minority of cases to be determined where an objection to an application is received from a third party. Land Registry's internal dispute procedures may assist in resolving disputed applications, but ultimately it may be necessary for the matter to be determined judicially. This judicial determination may be carried out by the court or, on reference from Land Registry, by the Adjudicator to HM Land Registry ("the Adjudicator"). **23–001**

Objections and disputes

Subject to two exceptions, anyone may object to an application to the registrar (s.73(1)). The exceptions are that: **23–002**

(1) in the case of an application to cancel a caution against first registration under s.18 (see para.4–008), only the person who lodged the caution or other person for the time being shown as the cautioner may object (s.73(2) and r.52); and

(2) in the case of an application to cancel a unilateral notice under s.36 (see para.16–011), only the person shown in the register as the beneficiary of the notice, or a person entitled to be registered as the beneficiary, may object (s.73(3) and r.86(7)).

An objection, whether to a notice served by the registrar or otherwise, must be in writing, signed by the objector or their conveyancer and must be delivered to the proper office, or, if different, to the office specified in the notice to which it is a response. It must state that the objector objects to the application, state the grounds for the objection and give the full name of the objector and an address for service in accordance with r.198 (r.19). The objection may be delivered in paper form or by e-mail or fax.

When an objection is received, unless the registrar decides that it is groundless, notice of the objection must be given to the applicant and the application to which it relates cannot proceed until it is disposed of (s.73(5)). An objection may be disposed of if it is withdrawn, or settled by agreement, or determined by a decision of the Adjudicator or of the court.

The notice of objection served upon the applicant by the registrar will invite them to either withdraw their application or indicate that they wish to proceed. If the applicant does not respond to the notice it will be assumed that they do not wish to proceed and the application will be cancelled.

If the applicant indicates that they do wish to proceed, the parties will be allowed time to negotiate. This will be done by inviting them to complete forms, confirming that they wish to negotiate (or continue to negotiate), at regular intervals. If they indicate at any time that they do not wish to negotiate, or fail to respond to the forms or it appears that negotiations are not progressing, the matter must be referred by the registrar to the Adjudicator on the basis that it is not possible to dispose of the objection by agreement (s.73(7)).

Referral to the Adjudicator is made under the provisions of the Land Registration (Referral to the Adjudicator to HM Land Registry) Rules 2003 ("the Referral Rules"). The referral is effected by means of a written notice to the Adjudicator informing him that the matter is being referred under s.73(7) accompanied by a case summary prepared by the registrar and copies of the documents listed in that case summary (r.5(2) and (3) of the Referral Rules).

The case summary must contain the names and addresses of the parties, details of their legal or other representatives, a summary of the core facts, details of the disputed application, details of the objection, a list of any documents that will be copied to the Adjudicator, and any other information the registrar considers appropriate (r.3(2) of the Referral Rules).

The purpose of the case summary is to give the Adjudicator brief details of the case being referred to him, to enable him to make an initial decision as to whether he will hear the case himself or direct one of the parties to start court proceedings. The case summary does not form part of the pleadings in the proceedings before the Adjudicator and it does not set out the parties' detailed arguments or evidence. The parties will be allowed to comment on the draft case summary before it is referred to the Adjudicator, but they are not entitled to insist on it being amended (r.3(3) of the Referral Rules).

When the case summary has been finalised the registrar will send it, with copies of the documents listed in it, to the Adjudicator under cover of the written notice informing him that the matter is being referred under s.73(7). At the same time the parties will be informed in writing that the matter has been referred to the Adjudicator and will be sent a copy of the case summary and documents (r.5(1) and (2) of the Referral Rules).

Adjudication

Before October 13, 2003, objections and disputes were referred to the Solicitor to HM Land Registry, who was a senior lawyer within Land Registry. **23–003**

The Act instead created a new independent post of Adjudicator to Her Majesty's Land Registry (s.107) to determine:

(1) objections referred to him under s.73(7); and

(2) appeals under para.4 of Sch.5 to the Act relating to e-conveyancing network access agreements (s.108(1)).

Also, the Adjudicator may make any order which the High Court could make for the rectification or setting aside of a document which effects a qualifying disposition of a registered estate or charge or is a contract to make such a disposition or effects a transfer of an interest which is the subject of a notice in the register (s.108(2)). For this purpose a "qualifying disposition" is a registrable disposition (i.e. one required to be completed by registration under s.27—see para.10–002) or a disposition which created an interest which may be the subject of a notice in the register (s.108(3)).

The Adjudicator may appoint such staff as he thinks fit (para.3 of Sch.9 to the Act) and, as well as support and administrative staff, he has appointed a number of full and part-time deputy adjudicators to assist him.

The Adjudicator will deal with the matter in accordance with the Adjudicator to Her Majesty's Land Registry (Practice and Procedure) Rules 2003 ("the Adjudicator Rules"), the overriding objective of which is to enable the Adjudicator to deal with matters justly. The Adjudicator may give directions to enable the parties to prepare for a hearing or to assist the Adjudicator to conduct the proceedings or determine any question in the proceedings with or without a hearing (r.20 of the Adjudicator Rules). The Adjudicator may impose a sanction upon a party who fails to comply with a direction, including a sanction that the application be cancelled in whole or part or that the registrar should give effect to the application as if the objection had not been made, as the case may be (r.55 of the Adjudicator Rules).

The parties will each be required to provide to the Adjudicator and each other party a statement of case and copies of the documents referred to in it (rr.12, 13 and 14 of the Adjudicator Rules). The Adjudicator has power to summarily dispose of the proceedings, or any particular issue in the proceedings if:

(a) the Adjudicator considers that the applicant or respondent has no real prospect of succeeding in the proceedings or on the issue; and

(b) there is no other compelling reason why the proceedings or issue should not be disposed of summarily (r.32A of the Adjudicator Rules).

The Adjudicator will normally hold a hearing, although in some circumstances he can also determine a dispute without holding a hearing. Hearings before the Adjudicator shall be held in public, except where he is satisfied that exclusion of the public is just and reasonable (s.109(1)).

A requirement of the Adjudicator is enforceable as an order of the court (s.112).

The Adjudicator may make an order for costs in proceedings before him (r.42 of the Adjudicator Rules).

A substantive decision by the Adjudicator, whether or not following a hearing, must be recorded in a substantive order which must be in writing, dated, sealed and state the name of the person making the order, state the substantive decision reached, state any steps that must be taken to give effect to that substantive decision and (where appropriate) state the possible consequences of a party's failure to comply with the substantive order within any specified time limits (rr.39 and 40(1) of the Adjudicator Rules).

The substantive order must be served by the Adjudicator upon every party to the proceedings and (where it requires him to take action) upon the registrar (r.40(2) of the Adjudicator Rules). If an order does not need to be served by the Adjudicator upon the registrar then the parties should send a copy of the order to the registrar so that he can take any appropriate action in the light of it.

On a reference under s.73(7), the Adjudicator may, instead of deciding a matter himself, direct a party to the proceedings to commence proceedings in the court within a specified time (s.110). In that case, the Adjudicator is likely to adjourn the proceedings before him pending the outcome of the court proceedings.

A person aggrieved by a decision of the Adjudicator may appeal to the High Court, but in the case of a decision relating to a network access agreement, an appeal can only be on a point of law.

Practical points

- Consider the possibility of an objection to an application being made and whether it is the applicant's best interests to proceed with an application,
- Be aware of the dispute and adjudication process which will apply if a valid objection is received which cannot be disposed of by agreement,
- Consider whether an application to the court would be more appropriate than an application to Land Registry (and referral to the Adjudicator), where a matter is in dispute.

Chapter 24

Alteration, Rectification and Indemnity

Introduction

24–001 The Act contains provisions relating to the alteration of the register, including rectification (s.65 and Sch.4 to the Act) and to the payment of indemnity, i.e. statutory compensation under the "state guarantee of title" where appropriate (s.103 and Sch.8 to the Act).

The Act makes a clear distinction between "alteration" generally and "rectification" as a specific type of alteration (see para.24–002), unlike the Land Registration Act 1925 where these two terms were used interchangeably. The distinction between the two is important in relation to both alteration of the register (where the power to rectify against a "proprietor in possession" of an estate in land is limited—see para.24–003) and entitlement to indemnity (which arises, in relation to alteration to correct a mistake in the register, where the register is rectified or there is a mistake whose correction would involve rectification—see para.24–005).

Alteration and rectification

24–002 Schedule 4 to the Act provides for alteration of the register for a number of purposes either by the registrar or in pursuance of a court order (see para.24–003). An alteration may or may not amount to "rectification", which is defined as an alteration of the register which:

(1) involves the correction of a mistake; and

(2) prejudicially affects the title of a registered proprietor (para.1 of Sch.4 to the Act).

Alteration by the court or by the registrar

24–003 The court may make an order for alteration of, or the registrar may alter the register to:

(1) correct a mistake;

(2) bring the register up to date; or

(3) give effect to any estate, right or interest excepted from the effect of registration (paras 2(1) and 5 of Sch.4 to the Act).

In addition, the registrar may also alter the register to remove a superfluous entry (para.5(d) of Sch.4 to the Act).

If the alteration of a registered estate in land would amount to rectification of the proprietor's title, no court order or alteration by the registrar can be made without the proprietor's consent in relation to land in their possession unless:

(a) they have by fraud or lack of proper care caused or substantially contributed to the mistake; or

(b) it would for any other reason be unjust for the alteration not to be made (paras 3(2) and 6(2) of Sch.4 to the Act).

A proprietor's title, for this purpose, includes their title to any registered estate which subsists for the benefit of their registered estate in the land, e.g. a benefitting easement.

Under s.131 land is in the possession of a proprietor if it is physically in their possession, or in that of a person who is entitled (other than as an adverse possessor under Sch.6 to the Act—see para.7–010) to be registered as the proprietor of the registered estate. In the following cases land which is (or is treated as being) in the possession of the second-mentioned person is to be treated for these purposes as in the possession of the first-mentioned person:

(i) landlord and tenant;

(ii) mortgagor and mortgagee;

(iii) licensor and licensee;

(iv) trustee and beneficiary.

Where there is power to do so, the court must make an order for alteration (whether or not rectification) unless there are exceptional circumstances which justify not doing so (para.3 of Sch.4 to the Act and r.126). Where he has power to do so, the registrar must approve any application for rectification made to him unless there are exceptional circumstances which justify his not making the alteration (para.6 of Sch.4 to the Act).

Applications for alteration

Whenever a case for alteration arises, an application should be submitted to Land Registry at the proper office at the earliest opportunity. Alternatively, application may be made to the court, where appropriate. **24–004**

If the court makes an order for alteration, the registrar must give effect to it when it is served on him (para.2(2) of Sch.4 to the Act). Service of the order on the registrar must be made by making an application for the registrar to give effect to the order, accompanied by the order (r.127(2)). The order must state the title number affected and the alteration that is to be made, and must direct the registrar to make the alteration (r.127(1)).

The application should be made in Form AP1 accompanied by the order. The application may be submitted without a fee and Land Registry will requisition for payment of any fee which may be appropriate.

An application for alteration by the registrar (otherwise than under a court order), should be made in Form AP1, supported by evidence to justify the alteration (r.129). The application may be submitted without a fee and Land Registry will requisition for payment of any fee which may be appropriate.

Unless he is satisfied that such notice is unnecessary, the registrar must give notice of a proposed alteration to:

(1) the registered proprietor of any registered estate and of any registered charge; and

(2) any person who appears to the registrar to be entitled to an interest protected by a notice and whose name and address for service is set out in the register in which the notice is entered, where that estate, charge or interest would be affected by the alteration (r.128(2) and (3)).

In deciding whether to make the alteration, the registrar may make such enquiries as he thinks fit (r.128(4)).

If a valid objection to the proposed alteration is received which cannot be disposed of by agreement, the matter must be referred to the Adjudicator (see Chapter 23).

Rule 130 relates specifically to any alteration made by the registrar for the purpose of correcting a mistake in any application or accompanying document. The alteration will have effect as if made by the applicant or other interested party or parties:

(a) in the case of a mistake of a clerical or like nature, in all circumstances; or

(b) in the case of any other mistake, only if the applicant and every other interested party has requested, or consented to, the alteration.

The requirement to serve notice under r.128(2) does not apply in this instance.

Indemnity provisions

24–005 Under Sch.8 to the Act, indemnity is payable by the registrar where a person suffers loss by reason of:

(1) rectification of the register;

(2) a mistake whose correction would involve rectification of the register;

(3) a mistake in an official search;

(4) a mistake in an official copy;

(5) a mistake in a document kept by the registrar which is not an original and is referred to in the register;

(6) the loss or destruction of a document lodged at Land Registry for inspection or safe custody;

(7) a mistake in the cautions register; or

(8) failure by the registrar to give notice of an overriding statutory charge as required under s.50 (see para.14–012).

A mistake means anything mistakenly omitted as well as anything mistakenly included (para.11 of Sch.8 to the Act).

A proprietor claiming in good faith under a forged disposition is, where the register is rectified, to be regarded as having suffered loss by reason of such rectification as if the disposition had not been forged (para.1(2)(b) of Sch.8 to the Act).

No indemnity is payable:

(a) under (2) above until a decision has been made about whether to alter the register for the purpose of correcting the mistake and the loss suffered by reason of the mistake is to be determined in the light of that decision (para.1(3) of Sch.8 to the Act);

(b) on account of any mines or minerals or the right to work or get them unless the title specifically includes mines or minerals (para.2 of Sch.8 to the Act—see paras 5–009, 11–012 and 12–012);

(c) on account of any loss suffered by a claimant wholly or partly as a result of their own fraud or wholly as a result of their own lack of proper care. Where any loss is suffered by a claimant partly as a result of their own lack of proper care, any indemnity payable to them is to be reduced to such extent as is fair having regard to their share in the responsibility for the loss (para.5 of Sch.8 to the Act).

There are limitations on the valuation of an estate, interest or charge where indemnity is payable in respect of its loss. Where the register is rectified, the indemnity cannot exceed the value of the property immediately before rectification. Indemnity payable in the case of a mistake, the correction of which would involve rectification of the register (but where the rectification is not effected) is not to exceed the value of the property at the time when the mistake which caused the loss was made (para.6 of Sch.8 to the Act).

For the purposes of the Limitation Act 1980 a liability to pay indemnity is a simple contract debt, and the cause of action arises at the time when the claimant knows, or but for his own default might have known, of the existence of his claim (para.8 of Sch.8 to the Act).

Interest may be payable on indemnity (para.9 of Sch.8 to the Act and r.195).

A person may apply to the court for the determination of any question as to whether they are entitled to indemnity, or the amount of such indemnity (para.7 of Sch.8 to the Act).

Where he has paid indemnity in respect of loss, the registrar has certain rights of recourse enabling him to recover indemnity:

(i) from any person who caused or substantially contributed to the loss by their fraud; or

(ii) by enforcing rights of action which the claimant would have been entitled to enforce had the indemnity not been paid, and where the register has been rectified, any right of action which the person in whose favour the register has been rectified would have been entitled to enforce had it not been rectified (para.10 of Sch.8 to the Act).

Costs and expenses

24–006 Claimants entitled to be indemnified will be paid their costs and expenses reasonably incurred in relation to the matter even if no other indemnity is payable (para.3 of Sch.8 to thc Act).

It is important to bear in mind that, under para.3(1) of Sch.8 to the Act, a claimant can only be indemnified against costs and expenses incurred with the consent of the registrar. If such consent is required, application should be made by letter to the proper office at the earliest opportunity.

Although the registrar may approve costs or expenses after they have been incurred, in which case they are treated as having been incurred with his consent (para.3(3) of Sch.8 to the Act), it is appropriate to seek consent beforehand wherever possible, as retrospective consent may not necessarily be given.

The need for consent does not apply where:

(1) the costs or expenses must be incurred urgently; and

(2) it is not reasonably practicable to apply for the registrar's consent (para.3(2) of Sch.8 to the Act).

The Act also contains provision for a discretionary payment in respect of costs in "non-rectification" cases, i.e. where indemnity does not apply. If the register is altered in a case not involving rectification, the registrar may pay such amount as he thinks fit in respect of any costs or expenses reasonably incurred, with the consent of the registrar, in connection with the alteration. Again, it is important that such consent is sought at the earliest opportunity wherever possible.

The registrar may make a payment notwithstanding the absence of consent if it appears to him that the costs or expenses had to be incurred urgently, and either it was not reasonably practicable to apply for his consent, or he has subsequently approved the incurring of the costs or expenses (para.9 of Sch.4 to the Act).

Unlike the payment of indemnity, there is no entitlement to payment in respect of such costs and payment is at the discretion of the registrar.

Provision is made under the Act for payment of costs in relation to an alteration of the cautions register (s.21(3)—see para.4–006).

Claims for payment of indemnity

A claim for indemnity should normally be submitted by letter, supported by relevant valuations, calculations and accounts, to the proper office. **24–007**

Almost all claims for indemnity are settled by agreement but if agreement cannot be reached, whether as to the right to or to the amount of indemnity, the question may be determined by the court. It is not necessary to obtain the registrar's consent to the costs of court proceedings relating to indemnity (para.7 of Sch.8 to the Act).

Practical points

- Be aware of the distinction between rectification and alteration generally,
- Bear in mind the limitation on the power of the court or the registrar to order rectification against a "proprietor in possession" of registered land,
- Consider whether an application to the court, rather than to the registrar, for alteration may be more appropriate in particular circumstances,
- Remember to request the consent of the registrar before incurring costs, as this may affect entitlement to indemnity for costs.

APPENDIX I

Postal and document exchange addresses and telephone and fax numbers of Land Registry Offices

Head Office
Lincoln's Inn Fields
London WC2A 3PH
DX No. 1098 London/Chancery Lane WC2
Tel: 020 7917 8888
Fax No: 020 7955 0110

Birkenhead Office
Rosebrae Court
Woodside Ferry Approach
Birkenhead
Merseyside CH41 6DU
DX No. 24270 Birkenhead (4)
Tel: 0151 472 6666
Fax No: 0151 472 6789

Coventry Office
Leigh Court
Torrington Avenue
Tile Hill
Coventry CV4 9XZ
DX No. 18900 Coventry (3)
Tel: 024 7686 0860
024 7686 0864 (enquiries)
Fax No: 024 7686 0021

Croydon Office
Trafalgar House
Bedford Park
Croydon CR0 2AQ
DX No. 2699 Croydon (3)
Tel: 020 8781 9100
020 8781 9103 (enquiries)
Fax No: 020 8781 9110

Durham Office
Southfield House
Southfield Way
Durham DH1 5TR
DX No. 60200 Durham (3)
Tel: 0191 301 3500
Fax No: 0191 301 0020

Fylde Office
Wrea Brook Court
Lytham Road
Warton
Preston PR4 1TE
DX No. 721560 Lytham (6)
Tel: 01772 836700
01772 836838 (enquiries)
Fax No: 01772 836970

Gloucester Office
Twyver House
Bruton Way
Gloucester GL1 1DQ
DX No. 7599 Gloucester (3)
Tel: 01452 511 111
Fax No: 01452 510050

Kingston Upon Hull Office
Earle House
Colonial Street
Hull HU2 8JN
DX No. 26700 Hull (4)
Tel: 01482 223244
Fax No: 01482 224278

Leicester Office
Westbridge Place
Leicester LE3 5DR
DX No. 11900 Leicester (5)
Tel: 0116 265 4000
0116 265 4001 (enquiries)
Fax No: 0116 265 4008

Nottingham Office
Chalfont Drive
Nottingham NG8 3RN
DX No. 10298 Nottingham (3)
Tel: 0115 935 1166
Fax No: 0115 935 0038

Peterborough Office
Touthill Close
City Road
Peterborough PE1 1XN
DX No.12598 Peterborough (4)
Tel: 01733 288288
Fax No: 01733 280022

Plymouth Office
Plumer House
Tailyour Road
Crownhill
Plymouth PL6 5HY
DX No.8299 Plymouth (4)
Tel: 01752 636000
01752 636123 (enquiries)
Fax No: 01752 636161

Portsmouth Office
St Andrew's Court
St Michael's Road
Portsmouth
Hants PO1 2JH
DX No.83550 Portsmouth (2)
Tel: 023 9276 8888
023 9276 8888 (enquiries)
Fax No: 023 9276 8768

Stevenage Office
Brickdale House
Swingate
Stevenage
Herts SG1 1XG
DX No.6099 Stevenage (2)
Tel: 01438 788888
01438 788889 (enquiries)
Fax No: 01438 785 460

Swansea Office
Ty Bryn Glas
High Street
Swansea SA1 1PW
DX No. 33700 Swansea (2)
Tel: 01792 458877
Fax No: 01792 473236

Telford Office
Parkside Court
Hall Park Way
Telford TF3 4LR
DX No. 28100 Telford (2)
Tel: 01952 290355
Fax No: 01952 290356

Tunbridge Wells Office
Forest Court
Forest Road
Tunbridge Wells TN2 5AQ
DX No. 3999 Tunbridge Wells (2)
Tel: 01892 510015
Fax No: 01892 510032

Wales Office
Ty Cwm Tawe
Phoenix Way
Llansamlet
Swansea SA7 9FQ
DX No. 82800 Swansea (2)
Tel: 01792 355000
01792 355095 (enquiries)
Fax No: 01792 355055

Weymouth Office
Melcombe Court
1 Cumberland Drive
Weymouth
Dorset DT4 9TT
DX No. 8799 Weymouth (2)
Tel: 01305 363636
Fax No: 01305 363646

Land Charges Department
Plumer House
Tailyour Road
Crownhill
Plymouth PL6 5HY
DX No. 8249 Plymouth (3)
Tel: 01752 636666
Fax No: 01752 636699

APPENDIX II

List of Forms

Schedule 1 Forms

ADV1	Application for registration of a person in adverse possession under Sch. 6 to the Act
ADV2	Application to be registered as a person to be notified of an application for adverse possession
AN1	Application to enter an agreed notice
AP1	Application to change the register
AS1	Assent of whole of registered title(s)
AS2	Assent of charge
AS3	Assent of part of registered title(s)
CC	Entry of a note of consolidation of charges
CCD	Application to cancel a caution against dealings
CCT	Application to cancel a caution against first registration
CH1	Legal charge of a registered estate
CH2	Application to enter an obligation to make further advances
CH3	Application to note agreed maximum amount of security
CI	Certificate of inspection of title plan
CIT	Application in connection with court proceedings, insolvency and tax liability
CN1	Application to cancel a notice (other than a unilateral notice)
CS	Continuation sheet for use with application and disposition forms
CT1	Caution against first registration
DB	Application to determine the exact line of a boundary
DI	Disclosable overriding interests
DL	List of documents
DS1	Cancellation of entries relating to a registered charge

DS2	Application to cancel entries relating to a registered charge
DS3	Release of part of the land from a registered charge
EX1	Application for the registrar to designate a document as an exempt information document
EX1A	Reasons for exemption in support of an application to designate a document as an exempt information document
EX2	Application for official copy of an exempt information document
EX3	Application to remove the designation of a document as an exempt information document
FR1	First registration application
HC1	Application for copies of historical edition(s) of the register/title plan held in electronic form
HR1	Application for registration of a notice of home rights
HR2	Application for renewal of registration in respect of home rights
HR3	Application by mortgagee for official search in respect of home rights
HR4	Application for cancellation of a notice of home rights
NAP	Notice to the registrar in respect of an adverse possession application
OC1	Application for official copies of register/plan or certificate in Form CI
OC2	Application for official copies of documents only
OS1	Application by purchaser for official search with priority of the whole of the land in a registered title or a pending first registration application
OS2	Application by purchaser for official search with priority of part of the land in a registered title or a pending first registration application
OS3	Application for official search without priority of the land in a registered title
PIC	Application for a personal inspection under s.66
PN1	Application for a search in the Index of Proprietors' Names
PRD1	Request for the production of documents
PRD2	Notice to produce a document, s.75 and r.201
RX1	Application to enter a restriction
RX2	Application for an order that a restriction be disapplied or modified
RX3	Application to cancel a restriction
RX4	Application to withdraw a restriction
SC	Application for noting the overriding priority of a statutory charge

SEV Application to enter a restriction in Form A on severance of joint tenancy by agreement or notice
SIF Application for an official search of the index of relating franchises and manors
SIM Application for an official search of the index map
ST1 Statement of truth in support of application for registration based upon adverse possession
ST2 Statement of truth in support of application for registration based upon adverse possession of a rentcharge
ST3 Statement of truth in support of application for registration of land based upon lost or destroyed title deeds
ST4 Statement of truth in support of application for registration and/or noting of a prescriptive easement
TP1 Transfer of part of registered title(s)
TP2 Transfer of part of registered title(s) under power of sale
TR1 Transfer of whole of registered title(s)
TR2 Transfer of whole of registered title(s) under power of sale
TR4 Transfer of a charge or portfolio of charges
TR5 Transfer of portfolio of titles (whole or part)
UN1 Application to enter a unilateral notice
UN2 Application to remove a unilateral notice
UN3 Application to be registered as beneficiary of an existing unilateral notice
UN4 Application for the cancellation of a unilateral notice
UT1 Application for upgrading of title
WCT Application to withdraw a caution

Schedule 3 Forms

Form 1 Certificate as to execution of power of attorney (r.61)
Form 2 Statutory declaration/certificate/statement of truth as to non-revocation for powers more than 12 months old at the date of the disposition for which they are used (r.62)
Form 3 Statutory declaration/certificate/statement of truth in support of power delegating trustees' functions to a beneficiary (r.63)
Form 4 Certificate as to Vesting in an Incumbent or other Ecclesiastical Corporation (r.174)
Form 5 The like certificate under r.175
Form 6 Transfer where the Tenant for Life is already registered as proprietor (r.186 and para.5 of Sch.7 to the Rules)

Form 7	Certificate of powers of overseas corporations (r.183)
Form 8	Certificate of powers of corporations other than overseas corporations (r.183)

Commonhold Forms

CM1	Application to register a freehold estate in commonhold land
CM2	Application for the freehold estate to cease to be registered as a freehold estate in commonhold land during the transitional period
CM3	Application for the registration of an amended commonhold community statement and/or altered memorandum and articles of association
CM4	Application to add land to a commonhold registration
CM5	Application for the termination of a commonhold registration
CM6	Application for the registration of a successor commonhold association
COE	Notification of change of extent of a commonhold unit over which there is a registered charge
CON1	Consent to the registration of land as commonhold land
CON2	Consent to an application for the freehold estate to cease to be registered as a freehold estate in commonhold land during the transitional period
COV	Application for registration with unit holders
SR1	Notice of surrender of development right(s)

Other Forms

ACD	Application for approval of a standard form of charge deed and allocation of official Land Registry Reference
DJP	Application to remove from the register the name of a deceased registered proprietor
DS2E	Application to cancel entries relating to a registered charge
ID1	Evidence of identity for a private individual
ID2	Evidence of identity for a corporate body
ID3	Evidence of identity for use with FR1 only
RD1	Request for the return of an original document(s)

APPENDIX III

Schedule 4 to the Land Registration Rules 2003

Standard Forms of Restriction

In the forms in this Schedule—

(a) words in [*square brackets*] *in ordinary type are optional parts of the form; the brackets are not to be included in the restriction;*

(b) words in [*square brackets*] *in italic type are instructions for completion of the form, and are not to be included in the restriction;*

(c) where (round brackets) enclose one or more words, the brackets and all words in ordinary type enclosed in them are part of the form and, unless also enclosed in [*square brackets*]*, must be included in the restriction; and*

(d) where a form includes a group of clauses introduced by bullets, only one of the clauses may be used; the bullets are not to be included in the restriction.

Rule 91A contains other permitted modifications of some forms.

Rule 91B contains provisions as to how a consent or certificate, required by the terms of a restriction to be given by a corporation aggregate, is to be signed on its behalf.

Form A (Restriction on dispositions by sole proprietor)

No disposition by a sole proprietor of the registered estate (except a trust corporation) under which capital money arises is to be registered unless authorised by an order of the court.

Form B (Dispositions by trustees—certificate required)

No [disposition *or specify type of disposition*] by the proprietors of the registered estate is to be registered unless one or more of them makes a statutory declaration or statement of truth, or their conveyancer gives a certificate, that the [disposition *or specify type of disposition*] is in accordance with [*specify the disposition creating the trust*] or some variation thereof referred to in the declaration, statement or certificate.

Form C (Dispositions by personal representatives—certificate required)

No disposition by the personal representative of [*name*] deceased, other than a transfer by way of assent, is to be registered unless such personal representative makes a statutory declaration or statement of truth, or their conveyancer gives a certificate, that the disposition is in accordance with the terms of: [*choose whichever bulleted clause is appropriate*]

- the will of the deceased [as varied by [specify date of, and parties to, deed of variation or other appropriate details]];
- the law relating to intestacy as varied by [specify date of, and parties to, deed of variation or other appropriate details],

or some [*further*] variation thereof referred to in the declaration, statement or certificate, or is necessary for the purposes of administration.

Form D (Parsonage, diocesan glebe, church or churchyard land)

No disposition of the registered estate is to be registered unless made in accordance with:
[*choose whichever bulleted clause is appropriate*]

- [*in the case of parsonage land*] the Parsonages Measure 1938;
- [*in the case of church or churchyard land*] the New Parishes Measure 1943;

- [*in the case of diocesan glebe land*] the Endowments and Glebe Measure 1976,

or some other Measure or authority.

Form E (Non-exempt charity—certificate required)

No disposition by the proprietor of the registered estate to which section 36 or section 38 of the Charities Act 1993 applies is to be registered unless the instrument contains a certificate complying with section 37(2) or section 39(2) of that Act as appropriate.

Form F (Land vested in official custodian on trust for non-exempt charity—authority required)

No disposition executed by the trustees of [*name of charity*] in the name and on behalf of the proprietor is to be registered unless the transaction is authorised by an order of the court or of the Charity Commission, as required by section 22(3) of the Charities Act 1993.

Form G (Tenant for life as registered proprietor of settled land, where there are trustees of the settlement)

No disposition is to be registered unless authorised by the Settled Land Act 1925, or by any extension of those statutory powers in the settlement, and no disposition under which capital money arises is to be registered unless the money is paid to [*name*] of [*address*] and [*name*] of [*address*], (the trustees of the settlement, who may be a sole trust corporation or, if individuals, must number at least two but not more than four) or into court.

[Note—If applicable under the terms of the settlement, a further provision may be added that no transfer of the mansion house (shown on an attached plan or otherwise adequately described to enable it to be fully identified on the Ordnance Survey map or title plan) is to be registered without the consent of the named trustees or an order of the court.]

Form H (Statutory owners as trustees of the settlement and registered proprietors of settled land)

No disposition is to be registered unless authorised by the Settled Land Act 1925, or by any extension of those statutory powers in the settlement, and, except where the sole proprietor is a trust corporation, no disposition under which capital money arises is to be registered unless the money is paid to at least two proprietors.

[*Note—This restriction does not apply where the statutory owners are not the trustees of the settlement.*]

Form I (Tenant for life as registered proprietor of settled land—no trustees of the settlement)

No disposition under which capital money arises, or which is not authorised by the Settled Land Act 1925, or by any extension of those statutory powers in the settlement, is to be registered.

Form J (Trustee in bankruptcy and beneficial interest—certificate required)

No disposition of the:
[*choose whichever bulleted clause is appropriate*]

- registered estate, other than a disposition by the proprietor of any registered charge registered before the entry of this restriction,
- registered charge dated [*date*] referred to above, other than a disposition by the proprietor of any registered sub-charge of that charge registered before the entry of this restriction,

is to be registered without a certificate signed by the applicant for registration or their conveyancer that written notice of the disposition was given to [*name of trustee in bankruptcy*] (the trustee in bankruptcy of [*name of bankrupt person*]) at [*address for service*].

Form K (Charging order affecting beneficial interest—certificate required)

No disposition of the:
[*choose whichever bulleted clause is appropriate*]

- registered estate, other than a disposition by the proprietor of any registered charge registered before the entry of this restriction,
- registered charge dated [*date*] referred to above, other than a disposition by the proprietor of any registered sub-charge of that charge registered before the entry of this restriction,

is to be registered without a certificate signed by the applicant for registration or their conveyancer that written notice of the disposition was given to [*name of person with the benefit of the charging order*] at [*address for service*], being the person with the benefit of [an interim *or* a final] charging order on the beneficial interest of [*name of judgment debtor*] made by the [*name of court*] on [*date*] (Court reference [*insert reference*]).

Form L (Disposition by registered proprietor of a registered estate or proprietor of charge—certificate required)

No [disposition *or specify type of disposition*] of the registered estate [(other than a charge)] by the proprietor of the registered estate [, or by the proprietor of any registered charge, not being a charge registered before the entry of this restriction,] is to be registered without a certificate signed by:
[choose one of the bulleted clauses]

- a conveyancer
- the applicant for registration [*or their conveyancer*]
- [*name*] of [*address*] [or their personal representatives] [or [their conveyancer *or specify appropriate details*]]
- [*name*] of [*address*] [or their personal representatives] and [*name*] of [*address*] [or their personal representatives] [or [their conveyancer *or specify appropriate details*]]

- [*name*] of [*address*] and [*name*] of [*address*] or the survivor of them [or by the personal representatives of the survivor] [or [their conveyancer *or specify appropriate details*]]
- [*name*] of [*address*] or [after that person's death] by [name] of [address] [or [their conveyancer *or specify appropriate details*]]

that the provisions of [*specify clause, paragraph or other particulars*] of [*specify details*] have been complied with [or that they do not apply to the disposition].

Form M (Disposition by registered proprietor of registered estate or proprietor of charge—if registered proprietor of specified title, number required)

No [disposition *or specify type of disposition*] of the registered estate [(other than a charge)] by the proprietor of the registered estate [, or by the proprietor of any registered charge, not being a charge registered before the entry of this restriction,] is to be registered without a certificate signed by the proprietor for the time being of the estate registered under title number [*specify title number*] [or [their conveyancer *or specify appropriate details*]] *that the* provisions of [*specify clause, paragraph or other particulars*] of [*specify details*] have been complied with [or that they do not apply to the disposition].

Form N (Disposition by registered proprietor of registered estate or proprietor of charge—consent required)

No [disposition *or specify type of disposition*] of the registered estate [(other than a charge)] by the proprietor of the registered estate [, or by the proprietor of any registered charge, not being a charge registered before the entry of this restriction,] is to be registered without a written consent signed by:
[*choose one of the bulleted clauses*]

- [*name*] of [*address*] [or their personal representatives] [or [their conveyancer *or specify appropriate details*]].
- [*name*] of [*address*] [or their personal representatives] and [*name*] of [*address*] [or their personal representatives] [or [their conveyancer *or specify appropriate details*]].

- [*name*] of [*address*] and [*name*] of [*address*] or the survivor of them [or by the personal representatives of the survivor] [or [their conveyancer *or specify appropriate details*]].
- [*name*] of [*address*] or [after that person's death] by [*name*] of [*address*] [or [their conveyancer *or specify appropriate details*]].

Form O (Disposition by registered proprietor of registered estate or proprietor of charge—consent of registered proprietor of specified title number or certificate required)

No [disposition *or specify type of disposition*] of the registered estate [(other than a charge)] by the proprietor of the registered estate [, or by the proprietor of any registered charge, not being a charge registered before the entry of this restriction,] is to be registered without a written consent signed by the proprietor for the time being of the estate registered under title number [*specify title number*] [or [their conveyancer *or specify appropriate details*]].

[*The text of the restriction may be continued as follows, to allow for the provision of a certificate as an alternative to the consent.*] or without a certificate signed by:
[*choose one of the bulleted clauses*]

- a conveyancer
- the applicant for registration [or their conveyancer]
- [*name*] of [*address*] [or [their conveyancer *or specify appropriate details*]]

that the provisions of [*specify clause, paragraph or other particulars*] of [*specify details*] have been complied with [*or that they do not apply to the disposition*].

Form P (Disposition by registered proprietor of registered estate or proprietor of charge—consent of proprietor of specified charge or certificate required)

No [disposition *or specify type of disposition*] of the registered estate [(other than a charge)] by the proprietor of the registered estate [, or by the proprietor of any registered charge, not being a charge registered before the entry of this restriction,] is to be registered without a written consent signed by the proprietor for the time being of the charge dated [*date*] in favour of [*chargee*] referred to in the charges register [or [their conveyancer *or specify appropriate details*]].

[*The text of the restriction may be continued as follows, to allow for the provision of a certificate as an alternative to the consent.*]
or without a certificate signed by:
[*choose one of the bulleted clauses*]

- a conveyancer
- the applicant for registration [*or their conveyancer*]
- [*name*] of [*address*] [or] their conveyancer *or specify appropriate details]]*

that the provisions of [*specify clause, paragraph or other particulars*] of [*specify details*] have been complied with [or that they do not apply to the disposition].

Form Q (Disposition by registered proprietor of registered estate or proprietor of charge—consent of personal representatives required)

No [*disposition or specify type of disposition*] of the:
[*choose whichever bulleted clause is appropriate*]

- registered estate by the proprietor of the registered estate
- registered charge dated [*date*] referred to above by the proprietor of that registered charge

is to be registered after the death of [*name of the current proprietor(s) whose personal representatives' consent will be required*] without the written consent of the personal representatives of the deceased.

Form R (Disposition by registered proprietor of registered estate or proprietor of charge—evidence of compliance with club rules required)

No [disposition *or specify type of disposition*] of the registered estate [(other than a charge)] by the proprietor of the registered estate [, or by the proprietor of any registered charge, not being a charge registered before the entry of this restriction,] is to be registered unless authorised by the rules of the [*name of club*] of [*address*] as evidenced by:
[*choose whichever bulleted clause is appropriate*]

- a resolution of its members.
- a certificate signed by its secretary or conveyancer. [*specify appropriate details*].

Form S (Disposition by proprietor of charge—certificate of compliance required)

No [disposition *or specify type of disposition*] by the proprietor of the registered charge dated [*date*] referred to above is to be registered without a certificate signed by:
[*choose one of the bulleted clauses*]

- a conveyancer
- the applicant for registration [*or their conveyancer*]
- [*name*] of [*address*] [or their personal representatives] [or [their conveyancer *or specify appropriate details*]]
- [*name*] of [*address*] [or their personal representatives] and [*name*] of [*address*] [or their personal representatives] [or [their conveyancer *or specify appropriate details*]]
- [*name*] of [*address*] and [*name*] of [*address*] or the survivor of them [or by the personal representatives of the survivor] [or [their conveyancer *or specify appropriate details*]]
- [*name*] of [*address*] or [after that person's death] by [*name*] of [*address*] [or [their conveyancer *or specify appropriate details*]]
- the proprietor for the time being of the sub-charge dated [*date*] in favour of [*sub-chargee*] [or [their conveyancer *or specify appropriate details*]]

that the provisions of [*specify clause, paragraph or other particulars*] of [*specify details*] have been complied with [or that they do not apply to the disposition].

Form T (Disposition by proprietor of charge—consent required)

No [disposition *or specify type of disposition*] by the proprietor of the registered charge dated [*date*] referred to above is to be registered without a written consent signed by:
[*choose one of the bulleted clauses*]

- [*name*] of [*address*] [or their personal representatives] [*or [their conveyancer or specify appropriate details*]].
- [*name*] of [*address*] [or their personal representatives] and [*name*] of [*address*] [or their personal representatives] [or [their conveyancer *or specify appropriate details*]].
- [*name*] of [*address*] and [*name*] of [*address*] or the survivor of them [or by the personal representatives of the survivor] [or [their conveyancer *or specify appropriate details*]].
- [*name*] of [*address*] or [after that person's death] by [*name*] of [*address*] [or [their conveyancer *or specify appropriate details*]].
- the proprietor for the time being of the sub-charge dated [*date*] in favour of [*sub-chargee*] [or [their conveyancer *or specify appropriate details*]].

Form U (Section 37 of the Housing Act 1985)

No transfer or lease by the proprietor of the registered estate or by the proprietor of any registered charge is to be registered unless a certificate by [*specify relevant local authority*] is given that the transfer or lease is made in accordance with section 37 of the Housing Act 1985.

Form V (Section 157 of the Housing Act 1985)

No transfer or lease by the proprietor of the registered estate or by the proprietor of any registered charge is to be registered unless a certificate by [*specify relevant local authority or housing association etc.*] is given that the transfer or lease is made in accordance with section 157 of the Housing Act 1985.

Form W (Paragraph 4 of Schedule 9A to the Housing Act 1985)

No disposition (except a transfer) of a qualifying dwellinghouse (except to a qualifying person or persons) is to be registered without the consent of the [Secretary of State *or* Welsh Ministers] given under section 171D(2) of the Housing Act 1985 as it applies by virtue of the Housing (Preservation of Right to Buy) Regulations 1993.

Form X (Section 81 or 133 of the Housing Act 1988 or section 173 of the Local Government and Housing Act 1989)

No disposition by the proprietor of the registered estate or in exercise of the power of sale or leasing in any registered charge (except an exempt disposal as defined by section 81(8) of the Housing Act 1988) is to be registered without the consent of the [Secretary of State *or* Welsh Ministers] to that disposition under the provisions of:
[*choose whichever bulleted clause is appropriate*]

- section 81 of that Act.
- section 133 of that Act.
- section 173 of the Local Government and Housing Act 1989.

Form Y (Section 13 of the Housing Act 1996)

No transfer or lease by the proprietor of the registered estate or by the proprietor of any registered charge is to be registered unless a certificate by [*specify relevant registered social landlord*] is given that the transfer or lease is made in accordance with section 13 of the Housing Act 1996.

Form AA (Freezing order on the registered estate)

Under an order of the [*name of court*] made on [*date*] (Court reference [*insert reference*]) no disposition by the proprietor of the registered estate is to be registered except with the consent of [*name*] of [*address*] or under a further order of the Court.

Form BB (Freezing order on charge)

Under an order of the [*name of court*] made on [*date*] (Court reference [*insert reference*]) no disposition by the proprietor of the registered charge dated [*date*] referred to above is to be registered except with the consent of [*name*] of [*address*] or under a further order of the Court.

Form CC (Application for freezing order on the registered estate)

Pursuant to an application made on [*date*] to the [*name of court*] for a freezing order to be made under [*statutory provision*] no disposition by the proprietor of the registered estate is to be registered except with the consent of [*name of the person applying*] of [*address*] or under a further order of the Court.

Form DD (Application for freezing order on charge)

Pursuant to an application made on [*date*] to the [*name of court*] for a freezing order to be made under [*statutory provision*] no disposition by the proprietor of the registered charge dated [*date*] referred to above is to be registered except with the consent of [*name of the person applying*] of [*address*] or under a further order of the Court.

Form EE (Restraint order or interim receiving order on the registered estate)

Under [a restraint order or an interim receiving order] made under [*statutory provision*] on [*date*] (Court reference [*insert reference*]) no disposition by the proprietor of the registered estate is to be registered except with the consent of [*name of prosecutor or other appropriate person*] of [*address*] or under a further order of the Court.

Form FF (Restraint order or interim receiving order on charge)

Under [a restraint order or an interim receiving order] made under [*statutory provision*] on [*date*] (Court reference [*insert reference*]) no disposition by the proprietor of the registered charge dated [*date*] referred to above is to be registered except with the consent of [*name of prosecutor or other appropriate person*] of [*address*] or under a further order of the Court.

Form GG (Application for restraint order or interim receiving order on the registered estate)

Pursuant to an application for [a restraint order or *an* interim receiving order] to be made under [*statutory provision*] and under any order made as a result of that application, no disposition by the proprietor of the registered estate is to be registered except with the consent of [*name of prosecutor or other appropriate person*] of [*address*] or under a further order of the Court.

Form HH (Application for restraint order or interim receiving order on charge)

Pursuant to an application for [a restraint order *or* an interim receiving order] to be made under [*statutory provision*] and under any order made as a result of that application no disposition by the proprietor of the registered charge dated [*date*] referred to above is to be registered except with the consent of [*name of prosecutor or other appropriate person*] of [*address*] or under a further order of the Court.

Form II (Beneficial interest that is a right or claim in relation to a registered estate)

No disposition of the registered estate, other than a disposition by the proprietor of any registered charge registered before the entry of this restriction, is to be registered without a certificate signed by the applicant for registration or their conveyancer that written notice of the disposition was given to [*name*] at [*address*].

Form JJ (Statutory charge of beneficial interest in favour of Legal Services Commission)

No disposition of the:
[*choose whichever bulleted clause is appropriate*]

- registered estate, other than a disposition by the proprietor of any registered charge registered before the entry of this restriction,
- registered charge dated [*date*] referred to above, other than a disposition by the proprietor of
- any registered sub-charge of that charge registered before the entry of this restriction,

is to be registered without a certificate signed by the applicant for registration or their conveyancer that written notice of the disposition was given to the Legal Services Commission, Land Charge Department, at [*address and Commission's reference number*].

Form KK (Lease by registered social landlord)

No deed varying the terms of the registered lease is to be registered without the consent of:
[*choose whichever bulleted clause is appropriate*]

- the Housing Corporation

- the Welsh Ministers of [*address*].

Form LL (Restriction as to evidence of execution)

No disposition of the:
[*choose whichever bulleted clause is appropriate*]

- registered estate by the proprietor of the registered estate
- registered charge dated [*date*] referred to above by the proprietor of that registered charge

is to be registered without a certificate signed by a conveyancer that that conveyancer is satisfied that the person who executed the document submitted for registration as disponor is the same person as the proprietor.

Form MM (Interest in beneficial joint tenancy subject to charge under section 22(1) of the Health and Social Services and Social Security Adjudications Act 1983)

No disposition of the registered estate made after the death of [*specify the name of the person whose beneficial interest under a beneficial joint tenancy is subject to a charge under section 22(1) of the Health and Social Services and Social Security Adjudications Act 1983*], or after that person has become the sole proprietor of the registered estate, is to be registered unless—

(1) the disposition is by two or more persons who were registered as proprietors of the legal estate at the time of that person's death,

(2) notice of a charge under section 22(1) or (6) of the Health and Social Services and Social Security Adjudications Act 1983 for the benefit of [*name and address of the local authority*] has been entered in the register or, where appropriate, such charge has been registered, or

(3) it is shown to the registrar's satisfaction that no such charge is subsisting.

Form NN (Disposition by registered proprietor of registered estate or proprietor of charge—consent or certificate required)

No [disposition *or specify type of disposition*] of the registered estate [(other than a charge)] by the proprietor of the registered estate [, or by the proprietor of any registered charge, not being a charge registered before the entry of this restriction,] is to be registered without a written consent signed by:
[*choose one of the bulleted clauses*]

- [*name*] of [*address*] [or their personal representatives] [or [their conveyancer *or specify; appropriate details*]],
- [*name*] of [*address*] [or their personal representatives] and [*name*] of [*address*] [or their personal representatives] [or [their conveyancer *or specify appropriate details*]],
- [*name*] of [*address*] and [*name*] of [*address*] or the survivor of them [or by the personal representatives of the survivor] [or [their conveyancer *or specify appropriate details*]],
- [*name*] of [*address*] or [after that person's death] by [*name*] of [*address*] [or [their conveyancer *or specify appropriate details*]],

or a certificate signed by:
[*choose one of the bulleted clauses*]

- a conveyancer
- the applicant for registration [or their conveyancer]
- [*name*] of [*address*] [or [their conveyancer *or specify appropriate details*]]

that the provisions of [*specify clause, paragraph or other particulars*] of [*specify details*] have been complied with [or that they do not apply to the disposition].

Form 00 (Disposition by proprietor of charge—consent or certificate required)

No [disposition *or specify type of disposition*] by the proprietor of the registered charge dated [*date*] referred to above is to be registered without a written consent signed by:

[*choose one of the bulleted clauses*]

- [*name*] of [*address*] [or their personal representatives] [or [their conveyancer *or specify appropriate details*]].
- [*name*] of [*address*] [or their personal representatives] and [*name*] of [*address*] [or their personal representatives] [or [their conveyancer *or specify appropriate details*]].
- [*name*] of [*address*] and [*name*] of [*address*] or the survivor of them [or by the personal representatives of the survivor] [or [their conveyancer *or specify appropriate details*]].
- [*name*] of [*address*] or [after that person's death] by [*name*] of [*address*] [or [their conveyancer *or specify appropriate details*]].

the proprietor for the time being of the sub-charge dated [*date*] in favour of [*sub-chargee*] [or [their conveyancer *or specify appropriate details*]].
or a certificate signed by:
[*choose one of the bulleted clauses*]

- a conveyancer
- the applicant for registration [*or their conveyancer*]
- [*name*] of [*address*] [or [their conveyancer *or specify appropriate details*]]

that the provisions of [*specify clause, paragraph or other particulars*] of [*specify details*] have been complied with [or that they do not apply to the disposition].

Form PP (Disposition by registered proprietor of registered estate or proprietor of charge—certificate of landlord etc, or of a conveyancer, required)

No [disposition *or specify type of disposition*] of the registered estate [(other than a charge)] by the proprietor of the registered estate [, or by the proprietor of any registered charge, not being a charge registered before the entry of this restriction,] is to be registered without a certificate signed by:
[*choose one of the bulleted clauses*]

- the proprietor for the time being of the registered estate comprising the reversion immediately expectant on the determination of the registered lease,

- the proprietor for the time being of the estate registered under title number [*specify title number*],
- [*name*] of [*address*] [or by [*name*] of [*address*]],

or by a conveyancer, that the provisions of [*specify clause, paragraph or other particulars*] of [*specify details*] have been complied with [or that they do not apply to the disposition].]

APPENDIX IV

Schedule 1A to the Land Registration Rules 2003

Prescribed clauses LR1 to LR14

- *All words in italicised text and inapplicable alternative wording in a clause may be omitted or deleted.*
- *Clause LR13 may be omitted or deleted.*
- *Clause LR14 may be omitted or deleted where the tenant is one person.*
- *Otherwise, do not omit or delete any words in bold text unless italicised.*
- *Side-headings may appear as headings if this is preferred.*
- *Vertical or horizontal lines, or both, may be omitted.*

LR1 Date of lease	
LR2 Title number(s)	**LR2.1 Landlord's title number(s)** *Title number(s) out of which this lease is granted. Leave blank if not registered.* **LR2.2 Other title numbers** *Existing title number(s) against which entries of matters referred to in LR9, LR10, LR11 and LR13 are to be made.*

LR3 Parties to this lease *[Give full names and addresses of each of the parties. For UK incorporated companies and limited liability partnerships, also give the registered number including any prefix. For overseas companies, also give the territory of incorporation and, if appropriate, the registered number in the United Kingdom including any prefix.]*	**Landlord** **Tenant** **Other parties** *Specify capacity of each party, for example "management company", "guarantor", etc*
LR4 Property *Insert a full description of the land being leased* *or* *Refer to the clause, schedule or paragraph of a schedule in this lease in which the land being leased is more fully described.* *Where there is a letting of part of a registered title, a plan must be attached to this lease and any floor levels must be specified.*	**In the case of a conflict between this clause and the remainder of this lease then, for the purposes of registration, this clause shall prevail.**
LR5 Prescribed statements etc. *If this lease includes a statement falling within LR5.1, insert under that sub-clause the relevant statement or refer to the clause, schedule or paragraph of a schedule in this lease which contains the statement.*	***LR5.1 Statements prescribed under rules 179 (dispositions in favour of a charity), 180 (dispositions by a charity) or 196 (leases under the Leasehold Reform, Housing and Urban Development Act 1993) of the Land Registration Rules 2003.***
In LR5.2, omit or delete those Acts which do not apply to this lease.	***LR5.2 This lease is made under, or by reference to, provisions of:*** ***Leasehold Reform Act 1967*** ***Housing Act 1985*** ***Housing Act 1988*** ***Housing Act 1996***

LR6 Term for which the Property is leased *Include only the appropriate statement (duly completed) from the three options.* *NOTE: The information you provide, or refer to, here will be used as part of the particulars to identify the lease under rule 6 of the Land Registration Rules 2003.*	From and including To and including *OR* The term as specified in this lease at clause/schedule/paragraph *OR* The term is as follows:
LR7 Premium *Specify the total premium, inclusive of any VAT where payable.*	
LR8 Prohibitions or restrictions on disposing of this lease *Include whichever of the two statements is appropriate.* *Do not set out here the wording of the provision.*	This lease does not contain a provision that prohibits or restricts dispositions. *OR* This lease contains a provision that prohibits or restricts dispositions.
LR9 Rights of acquisition etc. *Insert the relevant provisions in the sub-clauses or refer to the clause, schedule or paragraph of a schedule in this lease which contains the provisions.*	**LR9.1 Tenant's contractual rights to renew this lease, to acquire the reversion or another lease of the Property, or to acquire an interest in other land** **LR9.2 Tenant's covenant to (or offer to) surrender this lease** **LR9.3 Landlord's contractual rights to acquire this lease**
LR10 Restrictive covenants given in this lease by the Landlord in respect of land other than the Property *Insert the relevant provisions or refer to the clause, schedule or paragraph of a schedule in this lease which contains the provisions.*	

LR11 Easements *Refer here only to the clause, schedule or paragraph of a schedule in this lease which sets out the easements.*	**LR11.1 Easements granted by this lease for the benefit of the Property** **LR11.2 Easements granted or reserved by this lease over the Property for the benefit of other property**
LR12 Estate rentcharge burdening the Property *Refer here only to the clause, schedule or paragraph of a schedule in this lease which sets out the rentcharge.*	
LR13 Application for standard form of restriction *Set out the full text of the standard form of restriction and the title against which it is to be entered. If you wish to apply for more than one standard form of restriction use this clause to apply for each of them, tell us who is applying against which title and set out the full text of the restriction you are applying for.* *Standard forms of restriction are set out in Schedule 4 to the Land Registration Rules 2003.*	The Parties to this lease apply to enter the following standard form of restriction [against the title of the Property] or [against title number]
LR14 Declaration of trust where there is more than one person comprising the Tenant *If the Tenant is one person, omit or delete all the alternative statements.* *If the Tenant is more than one person, complete this clause by omitting or deleting all inapplicable alternative statements.*	The Tenant is more than one person. They are to hold the Property on trust for themselves as joint tenants. *OR* The Tenant is more than one person. They are to hold the Property on trust for themselves as tenants in common in equal shares. *OR* The Tenant is more than one person. They are to hold the Property on trust *Complete as necessary*]

APPENDIX V

Land Registration, England and Wales

The Land Registration Fee Order 2009 (SI 2009/845)

Made - - - - - - - - - - - - - - *1 April 2009*
Laid before Parliament- - - - - - *2 April 2009*
Coming into force - - - - - - - - - *6 July 2009*

The Lord Chancellor, makes the following Order in exercise of the powers conferred on him by sections 102 and 128(1) of the Land Registration Act 2002.

In accordance with section 102 of that Act, he has received the advice and assistance of the Rule Committee, appointed under section 127[1] of that Act.

Also in accordance with section 102 of that Act, the Treasury has consented to the making of this Order.

PART 1

General

Citation, commencement and interpretation

1.—(1) This Order may be cited as the Land Registration Fee Order 2009 and shall come into force on 6 July 2009.

(2) In this Order unless the context otherwise requires—

"account holder" means a person holding a credit account,
"the Act" means the Land Registration Act 2002,
"CLRA" means the Commonhold and Leasehold Reform Act 2002,
"charge" includes a sub-charge,

"common parts" has the same meaning as in the CLRA,
"a commonhold" has the same meaning as in the CLRA,
"commonhold association" has the same meaning as in the CLRA,
"commonhold community statement" has the same meaning as in the CLRA,
"commonhold land" has the same meaning as in the CLRA,
"commonhold unit" has the same meaning as in the CLRA,
"credit account" means an account authorised by the registrar under article 14(1),
"developer" has the same meaning as in the CLRA,
"large scale application" has the same meaning as in article 6(1)(b),
"monetary consideration" means a consideration in money or money's worth (other than a nominal consideration or a consideration consisting solely of a covenant to pay money owing under a mortgage),
"premium" means the amount or value of any monetary consideration given by the lessee as part of the same transaction in which a lease is granted by way of fine, premium or otherwise, but, where a registered leasehold estate of substantially the same land is surrendered on the grant of a new lease, the premium for the new lease shall not include the value of the surrendered lease,
"profit" means a profit à prendre in gross,
"remote terminal" means a remote terminal communicating with the registrar's computer system in accordance with a notice given under Schedule 2 to the rules,
"rent" means the largest amount of annual rent the lease reserves within the first five years of its term that can be quantified at the time an application to register the lease is made,
"the rules" means the Land Registration Rules 2003,[2] and a rule referred to by number means the rule so numbered in the rules,
"Scale 1" means Scale 1 in Schedule 1,
"Scale 2" means Scale 2 in Schedule 2,
"scale fee" means a fee payable in accordance with a scale set out in Schedule 1 or 2 whether or not reduced in accordance with article 2(6),
"scale fee application" means an application which attracts a scale fee, or which would attract such a fee but for the operation of article 6,
"share", in relation to land, means an interest in that land under a trust of land,
"surrender" includes a surrender not made by deed,
"termination application" has the same meaning as in the CLRA,

"unit-holder" has the same meaning as in the CLRA,

"voluntary application" means an application for first registration (other than for the registration of title to a rentcharge, a franchise or a profit) which is not made wholly or in part pursuant to section 4 of the Act (when title must be registered).

(3) Expressions used in this Order have, unless the contrary intention appears, the meaning which they bear in the rules.

PART 2

Scale fees

Applications for first registration and applications for registration of a lease by an original lessee

2.—(1) The fee for an application for first registration of an estate in land is payable under Scale 1 on the value of the estate in land comprised in the application assessed under article 7 unless the application is—

(a) for the registration of title to a lease by the original lessee or his personal representative, where paragraph (2) applies,

(b) a voluntary application, where paragraph (6) applies, or article 6(3) applies, or

(c) a large scale application, where article 6 applies.

(2) The fee for an application by the original lessee or his personal representative for the registration of title to a lease or for the registration of the grant of a lease, is payable under Scale 1—

(a) on an amount equal to the sum of the premium and the rent, or

(b) where

(i) there is no premium, and

(ii) either there is no rent or the rent cannot be quantified at the time the application is made,

on the value of the lease assessed under article 7 subject to a minimum fee of £50,

unless either of the circumstances in paragraph (3) applies.

(3) Paragraph (2) shall not apply if the application is—

(a) a voluntary application, where paragraph (6) applies, or

(b) a large scale application, where article 6 applies.

(4) The fee for an application for the first registration of a rentcharge is £50.

(5) The fee for an application for the first registration of a franchise or a profit is payable under Scale 1 on the value of the franchise or the profit assessed under article 7.

(6) The fee for a voluntary application (other than a large scale application, where article 6(3) applies) is the fee which would otherwise be payable under paragraphs (1) and (2) reduced by 25 per cent and, where the reduced fee would be a figure which includes pence, the fee must be adjusted to the nearest £10.

(7) In paragraph (2) "lease" means—

(a) a lease which grants an estate in land whether or not the grant is a registrable disposition, or
(b) a lease of a franchise, profit or manor the grant of which is a registrable disposition.

Transfers of registered estates for monetary consideration, etc.

3.—(1) Subject to paragraphs (2), (3) and (4), the fee for an application for the registration of—

(a) a transfer of a registered estate for monetary consideration,
(b) a transfer for the purpose of giving effect to a disposition for monetary consideration of a share in a registered estate, or
(c) a surrender of a registered leasehold estate for monetary consideration, other than a surrender to which paragraph (3) of Schedule 4 applies,

is payable under Scale 1 on the amount or value of the consideration.

(2) Paragraph (1) shall not apply if the application is—

(a) a large scale application, where article 6 applies, or
(b) for the registration of a transfer of a registered estate made pursuant to an order of the court under the Matrimonial Causes Act 1973 or the Civil Partnership Act 2004, where article 4(1)(h) applies.

(3) Where a sale and sub-sale of a registered estate are made by separate deeds of transfer, a separate fee is payable for each deed of transfer.

(4) Where a single deed of transfer gives effect to a sale and a sub-sale of the same registered estate a single fee is assessed upon the greater of the monetary consideration given by the purchaser and the monetary consideration given by the sub-purchaser.

(5) The fee for an application to cancel an entry in the register of notice of an unregistered lease which has determined

is payable under Scale 1 on the value of the lease immediately before its determination under article 7.

Transfers of registered estates otherwise than for monetary consideration, etc.

4.—(1) Unless the application is a large scale application (where article 6 applies), the fee for an application for the registration of—

(a) a transfer of a registered estate otherwise than for monetary consideration (unless paragraph (2) applies),
(b) a surrender of a registered leasehold estate otherwise than for monetary consideration,
(c) a transfer of a registered estate by operation of law on death or bankruptcy, of an individual proprietor,
(d) an assent of a registered estate (including a vesting assent),
(e) an appropriation of a registered estate,
(f) a vesting order or declaration to which section 27(5) of the Act applies,
(g) an alteration of the register, or
(h) a transfer of a registered estate made pursuant to an order of the court under the Matrimonial Causes Act 1973 or the Civil Partnership Act 2004,

is payable under Scale 2 on the value of the registered estate which is the subject of the application, assessed under article 7, but after deducting from it the amount secured on the registered estate by any charge subject to which the registration takes effect.

(2) Where a transfer of a registered estate otherwise than for monetary consideration is for the purpose of giving effect to the disposition of a share in a registered estate, the fee for an application for its registration is payable under Scale 2 on the value of that share.

Charges of registered estates or registered charges

5.—(1) The fee for an application for the registration of a charge is payable under Scale 2 on the amount of the charge assessed under article 8 unless it is an application to which paragraphs (2), (3) or (4) apply.

(2) No fee is payable for an application to register a charge lodged with or before the completion of either a scale fee application to which paragraph (17) in Part 1 of Schedule 3 applies ("the primary application") that will result in the chargor being registered as proprietor of the registered estate included in the charge unless—

(a) the charge includes a registered estate which is not included in the primary application, where paragraph (4) applies, or
(b) the primary application is a voluntary application, in which case this paragraph shall apply only if the application to register the charge accompanies the primary application.

(3) No fee is to be paid for an application to register a charge made by a predecessor in title of the applicant that is lodged with or before completion of an application for first registration of the estate included in the charge.

(4) Where a charge also includes a registered estate which is not included in the primary application ("the additional property") any fee payable under Scale 2 is to be assessed on an amount calculated as follows:

$$\frac{\text{Value of the additional property}}{\text{Value of all the property included in the charge}} \times \text{Amount secured by the charge}$$

(5) The fee for an application for the registration of—

(a) the transfer of a registered charge for monetary consideration, or
(b) a transfer for the purpose of giving effect to the disposition for monetary consideration of a share in a registered charge,

is payable under Scale 2 on the amount or value of the consideration.

(6) The fee for an application for the registration of the transfer of a registered charge otherwise than for monetary consideration is payable under Scale 2 on—

(a) the amount secured by the registered charge at the time of the transfer or,
(b) where the transfer relates to more than one charge, the aggregate of the amounts secured by the registered charges at the time of the transfer.

(7) The fee for an application for the registration of a transfer for the purpose of giving effect to a disposition otherwise than for monetary consideration of a share in a registered charge is payable under Scale 2 on—

(a) the proportionate part of the amount secured by the registered charge at the time of the transfer or,

(b) where the transfer relates to more than one charge, the proportionate part of the aggregate of the amounts secured by the registered charges at the time of the transfer.

(8) This article takes effect subject to article 6 (large scale applications).

Large scale applications, etc.

6.—(1) In this article—

(a) "land unit" means—

(i) the land registered under a single title number other than, in the case of an application to register a charge, any estate under any title number which is included in a primary application within the meaning of article 5(2), or

(ii) on a first registration application, a separate area of land not adjoining any other unregistered land affected by the same application.

(b) "large scale application" means a scale fee application which relates to 20 or more land units, other than an application to register a disposition by the developer affecting the whole or part of the freehold estate in land which has been registered as a freehold estate in commonhold land, or a low value application,

(c) "low value application" means a scale fee application, other than an application for first registration, where the value of the land or the amount of the charge to which it relates (as the case may be) does not exceed £30,000.

(2) Subject to paragraphs (3) and (4), the fee for a large scale application is the greater of—

(a) the scale fee, and

(b) a fee calculated on the following basis—

(i) where the application relates to not more than 500 land units, £12 for each land unit, or

(ii) where the application relates to more than 500 land units, £6,000 plus £6 for each land unit in excess of 500.

(3) If a large scale application is a voluntary application, the fee payable under paragraph (2) is reduced by 25 per cent and, where the reduced fee would be a figure which includes pence, the fee must be ajusted to the nearest £10.

(4) The maximum fee payable for a large scale application for first registration is £52,000 unless the application is a voluntary application in which case the maximum fee is £39,000.

PART 3

Valuation
(first registration and registered estates)

Valuation (first registration and registered estates)
7.—(1) The value of the estate in land, franchise, profit, manor or share is the maximum amount for which it could be sold in the open market free from any charge—

(a) in the case of a surrender, at the date immediately before the surrender, and
(b) in any other case, at the date of the application.

(2) As evidence of the amount referred to in paragraph (1), the registrar may require a written statement signed by the applicant or his conveyancer or by any other person who, in the registrar's opinion, is competent to make the statement.
(3) Where an application for first registration is made on—

(a) the purchase of a leasehold estate by the reversioner,
(b) the purchase of a reversion by the leaseholder, or
(c) any other like occasion,

and an unregistered interest is determined, the value of the land is the combined value of the reversionary and determined interests assessed in accordance with paragraphs (1) and (2).

Valuation (charges)
8.—(1) On an application for registration of a charge, the amount of the charge is—

(a) where the charge secures a fixed amount, that amount,
(b) where the charge secures further advances and the maximum amount that can be advanced or owed at any one time is limited, that amount,
(c) where the charge secures further advances and the total amount that can be advanced or owed at any one time is not limited, the value of the property charged,
(d) where the charge is by way of additional or substituted security or by way of guarantee, an amount equal to the lesser of—

(i) the amount secured or guaranteed, and
(ii) the value of the property charged,

(e) where the charge secures an obligation or liability which is contingent upon the happening of a future event ("the obligation"), and is not a charge to which sub-paragraph (d) applies, an amount equal to—

(i) the maximum amount or value of the obligation, or
(ii) if that maximum amount is greater than the value of the property charged, or is not limited by the charge, or cannot be calculated at the time of the application, the value of the property charged.

(2) Where a charge of a kind referred to in paragraph (1)(a) or (1)(b) is secured on unregistered land or other property as well as on a registered estate or registered charge, the fee is payable on an amount calculated as follows—

$$\frac{\text{Value of the registered estate or registered charge}}{\text{Value of all the property charged}} \times \text{Amount of the charge}$$

(3) Where one deed contains two or more charges made by the same chargor to secure the same debt, the deed is to be treated as a single charge, and the fee for registration of the charge is to be paid on the lesser of—

(a) the amount of the whole debt, and
(b) an amount equal to the value of the property charged.

(4) Where one deed contains two or more charges to secure the same debt not made by the same chargor, the deed is to be treated as a separate single charge by each of the chargors and a separate fee is to be paid for registration of the charge by each chargor on the lesser of—

(a) the amount of the whole debt, and
(b) an amount equal to the value of the property charged by that chargor.

(5) In this article "value of the property charged" means the value of the registered estate or the amount of the registered charge or charges affected by the application to register the charge, less the amount secured by any prior registered charge.

PART 4

Fixed Fees and Exemptions

Fixed fees

9.—(1) Subject to paragraph (2) and to article 10, the fees for the applications and services specified in Schedule 3 shall be those set out in that Schedule.

(2) The fee for an application is one specified in paragraphs (1), (2) or (10) in Part 1 of Schedule 3 affecting the whole or

part of the freehold estate in land which has been registered as a freehold estate in commonhold land registered in the name of the developer under more than one title number, the fee is to be assessed as if the application affects only one title.

Exemptions
10. No fee is payable for any of the applications and services specified in Schedule 4.

PART 5

General and Administrative Provisions

Cost of surveys, advertisements and special enquiries
11. The applicant is to meet the costs of any survey, advertisement or other special enquiry that the registrar requires to be made or published in dealing with an application.

Applications not otherwise referred to
12. The fee payable for an application in respect of which no other fee is payable under this Order shall be £50.

Method of payment
13.—(1) Except where the registrar otherwise permits, every fee shall be paid by means of a cheque or postal order crossed and made payable to the Land Registry.

(2) Where there is an agreement with the applicant, a fee may be paid by direct debit to such bank account of the Land Registry as the registrar may from time to time direct.

(3) Where the amount of the fee payable on an application is immediately quantifiable, the fee shall be payable on delivery of the application.

(4) Where the amount of the fee payable on an application is not immediately quantifiable, the applicant shall pay the sum of £50 towards the fee when the application is made and shall lodge at the same time an undertaking to pay on demand the balance of the fee due, if any.

(5) Where an outline application is made, the fee payable shall be the fee payable under paragraph (9) of Part 1 of Schedule 3 in addition to the fee otherwise payable under this Order.

Credit accounts
14.—(1) Any person may, if authorised by the registrar, use a credit account in accordance with this article for the payment of

fees for applications and services of such kind as the registrar shall from time to time direct.

(2) To enable the registrar to consider whether or not a person or firm applying to use a credit account may be so authorised, that person or firm shall supply the registrar with such information and evidence as the registrar may require to satisfy him of the person or firm's fitness to hold a credit account and the ability of the person or firm to pay any amounts which may become due from time to time under a credit account.

(3) To enable the registrar to consider from time to time whether or not an account holder may continue to be authorised to use a credit account, the account holder shall supply the registrar, when requested to do so, with such information and evidence as the registrar may require to satisfy him of the account holder's continuing fitness to hold a credit account and the continuing ability of the account holder to pay any amounts which may become due from time to time under the account holder's credit account.

(4) Where an account holder makes an application where credit facilities are available to him, he may make a request, in such manner as the registrar directs, for the appropriate fee to be debited to the account holder's credit account, but the registrar shall not be required to accept such a request where the amount due on the account exceeds the credit limit applicable to the credit account, or would exceed it if the request were to be accepted.

(5) Where an account holder makes an application where credit facilities are available to him, and the application is accompanied neither by a fee nor a request for the fee to be debited to his account, the registrar may debit the fee to his account.

(6) A registrar shall send a statement of account to each account holder at the end of each calendar month or such other interval as the registrar shall direct.

(7) The account holder must pay any sums due on his credit account before the date and in the manner specified by the registrar.

(8) The registrar may at any time terminate or suspend any or all authorisations given under paragraph (1).

(9) In this article "credit limit" in relation to a credit account authorised for use under paragraph (1) means the maximum amount (if any) which is to be due on the account at any time, as notified by the registrar to the account holder from time to time, by means of such communication as the registrar considers appropriate.

Revocation

15. The Land Registration Fee Order 2006 is revoked.

Signed by the authority of the Lord Chancellor

Michael Wills
Minister of State, Ministry of Justice

Dated 31st March 2009

We consent

Tony Cunningham; Frank Roy
Two of the Lord Commissioners of Her Majesty's Treasury

Dated 1st April 2009

SCHEDULE 1

SCALE 1

NOTE 1: Where the amount or value is a figure which includes pence, it may be rounded down to the nearest £1.

NOTE 2: The third column, which sets out the reduced fee payable where article 2(6) (voluntary registration: reduced fees) applies, is not part of the scale.

Amount or value £	*Fee* £	*Reduced fee where article 2(6) (voluntary registration: reduced fees) applies* £
0–50,000	50	40
50,001–80,000	80	60
80,001–100,000	130	100
100,001–200,000	200	150
200,001–500,000	280	210
500,001–1,000,000	550	410
1,000,001 and over	920	690

SCHEDULE 2

SCALE 2

NOTE: Where the amount or value is a figure which includes pence, it may be rounded down to the nearest £1.

Amount or value £	*Fee* £
0–100,000	50
100,001–200,000	70
200,001–500,000	90
500,001–1,000,000	130
1,000,001 and over	260

SCHEDULE 3

PART 1

Fixed Fee Applications

Fee

(1) To register:

(a) a standard form of restriction contained in Schedule 4 to the rules, or

(b) a notice (other than a notice to which section 117(2)(b) of the Act applies), or

(c) a new or additional beneficiary of a unilateral notice

— total fee for up to three registered titles affected. £50

— additional fee for each subsequent registered title affected £25

Provided that no such fee is payable if, in relation to each registered title affected, the application is accompanied by a scale fee application or another application which attracts a fee under this paragraph.

(2) To register a restriction in a form not contained in Schedule 4 to the rules—for each registered title . . £100

(3) To register a caution against first registration (other than a caution to which section 117(2)(a) of the Act applies). £50

(4) To alter a cautions register—for each individual cautions register £50

(5) To close or partly close a registered leasehold or a registered rentcharge title other than on surrender—for each registered title closed or partly closed £50

Provided that no such fee is payable if the application is accompanied by a scale fee application.

(6) To upgrade from one class of registered title to another £50

Provided that no such fee is payable if the application for upgrading is accompanied by a scale fee application.

(7) To cancel an entry in the register of notice of an unregistered rentcharge which has determined—for each registered title affected £50

Provided that no such fee is payable if the application is accompanied by a scale fee application.

(8) To enter or remove a record of a defect in title pursuant to section 64(1) of the Act £50

Provided that no such fee is payable if the application is accompanied by a scale fee application.

(9) An outline application made under rule 54:

(a) where delivered from a remote terminal £3

(b) where delivered by any other permitted means £6

Such fee is payable in addition to any other fee which is payable in respect of the application.

(10) For an order in respect of a restriction under section 41(2) of the Act—for each registered title affected £50

(11) To register a person in adverse possession of a registered estate—for each registered title affected £150

(12) For registration as a person entitled to be notified of an application for adverse possession—for each registered title affected £50

(13) For the determination of the exact line of a boundary under rule 118—for each registered itle affected £100

(14) To register a freehold estate in land as a freehold estate in commonhold land which is not accompanies by a statement under section 9(1)(b) of the CLRA:

(a) up to 20 commonhold units £50

(b) for every 20 commonhold units, or up to 20 commonhold units, thereafter. £15

(15) To add land to a commonhold:

(a) adding land to the common parts title £50

(b) adding land to a commonhold unit	£50
(c) adding commonhold units	
— up to 20 commonhold units	£50
— for every 20 commonhold units, or up to 20 commonhold units, thereafter.	£15
(16) To apply for a freehold estate in land to cease to be registered as a freehold estate in commonhold land during the transitional period, as defined in the CLRA	£50
(17) To register a freehold estate in land as a freehold estate in commonhold land, which is accompanied by a statement under section 9(1)(b) of the CLRA	
— for each commonhold unit converted	£50
(18) To register an amended commonhold community statement which changes the extent of the common parts or any commonhold unit:	
(a) for the common parts	£50
(b) for up to three commonhold units.	£50
(c) for each subsequent commonhold unit	£25
Provided that no such fee shall be payable if, in relation to each registered title affected, the application is accompanied by a scale fee application or another application that attracts a fee under this Part.	
(19) To register an amended commonhold community statement, which does not change the extent of a registered title within the commonhold	
Provided that no such fee shall be payable if, in relation to each registered title affected, the application is accompanied by a scale fee application or another application that attracts a fee under this Part.	
(20) To register an alteration to the Memorandum or Articles of Association of a commonhold association. .	£50
(21) To make a termination application	
— for each registered title affected.	£50
(22) To note the surrender of a development right under section 58 of the CLRA.	£50

PART 2

Services—Inspection and Copying

NOTE: In this Part "lease" means a lease or a copy of a lease.

	Fee
(1) Inspection, from a remote terminal:	
(a) for each individual register	£4
(b) for each title plan	£4
(c) for any or all of the documents (other than leases referred to in an individual register—for each registered title	£6
(d) for each lease kept by the registrar which is referred to in an individual register or which relates to an application to him...............	£12
(e) for the individual register and title plan of a commonbhold common parts title—for each registered title.............................	£4
(f) for each individual caution register...........	£4
(g) for each caution plan.........................	£4
(h) for any other document kept by the registrar which relates to an application to him—for each document..................................	£6
(2) Inspection (otherwise than under paragraph (1)):	
(a) for each individual register	£8
(b) for each title plan	£8
(c) for any or all of the documents (other than leases) referred to in an individual register—for each registered title	£12
(d) for each lease kept by the registrar which is referred to in an individual register or which relates to an application to him..............	£24
(e) for the individual register and title plan of a commonhold common parts title—for each registered title............................	£8
(f) for each individual caution register	£8
(g) for each caution plan	£8
(h) for any other document kept by the registrar which relates to an application to him—for each document..................................	£12
(3) Official copy in respect of a registered title:	
(a) for each individual register	
(i) where an official copy in electronic form is requested from a remote terminal........	£4
(ii) where an official copy in paper form is requested by any permitted means	£8
(b) for each title plan	
(i) where an official copy in electronic form is requested from a remote terminal.......	£4
(ii) where an official copy in paper form is requested by any permitted means	£8

(c) for each commonhold common parts individual register and title plan

(i) where an official copy in electronic form is requested from a remote terminal........ £4

(ii) where an official copy in paper form is requested by any permitted means........ £8

(4) Official copy in respect of the cautions register

(a) for each individual caution register

(i) where an official copy in electronic form is requested from a remote terminal........ £4

(ii) where an official copy in paper form is requested by any permitted means £8

(b) for each caution plan

(i) where an official copy in electronic form is requested from a remote terminal........ £4

(ii) where requested by any other permitted means £8

(5) Official copy of any or all of the documents (other than a lease) referred to in an individual register—for each registered title

(a) where an official copy in electronic form is requested from a remote terminal............ £6

(b) where an official copy in paper form is requested by any other permitted means £12

(6) Official copy of a lease kept by the registrar which is referred to in an individual register or which relates to an application to him—for each lease

(a) where an official copy in electronic form is requested from a remote terminal and a copy of the lease is held in electronic form by the registrar £12

(b) where an official copy in electronic form is requested from a remote terminal and a copy of the lease is not held in electronic form by the registrar £24

(c) where an official copy in paper form is requested by any permitted means £24

(7) Official copy of any other document kept by the registrar which relates to an application to him—for each document

(a) where an official copy in electronic form is requested from a remote terminal and a copy of the document is held in electronic form by the registrar £6

(b) where an official copy in electronic form is requested from a remote terminal and a copy of the document is nt held i electronic form by the registrar £12

(c) where an official copy in paper form is requested by any permitted means £12

(8) Copy of an historical edition of a registered title (or of part of the edition where rule 144(4) applies)—for each title £10

PART 3

Services—Searches

(1) An official search of an individual register or of a pending first registration application made to the registrar from a remote terminal—for each title £4

(2) An official search of an individual register by a mortgagee for the purpose of section 56(3) of the Family Law Act 1996 made to the registrar from a remote terminal £4

(3) An official search of an individual register or of a pending first registration application other than as described in paragraphs (1) and (2)—for each title £8

(4) The issue of a certificate of inspection of a title plan.. £8

(5) An official search of the index map

(a) where no or not more than five registered titles are disclosed £5

(b) where more than five registered titles are disclosed

(i) for the first five titles £5

(ii) for every ten titles, or up to ten titles, thereafter £3

(6) Search of the index of proprietors' names—for each name £12

(7) An official search of the index of relating franchises and manors—for each administrative area:

(a) where the application is made from a remote terminal.................................... £4

(b) where the application is made by any other permitted means £8

PART 4

Services—Other Information

(1) Application for return of a document under rule 204	£10
(2) Application that the registrar designate a document an exempt information document	£26

SCHEDULE 4

Exemptions

No fee is payable for:

(1) reflecting a change in the name, address or description of a registered proprietor or other person referred to in the register, or in the cautions register, or changing the description of a property,

(2) giving effect in the register to a change of proprietor where the registered estate or the registered charge, as the case may be, has become vested without further assurance (other than on the death or bankruptcy of a proprietor) in some person by the operation of any statute (other than the Act), statutory instrument or scheme taking effect under any statute or statutory instrument,

(3) registering the surrender of a registered leasehold estate where the surrender is consideration or part consideration for the grant of a new lease to the registered proprietor of substantially the same premises as were comprised in the surrendered lease and where a scale fee is paid for the registration of the new lease,

(4) registering a discharge of a registered charge,

(5) registering a matrimonial home rights notice, or renewal of such a notice, or renewal of a matrimonial home rights caution under the Family Law Act 1996,

(6) entering in the register the death of a joint proprietor,

(7) cancelling the registration of a notice, (other than a notice in respect of an unregistered lease or unregistered rentcharge), caution against first registration, caution against dealings, including a withdrawal of a deposit or intended deposit, inhibition, restriction, or note,

(8) the removal of the designation of a document as an exempt information document,

(9) approving an estate layout plan or any draft document with or without a plan,

(10) an order by the registrar (other than an order under section 41(2) of the Act),

(11) deregistering a manor,

(12) an entry in the register of a note of the dissolution of a corporation,

(13) registering a restriction in form A in Schedule 4 to the rules,

(14) an application for day list information on any one occasion from a remote terminal,

(15) an application to lodge a caution against first registration or to make a register entry where in either case the application relates to rights in respect of the repair of a church chancel.

Notes

[1] Section 127 was amended by the Constitutional Reform Act 2005 (c.4), s.15(1) and Sch.4, Pt 1, paras 301 and 302.

[2] Relevant amending instruments are S.I. 2005/1766, 2005/1982, 2008/1750 and 2008/1919.

Index